MAYA ATLAS

LIVE AND
CUXLEN COSH
CUAN COH'K
UT

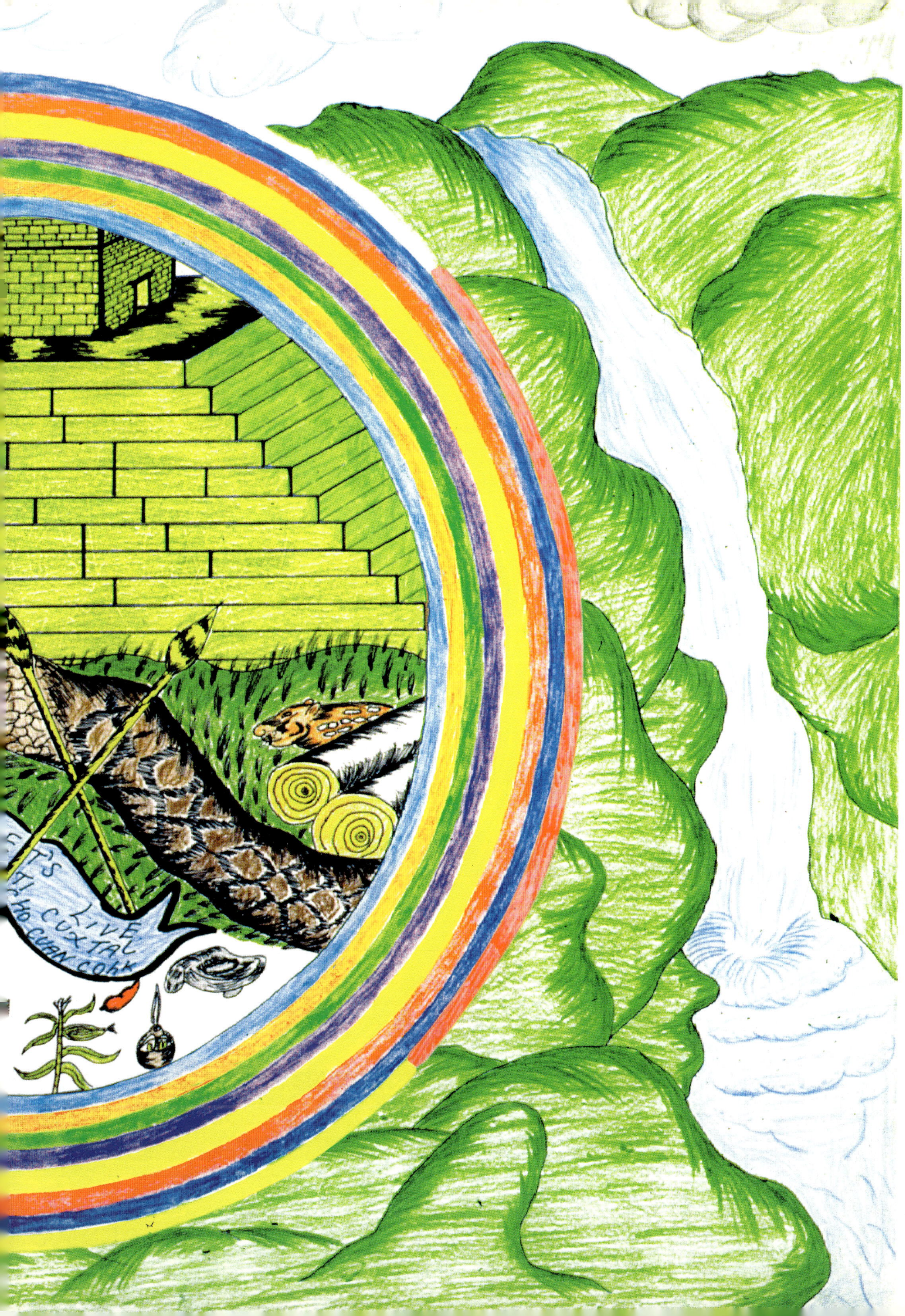
LIVE
CUXTAL

This Atlas is dedicated to

The Maya Children and their Environment

The Maya have certain colors with significance to their livelihoods. There are four primary colors—red, white, black, and yellow—and two secondary colors: green and blue. These colors are represented in the Mayan flag on the preceding pages.

The four primary colors are associated with the various groups of elements sacred to the Maya and organized in groups of four: (1) the four varieties of corn grains, (2) the four cardinal points, (3) the four roads mentioned in the *Popul Vuh*, and (4) the four biological elements of the human body—blood, bone, hair, and skin.

The secondary colors represent the overall source of life. Green—rainforest, environment, and mother earth. Blue—heaven, god, or overall creator. These two secondary colors are normally placed in the center of the four cardinal points, representing the center of the universe.

MAYA ATLAS

The Struggle to Preserve Maya Land in Southern Belize

compiled by

The Maya People of Southern Belize

in conjunction with

The Toledo Maya Cultural Council

and

The Toledo Alcaldes Association

With the Assistance of

Indian Law Resource Center
GeoMap Group, UC Berkeley
and
Society for the Preservation of Education and Research

North Atlantic Books, Berkeley, California

Maya Atlas
The Struggle To Preserve Maya Land in Southern Belize

Copyright © 1997 by **The Toledo Maya Cultural Council and Toledo Alcaldes Association.**
All rights reserved. No portion of this book, except for brief review,
may be reproduced, stored in a retrieval system, or transmitted in
any form or by any means—electronic, mechanical, photocopying,
recording, or otherwise—without written permission of the publisher.

Published by
North Atlantic Books
P.O. Box 12327
Berkeley, California 94712

Cover and book design by
GeoMap Group
University of California at Berkeley
Department of Geography
Berkeley, CA 94720
weaving by the Maya Women of southern Belize
photo: Bernard Nietschmann

Printed by Global Interprint in Hong Kong

Maya Atlas is sponsored by the Society for the Study of Native Arts and Sciences,
a nonprofit educational corporation whose goals are to develop an educational
and cross cultural perspective linking various scientific, social, and artistic fields;
to nurture a holistic view of arts, sciences, humanities, and healing; and
to publish and distribute literature on the relationship of mind, body, and nature.

Library of Congress Cataloging-In-Publication Data

Toledo Maya Cultural Council
    Maya atlas : the struggle to preserve Maya land in southern Belize
/ Toledo Maya Cultural Council [and] Toledo Alcaldes Association.
       p.   cm.
    Covers human, natural, and cultural resources, history, rainforest
management, and current problems in Maya lands.
    Data collected and mapped by Mayans of the Mopan and Kekchi
villages of the Toledo and Stann Creek Districts.
    ISBN 1-55643-256-9
    1. Mayas--Belize--Maps. 2. Mayas--Land tenure--Maps 3. Mayas-
-Government relations. 4. Mayas--Social life and customs.
I. Toledo Alcaldes Association. II. Title.
G1561.E1 T6 1997 <G&M>
912.7282--DC21   97-15801
                                                           CIP
                                                           MAPS

1 2 3 4 5 6 7 8 / 00 99 98 97

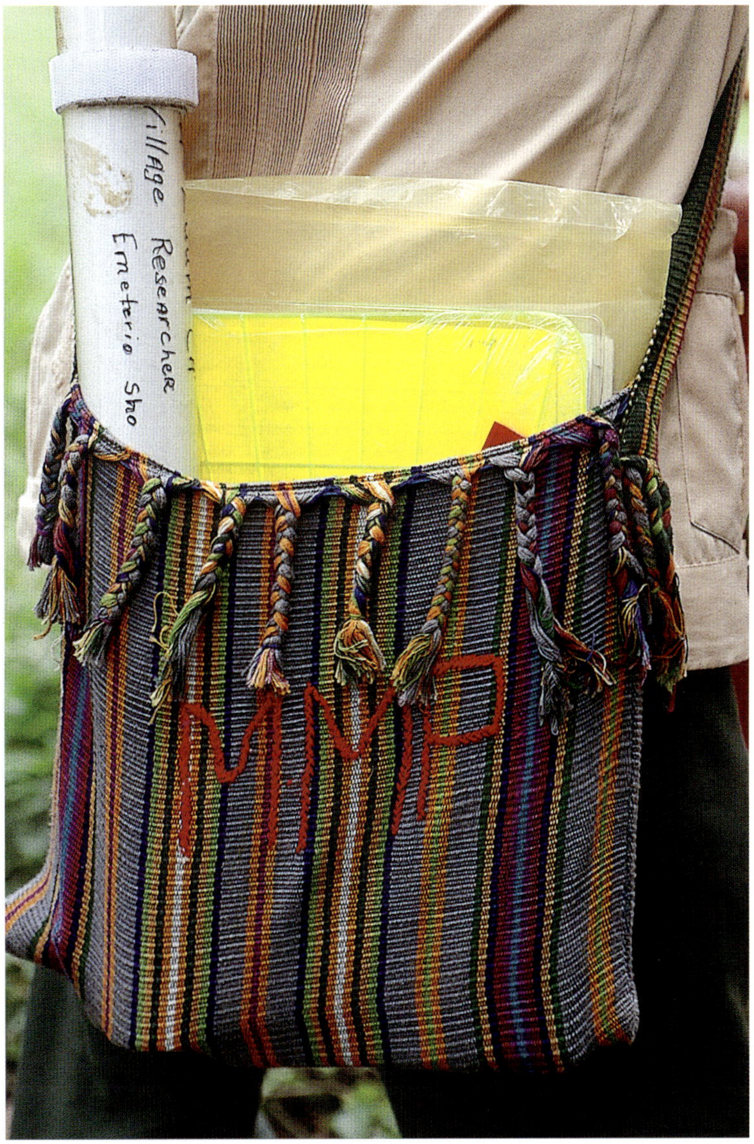
Village Researcher
Emeterio Sho
MMP

Acknowledgments

Toledo Maya Cultural Council and Toledo Alcaldes Association wish to thank the following people and organizations:

Amalia Mai and *The Belize Times*, Andres Coh, Curtis Berkey, Armstrong Wiggins, Audubon Society, Aurora Coc, Basilio Ah, Carlo Krieger, Charles Tambiah, Charles Wright, Clara Bol, Crecencio Cho, Dean Roches, Deborah Schaaf, Diego Bol, Domingo Pau, Dr. Bernard Nietschmann, Estevan Assi, Evan X. Hyde, Dr. George E. Stuart, Geronimo Coc, Harry Lawrence of *The Reporter*, Inter-American Foundation, James Anaya, Joël Wainwright, Juan Ash, Julian Cho, Julio Sanchez, Leonardo Acal, Linadora Bol, Lisa Shoman, Machaca Outreach Center, Madison Roswell, Marcello Cho, National Geographic Society, Pio Coc, Punta Caliente Hotel and Restaurant, Republic of Luxembourg, Santiago Coh, Simeon Sampson, Sophia Cho, Steve Rose, Steve Tullberg, Teodora Castellano, *The Amandala*, the John D. and Catherine T. MacArthur Foundation, Tim Norris, Widdicombe Schmidt

GeoMap wishes to thank the following people and organizations:

National Geographic Society, George E. Stuart, Bill Johnston, Mac Chapin, Bill Threlkeld, Charles Tambiah, Jennie Freeman, Amy Moses, Andrew Nystrom, Heidi Quante, Don Bain, Cherie Semans, Jenna Loyd, Carey Pelton, UC Berkeley Geography 177 students (Fall '96), Anastasia McGhee, Susan Bumps, Richard, Lindy, and Robin Grossinger, Kathy Glass, Catherine E. Campaigne, Ken Coburn, Macromedia Freehand, Alan Abruzzo, Francis Smith, Dan Plumlee, Natalia Vonnegut, Charlie and Barbara Haddenfeldt, Luda Redquat, Karl, Frances and Daniel Malamud-Roam, Joel, Christine, Maya and Zoe Medina, Jesus Lopez, The Pew Charitable Trusts, Margaret MacKenzie-Hooson, Punta Graphics

Many thanks to these organizations for funding this project:
Inter-American Foundation
The John D. and Catherine T. MacArthur Foundation
The Republic of Luxembourg
National Geographic Society
Lannan Foundation

Table of Contents

	Maps	x
	Foreword	xi
1.	Introduction	1
2.	History	3
3.	Maya Homeland	7
4.	People and Place	11
5.	Land Use	19
6.	Culture	25
7.	Village Maps	43
8.	Community Services	119
9.	Tourism	120
10.	Outside Problems	122
11.	Special Topics	128
12.	The Making of the MAYA ATLAS	136
13.	Group Photos	148
	Afterword	150
	Index	151

Maps

Proposed Cultural Homeland *	4
Southern Belize and the World †	12, 13
Maya Population in the Toledo and Stann Creek Districts †*	15
Neighbors of the Maya †	16
Mountains, Rivers, and Valleys †	17
Land Use †*	18
Annual Rainfall †	22
Regions *	42
Village Maps *	45-115
Satellite Image of Southern Belize ‡	116
Community Services †*	118
Travel Time †*	119
Tourism †*	121
Maya Communal Lands, Reservations, and Logging Threats †*¥	123
Outside Threats to Maya Lands †*	124
Sanctuaries, Reserves, and Parks †*°	126
Maya Land Use and Outside Threats †*	127

† Basemap data from *Belize*, Directorate of Overseas Surveys, 1991, series D.O.S. 649/1, sheets NORTH and SOUTH, edition 2-O.S. 1991
¥ Data from Belize Centre for Environmental Studies
° Data from The Land Information Centre, Ministry of Natural Resources, Belize, C.A.
‡ Image acquired from The National Geographic Society

All Data compiled by Maya Mapping Project(MMP) © 1996, Basemap Data from (1) *Belize* 1:250:000, Directorate of Overseas Surveys, 1991, series D.O.S. 649/1, sheets NORTH and SOUTH, edition 2-O.S. 1991 or (2) *Belize* 1:50,000, Directorate of Overseas Surveys, 1991, series E775(DOS4499), Sheets 30-44

FOREWORD

FROM ALL THAT WE KNOW from the patterns that appear among the archaeological sites, hieroglyphic texts, paintings, and monumental sculptures, the ancestors of the present-day Maya built much of their own greatness upon the idea of regions and regional states within the great area that they occupied. Defined by the presence of both the ancient and the modern Maya, that area embraces the Yucatán Peninsula and its broad base and includes the present Mexican states of Chiapas, Campeche, Yucatán, and Quintana Roo, along with Guatemala, Belize, and the western reaches of Honduras and El Salvador. On this landscape the idea of regional political systems began to take tangible form some 2,500 years ago at such places as Calakmul, Nakbe, and uncounted other cities, now long abandoned, that dot the Maya lands from the volcano-studded highlands of the south to the vast lowlands of the north.

In what is now central and southern Belize, the Maya ancestors created powerful regional capitals at Caracol, Lubaantun, and other places. From such centers, the ruling elite traded, waged war, and governed a complex society firmly founded on the extraordinary talents of the ancient Maya farmer who overcame the caprice of tropical rainfall patterns to successfully cultivate maize, beans, squash and other staples.

An extraordinary knowledge of local and regional geography—locations of raw materials for manufacture and trade, water sources and drainage topography, strategic placement of trails and portage routes—is implicit in the ancient success of the Maya. This achievement is particularly evident in the numerous and imposing remains of the Classic Period (ca. AD 250-900). In short, and to anticipate a point made in the introduction that follows, in order to govern successfully, the ancient Maya kings needed to know what they were governing. And so do the local Maya who led the effort that resulted in the present work.

Behind the *Maya Atlas* lies the desire for a better understanding of region. As a product of the local Mopan- and Ke'kchi-speaking Maya of forty-two communities in southern Belize, it is an appropriate and effective extension of the work of the ancestors who early on sought to realize the urgency of regional geographic knowledge to the successful inter-relationship of themselves and their environment.

The *Maya Atlas* appears in a time of an ever-changing and continually threatened environment, and is nothing short of a miracle—a brilliant model of what can be done to increase and diffuse geographic understanding on the all-important level of the small regions upon which the world depends. For the Maya and their neighbors in southern Belize, the contents of this atlas will allow a far better understanding of regional landscape in terms defined by the people themselves. They will be better equipped than are many of us to address issues which affect their future well-being—logging, toxic waste, agricultural practices, and land use in general. Sheer endurance has ever been the greatest hallmark of Maya culture. This work by the Maya people and for the Maya people only underscores that essential characteristic.

George E. Stuart
Vice President and Chairman,
Committee for Research and Exploration
National Geographic Society

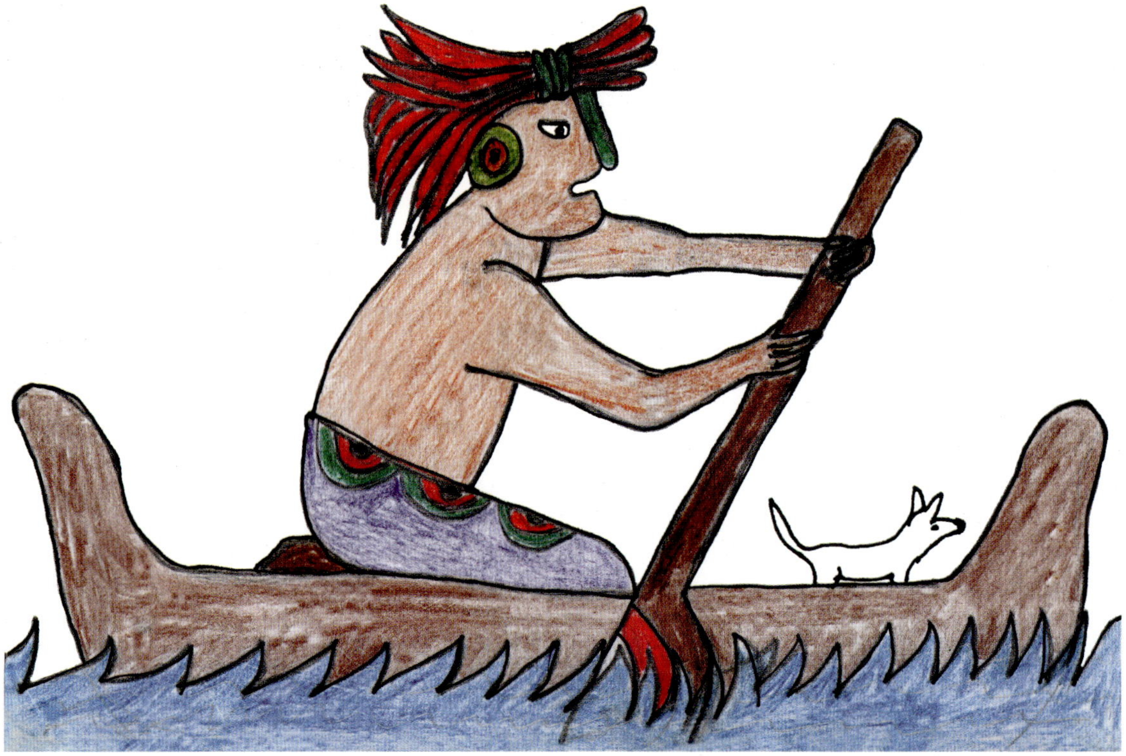

Introduction

The creation of a Maya map was an idea brought up by the previous leaders of the Toledo Maya Cultural Council (TMCC) under the chairmanship of Mr. Estevan Assi.

However, the idea of a Maya map did not come to fruition until a new TMCC Board of Directors was constitutionally elected on December 31, 1995. This new board was spearheaded by Mr. Julian Cho, who got to work revitalizing the Maya organization and implementing the historical work on the map to be produced by the Mayas. The TMCC asked the Toledo Alcaldes Association (TAA) to help, and a partnership was born.

The plan for the much-needed Maya map included the full participation and efforts of all thirty-six communities and leaders thereof in the Toledo District and the five communities and associated leaders in the Stann Creek District. The Mayas of southern Belize realized that having such records would help them know the historical boundaries of their land which, until recently, had never been delineated, as boundaries are a European concept.

We also needed this information to help us press our claim for legal rights to our land. Although we Maya have lived in and around southern Belize for many centuries, the laws of the government of Belize do not recognize our rights to this land. There are ten Indian reservations in the Toledo District which were created by the British colonial government, but most Maya villages are not within these boundaries. According the information collected during the Maya Mapping Project, only 51 percent of the Maya live on one of these reserves and twenty-one villages are outside the boundaries. But, according to Belize law, the Maya do not have legal rights even to the land within the reservations. The government can sell the land where our villages are and where we farm, hunt, and fish without asking us.

But we have been here long before this government or any other government, living on and protecting this land. It has supported us as it does now. International law recognizes these ancestral rights. So we also wanted to map our land so we could show what part of the land is ours.

Through this attempt to show where the Mayas of the Toledo District live and the areas in which we make our living, the Maya Mapping Project was begun. The end result would be the demarcation of the proposed Maya Homeland. But we wanted more than a map showing where the Mayas hunt, fish, farm, and live.

So the TMCC, the TAA, and all of the communities involved with the mapping project decided to add flesh or life to the Maya map by undertaking to make an atlas. Such an atlas would include the history as told by the Mayas, individual village histories as told by the residents, and descriptions of culture, folklore, and the Maya way of life. And by developing an atlas of our land, people throughout Belize and the world will be able to appreciate our unique way of life and respect indigenous land rights.

As an outcome of continuous collaboration and consultation with the Mayas, the TMCC, the TAA, the Indian Law Resource Center (ILRC), and GeoMap from the University of California at Berkeley, the *Maya Atlas* has become a much more important document containing many useful facts—for example, Maya population, Maya stories, Maya photos, Maya artwork, and a series of maps showing the Maya way of using the land.

In June and July of 1996 a number of training workshops were conducted in conjunction with a team of geographers from the University of California at Berkeley. The people involved were the executives of the TMCC and TAA, the Maya Mapping Project administrators and coordinators, and one person from each village called community researchers. At these workshops the leaders and the researchers were trained as cartographers and immediately spread out into all of the Mayan communities to begin researching the atlas, which has now been completed by the Mopan and Ke'kchi Mayas of southern Belize. This is what you are holding in your hands.

Funding for this mapping project has been provided largely by the Inter-American Foundation and the John D. and Catherine T. MacArthur Foundation, both based in the United States. The TMCC and TAA voluntarily contributed and invested their time in this important project.

In recent years the government of Belize began granting massive long-term logging concessions in our Maya territory to foreign-owned companies without any consultation with the Maya. If the government is allowed to continue the granting of logging concessions within our territory, we will lose our Maya culture and land. We asked the Indian Law Resource Center in the U.S.A. to file a lawsuit challenging the government's right to grant concessions on our land, and to assist us in gaining legal security for our ancestral land; we want to establish a homeland that will also be an environmentally protected area under the management of the Maya.

Juan Choc, Santiago Coh, Santos Coc, and Julian Cho at the Atlantic Industries sawmill, Big Falls, April 1996

This atlas aims not only to show the boundaries of the Maya Homeland but to bring out the dynamic interactions of the various communities and their relationship to the environment. In the *Maya Atlas*, we explain current challenges to our traditions and the struggle to preserve our religious beliefs and relationship with Mother Nature. In addition, the atlas gives us an opportunity to explain our links to the sacred Mayan temples dotting the country of Belize and tell you how we have preserved our tradition and culture.

We believe that because such historical and cultural information placed in the *Maya Atlas* is coming from the Maya ourselves, it will have a greater impact on our future generations. Those who exploit our rainforest and environment are brought to light. Moreover, the *Maya Atlas* serves as evidence of the existence of the Mayas as living people, and may clear the notion of the Mayas being an ancient race known only through archaeological sites or recent immigrants to Belize. How can we, Mayas, be considered immigrants? We are the original inhabitants of Toledo Belize who know no boundaries. The concept of putting down boundaries is European.

The Mopan and the Ke'kchi Mayas have always lived in harmony until the coming of the Europeans. Our religious beliefs and traditions are the same. The concept of one ethnic group being superior to the other started when the Europeans began their Christianization crusade. The Ke'kchi resisted Christianization more than the Mopan. The Christianized Mopan were made to feel superior to the "pagan" Ke'kchi. Thus began the rule of divide and conquer.

Today, the Mopan and Ke'kchi Maya recognize each other as Brothers. The bottom line is that all are Mayas and we are bent on resolving the problems that differences make in the communities.

The greatest strength of the Maya Atlas is that it was created by many different people, bearing the imprint of multiple voices. You will hear those voices when you read our book, and they will not always sound the same. Our elders will tell you about our traditional ways because their perspective is traditional, while our young people may describe the problems we face from a different point of view. The village histories were written by a member of each village. They are not uniform because they relate what is significant to the people of the village. Some of the sections contain information that was taken in substantial part from interviews with elders and village leaders, and we have given you their words as they were spoken. Every person who participated wrote with their own eyes and their own heart. They are not always the same, but they are the eyes and the hearts of the Maya. We hope you will appreciate the rich texture and experience we offer in this book. You are learning about the Maya of southern Belize in a way that no one has before, and we welcome you to our world.

Juan Cal, Eduardo Salam Jr., and Diego Bol—founding members of the TMCC, at the TMCC office in San Antonio, July 1993

Santos Coc, Estevan Assi, and Juan Choc at the Atlantic Industries Sawmill, Big Falls, May 1996

History

The Mayas of Toledo are the direct descendants of the ancient Mayas whose civilization reached its peak around A.D. 900. The continuous use of the Maya temples for religious purposes is testimony to their connection with the past. Present-day Mopan Maya descendants were found living in the vicinity of the Moho River by the Spanish missionaries, and present-day Mopan and Ke'kchi Mayas speak about the Christianization ordeal in Punta Gorda Town. Many of the Mayas who refused to be Christianized fled into the interior to take refuge in the Maya Mountain range. The Mopan call these people *Che'il* and the Ke'kchi call them *Chol*.

Both Ke'kchi and Mopan continue to look up to these unconverted Mayas. They speak to their leaders through prayers and incense burning, exhorting their names— *Wal Itza*, *Wal Shucaneb*, *Wal Taca*, and *Wal Cua*. These Mayan leaders are considered to be the caretakers of wild animals. They live in caves and were often contacted in the past to assist hunters and chicle workers. Present-day Mayas speak of their contact with them during the period of mahogany and chicle operators. When workers came down from the forest for Christmas or Easter vacation, the forest would become silent, and the few Mayas who stayed behind speak of seeing Mayan children cracking cohune nuts on foot trails used by mahogany workers. A few chicle workers speak of being assisted by these wild Indians in bleeding of chicle trees in return for salt. Hunters have also met these *Che'il* and made secret agreements to exchange meat for salt.

Anthropologists and Mayanist Dr. Leventhal wrote a report for the Supreme Court of Belize supporting our claim to our land. In it he states that Maya were living in what is now the Toledo District of Belize when the Spanish first arrived here. "There is clear reference [in the 16th century] to small numbers of Maya people living within the Pusila River area of this Toledo District region of Belize. These people are described as Manche-Chol Maya living in very small communities, perhaps of not more than 10-20 people in each cluster." Mayanist, Dr. Grant Jones stated to the Court in support of our lawsuit, "The principal inhabitants of the Toledo District during the 16th through 18th centuries were Mayas who spoke Yucateca languages, Chol, and Mopan. Peoples of Kekchi Chol ethnicity may have been moving in and out of the area long before the well-known migrations from Guatemala during the late 19th century."

A western boundary to limit the expansion for British settlement did not appear on maps until 1850, but it was a hypothetical line on paper only. It was not until 1934 that a western boundary was surveyed separating the colony, British Honduras, from neighboring Guatemala and Mexico. Thus the much-discussed boundary has only been a reality for the past 63 years.

The Toledo Maya Cultural Council

The Toledo Maya Cultural Council (TMCC) was created on April 15, 1978, in response to the systematic destruction of Mayan culture by the government of Belize. The Mayan land began to be parceled out to political friends without consultation of the *alcaldes* or Mayan communities. The *alcalde* system was being gradually eroded, and more power given to the village councils. The process of forced assimilation and acculturation was intensified.

The *alcaldes* became concerned and thus called a meeting in 1978 to discuss the issue, giving birth to the Toledo Indian Movement. The Toledo Indian Movement was immediately branded by the government as subversive. To remove the stigma, in 1982 the name was changed to the Toledo Maya Cultural Council.

The Toledo Maya Cultural Council is a representative body for cooperation among the Mayas of the Toledo District. The Council was set up to safeguard and promote the economic, social, and educational interests of the Mayas. The Council also endeavors to support and strengthen unity and mutual understanding among the Mayas and to publicize the situation and the aims of the Mayas. The Council seeks recognition of the special position of the Mayas and works toward measures to ensure that they may continue to live in their ancestral territory. The Council aims to coordinate actions by the Mayas of Toledo in the solution of common problems.

On August 29, 1986, the Toledo Maya Cultural Council was registered under the Companies Ordinance Chapter 206 of the laws of Belize.

According to the mission statement, the main objectives of the TMCC are:

1) To ensure unity among the Mayas of Toledo.

2) To strengthen the concepts of indigenous and cultural rights based upon the principle of equality.

3) To represent all Belizean indigenous Mayas of Toledo in international and national forums.

4) To be a non-religious, non-governmental, and non-profit-making organization.

5) To participate in international forums concerned with solving the issues of human development and solidarity.

6) To assist Maya communities in identifying and implementing projects with a view of creating employment, self-reliance, and improvement of the quality of life.

7) To promote, coordinate, and supervise cooperative ventures.

8) To take steps for the recognition of the Council in government policy decisions in matters relating to the well-being of the Maya People, e.g. Indian land rights, archaeological sites, museums, etc.

9) To preserve the archaeological presence of the indigenous people and to obtain a leading role in its management.

10) To promote the Maya languages and to encourage cohesion among Maya through cultural activities such as the arts, music, drama, craft, science, and ceremonies.

11) To promote activities that will strengthen the cultural base of the indigenous people in their struggle to preserve their values and identity.

12) To seek and raise capital and financing from person(s) or agencies in Belize or elsewhere for the purpose of aiding or carrying into effect projects or undertakings to

realize the objectives of the Council.

13) To abolish the possibility of physical and cultural genocide and ethnocide wherever it may occur.

14) To combat racism and ensure political, economic, and social justice.

15) To promote the respect and understanding of other cultures, national and international, to collaborate in the solution of problems that inhibit the development of humanity.

16) To promote and seek adequate health, housing, education, and all necessary means to realize the Mayas' full human potential and dignity.

17) To do such other lawful things as may appear to be incidental or conducive to the achievement of the above objectives.

At the inception of the Toledo Maya Cultural Council in 1978, members of the Executive Council were elected without regard to whether they were Mopan or Ke'kchi. However, in 1986, to ensure that all our Maya communities would be represented, the TMCC provided that the executive committee would have six Mopan and six Ke'kchi members. The Toledo Maya Cultural Council, along with the thirty-six village leaders *(alcaldes)* of the Mayan communities, have successfully thwarted the erosion of the *alcalde* system. In 1992, the Toledo Alcaldes Association was established as the legal representative of the Mayan communities and given recognition, in principle, by the government. Bi-monthly meetings and workshops are carried out to educate the *alcaldes* and to inform them of current developments.

Through lobbying visits to Belmopan, the capital of Belize, the Toledo Maya Cultural Council, through the help of Diego Bol, was able to secure in 1983 thirty scholarships and bursaries for Mayan students to attend the Toledo Community College in Punta Gorda. Thereafter, thirty Mayan students were awarded assistance yearly. In 1986, the TMCC initiated, through a private enterprise, the first student bus service to Toledo Community College. Presently there are six government-run school buses, shuttling Mayan students to high school.

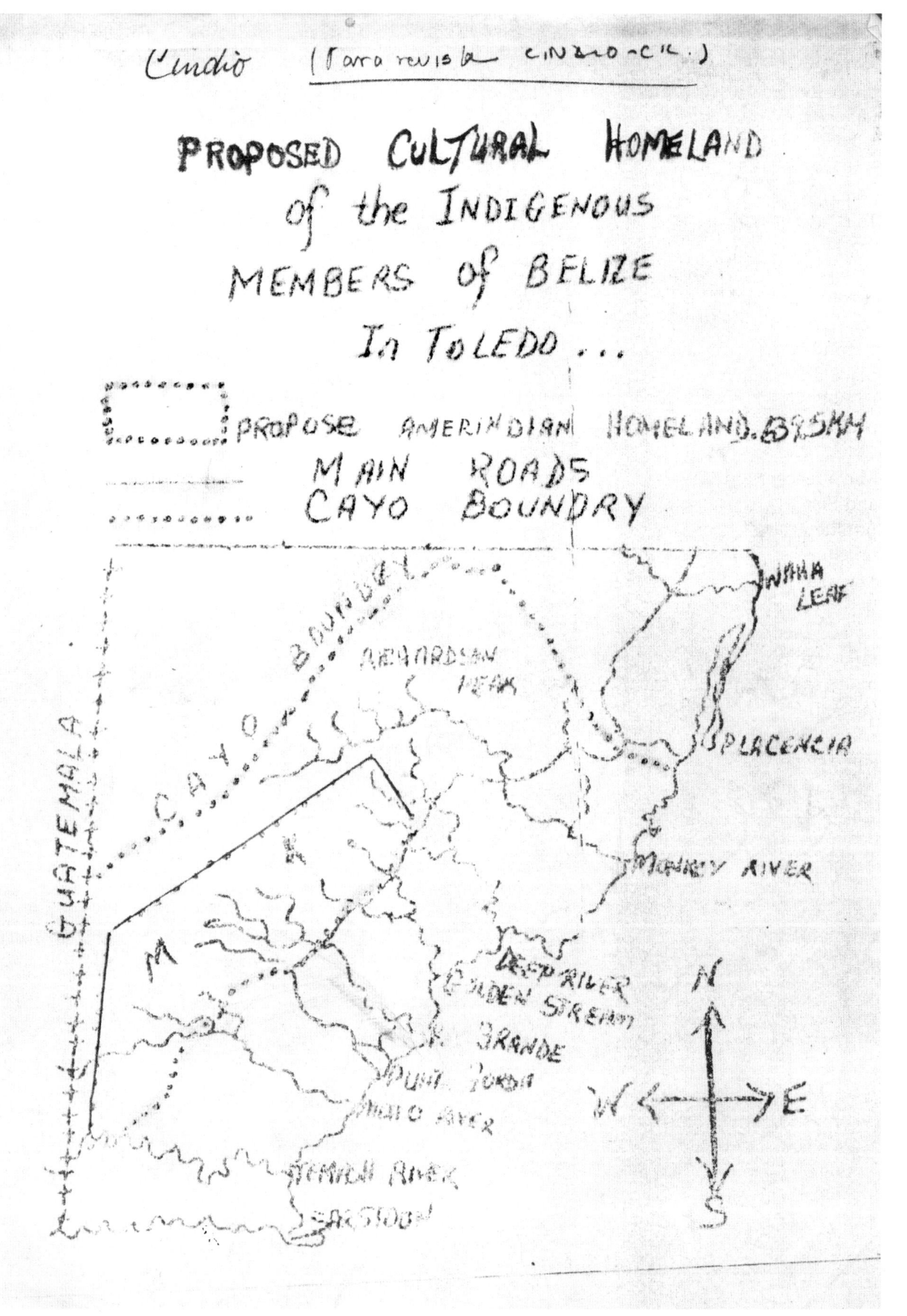

Julian Cho and Diego Bol drafted the homeland sketch map in 1986 in San Antonio village.

In the past, the Maya never had the opportunity to progress in the educational field. In part through the TMCC's efforts, approximately 300 Maya students are currently receiving secondary education at the Toledo Sister Caritas Lawrence CSC and the Toledo Community College in Punta Gorda each year. TMCC has also challenged the government of Belize to upgrade and create schools in Maya communities and to make scholarships available to young people beyond primary school. We fought for a place for Maya teachers in schools. The late Fr William Mesmer SJ, manager of Catholic primary schools in Toledo, was open to TMCC's suggestion in the 1980s of allowing Maya teachers to teach their own people, and Sister Caritas encouraged Maya girls to pursue secondary education. However, much more needs to be done if we, the Maya, are to advocate effectively for our human rights to pursue sustainable economic development. We would like to train our young people in conservation management, in administration and managerial tasks, in the political process, and in other ways that will make it possible for us to solve the problems our people face.

The Mayas of the Toledo District of southern Belize are faced with severe socio-economic and political problems. The education system is woefully inadequate, and consequently the illiteracy rate is the highest in the country. The Mayas are often called "the poorest of the poor" in Belize, with government statistics indicating that the average annual family income is only US $600. Basic social infrastructure, including health care, transportation, and community services, is sorely underdeveloped. To compound these problems, the Mayas lack a means to redress their grievances, as we have absolutely no political representation in the government of Belize and are treated as a "forgotten people" of our own country. The TMCC wants to change that.

In its attempt to alleviate the economic hardships faced by the Mayas, the TMCC has secured funds for the Cedar Farmers Group to establish a small sawmill project to harvest logs on areas cleared for farming.

Geronimo Coc (project coordinator) and Julio Sanchez (cartographer) at the TMCC office in Punta Gorda

The TMCC acquired funds for a video project and trained and provided jobs for Mayan youths in the documentation of Mayan culture. The Toledo Maya Cultural Council assisted women's groups to improve the quality of their native crafts through workshops and exchange visits. In 1993, the TMCC was able to secure a British market for organically grown cacao beans. Some 40,000 pounds of cacao beans are exported to England annually.

Through a Bi-annual General Assembly, community workshops, and involvement in community affairs, the Toledo Maya Cultural Council was able to bring back to the communities an awareness of Mayan identity and pride in their culture. Mayan cultural dances are revived and many other indigenous organizations sprang up: the Belize Maya Institute in Belmopan, the Sucootz Maya Organization in the Cayo District, The Mayan Association of Belize City, The Ke'kchi Council of Belize, and the Maya Centre Indigenous Organization.

The Toledo District contains the most intact tropical wet forest remaining in Belize, and possibly all of Central America. The majority of the inhabitants of the Toledo District are indigenous Maya people, most of whom subsist through *milpa* (slash-and-burn or slash-and-mulch) agricultural production, growing maize (corn) as the staple crop. The land the Maya live on and that has sustained us for centuries still retains abundant forests, but these are threatened more every day. A recent report by World Resources Institute states that Belize has already lost 65 percent of its frontier forest, and 66 percent of the remaining forests are threatened.

The ultimate dream of the Mayas is yet to be achieved—the security of tenure to their lands and the creation of a 500,000-acre Maya Homeland. To achieve this, the Mayas have obtained legal assistance and are developing a practical, long-term sustainable development plan for control of their homeland. The government of Belize can rest assured that the Mayas are not seeking the establishment of a separate state, but merely secure land tenure, a fair share of the Mayas' patrimony, and a meaningful sustainable relationship with Mother Nature. The development envisioned is one that would preserve humanity and nature, not the reckless use of resources, based on greed, that hastens the extinction of our way of life and that of humankind.

We are now working harder than ever to help our people participate in all levels of the political process. More recently, the TMCC has taken a direct interest in environmental affairs, understanding the relationship between clean and protected natural environment and the well-being of our people. We are currently confronting several urgent problems that threaten our environment and lands. Since 1993, the government of Belize has granted seventeen logging concessions on Maya land—over 500,000 acres of rainforest. One 48,000-acre concession is in the Columbia River Forest Reserve. Local communities can expect nothing more than a few very low-wage jobs in return for muddied rivers, damaged roads, loss of wildlife, and social disruption caused by logging. Given the tenuous legal status of Maya land claims in the region, an intrusion of exploitative, land-destroying operations directly threatens the Maya communities. The TMCC has led an historic campaign to protect our natural heritage. We organized a successful public demonstration; published several articles in the national and international press; negotiated with the Prime Minister of Belize; and traveled to Washington D.C. twice to seek support for our efforts. The TMCC will continue its struggle to achieve the goals of the Maya as long as it is necessary.

Toledo Alcaldes Association

"Alcalde" is not a Maya word. In the Maya world, many centuries ago, the law used to be within the hands of Mayan Kings, Chiefs, Queens, Mayan priests, the *Hun Utchben Ilma* [Mopan], and *Hun Shil* [Ke'kchi] (shamans), and their elder warriors, for it was a communal duty to see things go right at that time. Around the year 1500, this system began to change when the Maya were found by the people who came from across the sea [from Europe]. These new people exploited everything the Maya knew for their own greed.

In times past the Maya chiefs served for life. Today leadership is limited to two years by a recent amendment of the Belize Constitution. The difference was that in the old days, Maya leaders lived in independent nations by themselves—free. Today, Mayas live in an oppressive situation where a non-Maya government dictates to them how to live.

Children of San Miguel collecting firewood

Today we know our law men as *Notch Winic* or *Pohlil Kah* [Mopan], and *Mamah* or *Ruj'il* [Ke'kchi] in the Maya language. In the Maya communities the word *alcalde*, which is Spanish, is still used today. This *Pohlil Kah* is a person on whom villagers depend for the smooth governing of all indigenous communities. He is very important and carries a lot of responsibilities for his Maya people. When one of his subjects misbehaves, he judges the misdeeds committed. The punishment is to pay fines or to work for a certain time cleaning in the community.

This chief must work hard. Sometimes, if weather permits, he assembles the villagers for a vigil night to bring down rain. He calls the communal cleaning of his village, the *fajina*. He manages the Maya's communal land. He is the Maya inspector of schools. He takes care of the dead. His term of office was one year, but now by law, he is to serve two years. Traditionally, when the *alcalde's* or the *Pohlil Kah's* term of office expired, he summoned his people to a very important meeting to select a new leader. To contest the post, four persons were nominated by one person among the crowd. Then by secret ballots they voted and the person who received the majority became the chief; the second-place person became his deputy *Pohlil Kah*; the third became the chief of Maya police. Then the swearing-in is set, where each *alcalde* makes an oath to serve his people to the best of his ability. This is a modern-day practice.

In March of 1992, *alcaldes* from several villages—San Pedro Columbia, San Miguel, Silver Creek, and Big Falls—met to form a steering committee that was tasked to organize the Toledo Alcaldes Association. This steering committee was chaired by Santiago Moh, Jr., *alcalde* of Big Falls. On December 12, 1992, a General Meeting was held for the first time to form the Toledo Alcaldes Association. Santiago Moh became the first chairman. His term of office ended on December 31, 1992. In January 1993 Lorenzo Pop was elected chairman. In January 1994 Mr. Santiago Coh, *alcalde* of Silver Creek, was elected chairman. In January of 1995 he was re-elected and served for two more years. Then on January 11, 1997, Leonardo Acal was elected as the new chairman.

Recognition of the Toledo Alcaldes Association, February 24, 1994

The TAA would not have become a reality were it not for the TMCC and the Ke'kchi Council of Belize (KCB).

Goals and Objectives of the TAA

1) To educate the public on the significance and importance of the *alcalde* system.
2) To promote recognition from the government of Belize of the invaluable contribution the *alcaldes* have made to the country.
3) To organize a reputable swearing-in ceremony for new *alcaldes*.
4) To address the concerns of the communities in general.
5) To lobby the government of Belize for Maya development (e.g. scholarships to the Toledo Community College)
6) To promote the recognition of the TAA by international governments.

Achievements of the TAA

1) A swearing-in ceremony is now conducted every two years and has the participation of the Solicitor General of Belize and all the *alcaldes* and the general public.
2) The TAA was given recognition and a scroll by Queen Elizabeth II on February 24, 1994.
3) The TAA obtained a grant for 40 scholarships for underprivilegded children to attend secondary school.

Maya Homeland

The Mayas will undoubtedly remain a distinct ethnic group for generations to come, continuing to press for equality in educational standards, occupations, and social life. They strive to retain the right to maintain their own identity and develop their lives as they wish within the framework of their culture and Belizean society.

It is with these goals in mind that the Mayas claim a Homeland to preserve their culture, land, freedom, and democracy. The idea was born among the Ke'kchi and Mopan Mayas of the Toledo District, developed by the Toledo Maya Cultural Council, and endorsed by the Toledo Alcaldes Association. The Homeland would encompass all the Maya villages and geographical areas traditionally used by the Mayas. Since our ancestors were the original inhabitants of Belize, and because we are still using the land, we have a legal claim to the land based on ancestral rights.

Encounters between the Maya and the British woodcutters were not peaceful. The Mayas were forced to retreat into the interior to accommodate logging. The British, in an attempt to subdue the Mayas, created ten Maya reservations amounting to about 77,000 acres. The reserves were never physically demarcated nor defined in the country's constitution as the communal property of the Mayas. The reservations constructed by the British to subjugate the Mayas were not honored by the Mayas. Many villages were constructed outside of the reservations without the government's approval, as the Mayas regard all of these lands as their own, the home of their forefathers, who built magnificent temples to manifest their presence.

Despite the neglect of regional infrastructure by the central government, the Mayas flourished in these lands by being self-sufficient like their ancestors thousands of years ago. They planted their corn, beans, and fruit trees and built their houses out of materials from the forest. The Maya traditional healers treated ailments among the populace. The communal land system was the norm. Law and order was kept by the *alcalde*. The first two villages to be opened to Western civilization, by the introduction of primary education in the 1940s, were San Antonio and San Pedro Columbia.

In 1974 the Honorable Florencio Marin, Minister of Lands in the government of Belize, initiated plans to abolish the reservation system and to open the Toledo District to foreign investors. The TMCC opposed such a move, arguing that once the reservation system was abolished, the *alcaldes* would have no role in determining who gets land in the villages, and law and order would not be respected. The government of Belize regards the communal land system as an obstacle to development.

The TMCC is willing to accept the abolition of the reservation system on the condition that a Maya Homeland is secured. Only a Homeland would guarantee adequate land distribution for the Mayas. Under a Communal Homeland proposal, those who prefer to work the land communally would have that privilege. The Homeland would accommodate Mayas who want to lease land for *milpa*, tourism, or other meaningful development.

It is the philosophy of Mayas that land cannot be bought or sold. The land is sacred. For example, can we buy air?

Children of San Miguel

Maya Temple

Clouds? Rain? Sunshine? In the same way land cannot be sold. Individuals who may want to sell a parcel of land within the Homeland can only sell it to other Mayas or leave the land for the benefit of the community.

The *alcaldes* and the Land Trust Committee, duly elected democratically by all village leaders, will decide how land is distributed in the Maya Homeland. The Land Trust Committiee stresses that the Homeland must be developed and managed by the indigenous occupants for their own economic development. All places considered to be sacred resources for the community would not be used. The *alcaldes* and the Land Trust Committiee would decide which land or resources would be co-managed by the government and Mayas.

The Homeland proposal has the support of all the villages in the Toledo District. In order to achieve a Maya Homeland, the TMCC asked the Indian Law Resource Center to do an extensive search on the historical land rights of the Mayas in collaboration with Belizean attorney-at-law Lisa Shoman. Upon the completion of the report showing that the Maya have a valid claim to their land based on ancestral rights, the TMCC held a series of workshops to educate the local communities.

The creation of a Homeland under the status of a "Freehold Title" is the ultimate goal of the Mayas. The production of permanent crops such as citrus, cacao, spices, and *achiote* is encouraged. The Land Trust Committee would endorse areas to be surveyed for such use through individual or group effort. This system would give the Mayas time for transition into the free-enterprise market economy without being exploited, thereby becoming the direct beneficiaries.

Existing private properties will be respected. Village land committees along with the village *alcalde* would plan the village, parceling the lot for better management. One hundred acres would be left around the village to accommodate future expansion and for the poor, the disabled, and the aged to collect firewood. Streams must be protected from erosion and forest preserved along the river banks. Forests should not be cleared for plantations, but may be used for selective logging on a small scale providing the community benefits. Ruins will be preserved and improved for tourists' attraction by the Land Trust Committee.

Community property will be tax-free, but any land parceled out for individual or group possession will be taxed and payable to the government of Belize. This is a gesture of working in cooperation with the government of Belize for the development of our country.

The Mayas are not proposing to be an autonomous body, but rather the right to be consulted about our future. This is a move to guarantee that every Maya has an inalienable right to a piece of land no matter what his or her financial status.

Finally, the Mayas do not want anything extravagant, nor do we want anything harmful to the legitimate interests of non-Mayas. We want our rights determined and recognized. We want a settlement based upon justice. We want a full opportunity to make a future not only for ourselves but also our children. It is having a small portion of this country and this world that we call our home that will guarantee our culture's survival in the next century and beyond. We want this done in such a way that in the future we shall be able to live securely and work with all the people as our brothers and sisters and fellow citizens of this global village.

Crystal-clean Poite River

Mrs. Sho, Eleuterio Cho (former chairlady), and Isabella Coc (present chairlady) of the Women's Group in Maya Mopan, Stann Creek District

The Oldest Village

Pueblo Viejo is considered to be one of the first settlements in what is now southern Belize. Returning to our ancestral lands in the year 1840, our forefathers settled near the western border of neighboring Guatemala, approximately two and one half miles to the east. Later the community began to expand and grow rapidly in population, and it now houses about one hundred seventy-five families.

Most of the Ke'kchi and Mopan Maya came in groups from neighboring Guatemala to find their roots here in Belize. At present Pueblo Viejo has gone through many changes; development is taking place very quickly. Services for health have been placed within the community. There is now a new school, a police station, a community telephone, and water pumps. All-weather roads are also in place.

Transportation of crops is done by people who own bus services, and other small vehicles that go to and from Punta Gorda Town. Many Maya students travel by schoolbus on a daily basis to educational institutions in Punta Gorda Town.

Corn in the Cave
A Story

Once upon a time, there was an old man named Mr. Shucaneb. He had a daughter named Miss Abas. A boy named Quix Mes came to Mr. Shucaneb's house looking for his daughter and went away with her into a mountain cave called Sak-lege, along with all Mr. Shucaneb's riches and belongings.

Mr. Shucaneb did not know what had happened. Somebody gave him the news that his daughter and all his riches were stolen by Mr. Quix Mes and carried into the mountain cave called Sak-lege.

He was told that he should send a messenger to check things to prove if it was true. He sent two dogs. In those days they called a dog a tiger, so the messengers were tigers [jaguars]. He sent the two tigers, but he was told that if his daughter is there at the cave, the dogs (tigers) will not come back.

The dogs (tigers) stayed a long time. It was a month or two until they came back. The dogs gave the news that Mr. Shucaneb's daughter was at the Mountain Cave with all his riches and belongings. But he was not satisfied with the dogs' message. He sent more messengers—a big hawk and a small hawk—back to the Mountain Cave Sak-lege to check on all his riches and belongings.

When the two hawks came back they told Mr. Shucaneb that everything was there, stored by Mr. Quix Mes at the mountain cave called Sak-lege, and his daughter also. In that cave many kinds of animals were there: the raccoon, peccary, gibnut [paca], rabbit, and quash [coatimundi].

Among these animals in the cave, no one knew where this Rabbit went out or when he comes back. They usually slept together. In his sleep, the Rabbit fart himself, and all of them said to him, "Your fart stinks." They asked him what he ate. He answered, "Some fruits." He did not tell them exactly what he ate. After that they started to track him. Everywhere he went, they went along with him because they wanted to know where he went and what he ate. After they stopped to watch him, he squatted down by a wee-wee ant trail, when the wee-wee ants [leaf-cutter ants] were backing more corn off [carrying] from the cave called Sak-lege.

The Rabbit took away the corn from the wee-wee ant and ate it, but the others were tracking him, and they told the Rabbit, "Now we know what you eat." And they knew that corn was in the Mountain Cave.

The Rabbit pushed his hand in the cave, but the wee-wee ants bit him and he jerked his hand from the ground. All kinds of birds were there to eat corn. There they found corn and they brought back the news to Mr. Shucaneb.

He knew that all his belongings were there.

Then Mr. Shucaneb chose three young strong men to break into the Mountain Cave and take away all his riches, his belongings, his daughter, and the corn that was discovered.

These three young men are named Sext: first, second, and third Sext. They tried and tried to break into the cave. They could not. They finally gave up. Discouraged, they came up with a plan. They had a younger brother named Puc-Bulum, but Puc-Bulum had a sickly, swollen foot. He was weak, but at last the three young men went and told him to break into the cave. He responded, "What will I do? I am not strong. I am sick." But finally he said he could try. "But don't depend on me," he added.

Puc-Bulum had an idea. He did not go immediately. He set a date and time. He thought first how he would do it. He went to the cave. He went over it to find which side of the cave was shallow. But this Puc-Bulum is really the thunder.

While watching the cave, he saw a woodpecker. He told the woodpecker to check out which side of the cave was shallow. Finally, the woodpecker found the

Maya King in ceremonial dress (historical)

shallow part, but Puc-Bulum told the woodpecker to be careful; if he saw lightning, he should fly downward. When Puc-Bulum flashed lightning, the woodpecker flew upward and was hit by the lightning. The woodpecker's face dropped half-dead. Puc-Bulum cracked open the mountain by striking it with lightning and all the corn was revealed. Some corn was half roasted, some was burned, and some was left untouched; this is the origin of the different types of corn.

Puc-Bulum went far.

But the three young, strong men went ahead picking up all the corn and left a bag of bad corn for Puc-Bulum.

Now the three young, strong men went ahead and planted the corn they picked at the cave. They planted before Puc-Bulum. They planted healthy corn, but none of it germinated or grew.

Puc-Bulum planted afterwards. He planted the bad corn. All of it germinated and grew well.

Now the three strong men were surprised at what had happened. Their corn did not grow at all. So they went to Puc-Bulum to ask him a question: "How did you plant your corn field?"

Puc-Bulum answered, "Probably you have to burn the corn first." They burned their corn, but it made it worse, and none grew. They went to ask him a second time. Puc-Bulum said, "Probably you should boil the corn first, then plant." They did it again. . . none grew again.

They went to him a third time. Puc-Bulum told them to bathe and wash and change clothes, which they did. Nothing.

They went to him a fourth time.

Then Puc-Bulum had mercy on them. He explained to them how to plant corn. Puc-Bulum used a trick on them because the three strong men tricked Puc-Bulum at the beginning.

So that is the story of how they discovered corn.

Traditional Hunting
A Story

Once upon a time, a man used to hunt. He hunted all the time but could not catch anything. He would just go hunt; he did not pray every time he went. He met some country people who came home with game meat, but he could not catch his own.

He used a shotgun from others, but he could not catch or shoot anything. He did not pray or burn incense, asking the Hills and Valleys. He hunted in the same places where others hunt.

One day while he was in the bush hunting, he started to curse bad words, cursing the Hills and Valleys. All of a sudden he saw a boy in front of him asking what he was doing. He answered, "I am hunting some game meat for myself, but I did not catch anything. I see my country partners—they catch meat for themselves, but I can't."

The boy told him to come along with him because his father told him to do so.

The boy said his father wanted to talk to the man. The man asked how he should go. The boy told him to close his eyes. So the man closed his eyes and when he opened them again, he was in a different place. The boy told his father that the man had arrived.

The boy's father, an old man, said, "OK." An old lady began to talk to the man, saying, "Now I sent for you, because you want to hunt, but you do not pray and burn." which means he did not ask in prayers or burn incense to the Hills and Valleys. He was told by the old lady, "You did not think about anything, why it's important. Burning incense is like feeding me, it's like I eat and drink. You are always hunting without giving anything."

Three days he was there with the old man and lady. He was with them when a hunter appeared in a dream and the hunter began to pray and burn incense. In his dream he saw what the hunter man was doing.

After the hunter finished praying and burning incense, all of a sudden curassow, quam, and peccary, all game animals, started to come out. The hunter started to shoot. He got all he needed. He went home loaded with meat for himself. That is how the man learned how and what it means to hunt. He was told by the old man and old lady that he should do likewise and that he should tell the story to all his friends or anybody, that it is important to pray and burn incense.

So the man headed home, but he was lost for three days. When he reached his house he was asked where he had been. He began to explain the story, how to hunt and how to pray for anything you wish to do. After three days the man died. He went back where he came from, to the Hills and Valleys.

It is still our Mayan tradition to burn incense and pray to the Hills and Valleys.

Yum Kax, the corn god

People and Place

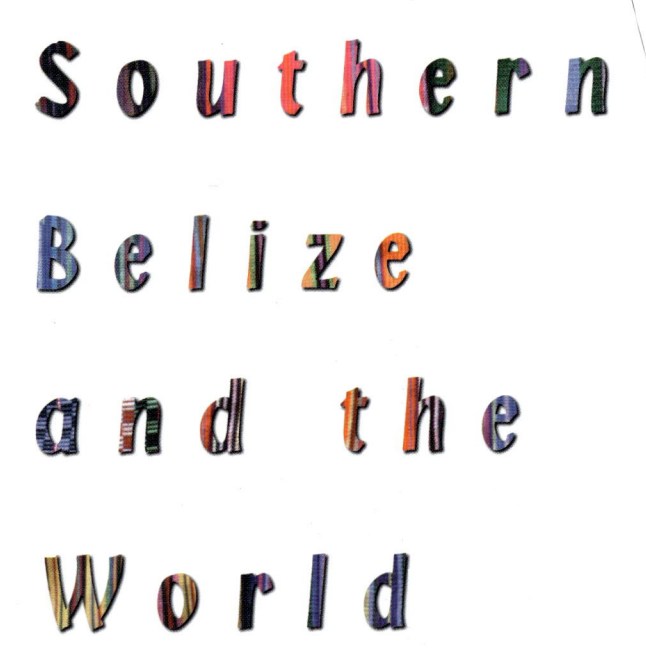

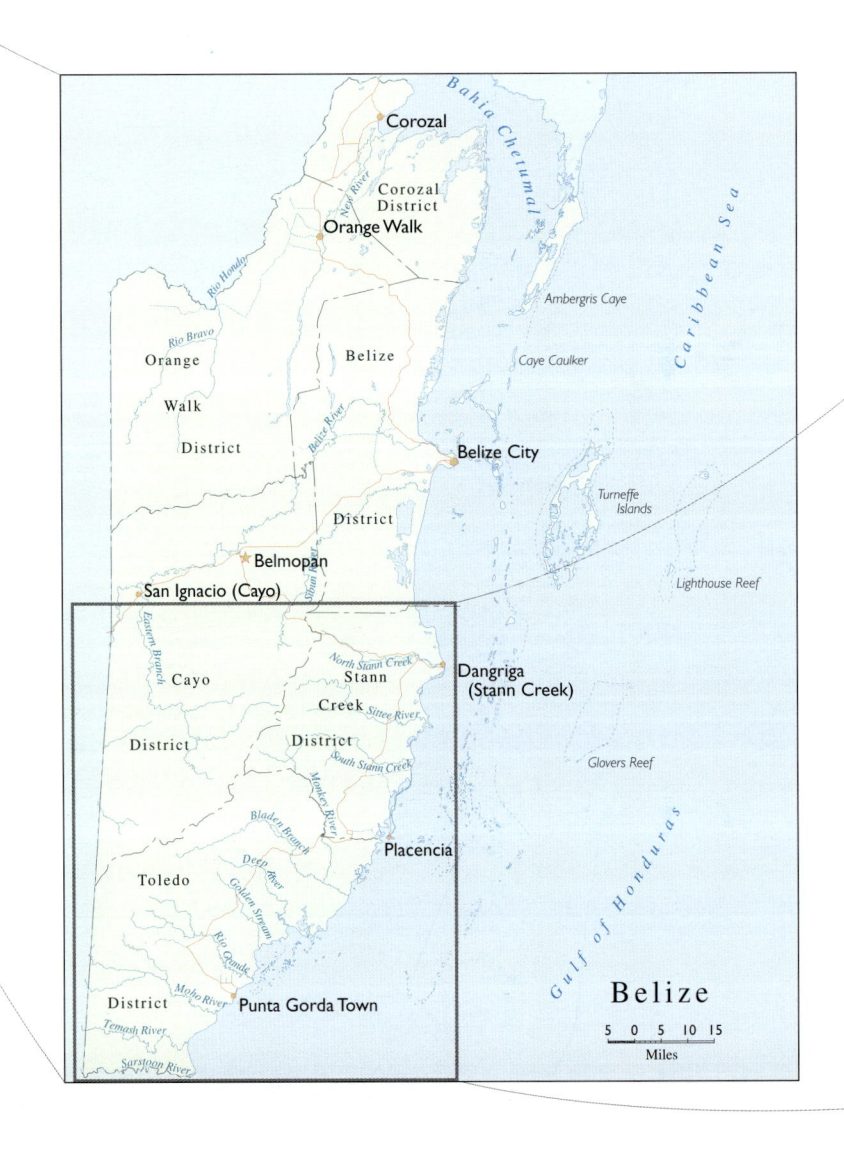

Southern Belize and the World

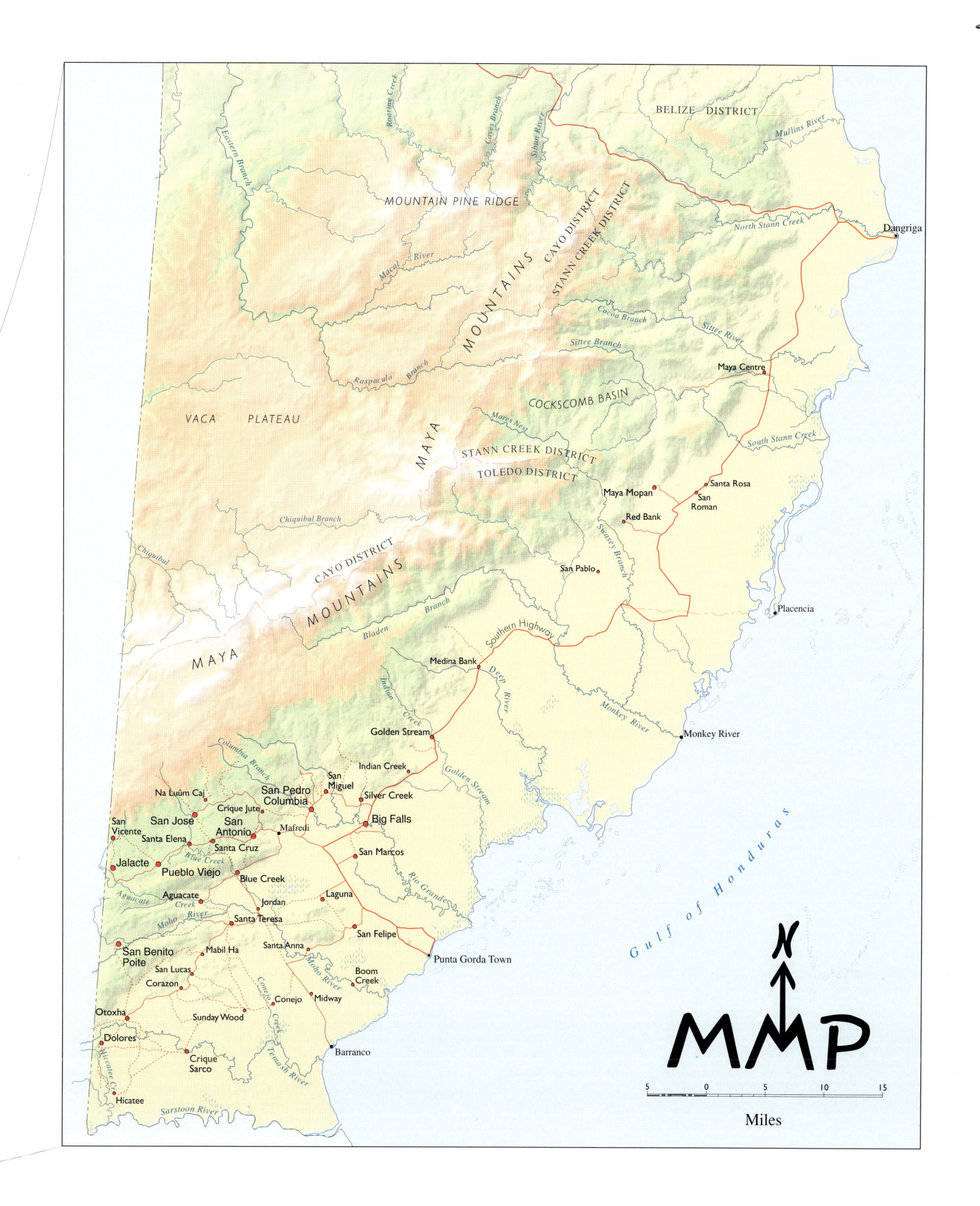

Population

Southern Belize is home to approximately 14,000 Maya (nearly 11,000 counted in this survey). Two Maya peoples—the Mopan and Ke'kchi—live in southern Belize. The Ke'kchi have the most numerous villages and population; the Mopan have the largest villages and most concentrated population. Most villages today are expanding and the population growth is obvious. In 1996, the Maya Mapping Project(MMP) census counted 10,694 individuals from some 2,004 households in southern Belize.

Southern Belize has two administrative districts, Toledo and Stann Creek. Bordering Guatemala on two sides, Toledo is comprised of thirty-six Mayan villages located in the lowlands and uplands throughout the region; twenty-four are Ke'kchi villages, six are Mopan, and six are mixed Mopan and Ke'kchi. Immediately north of Toledo District is Stann Creek District where six Maya villages are located. Five are Mopan and one is Ke'kchi.

The Toledo District has been Mayan territory for many centuries. Mayan people were the first to occupy and use the land for subsistence agriculture. Four thousand years ago, the Maya were occupying the land that is now known as Belize.

The Maya have had continuous occupation and use of these lands that are known today as southern Belize. This gives us right to ancestral claims and we are working to gain legal recognition for those rights from the government of Belize

Regional Identity

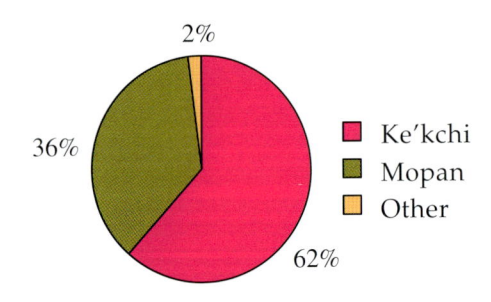

- Ke'kchi: 62%
- Mopan: 36%
- Other: 2%

Regional Age Distribution

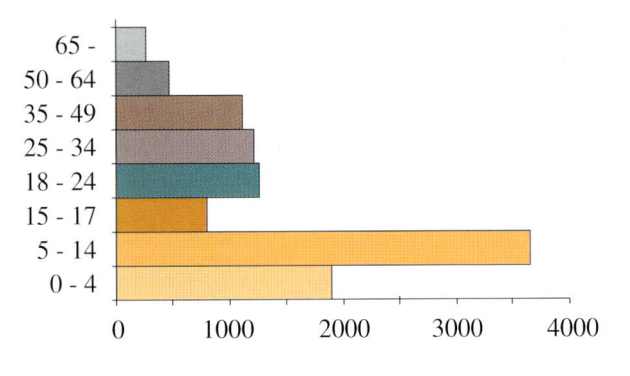

Age	
65 -	
50 - 64	
35 - 49	
25 - 34	
18 - 24	
15 - 17	
5 - 14	
0 - 4	

(0 to 4000)

Regional Religious Practice

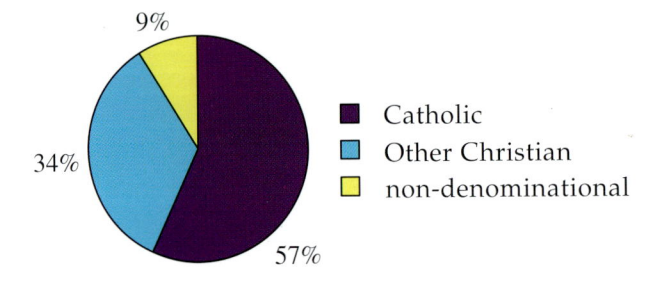

- Catholic: 57%
- Other Christian: 34%
- non-denominational: 9%

Poite River

Maya Population in Toledo and Stann Creek Districts

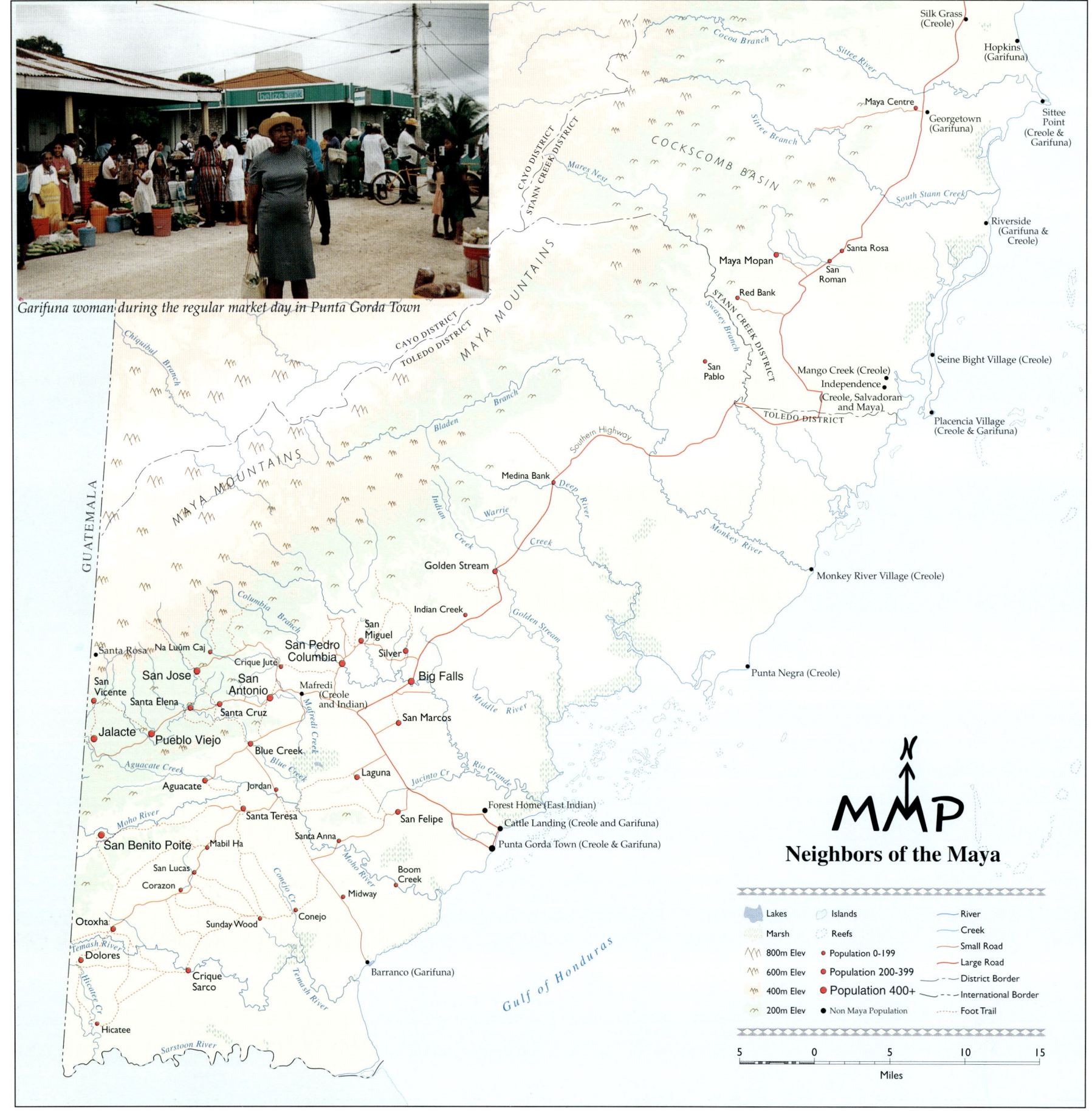

Garifuna woman during the regular market day in Punta Gorda Town

MMP
Neighbors of the Maya

Mountains, Rivers, and Valleys

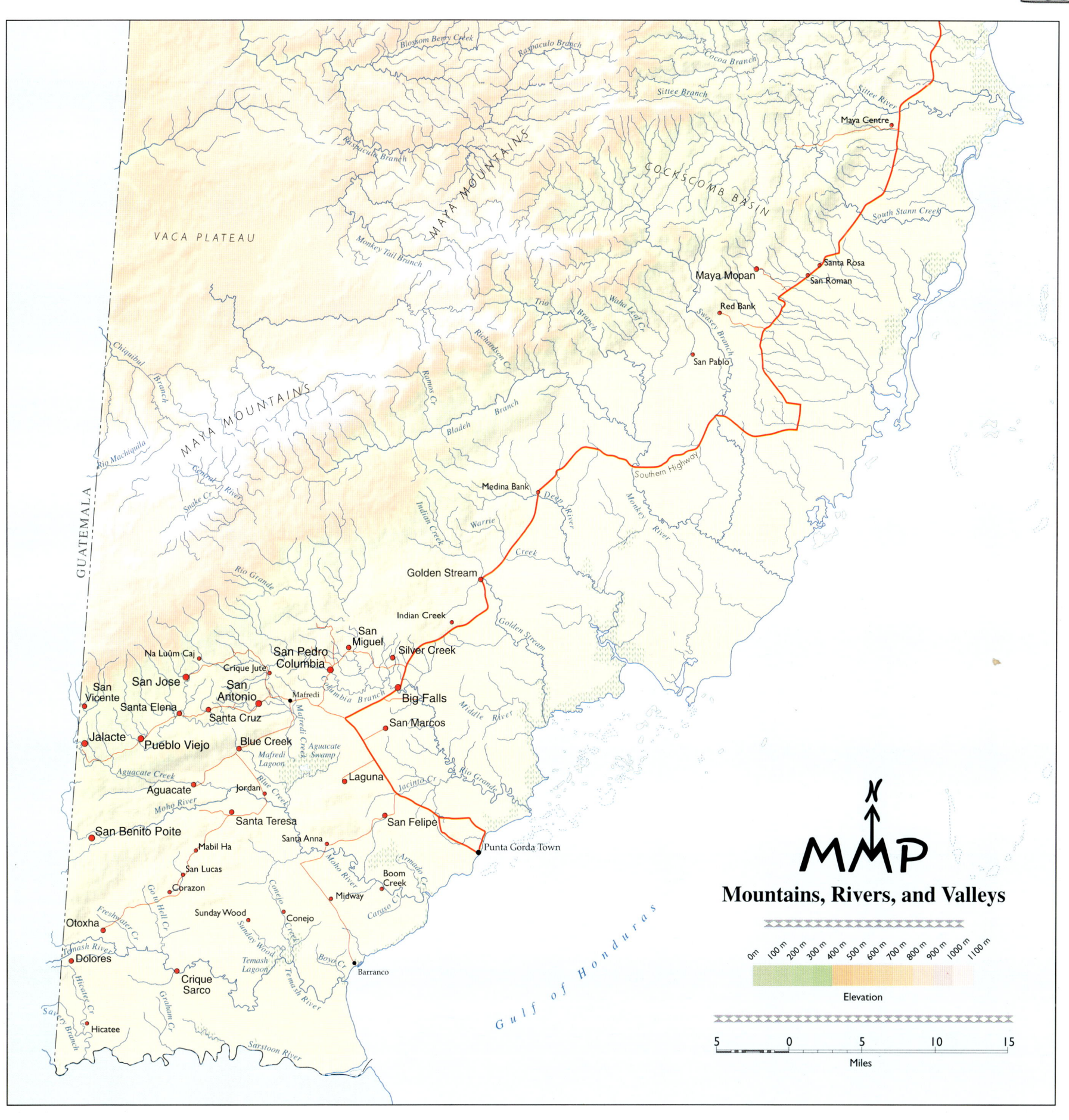

Maya Land Use in the Toledo and Stann Creek Districts, Southern Belize

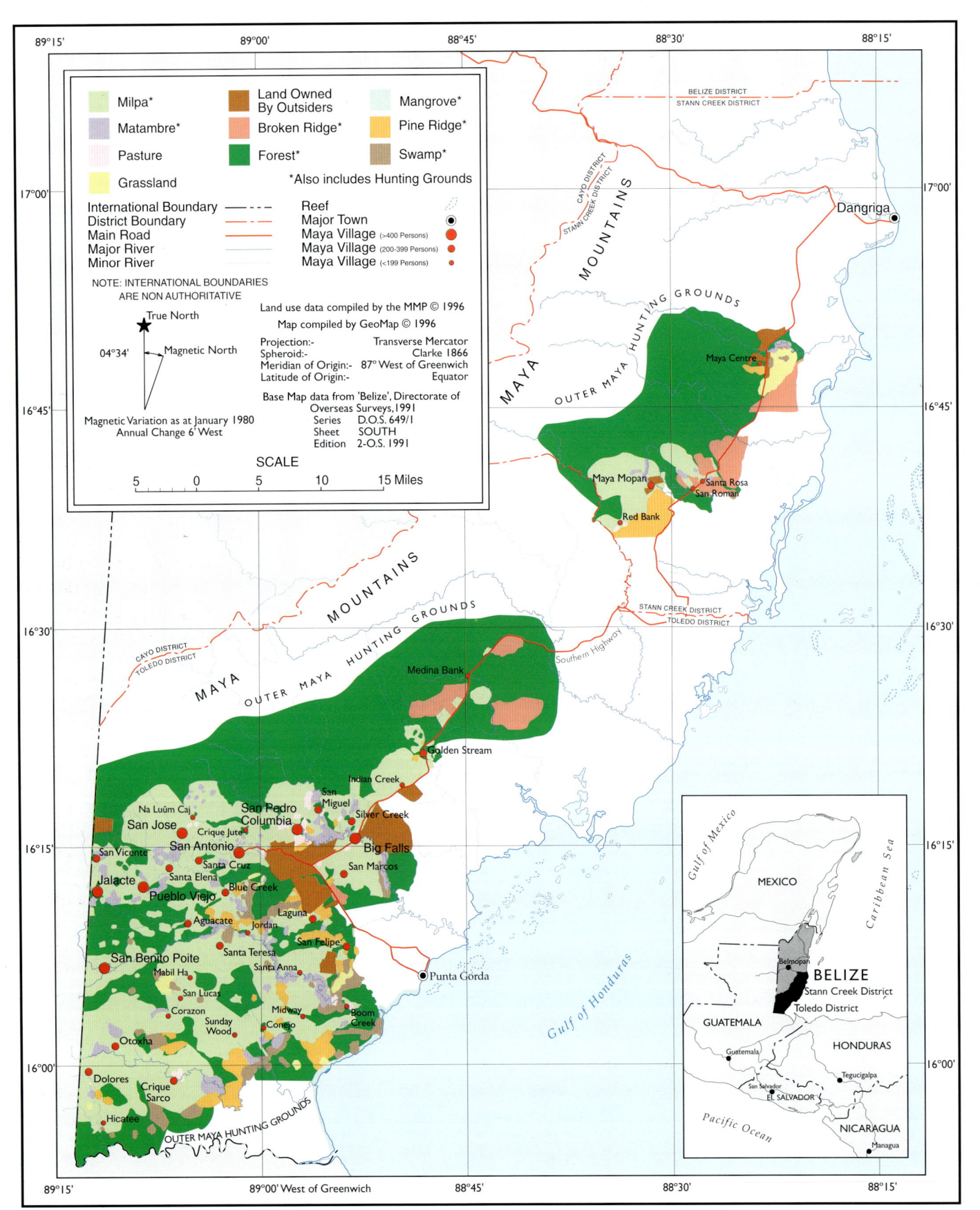

Definition of Terms

Milpa: Plantation of corn or rice done by the slash-and-burn method. The bush is cut down in late January to the end of February and burned in April. (*Milpa* is the Spanish word for plantation.)

Matambre: A second corn crop or plantation worked in October using the mulching method. It is usually done along the riverside in the lowland area or in upland areas of bush one—or two-years-old. This is carried out when it is presumed that the supply of corn for home use will not be sufficient.

Pasture: An area where cattle, horses, or mules are confined to graze.

Grassland: An area covered by grass not suitable for grazing; it can be natural or caused by overuse of the land. Also, an area covered by grass during the dry weather that is good for grazing, but covered with water in the rainy season.

Land Owned by Outsiders: Land leased or owned by a non-Maya within the area where the Maya live.

Broken Ridge: An area not suitable for the cultivation of corn, rice, or etc.; usually water-logged, heavy clay with high or low bush.

Forest: An area that has not been used for plantation since the establishment of the present village; any area that if cleared needs the use of an axe to fall big trees of a diameter of greater than one foot.

Mangrove: An area where mangroves grow, usually along the sea coast or where rivers and sea meet.

Pine Ridge: An area that is low, covered with grass, pines and other small shrubs with wide open spaces

Swamp: Any area covered with water throughout most of the year.

Hunting Grounds: Areas where the Maya look for game meat to supplement their diet. This would also include areas where they they look for wild fruits and plants that are edible; fishing grounds are also hunting grounds.

Land Use

Mayas live in a communal land system. This Maya system is basically still run by the rules of the traditional Mayas, although this is not recognized by the present Belizean government. The Maya do not know about lease land. This information is for today's children of the Maya.

The Maya do *milpa*, or slash-and-burn farming. For a plantation of corn or rice, we cut an area in late January, burn the dried materials in April, and then plant it for a season. We don't cut it again until it grows back. We also plant corn along the river. This is called *matambre*. For this we do not burn, but mulch instead.

Land management is carried out through the village leader, called an *alcalde*, with consultation of the villagers. Although the *alcalde* has a guide book to help him solve social and legal problems, when difficulties arise regarding land, he must consult the village.

To start a new plot of land to make a farm, it is necessary to create a posting on the land. The farmer simply marks the spot by cutting a line to surround the plot. The land use rules here are: do not burn the area without a proper fire line to prevent the fire from escaping to burn the uncultivated areas. Do not enter a line that was marked earlier by a neighboring farmer. By tradition this marking of an area of operation is done annually in late December or early January. Even when the lines are not there, somehow the Mayas are conscious as to how far they can go before crossing into their brother's land.

The other rule worth mentioning is if a farmer has farmed virgin land (forest), he will be expected to work on this land for seven or more years; after this is completed the farmer may leave the area free to be cultivated by other farmers in the future.

If a family from one village wishes to live in another village, it is possible only through consultation with the leader of the community; then, if the family and the village agree, it becomes legal to access the village. The Maya tradition is to have one's son inherit almost everything they have; if a father has no son, then his daughter. The daughters enjoy some inheritance along with their future husbands. The Maya have their local justice of the peace appointed by the political government. If a person wants to, he can execute his will in writing. If conflicts arise from the willing of property to certain members of a family, then again the right person to solve this problem is the *alcalde*.

Single women and widows seek the help of the *alcalde* if they want to build their houses or want to clear a farm. The villagers volunteer for one day to help them. In certain cases, the widows are helped by their sons or by a religious group, but the villagers always help. Because the Maya use a communal land system, our women are free to cultivate anywhere surrounding their village. If a woman's deceased husband owned land, she can continue to use it.

We have caves, hills, and rivers to be used as demarcation lines that separate one community from another. If a problem arises, first we consult the leader of each community. We argue among ourselves about the demarcation lines formed by the Moho River, Black Creek, the hills, and Jacinto Creek. For every problem that affects all of us, we consult each community leader. A joint solution is found. Then we educate the villagers about the discussion.

When non-Mayas have a problem with us over land, we have to solve it differently. For example, a foreign citrus company began operating in the area of San Felipe village. We were against this, because it is our land. But when the Government Lands Office was consulted concerning the matter we were told that the land is not ours, that it is not even a reserve, but crown land. At one time, ten Indian reserves were demarcated by the British colonial government. But the Maya have many villages, like San Felipe, that are not within the reserves. We use our traditional communal system everywhere.

Corn plantation

Milpa near Santa Cruz

Corn Planting

Corn is the staple food of the Mayas. The Mayas plant corn the way our elders taught us. It is very important to do it right because it concerns life. Seed selection is crucial. The farmer first chooses the biggest corn. When the corn seeds are ready, the farmer and his wife set a date for the planting and find an additional man to help, while the wife gets the other women to help her cook meals for that special corn-planting day.

Bathing, changing, and washing of clothes is the beginning of planting corn. When a family schedules to plant corn, the

Maya farmer with horse

date and time begin seven days before planting. They collect corn seed three days before planting. The man and his wife each carry their candle and go to church to pray for their corn planting. They pray to the Gods, asking to plant corn. They want the corn to grow well so that nothing will hamper it: no birds, no pests, and no diseases, because they want family food for one long year. They also pray to the Mountains and Valleys, burn their candle and leave the candle in the church. They both finish praying. They come back home and start to shell their corn seed. While getting ready to shell the corn, they first put five coals into burning incense to smoke the selected corn seed. A candle is burned on the table for light. They sit down to shell the corn, but first of all the man loosens his belt; that is to call the corn so it will not be tied to the cob. After finishing shelling corn, they collect the corn cobs, sweep the place, and collect the corn seed. They put it in bags under the table for three days. Traditionally the corn cobs are put away in various ways. Some are thrown into a river or put permanently under a cool place in the forest.

If the corn seed is abundant, two or three men could help shell corn and eat something after they finish. After all this happens, ladies come in and help the owner of the corn field grind corn to make some tamales called *pooch*. When the corn seeds are ready, the woman grinds a couple of green cacao seeds and mixes them into the corn seeds in the bags. This corn seed is special; it is nothing to play with.

The day before the corn planting, the corn seeds are placed into a bag to be carried before daybreak to the area to be planted. The evening before, the corn seeds are placed on a table and one candle is placed standing by them, to be ignited later in the evening, together with the copal incense and the incense burner. This day is very busy for the man and wife. Today the wife cooks the corn to be used for the *pooch* or *ko'yem* drink and also the corn to be used for *wah* or tortillas, and the chickens are to be killed and hung to bleed in the morning on the planting day if they are to be used. If not, the husband butchers a pig in the evening. Now the owner of the field has to have a wake. They could play harp or marimba, and they may play a game called *buluuk* [Ke'kchi] or *buul* [Mopan]. This wake is to take care of the cornfield so that nothing could happen. The owner of the field should not sleep at all. At 3 AM the man should be burning incense outside and praying to the Hills and Valleys. Some friends are invited to this evening's activities. Then at about 6 or 7 o'clock a small spiritual ceremony is performed on the seeds to be planted the next day. Firstly, the woman brings the lighted candle and puts the copal incense on the fire, followed by the sign of the cross, spiritual cardinal signs on the body, then the traditional Mayan prayers, and lastly the passing of the copal smoke on the corn seeds.

Yum Kax—corn god

During this special short devotion, communication is made with the divine spirits of corn and the great spirit of creation, to beg a blessing on the corn plants. The people wait for the evening meal that will be served hot, with cocoa drinks and of course a lot of tortillas. At this night meal, it is a practice to bless the food with incense for thanksgiving before it is eaten.

Corn Planting Day: The wife gets up at about 2:30 in the morning to prepare her husband's necessary things to carry to the planting area. She grinds the *posol* to wrap in *waha* leaves. The man wraps a piece of

Rice storage inside a house

copal to burn in the center of his field. When it is almost daylight the husband takes a few corn seeds in his bag to his cornfield. He carries a planting bag, machete, cups, and other items. The man leaves his home at approximately 4 o'clock in the morning, because the area of work is quite far from home.

Upon reaching his cornfield, he walks into the middle, he stoops down while the sun is rising to pray again, and to burn incense again to call all the Hills and Valleys. In his praying he calls all the names of the hills and mountains: Ka'na Santa Maria, Ka'cua Cojak, Ka'caw Shucaneb, Ka'caw Chixim, Ka'caw Xacab Yut, Ka'caw Yequikee, Kacaw Santiago, Ka'cuc Raxhon Zunœm, Ka'caw Siyab, Ka'caw Cahibay, Ka'caw Caxlan Jeen, Ka'caw Lege, and Ka'caw Chi Chen. These are the names of all the mountains and valleys. When a person plants corn traditionally, these names should be called. After the person calls all these names in the middle of his field, he digs seven holes for corn with a maximum of four to six grains in each hole. The man begins to plant, taking a deep breath because he is sorry about piercing the face of the earth with a planting rod. But this person should not eat anything until after he has done all this praying and planting. He should carry something to eat afterwards. Traditionally, some planters get their corn seeds at home, and they probably will eat first. The other friends continue the work until the field is planted.

During the morning, the woman selects two or three old women to grind cacao and hoddle. After it is ready, all the women drink their cocoa drink apart from that of the owner of the house or planters at about 11 AM. The woman burns incense again and puts some meat in a bowl and tortillas and cacao and burns a candle and sets it on the table—that is the Gods' food because it is showing thanks to the Hills and Valleys for taking care of the corn in the field. At about 10 o'clock, the woman may carry food prepared in the village to feed the men. If there are mounds of wee-wee leaf-cutting ant nests in the area, the dinner will be postponed for a few minutes while the youngest first-born female carries bits of food to the ant nest. Inside a bowl, twelve pieces of meat from the chest of a chicken are used, with water in which the meat is cleaned and bits of tortilla. The first-born female will sprinkle this *cumla* on the ant nest, saying, "*Mash que i cah ah th-lesh ma me, ma ma,*" three times. This is done to prevent the ants from destroying the plants. Now the planters may eat dinner. The women eat afterwards. If the area is planted and done all may go home. But if not, the planters will stay until evening to complete the job.

When the men from the field arrive at the house for which they planted corn, they all wash their hands. They all sit down together, getting their dish one by one until all have food. Then the owner of the house gets his little bowl with fire coals and puts some incense into it. He passes the burning incense over all the planters and their food dishes, then he goes outside to pray to the Hills and Valleys, telling the hills to take care of the planted corn in the field.

After doing all this, he comes inside the house to tell his planters to go ahead and eat, but he should be the first one to eat a piece of his tortillas. After all finish eating, the owner of house should remain silent—no playing, no fuss. He then collects all the incense leaves that have been used and puts them under the table, until three days later; then they are able to throw them away, far into the shade jungle. During the same three days, he also will go and visit his cornfield to make sure that everything is all right.

Each family should do likewise. That is the traditional way of planting corn among the Mayas. It was inherited by our fathers and has been passed on by generations.

Traditional corn storage

More on Maya Agriculture

Besides the corn which the Maya plant, there are other grains and ground foods planted. This includes rice and beans, which come in different varieties. The different types of beans are red kidney beans, black beans, white beans, pinto beans, and string beans. These are some of the many kinds of beans produced by the Maya people for home use and for the local markets.

The ground food includes sweet potatoes, cassava, soup yam, coco yam, spinach, yampi, bananas, and plantains. Most of these are planted for the local markets. In these modern times the Maya people are expanding agriculture by planting citrus or cacao orchards and raising cattle, but not forgetting their traditional way of life.

Path to a plantation

The Maya Year

January: Maya prepare for the New Year by doing an individual mini-ceremony, burning incense, and a few days after that one can go work for a few weeks. Farmers continue to search for new areas to cultivate. Hunting goes on the whole year. The Maya have market days on Wednesdays and Saturdays.

February: Clearing of low *wahmil* [secondary fresh-scrub] begins for various kinds of crops, but mostly for corn in mid-February when the summer dry weather begins.

March: The second corn crop begins to be harvested and also red kidney beans and other kinds of beans are reaped, too. Burning of fields begins for the first corn crop.

April: Corn harvesting continues. Burning of fields continues. Mid-month, corn planting begins. The families thatch their homes and new houses are constructed, and renovation is done on the old ones. April is the month for fasting and prayers. Sometimes cultural dances are performed during this month to honor the great spirit, the Divine. Many kinds of seeds are sorted in plastic bags to be planted in June.

May: Corn harvest and the burning of fields continue. Corn planting continues. Rice fields are planted. Construction is done of temporary storage bush houses for corn.

June: Heavy rain season begins. Fish trapping, hook fishing, and fishing with nets and spear are done in the month of June. Weeding fields and planting ground food under the corn, cacao, and citrus are done in this month. Rice fields are cleared. The season for crab hunting begins. Floods occur.

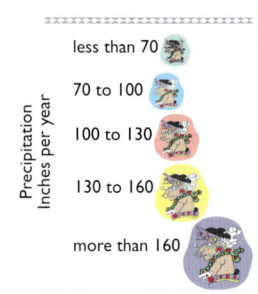

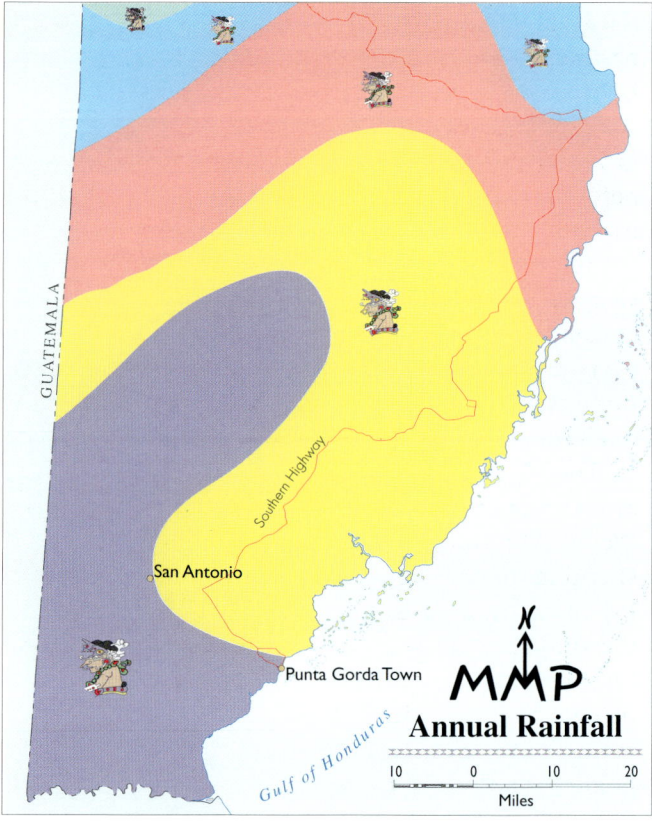

July: Rice ground clearing continues. Most farmers stay home during the rainy season. They sample the new, green corn. Flooding continues.

August: A short dry period occurs in this month. Corn is mature. Social dancing and the Deer Dance Festival begin to be performed. During the last week of the month, corn and rice harvesting begins. Thanksgiving is conducted at the individual Maya houses.

September: Corn and rice are harvested in the month of September. The clearing of *begga* bush begins among planted fields and *kudzo* [legume used for fertilizer] is grown. Planted fields are cut down in preparation for a second crop of corn. A variety of beans is planted for the biggest crop in the dry season of the year.

October: Rice and corn are still being harvested; more land is cleared to continue the planting; corn planted in September is cleared in the month of October. On the last day of the month, people traditionally honor the dead by offering favorite foods at home.

November: Farm activities continue on many farms. At this time, harvesting is done of corn, rice, and red kidney beans, and land clearing is carried out to plant corn again. Beans for the off-season will soon be planted and the fields are cleared.

December: Corn is planted again in early December. More land is cleared by hand this month for the planting of corn, vegetabls, and fruit. These are planted on a rotational basis for a March and early April harvest the following year, so the cycle never ends. Thanksgiving festivals are conducted and social dances are performed. In December cash crops are transported to market. Relatives visit each other.

Man using mortar and pestle to mill rice

Milpa plantation

Hunting

The Mayas love hunting as a sport and as a way of walking in the forest to be close to nature. We also hunt to feed our families. Before venturing out, the hunter must prepare for the long journey to the hunting grounds. First, he fasts on earthly things before the day of departure. Traditionally, early that same morning, the wife in her white garment burns incense towards the eastern direction, along with saying a few ancient prayers. The departure morning preparation includes making food for the hunters; a special kind of tortilla (sikpet) is made to last for three to four days.

The Maya people have many areas where we hunt. We hunt by trapping, shooting, poisoning, the use of hunting dogs, and the slingshot. On this hunting trip we will be using a shotgun with extra shells, for we are going for a two- or three-day walk. We have food in our camping bags, matches and preventative medicines, especially to keep the poisonous snakes away from us during the journey and at the camping area where the hunters rest at night.

The first day traveling will be about eleven hours, beginning at 4 o'clock that morning. During the day sometimes you meet various kinds of animals that you may shoot. The hunters use the meat of the *wari* [white-lipped peccary] that roam in the woods by the hundreds. Also, we hunt peccary, deer, antelope [brocket deer], quam [a bird], curassow, monkey, baboon [howler monkey], wild turkey, gibnuts [paca], agouti, quash [coatimundi], mountain cow [tapir], wild ducks, *ah poom* the *kolol* [Ke'kchi] or *ixkolool* [Mopan], and many others.

At the end of the day's journey we search for a place to build a temporary camp with cohune leaves to thatch a shelter. We build a fire together and clean the animal and season it with a lot of herbs for the evening's supper. After the meal a storytelling might be held for an hour; if not you can just be comfortable in your bed made of bush and listen to the sound of the jungle at night. Early the same evening you would hear the howler monkeys; later it would be the owls and night walkers (*kinkajous*), chirping among the trees and cohune palms in search of food. Eventually you will hear the gibnut and the tiger [jaguar] call; at night jaguars are noticeable by their whistling sound.

Deer by Marcello Cho

Since most parts of our hunting grounds are within the areas of ancient temples and the local buildings of the Maya, some of these places are in fact enchanted by the invisible living spirits. These places are for our ancestors. We Mayas believe so, because our religion tells us that there is an afterlife, that you live again after you die. During this night, you may hear these sounds. It's really interesting indeed, when you drop into a deep sleep.

Then at the dawning of the new day, you might hear the whistle of the *kolol* [Ke'kchi] or *ixkolool* [Mopan] bird. If you do, that's 4 or 6 o'clock in the morning. The fire is lighted once again for the preparation of breakfast. After breakfast, the trip can be very interesting if you happen to come face to face with our local Big Foot Hairy Man of the forest. He makes no secret of his presence. You will know when you hear him screaming like a human being. Their area is among the rugged, rocky mountains, where caves are found.

The hunting today is very selective. Most of us like to track down wild pigs. We have three kinds—the pure black, the white shoulders, and the red one. The black and white shoulders are our favorite wild meat, while the red ones are small and dangerous.

Tonight then can be very tiring, because if we have a lot of meat, it will have to be smoked to make it lighter for us to carry home on our backs. We collect a lot of firewood for the meat preparation. We stay up until about midnight and then sleep on our bush beds. Only a few hours' rest will be taken tonight. At about 3 in the morning we get up to have an early breakfast and at the latest, 6 o'clock in the morning, we begin our journey back home to our families. You can imagine how happy our families will be to see us with some meat, and still standing on our feet. On every hunting trip two things may occur, a snake bite or no meat. But the family will be extra happy to see you return with no harm.

Hunting in Maya Land sometimes is difficult due to a few Maya hunters inviting more Mayas to areas used as their hunting grounds. As was mentioned above, we do not hunt for commercial use but only to satisfy the family and neighbors.

It so often occurs that once outside hunters get to know the Maya hunting grounds, they will go into these areas to overhunt the animals available in order to sell game meat to shops in larger towns. We do have areas where game animals are in abundance, but maybe not for long.

A point to be made in this atlas for the upcoming young Maya generation is that this kind of exploitation should be prevented. At this time of writing, a recent report told of a hunter visiting one of the many hunting grounds, where he was greatly annoyed with what he saw. He counted many recently hunted wild pig heads. This is commercial slaughter, which should not have occurred and must not happen again. We must not invite outside hunters—this is the only way to stop this kind of animal destruction in the wild lands. Logging and large commercial agricultural operations are also threatening our hunting grounds.

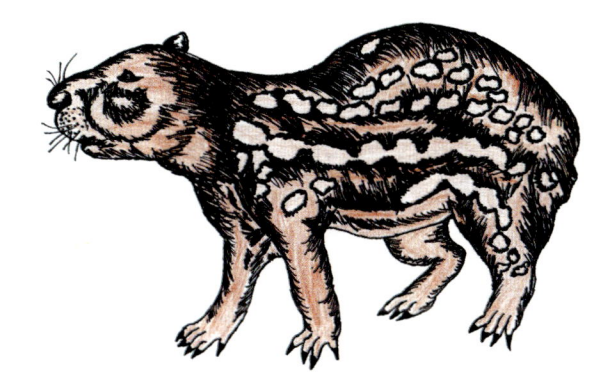

Gibnut (Paca), a Mayan delicacy

Fishing

Fishing is widely enjoyed by Maya people. Fish are caught many different ways, such as by trapping, hook, poison, net, gun, speargun, and the bamboo spear. I'll tell you about poisoning the river—a tradition that is not common today. Traditionally, the leader for this fishing trip brings about twenty to twenty-five men along (it depends upon the size of the river). The night before, a vigil night is held in one of the participants' houses until midnight. Then early the next morning all twenty men journey together to the river that is to be poisoned for its fishes. On this fish hunt the men involved carry some food for a two-day stay. As they reach the river, all the food bags will be put in one area, then off they go to hunt for *bolouyuuk ikilab ixchquow chalaam*, the vine that is used as the poison, and *kumum*, a palm whose leaf is used as a broom to prepare the area intended for fishing. By the day's end, all bundles of this necessary medicine will be brought to the river. This method for fishing is seasonal. It can only be done during the summer when rivers are very low.

Everything is now ready. Tonight some men will catch fish, crabs, and eels for a late dinner, and a few women will come along to cook, too. At this time a covered camp is not necessary; one can sleep almost anywhere, for it is dry enough.

Then it happens. The following morning early to rise, early to breakfast. The elder, the leader of this hunt, gets his copal incense and candle to burn. He gets a dry base of a cohune leaf *(becan)* that can float on the river's surface to journey downstream. The candle is placed on the bark to float down the river. The bark candle boat is called *becan* in Ke'kchi and Mopan. A small ritual is held for the success of this fish hunt. Immediately after this spiritual exercise, the poisonous vines are pounded onto the river's surface with stick clubs to extract the liquid by twenty people. Each person has a bundle. In an hour's time

Fishing on the Poite River

the river begins to change to a brown color. This is the sign that the big fishes will appear, jumping from the river trying to get away. This is the time that all or some can gather these fishes. The *machac*, snook, and *tze'h* [Mopan] or *chachi'* [Ke'kchi] are the main ones collected. By this time the women begin to prepare fresh fish soup for lunch. Fish collecting is done rapidly and ends quickly. The distribution of the catch is made to all men, excluding the women because their husbands are among the crowd. Everyone gets an equal share of the fishes collectively worked for.

Immediately after distribution, all begin to extract the unwanted parts within the abdomen. Soon after the fish cleaning, some may be salted, some smoked, a few can end up inside a *waha* leaf with a mixture of seasoning herbs, salt, and pepper to be cooked over the fire at night. Afterwards, everyone lies down to rest till the following morning, when they return home. Upon reaching their individual homes, the entire family begins to make hot tortillas— *wah* [Mopan] or *kua* [Ke'kchi]— to begin enjoying the delicious, fresh, smoked river fish.

Maya boy carrying firewood

Firewood

In every Mayan community, firewood is the main fuel source used for cooking. It is collected from dry limbs of trees in clearcuts made for plantation (a small subsistence farm). Firewood is removed from the area before or after planting, so that it can be kept away from the rain. It is usually kept in the house, where it dries. The best firewood comes from the *bri-bri* tree, also known for its *bitz* [Ke'kchi and Mopan], the tasty fruit from the pods. The tree is good for charcoal.

Firewood is cut up in sizes that enable the user to handle it easily. Some people cut pieces four or five inches in size, then place them in a pit where they can be buried to produce charcoal, which is used for cooking. Charcoal is rendered by burning the hard wood in a pit about six feet deep and six feet wide where the *bri-bri*, *craboo*, *subbim* tree, cockspur, fire ants tree, and many more are packed and covered with earth to be burned. After burning, it is allowed to cool and then packed and stored in bags ready for market. Charcoal is used to cook barbeque and as a substitute when firewood is not available.

Firewood is the key source of fuel for cooking and baking in a Mayan home. Only in recent times have Maya people begun to adopt the use of propane gas ranges, gas stoves, and kerosene stoves when it became inconvenient for people to obtain firewood due to limited vegetation (and lack of trees that are cut for firewood). This is occurring due to population growth and land use changes. As population grows, more fields are cut down each year, contributing to the scarcity of the trees used for firewood. However, this does not occur in places that have a proper agenda for land use—that is, people taking care of their resource and not allowing it to burn down, but instead cutting a fire break at the edge of the plantation to avoid a fire from breaking into the *wahmil* [secondary growth].

Culture

Manuela Tzub and family

Dominga Mas and child from Sunday Wood

Emelio Choco and Eulavia Sho

Emiliano Sho, Jesus Tush, and Pablo Ical, marimba.

Music and Instruments

Leonardo Acal playing the harp

Pedro Che playing violin

Marimba

Marimba is a musical instrument used by the Mayas for entertainment, dance, drama, special activities, and ceremonies. It produces the most unique sounds, especially when sacred music is played during rituals offered in ceremonies by a Maya shaman. This sacred music, *Marcha*, is the Mayas' Anthem. It is *Marcha* in Mopan and *Ixbenil Son* in Ke'kchi. A *Marcha* is a sacred song played when a ritual is taking place. About one hundred and fifty or more rhythms of music can be played on this musical instrument. The marimba is made from a combination of wood known locally as *qku'tej* and *sankil che*. *Qku'tej* is a tree that resembles the rosewood tree and is known for the color of the heart. *Sankil che's* heart is colored dark red; this tree is used mostly for firewood to produce charcoal. The heart of this wood is cut in thin lengths to suit the key that produces this mystical music. Used also are the local beeswax and the thin membrane of a pig's intestine. Each key produces a different sound.

The music is played by three or four men, who have the options to play superior, alto, tenor, and bass. This decision is made according to the music chosen.

Alfonso Pau playing bass (base of the harp)

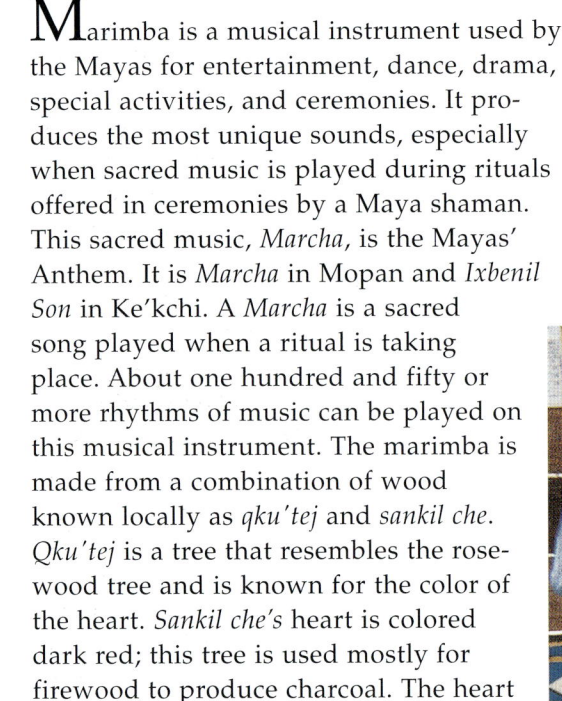

Marcos Coc and sons playing the marimba in Conejo

Harp

Harp is a musical instrument made by the Mayas and used for entertainment, religious ceremonies, cultural dances, drama, and other special activities. It is played with at least two other instruments, a four-string guitar and a violin, which blend the music of the harp. The harp contains about fifty lyres. The music is played by four men; one plays the harp, one the violin, one the guitar, and one the bass.

A harp is made of mahogany or cedar. Symbols of snakes, eagles, tigers, and other brave animals are carved on the neck of these instruments. These symbols go back in history to the Gods of Peace called *KuKue Can'*. Harps are set up when a lot of music will be played. They make the music special and really enjoyable.

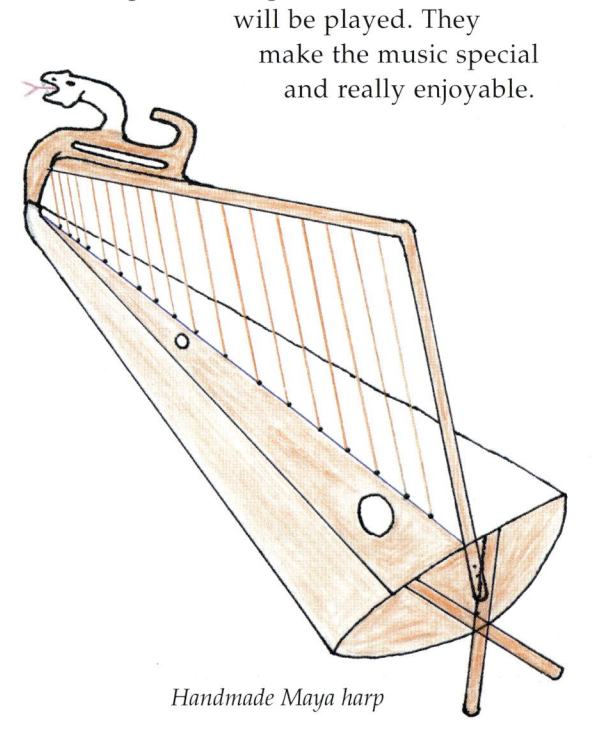

Handmade Maya harp

Teodora Castellano with a basket

Arts and Crafts

Most women in the rural area contribute significantly in the making of traditional handicrafts. They devote considerable time to creating woven materials from beautiful colors of thread. These products are used at home or they may be marketed to supply family income. A product commonly made is a shoulder bag called a *cuxtal*, in both Mopan and Ke'kchi.

It takes a Maya woman at least two or three days to weave a *cuxtal*. It is used to carry corn seed for planting, for souvenirs, and as a gift. Some *cuxtal* carry inscriptions regarding the bag's purpose. How beautifully the *cuxtal* will be crafted and the different inscriptions depend on its purpose. Recently craft centers were constructed in Maya Centre and Punta Gorda Town for the marketing of these products. The centers buy in bulk from the village women.

Along with the *cuxtal*, earthen wares including pots, plates, and other handicrafts are sold.

Cornmill projects in rural areas have injected quite a bit of income for the women involved in these groups. Cornmills have helped to reduce the hard work usually done manually by women. The cornmill projects were funded by outside agencies. Much effort was given to these projects to make them a reality.

The funding is based on the amount of labor a group can provide to build a cornmill shelter and the concrete base to bolt on a cornmill. Centers are constructed by husbands of the women in the group.

A women's organization is comprised of many women. Leadership is difficult because of the diverse opinions that may be held by members of a group. Good leadership can determine the rise and fall of the cornmill projects in the various villages. These cornmill projects enhance development among Maya women despite some problems.

Mrs. Salam talks about women's economics with Deborah Schaaf of the Indian Law Resource Center as the final touches are put on a cuxtal

The finances collected are shared equally among the members of the group after all the expenses are defrayed. Examples of expenses for a cornmill are diesel fuel, grease, parts, and engine repair.

Sewing is also a part of these projects. Sewing machines are given to the villagers or purchased from grants made to these projects. A leader is selected who is capable and has a broad knowledge of sewing and the technical difficulties that are encountered with the machines.

Materials are sewn in different styles, and where women take the initiative, they sell these clothes to other people in the village. The money collected is for reinvestment by the group.

Arts and crafts centers in villages have struggled their way out of muddy waters to a bright horizon by making clay pots. Clay pots and dishes earn a fair return within the group. The arts and craft centers have come a long way since the early 1980s when some village members first began these groups. Voluntary labor increased the production of items and sales. Only 10 percent goes to the individual; the rest goes to women's group projects. Meetings are convened to discuss the type of building used or expansion is also decided if additional membership is needed. Money is available for the expansion of buildings. Out of the many groups involved in making clay pottery, the beautifully made bear claw bracelet was developed. Since the bear claw bracelet is popular in the market, the clay pots are no longer in abundance.

Cuxtals and the colors of the Maya

Maya Centre craft center

Baskets are made from the twine called *bial* in Ke'kchi and *buyul* in Mopan. These baskets are used for storage or as containers for carrying things most used by the Mayas. They store corn when shelled or can be used to wash corn when preparing to make corn tortillas.

Embroidery is made by stitching designs with a marking thread on cloth around the collar and sleeves of blouses for Maya women. The designs are in the form of animals, ancient figures, and many other symbols with special meanings.

Bernarda Pop from Maya Centre Women's Group

Maya Clothing

Maya women wear clothing called *pic* and *koton* (Mopan for skirt and blouse) and the *suc pic* (Mopan for slip); it is called *ûûk* and *pôôt* (Ke'kchi for skirt and blouse) and *sa'il ûûk* and *pic* (Ke'kchi for slip). The materials are bought in stores and are available all over Maya land. *Pic*, the material used, is about five yards long. It is decorated with lace and ribbon of one's favorite color. The lace is sewn around the *pic* in three locations, at the lowest part, the middle, and upper part. This skirt reaches the ankle. *Suc pic* is the underwear worn to about mid-calf.

The *koton* is the blouse, decorated with embroidery around the shoulders and featuring a short sleeve that is also decorated with embroidery, narrower than that on the shoulder. The color of the cloth used is white. This is worn mainly by Mopan women.

The Maya Ke'kchi weave the clothing they use. This is the product of the cotton tree and is dyed with beautiful colors. The Ke'kchi women wear a garment called *ûûk* to about mid-calf in length. *Pôôt* is the blouse lace that is sewn beautifully around the shoulder and front part; there is a short sleeve. The blouse has a decoration to match the colorful dress used. *Sa'il ûûk* is the underwear worn to about mid-calf. Ke'kchi women are very industrious and clever weavers, who cleverly select the colors of beautiful thread needed. Presently only the Ke'kchi do this type of weaving. This material can be bought where it is in abundance.

Petrona Ack from Santa Teresa

Incense Burning

Like the ancient Maya people, the modern Maya are very religious. To the Mayas everything is living matter and all life is sacred, whether visible or invisible. We respect these living forces. A special and foremost respect is offered to our God, the great Spirit God of Creation. For this tree resins and a special bark are used from ancient times. Incense burning is very common among our people. Now it is appreciated even within our modern-day churches by burning the incense as the Mass begins.

Incense is essential in hunting, fishing, healing, corn planting, marriages, baptisms, to discourage evil spirits, in newly constructed homes, on special days, in death, and for other reasons. Its aromatic scent ascends to the heavens in smoke form along with prayers to make the divine invisible spirits happy to be remembered. In order to achieve success in using incense we prepare the items and ourselves. The *chúyubac'* [Mopan] or *ushb'* [Ke'kchi] trees are used for these special events at all times. Only an elder, through fasting and prayers, can prepare the incense.

Petrona Ack demonstrating the first step of weaving a basket

Weaving Baskets

The Mayas make baskets of different patterns and sizes. Materials used are *jipijapa*, *bayal*, and *tie-tie*. The *jipijapa* grows in almost all areas of the Maya lands. This material is prepared by hand and knife and then boiled for about a half hour. Then the *jipijapa* is dried in the sun one day and one night outside for the dew. After this curing, it can begin to be woven into baskets. When completed, the baskets are once more placed in the sun. Then they are marketed locally or to tourists. The *bayal* [Ke'kchi] or *buyul* [Mopan] is a prickly vine that is a bit difficult to prepare. It sometimes grows to thirty feet in length. The *tie-tie* vine is cooked like the *jipijapa*. *Tie-tie* is actually a resin collected from sacred tree extractions. It is dark brown in color and the *jipijapa* is pure white.

Weaver midway through a basket

Prudencia Canti from Maya Centre with a Mopan koton

Teodora Castellano (chairlady of Tapir Women's Group, San Antonio) weaving a basket

Weaver finishing a basket

Pottery

To make a clay pot, one needs to collect at least fifteen pounds of good clay. It is taken home and mixed with water, so the clay will become soft, and one can easily take out pieces of dirt and grass. After cleaning, the clay is ready to be shaped for a pot.

The clay will need something underneath like a leaf to keep it moist. The clay will first be pulled down and then pulled at the top. The potter starts hollowing the clay to go at least five inches deep. But the sides must be left a little thick. While it dries, the potter smoothes the inside and outside of the clay pot. If one wants to draw Maya designs on the pot, it can be done with a pen or pencil.

Upon finishing the pot, one would want to put it in a safe place to dry, so that later it can be baked. But the potter needs to try to smooth it every day with bottles, shells, etc., for at least two weeks before the pot can be baked in fire.

To fire the clay pot, one places it in the center of a fire pit and surrounds it with sticks, then lights the fire. It is baked for at least half an hour. One could put some *masa lab*, a corn beverage, in the clay pot after it is baked to facilitate cooling without cracking. After the work the potter wins a beautiful clay pot. One can either cook in it, or sell it.

Front view of a trapiche

Manuela Cus making pottery (Silver Creek)

Trapiche

In the land surrounding Maya villages, the extraction of sugar from cane is carried out by the use of a locally made trapiche cane press operated by three people. One person feeds the cane into the trapiche, and one person on either side pulls in opposite directions to make the process smooth. The cane juice is collected in a large plastic container or galvanized bucket, ready to be cooked or fired. The Maya use the cane juice to make sugar. They use the sugar for a variety of purposes, including a sweetener for corn wine, or *boh*, a local rum.

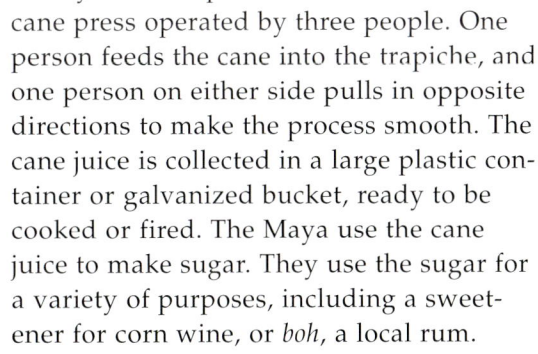

This manually operated tool is made from the heart of a very hard wood known traditionally as *naba* in both Ke'kchi and Mopan, a tree sacred for the Maya. When dry, the wood is cut to a size specified by the maker. The trapiche is a two-piece tool mounted on vertical posts strong enough to hold all the tension. The two pieces must be properly aligned in notches carved into the posts so the manual turning operation is not difficult. Every Maya household use to have a trapiche, which was usually made by the head of the family. Later a few Maya used mule-operated mills to grind cane. Today the trapiche is not common since most Mayas are purchasing sugar from stores.

Trapiche with a piece of cane

Hammock Making

The material to make hammocks comes from a henequen plant, which consists of many thick green leaves. When the leaves are mature they are cut and then cooked over the fire. Then the tiny fiber threads are processed. First the half-cooked thick leaves are scraped to remove the waste tissue or flesh. Only the fine fiber material is collected in small bundles. In Ke'kchi they call it *pohoc*. It is properly washed and then hung out in the sun to dry for a few days so the fiber will become white and strong. This is done until there is a sufficient amount of fine fibers to work with.

In the second step a hammock maker curves a light piece of wood and places it on their knees while pressing the fiber backwards. Ashes rubbed into wood roughen it so that fibers in contact with the wood tighten and increase in size

Santo Coc, oldest man in Laguna, making a hammock

Maya hammock

to become strong string. In Ke'kchi they call the string *ba cajhoc*.

When the materials are prepared, four round sticks are used to make the frame for stringing. They are arranged in order while stringing the hammock. In Ke'kchi they call the frame *tzuluc*. The length and width for an adult hammock is about eight feet by three feet. It takes about three days to complete a hammock this size. The hammock has long been very essential to the Maya people for sleeping and resting.

The same material is used to make string bags. In Ke'kchi they call it *champa*. They are useful bags for carrying ears of corn.

Wood Carving

The sound of chisel, carving knives, and various electric tools used for design and shaping can be heard here and there as Maya carvers are busy at work. They might carve the image of an ancient Maya god, a shaman performing a ceremonial ritual, or perhaps the image of a Maya chieftain. We Maya also carve figurines and ancient animals and birds, like *mescar*, *bicrod*, and *mischep*. We do this for our own use, and we also sell some of the carvings to tourists.

The type of wood we use for carving is mahogany or cedar, both high-priced and valuable woods. These woods can be obtained at the local sawmill in a larger village, where they are sold for about BZ$2.50 [US$1.25] per board foot. Of course, we also cut the wood from the forest ourselves. Mahogany and cedar are preferred because they are hardwoods and appropriate to work on.

The quality of the carvings depends on our artistic work. It requires skillful drawings and designs. It takes about three to four days to carve the figure, and about half a day to sandpaper and varnish it. Most carvings are about 12 x 10 inches, but some are even bigger.

Both wood and rock carving, can generate a healthy supplemental income for the Maya. It also attracts tourism.

Thread Making

We Mayas plant cotton, which takes about eight months to produce the fruit that dries to give cotton. Its flowers are a white-pink. We extract the seeds from the cotton boll to leave the pure white cotton.

Our equipment includes a small hand-made spindle about half-a-foot long with a marble in its middle to hold the thread. Our second tool is a calabash; we spin the spindle in it so that while spinning or darning it won't run away. Older Mayan women do most of this kind of work. It takes a lot of cotton to produce enough for one dress or pair of pants.

The middle part of the spindle is made from the *supa*, a palm tree with long spines. Its fruit contains a shell, a gum, a kernel, and a nut. The kernel of the *supa* palm fruit is used on the spindle, with a hole punched in the center of the kernel to fit the spindle. It was chosen because of its durability.

Emelio Choco making rope from the fibers of the ique'h plant (1) putting ash on a board for the twisting of the twine

Separating the fibers into different strands (2)

Anna Bolon of Maya Centre with a rock carving

Maya Centre craft shop

Twisting the rope (3)

Use and Preparation of Calabash

Calabash, named after the fruit of the tree they came from, are containers used by the Maya on a day-to-day basis. They are used as drinking vessels or to carry hot liquids, and for all sorts of domestic needs. There are two types of calabashes used in Maya land. A thin calabash is used for light domestic work, while a thicker one is used for heavier needs. Calabashes are more durable and more efficient than plastic wares. They are used by both Mopan and Ke'kchi Maya.

To make a calabash, we cut the fruit into halves, then heat it about two hours to harden the shell. It is removed from the fire and cleaned with a carving knife, then sanded and left in the sun to dry. When dry it can be used for as long as one year. The calabash tree is very durable. The limbs can be cut off and replanted just like seeds are planted. It can withstand the long dry season we have in Belize.

The dory is made from emery, Santa Maria, mahogany, or cedar trees. The artist carefully carves out the inside of the log to design the dory. Dories are used for fishing, hunting, and transportation. Mayas use the rivers as key transportation routes.

Landelaria Cal and family weaving a cuxtal

Cuxtal

The *cuxtal* is a colorful braided pouch-like cultural bag used by the Mayas. Its colors play a major role in Maya livelihood. The *cuxtal* is used for carrying food, planting materials, and other small things. The materials (cotton) are bought from *cobañeros* (Maya merchants from Petén, Guatemala) and local shops. The sticks used for braiding the *cuxtal* are straight and smooth. Two sticks are placed a distance apart and the cotton is strung around them in a figure-eight shape *(quimbal)*. The material from the first two sticks is transferred to two other sticks with knobs on the ends and then it is hung on the wall. Two more sticks are placed between the second two sticks; the one on top is a light stick, usually a *macapal*, the other is used to braid the material properly. Between these two sticks is yet another stick which is used to pass between the material *(samilakil)*. The other small stick is surrounded by cotton and goes from side to side to feed and build up the *cuxtal's* body until it is complete. It takes two normal pieces of material to produce one *cuxtal*. The *samilakil*, the stick first used, is used again to remove the material from the other sticks. A sewing machine is then used to complete the *cuxtal's* shape, along with fixing the strap. The *cuxtal* is now ready for its use or sale.

Elena Tzub from San Marcos embroidering

Lady from San Marcos making thread

Teresa Coc from Laguna weaving a cuxtal

Manuela Tzub embroidering

Petrina Posh from Otoxha weaving a cuxtal

Teresita Choco from San Miguel weaving a cuxtal

Marisa Choco from San Miguel weaving a cuxtal

Ix Chel, goddess of healing

Traditional Healing

In the world of the Maya, health is one of the most important basic elements of life. Health concerns the planting of seed, the germination at birth, the growing, the teaching, and eventually the death of a human after the blessing, after existence for a certain period. This wonderful knowledge, this wisdom, this mystery of life is a practice and theory for the Mayas. The origin of our knowledge of healing ways is obscure, but it developed even before Christ visited the Earth. To obtain this knowledge an individual must be qualified, and be prepared to listen closely if he or she becomes an apprentice. If a traditional healer is a family man or woman, then he or she can mold their children early to become healers.

To begin on the path of an adept, a small ritual must be performed to introduce the beginner into this unknown realm dealing with life and death, and the traditional knowledge of natural wild-grown healing plants and their incantations. This practice is linked with fasting and prayers. There are commandments to all who practice, for example, do not have sex during the time caring for a sick person. As tradition states, any such practice will harm and perhaps kill your patient. It takes about ten years to really get acquainted with all the many kinds of herbs, barks, roots, resins, fruits, flowers, prayers, and how to prepare and apply medicinal substances to an illness.

Marriage System

The preparation of marriage is very important within Maya culture, for it is a lifetime joint venture of man and woman. Today's marriage system is a mixture of traditional and modern ways. At age 14 the female may qualify for marriage and the males at age 19.

Traditionally a young man decides which girl he wants to marry before informing his parents about his choice. Then, the parents set a date for their visit to make known their son's intention concerning the young woman's hand for marriage. This visit usually is made at night. On the first visit, discussion ends with a promise that the young woman's parents will consider the marriage, and that the young man's parents may visit again to discuss the proposal at length. During the young man's parents' second visit, the proposal is finalized. This marriage decision is made by the young woman's parents without questions from their daughter.

At this second visit the young woman's parents are informed about a third visit the young man's parents will make. This visit occurs in two weeks, or at the latest, in a month's time. The preparation for this visit will cost a few dollars for items to offer the young lady, including half a dozen dresses, undergarments, hair pomades, shampoos, and other simple gifts to make the young lady happy with her future husband. These items will send lots of love messages. Everything is ready once the third visit is initiated. Invitations to relatives of both parents have been made so that a lot of people will participate in this occasion and be assembled at the young woman's home. Discussion begins early in the day and almost every person is recognized by both families.

Traditional healer collecting herbs

Juan Cal and family

In Maya marriage (and engagement), brothers, aunts, nieces, uncles, grandmothers, mothers, and fathers promise from this time forward they will at all times respect each other in a special manner—in words, thoughts, and in actions—till death in the name of the divine great Spirit God of creation. This is a solemn promise made by all involved and is still kept from a time long past. Everyone holds their hands together to show the respect each gives.

After this ritual is performed, it is time to eat. One parent begins passing dinners of *caldo*, rice, beans, pork, tortillas, chicken, or sometimes *escabeche*, a Mayan variation of a *caldo* dish. Then in the afternoon the girl's parents also serve food to all their visitors.

After these activities are over, another announcement is made by the young man's parents as to when the marriage will be performed. Now the couple to be married can make choices for their wedding day, including who will be their witnesses. After this is done the wedding day is set. The day before the marriage, a bull or a pig is butchered. Early the next morning both parents, the two witnesses, and the young couple walk to the place where the marriage will be performed.

For the wedding day, incense is used to march all participants to the altar where Mass will be held. In the midst of this ceremony the parents carry the offering with incense burning. Then the blessing and the receiving of the sacred bread are done. At the end of the ceremony everyone walks outside to journey to the house where this wedding day will be celebrated. Sometimes at this point the married couple walks hand-in-hand along with marimba or accordion music. As they reach home an elder, who has been appointed by the parents, covers the couple with incense as they enter the dwelling place. This day is celebrated with a lot of food and drink till evening arrives and everybody leaves for their respective homes, wishing this couple a long-lasting, loving married life. Till death do us part.

Juan Cal and Manuela Tek with a young wedding couple.

Man, Wife, Animals
A Story

This is the story of a family living in the forest, all alone. Many moons ago, when the land of the Mayas was still new after creation, there was a couple living alone in the forest. At the beginning of their life, they loved each other. It wasn't too long, however, before things began to change and at this same time they began to raise some chickens. They were so blessed that their poultry rearing became abundant. But the wife became so dictating to her husband that for every little mistake, she scolded the man. And that became a habit. Not much peace existed in this house, and the man began to worry because his wife became unbearable. But he had no choice—he was unable to leave her because he loved her so much and he wanted to continue their life together.

Sometimes he sat at his door, just staring out into empty space, lost in his mind, trying to think of a way to get his wife to be as she was in the beginning of their life together. Every day, coming from his farm, he would just sit, same place at his door, worrying for hours. During these unpeaceful times, he was not alone, for even the roosters among his animals seemed to know and to understand what was happening, but they were unable to speak to their father, the man. The roosters and the hens respected the man and the woman because they were fed well. These animals began to think of a way they could help the poor man. In their language, they always communicated among themselves. They wished they could talk Mopan Maya as their human parents did.

Everybody was worried—the man and all the animals—about this unfavorable way of life. Then one day, unexpectedly, something happened, and a miracle took place. Two old roosters found themselves talking in the Maya language to each other. At once it came to their minds—that this was the time to speak to their father, to show him how he, as a man, can control his wife's very bad ways.

The following morning their man-father was feeding them with new corn and was surprised to hear his two beautiful roosters call him: "*Tup, tup,* father, father," they said, "listen to us, we don't understand why our mother no longer loves you like after the wedding." The man could not believe his ears. "Who are you?" he asked. The roosters answered, "We are your children. You have been kind taking care of us all. We love you as a father and we want to help you correct our mother's ways. Be a man of correction, once again, with a bit of disapproval of our mother's bad ways. You were once like us living together, happily because you obeyed the great kind spirit as to how to live with a woman." "Ooh," said the man, "tell me your secrets then." "It's not a secret," said one of the roosters, "you used to do it when you were younger. What we will do is just show you an example which we keep with our many wives, then you will remember. After that then go back, at once, to the good old ways."

"Now," said the rooster, "watch me." The rooster stood straight, put out and beat his chest, and sang "San Perinco" and said, "doc doc doc doctore." At once, all over the place, the hens and chickens, young and old, came running and flying to the call of the male rooster. "You see," he said, "I have many wives and children and when I call, everyone comes to my command, and you my father only have one wife."

Once again the man remembers, kindly and patiently, regaining that which was forgotten many moons ago. Even the forest, the trees, and the animals surrounding his dwelling place were happier now to see happiness roam again among themselves with man and the wild. That's the end of this story.

Saddle Making

Saddle making depends on availability of a variety of materials. Most saddles are made from quality cattle hides and graded with the plain white board cut from the emery—a tree valued for construction because it does not break when nailing, cutting, and planing the finished product. When cattle are dressed for market, the outer skin is removed and left in a container of water mixed with white lime for a number of days. This is done so that the hair and other foreign matter will be easy to remove. After the skin is scraped properly, it is hung in the sun for about six days to dry. The skin is then cut to suit the size needed and nailed to the board. Designs are often carved in the leather; afterwards the saddle is assembled.

A saddle can serve for four years. It is valued at about BZ$100 [US$50].

Wooden horse saddle used for riding and carrying loads

Tools for leather-working, both for saddles and scabbards

Maya House Framing

In preparation for a Maya house frame, all the wood materials are first gathered from the forest. This includes the main posts, which are chipped flat from logs into posts six to eight inches thick, nine feet in length, and eight inches wide. The posts are mostly selected hardwood such as sapodilla, candlewood, ironwood, and rosewood. These are the woods mostly used by the Maya people. For the skeletal frame the sticks are selected from among other hardwoods from the forest.

The house frame begins to take shape after the posts and beams are in place. The beams are bound to the posts with a special kind of twine selected among the forest vines. After the beams and posts are in place, the rafters are built. The rafters are mostly round sticks. The length depends on the height of the frame. These round sticks are tied to form an A-frame on top of the beam. The roof is completed by thatching.

Communal work among Mayas is still practiced today. Here a group of men build the frame of a thatch house in Laguna.

Maya traditional bench

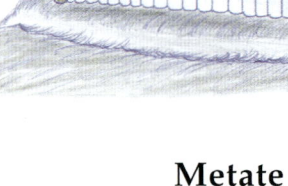

Metate

The corn grinding stone, the *metate*, is very important to the Maya way of life. Without this equipment, no corn tortilla, no *tamal*, no *posol*, no corn *lab* can be made; no *chicha*, the traditional drink used when the Maya elders do a ceremony for the sun when summer begins. The various sizes of *metate* stones are made from volcanic rocks and white sandstones, and they last a lifetime. They are also commonly found in the Earth, abandoned by ancient Maya.

Maya woman with a traditional grinding stone, known as kaaj (Mopan/Ke'kchi) or metate (Spanish and English)

Maya Food

Corn is the staple food used by the Maya in many forms for both food and beverage. Corn is prepared in the form of tortillas baked by hand on the *comal* (*sh'mm'ch* in Mopan and *k'el* in Ke'kchi), a thin flat sheet of metal that cooks the tortillas, or they can be rolled and wrapped in a *waha* leaf and cooked on the fire or boiled in a pot. This is called *pooch* in both Mopan and Ke'kchi. These can be eaten with stewed or roasted meat.

On special occasions sweet tortillas are made to mark a special happening and are served with coffee or cocoa sweetened to taste. These are called *ch'ukcua* in both Mopan and Ke'kchi.

Cornsham (roasted corn grain) is used to make a beverage in the same manner as coffee or cocoa. Cornsham can be boiled until thick and served as *lab*, a type of corn beverage, sweetened to taste. This is called *pinol* in Mopan and Spanish and *k'ah* in Ke'kchi.

Sweet corn *lab* is also used to make a beverage for some occasions and is seasoned with beans to taste. This is called *sa'h* in Mopan and *matz* in Ke'kchi.

Cocoa is used mostly for drinking. It is prepared in a special form when one has engaged a worker on one's farm or plantation. Cocoa has a rich taste and can be served hot or cold.

Other foods for the Maya are ground foods such as yams, coconut, cassava, rice, beans, plantain, banana, and fruits such as papaya, pineapple, and watermelon.

Modern Maya kitchen

Roasting peppers over a grill. The roasting process takes three days, and then the peppers are ground for caldo, a traditional stew dish.

The Maya also go to the forest to find subsistence for their families, such as cohune cabbage, *jipijapa*, fruit from palm trees used as meat, and many wild plants that can be used as food. Animals are hunted, such as peccary, wari, gibnut, curassow, quam, partridge, and many more.

The main dish used in Maya land is *caldo* (Spanish for stew). The Mopan word for this dish is *ca'intzle*; it is *tiââlinbil* in Ke'kchi. This thick stew with meat is seasoned with the following herbal ingredients: (1) mint or *isk'ih* in Ke'kchi; *isk'ih* has a very sweet-smelling aroma; (2) *samaat*, a name in Maya, can be found in every Maya home to use for the *caldo*; this plant is known by its long thin black leaves, and it can be grown on plantations or found in the wilds; (3) cilantro is a herbal ingredient very useful to the Maya for their cooking, and grown on plantations; (4) *orego* [Mopan] or *che'oreg* [Ke'kchi] is a herb that grows to a height of about five to six feet; the leaves are used to season the *caldo*; (5) *teb* is a round leaf from a thick, dark plant grown around homes in containers. Many other plants are used by the Maya for seasoning foods.

The Mortar and Pestle

The mortar or *pilón* [Mopan and Spanish] or *tenleb* [Ke'kchi] is a chalice-shaped hollow log, approximately thirty inches in height, mostly used by the Maya people for the purpose of threshing rice grain or coffee beans. The idea of the mortar began a long time ago. Where did the idea come from? No one knows, but today the mortar still exists widely among the Maya people.

The grain is placed in the hollow, whatever amount it can take, and then pounded with a pestle. The pestle is a three-foot wooden bar shaped like a drumstick. The pounding removes the pod or husk from the grain. The mortar is generally made from a mahogany or cedar log.

To make a mortar, a log is hollowed by burning the top with cohune nuts. The charcoal is dug out progressively with a machete or sharp object. The burning continues until the required depth is burned out. The burned charcoal is dug out, this time giving the sides of the hollow a perfect smooth clean-out. The mortar is rinsed with water and then is ready for use. The procedure takes two to three days. Burning the top of the log is the Maya way of making the mortar. Professional carpenters use carpentry tools to dig out the hollow in the wood. The hollow is basically about twelve inches deep.

Teresa Coc from Laguna demonstrating the use of the mortar and pestle.

Juana Sho making pooch (favorite corn dish)

Drying cacao in the sun for making cacao drink. Cacao has been used in ancient Maya traditions as money and is still a favorite beverage.

Apolonia Sho from Maya Centre demonstrating the use of the mortar and pestle.

Maya Dance

There are several kinds of Maya dance. The musical instruments used are harp, violin, guitar, marimba, flute, and drum. The Maya dance only on special days, such as weddings, birthdays, ceremonies, and cultural events like the Deer Dance.

Mayas dance the *Morros*, Monkey Dance, Torro Dances, Cortez Dance, and the Devils Dance. These dances use the flute, drum, and a special kind of marimba.

The social marimba is used for the local men and the women to dance in the community hall. As the music begins, the man puts a handkerchief in his hand and waves it in front of the woman, calling her to dance. She comes to him, goes to the center of the hall, and both of them turn around, and the dance is on. Now the man puts his hand behind his back and dances to the tune of the music until it ends. Then finally both of them stop dancing and both of them make a contribution of money to the host, who in turn pays the musicians.

The Deer Dance Festival

This is the story of the Deer Dance Festival, celebrated on the day of the San Luis Rey, patron saint of San Antonio village.

This morning, the 15th of August, is special because it is the day before we commence the performance of many traditional spiritual rites of the Maya. Tonight will be an all-night vigil, from early morning until the midnight meal, where the deer dancers in costumes and masks will be the first to have their meals, and to be blessed with the incense of *naba*, fire, in the specially made clay incense burners. The nine *chinams* (treasurers or persons responsible) will have their meal next.

The Deer Dance is a traditional spiritual ceremony. Since our high Mayan civilization collapsed we have retained recollections and practices from our glorious past. This Deer Dance ritual is celebrated here in our Mopan Mayan village of San Antonio, Toledo District, Belize. Our Mopan village has about two thousand Maya people.

Around the 1980s Lucio Sho was the last elder to have coordinated the Deer Dance sacred spiritual festival. On one of the last night's vigils, one of our own people struck a match to the traditional thatched-roof house where the costumes, harp, fiddle, guitar, and marimba were all destroyed by the fire.

Due to the ongoing influence of foreign missionaries, some of us Maya are losing

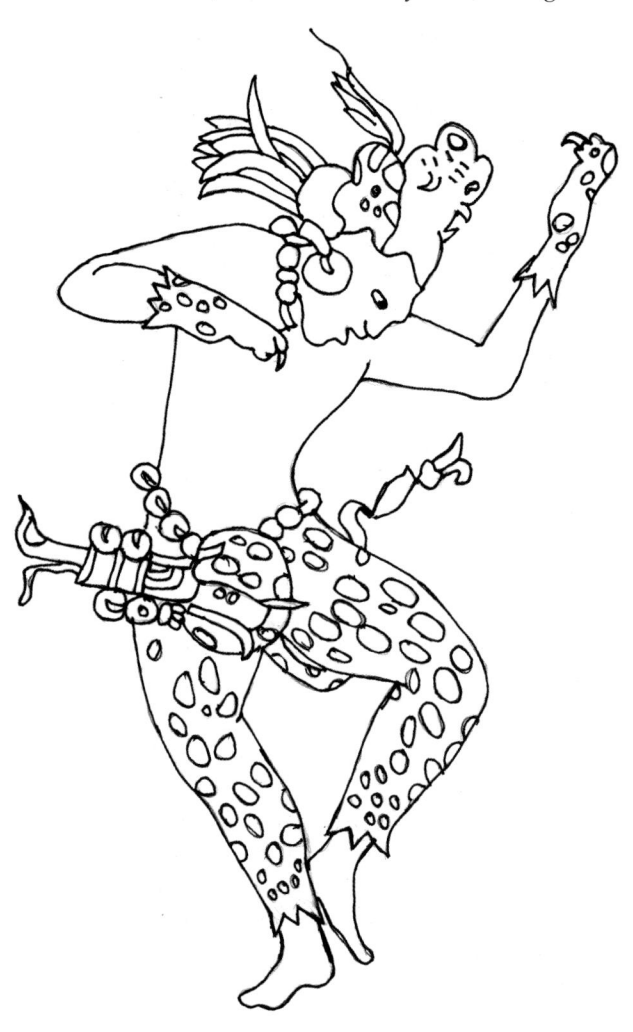

Jaguar Dancer image from an ancient Mayan artifact

interest in our traditional festivals. The deer dancers will be dancing from the 15th of August until the Festival of the Village Patron, San Luis, on the 25th. But the actual night to celebrate will be the 23rd. That evening all will dance to the harp and the marimba. Then at midnight incense is burned at the Maya traditional altar and the image of San Luis the King will be performed.

The Deer Dance Festival includes dancing to the lively music of the social marimba, harp, violin, mandolin, and the drum. The harp box also serves as the drum when hit with the fist of the *pash* (Mopan) or *ah'cuab* (Ke'kchi), meaning musician.

On this vigil evening of the 15th, the masks and costumes were blessed with the smoke from specially made clay incense burners. Within these burners, fire is placed in the *naba* bark. Each of the nine days of the festival, the sound of the drum announces the procession to the home of the *preiosta* or the elder sponsoring for that day.

Leading the procession will be the holy deer followed by the other eleven dancers and the marimba playing special music, reserved for that time when the deer music is played. There will be twelve dancers in two lines of six, which face the ceremonial marimba played by one man. The left line is where the elder brothers and sisters take their position. Tiger on the right and the holy deer on the left. Four red men, two women played by men, the two dogs and the two hunters in black. Six men play rattles and chant, adding to the music. The two lines formed by the dancers represent the four cardinal points: East, West, North and South. The tiger begins to dance, usually at a point or corner going to the East. When tiger whistles, it is done in the center, the fifth Mayan cardinal point.

Eventually, the four men in red costume chase tiger in all four corners and the center of the dancing area. Throughout the tiger's performance, he teases the hunters, stealing their rattles and hats. At the end the black hunters chase the tiger to all four directions and the center, completing the cardinal points he captured. The dancer steps out of the tiger skin costume. The hunters then enact killing and skinning the animal. They sell the meat but not before their wives get their share of the kill. It is a part of the dance that the young and old enjoy because the hunters talk about their kill, talk about all the parts of Mister Tiger, how to cook it and how to eat the soup, the *caldo* with the *wah*, corn tortilla. Most of this is done in Ke'kchi and a little in the Mopan language. This part of the dance lasts about a half hour, then the tiger skin is delivered to the two dogs to give it back to the tiger.

The holy deer begins dancing, prancing around on the five Maya cardinal points and also giving recognition to the other dancers. It eventually runs away to hide in the woods. Immediately the two dogs follow the footsteps of the deer, running around towards the same cardinal directions. During this moment the two black-costumed hunters begin chanting in Maya to their dogs, commanding them to seek and find the holy deer: Among the hills, among the valleys, rivers, and in the wild lands, they sing, calling the dogs by name, *Shu lay barcin shulay tu cu* and other names they give their dogs.

Then the hunting of the deer begins with the following of the deer tracks and the scent. In about fifteen minutes deer and dogs appear to continue dancing, chasing the deer, while the hunters wait for the appointed time to make the kill. Then it happens. The hunters capture the deer, kill it, and the dancer slips out of the skin. The hunters skin it in seven parts to represent now the seven Maya cardinal directions: the center, below, above, East, West, North, and South. They cut the head, two shoulders, the heart, the vertebrae, the two hind legs, and the distribution begins to their wives. The balance of the deer meat is then sold to the community, audience, and spectators.

The seventh day of the festival, which is always the 22nd of August, is the second vigil night. During this day, about eight elders assemble at the chief's house, with the drum announcing they are about to construct a Mayan traditional spiritual altar with local, wild-grown materials, namely, cohune stalks, *ohleche'*, *ohlay acer*, and *ochehelestûk*, and the *moho* bark to tie with. Tonight fifty or so men will embark to bring the greasy pole from the wild forest. They will first participate in the whole night's vigil, so as to gain the power, courage, and strength to carry this pole on their shoulders from the forest to the Maya village. In the morning, before leaving, the pole bearers light a candle to the great creator spirit to ask for safety in transporting the sixty-foot pole.

Jose Salam-the Deer Dancer, San Antonio.

The eighth day of the Maya ceremony, August 23rd, is the most important part of the Deer Dance Festival. Many things occur. First, early this morning, San Luis, patron of the Maya villagers, visits his people from house to house. Second, the pole or *sa'yuk* [Mopan] or *cha'kop* [Ke'kchi] arrives. Third, the prize to be placed at the tip of the pole is brought to the church with a procession featuring the deer dancers, marimba, drum, and the elders to spread incense from the donor's house. Finally, in the evening, the statue is carried from the church to the senior elder's house through a large crowd of people flanked by various colors, kerchiefs, and under a canopy to bless the pole. Included in this procession is the prize carried on a ten-foot pole by one man.

They leave the village in a procession. Leading them is the drum and the senior elder of the Deer Dance Festival, carrying a clay incense burner and a lot of incense to smudge or smoke the *sa'yuk* tree. The trunk of this tree was smoked by an elder who speaks to it asking the favor of forgiveness in the name of the great divine spirit of the mountain and valleys, that all may be done in harmony, peace, and safety during the spiritual occasion. Lastly, this tree is rubbed three times. Traditionally, on this morning, the dancers went house-to-house to assemble the other characters for the day's event. The dancers, after completing the house-to-house collecting of their fellow participants, then go to the sponsors—the *preiosta* (Spanish for festival host) or *yummil oku't* [Mopan] or *qh'echal sha'leb* [Ke'kchi]—to perform until the pole arrives at about eleven o'clock.

Within these hours, from dawn until the eleventh hour, the social marimba and the harp are played and the statue is at rest in the house. The pole travels approximately four to five miles. It is quite a distance. Arrival time must be eleven o'clock. Upon arrival this pole rests by the house of the sponsor, while refreshments are served. First, a gallon of rum is distributed to the pole carriers for an appetizer. Then lunch follows in which they are given pork or chicken. Corn cake, *pooch*, rice, and beans are served and to wash it down, made freshly toasted cacao beans or corn *lab*, coffee, and sugar—all food of the Gods eaten at this special festival. There are hundreds of spectators to this annual spiritual event.

Immediately upon the pole's arrival, the senior elder, his wife, and other elders smudge the pole to bless it with the *naba* bark. Sometimes a dump truck is requested to help bring the pole to arrive on the specified hour. On this 23rd day of August—the special day—the drum, the *pash*, and the marimba for deer are all playing. Immediately after lunch, the elders, who have prepared the food now, will approach the statue in the house. First, they make the sign on the body of four cardinal points. They kiss the feet of San Luis. Then they give their offering in the form of eggs, money, cacao beans, candles, or incense. The last leg of the journey with the pole is about to begin.

The elders get charcoal and incense. The greatest procession begins with the deer leading, followed by the two dogs, the tiger, and the two hunters chanting as the procession proceeds. This huge pole will be carried to the church compound. Two to three times the pole is put down to be blessed by the incense burners. On reaching the church the pole is again blessed with incense. Then, at this point, yet another procession is coordinated by the same elders to fetch a beautifully hand-made prize which includes a bottle of *rah* rum, some money, some small kerchiefs, and colored ribbons, symbolizing the four Maya cardinal points: yellow for the east; black for the west; white for the north; and red for the south. Also, a small statue in a metal case is set in the middle of a ring of vines and this vine also symbolizes the universe. On this ring of vine, the ribbons and the kerchiefs are hanging. This procession, when concluded, reaches the church.

Finally, a procession transfers the Patron Saint and the prize to the senior *preiosta* house for a one- to two-night celebration. This is the time when all may dance all night to the tune of the social marimba and harp. The dancing hall tonight is covered with freshly hand-picked all-spice and cooked *naba* leaves that produce a fragrant scent. A male dancer accompanied by a female contributes money after each song is played. There are dances involving everyone on both evenings, the 23rd and the 24th.

On the dawning of the 25th, preparations for raising the greasy pole begin early to the steady beat of the drum. A few men, specially appointed by the senior *preiosta*, cut grooves for the support rope and the prize. Some men construct supports for the cradle in the hole where the pole will be raised. The *sa'yuk* bark is removed. Then soap is dissolved in water and melted lard is added. This is applied to the massive *sa'yuk* pole. Once the slippery mixture is well mixed it is utilized to grease this pole.

Upon completing the greasing of this massive pole, a messenger informs the elders that are assembled at the senior *preiosta* house. It is now approaching the two o'clock hour. The pole begins to be raised and other preparations commence as soon as the messenger delivers the message to the *preiosta*. The pole raising creates a most striking effect, and is a powerful voice, part of a very dramatic event to the Maya people. The *sa'yuk* pole goes up as the black-costumed dancers chant, and the drum and bells announce that this most sacred part of the event has begun. Some men use forked sticks to guide the pole and to prevent it from swaying, while another crowd of men pulls on the ropes. Eventually the men with forked sticks drop these and move from under the pole. Most of the time, the giant pole sways dangerously while the whole crowd watches in awe and wonder until the pole finally rights itself and settles down into the hole.

What does the mighty *sa'yuk* pole symbolize? Our ancient Mayan ancestors and we today believe that the great spirit, the creator of all visible and invisible things, created the forest trees of all various kinds that bear fruits before creating man. All foliage, we Mayas believe, is sacred to us, because vegetation sustains us in our lifetime. They were our eldest brothers and sisters, even older than the animals of the earth. All was created before man. Every creation is sacred to us because they were blessed by the great god spirit after he saw all his works are good. The *Sa'yuk* pole represents our connection with and responsibility to nature and the Earth.

A procession is once again is on its way to the village church to return the Patron San Luis. This is the final procession, with the image of the Saint under his canopy, flags flying, and in the midst of a huge crowd assembled to mark the Saint's Day. Upon arrival of this procession at the church compound, the *sa'yuk* pole is ready and waiting with ropes tied to the top. The San Luis image, the deer dancers, the elders, men, and women are blessed with incense. The drum pounding and bells ringing celebrate this special Mayan traditional ceremony. The bells also represent history: when the Maya people fled oppression in their own land, they brought the bells along.

Once the pole is up, the deer dancers, especially the tiger and the black hunters, are the first to attempt to climb. Several other villagers now join to attempt to get the prize. Some, or all, are previous climbers, and traditionally a participant must act three consecutive times. Possibly a successful climber can fetch the prize, this same day, the 25th of August, but if not, it must be brought down early the next day, the 26th. When the successful candidate reaches for his prize at the top of the pole, the church bells ring out to announce the prize has been won.

During this ongoing effort to climb the greasy pole, the Deer Dance continues. In this last act of the Deer Dance, the tiger runs away and climbs a big tree to hide among its limbs, followed by the two dogs; tiger is captured on this special day, the twenty-fifth. The only time it occurs is in this last act.

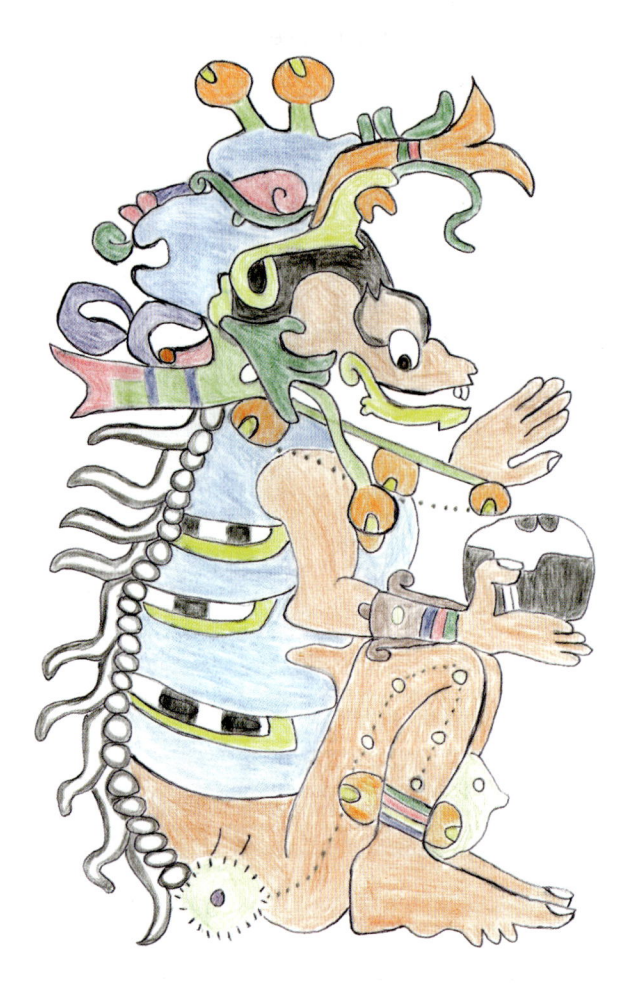

Ah Puch, the god of death

The two hunters begin to track down the tiger to save their hunting dogs, Barcin and Tonko, spotty and charred tail. In about half an hour, they find the tiger by hearing tiger's call. While in the tree, the tiger whistles loudly. As the hunters reach the trunk of the tree, they shoot tiger with bows and arrows. Eventually, tiger escapes, leaving the dogs on the tree branches, wounded and half-dead. The hunters save the two dogs, both at the point of death. It is at this point that traditional healing is performed on the dogs. The hunters, seeing the predicament of their great hunting dogs, medicate them with traditional healing herbs. There are pure and natural spirits which they search for and find among the rocks, valleys, and mountains in the forest, and the dogs revive to hunt for the last time.

Deer now are to be hunted, in the old style of trapping them with ropes. A medium-sized tree and a hole dug in the ground creates this trap for the holy deer. Deer prances around this trap for a few minutes, then eventually gets caught. After this act the spectators are covered with incense and smudged with hot pepper by the woman dancer and one of the hunters. Then, for the very last dance, the two hunters set off to return home after a successful hunt with the tiger and holy deer. These two hunters are in the wildlands, far from their village, but before starting the long journey, they have to celebrate because they have a lot of meat to carry to their wives and families. They are so happy that they begin to drink the *chicha* (homemade corn beer) and alcohol made from cane and corn. With this spirited drink, they become *nisop*.

All during this Deer Dance, the marimba plays a special music for the two hunters. They kneel down to pray and chant for a safe journey home. They sing their own music, the exact sound of the deer marimba. Then one of the hunters tries to get up under the load of deer meat, with the help of his brother. After the elder brother is up, he in turn helps the other hunter to get up with a load of tiger meat. Now both of them are on their feet to begin the long journey back home. Staggering with the paper bark still in their hands, they continue to pray, chant, and sing, and eventually they, too, get covered with incense and smudged with hot pepper while singing and praying. The dancers return to the *preiosta* house after the dance is over. The following day, they go back to the *preiosta* house to wash their individual costumes. So ends the enactment of one of many historical and ancient traditions of the Maya.

The question now arises, what is the meaning of this spiritual ceremonial festival? A ceremony is a poor trial of life itself. That is distinct. A ceremonial preparation is very important to make our prayers real and successful. We smudge ourselves and our homes with *copal* and *naba* incense to drive away the bad, wicked spirits. Then the elders that coordinate this event set a time for fasting. All our ceremonies are for thanksgiving. We Maya people are always thanking the spirits for the conditions of our life. We Mayas are thankful because we are given many opportunities—for instance, to heal by incantations and herbal medicines through our ceremonies. We request the great spirit, the creator, to bless every undertaking in life, for planting Mother Corn. We Mayas believe corn is the mother of all vegetation. We depend on her for sustenance. Corn grows according to the seasons. During a Maya ceremony, we believe all the life forces, all the divine great spirits, are present.

Our emotional state is very important. We do our ceremonies with all our mind, heart, soul, and strength. Spiritual ceremonies are a means to communicate with the higher spirits. Celestial sanction, the cosmos, the universal mind—to this we represent ourselves in general, for our dead ancestors, for our sick people to get help, for peace, for the right of the indigenous Maya (for we are a people too), for rain and sunshine, for abundant crops, for the harvest, to show our love to the creator, and many other good things in life. That is what the Maya ceremonial *limosna* [Mopan] or *si'maatou* [Ke'kchi]—a gift from someone—is all about, in brief. I hope this history of the Deer Dance Festival, one of many, will encourage a deeper respect for and understanding of the Mayan ancient wisdom and traditions of the indigenous people of this land.

Cortez Dance being performed in San Roman, Stann Creek District

The Cortez Dance

In the ancient days the Mayas did not use obscene language. They loved one another every day. They praised a Mayan God and each other early each day. Every feast they all came together into their own temple. They built temples in every place.

In their temples they celebrated, feasted, and danced their Cortez. The Cortez is a dance done by individuals. Once during the Cortez dance, a dancer named the *C'ooxol* (a Mayan king) came in and asked Cortez if he could dance among them.

This *C'ooxol* dancer taught the Cortez dancers that they should dance in unity, making a peaceful dance. He gave them a speech about the sunrise, their God the Father, and the sunset as part of each of us. He also taught them to praise and worship God the Father, morning and evening. The names of Cortez dancers are *K'eche Cuink*, *Cha'n'al*, *C'ooxol*, and *Mutuzum*.

The *C'ooxol* explained that the angels of God are in the mid-sky where the Sun houses them. The dancers praised the four corners of the Earth. They knew exactly how to praise and worship the Sun and the Earth at the four corners.

These Cortez dancers and the *C'ooxol* really knew what was best to do.

While they were in harmony, dancing, here comes the Spaniards to distract them. They were amazed. Nevertheless, the Spaniards asked, please, could they dance with the Maya, so the Cortez responded, "If you do not beat us, you are all welcome." Because the Spanish soldiers asked please, they were welcome. The Cortez dancers called the Spanish soldiers *c'axlan quink*, meaning stranger in Ke'kchi. The Spaniards started to mix, to dance among the Cortez. But the *c'axlan quink* had their guns and machetes. Apparently they started to dance in harmony, the Cortez and the twelve *c'axlan quink*, together. Now here comes the tiger *(hix)* and the *carajay*, and the girls *(ix'-ca'al)*.

So the *carajay* (Ke'kchi term for the boy illustrating the young sexy boy taking part in the dance on Cortez' side, symbolizing the westerner) comes to dance to sweeten the Cortez and show love to the Cortez. The *carajay* is from the *c'axlan quink*.

After they mixed up to dance, the Cortez started to fear, because the *c'axlan quink* have a dance called *hass*, the priest. The priest started to bless the Cortez; some Cortez received blessing and some were afraid so they ran away. They feared being killed. The tigers *(hix)* tried their best to defend them, but they were unable.

This happened about five hundred years ago, that our kings were being was killed. Those are the things that happened among the Maya before they used to worship with candles and burn incense; that was God's likeness.

This was *C'ooxol's* story, but when they caught him, he surrendered. After they blessed him they turned him loose and he ran away and disappeared and went into the hills or heaven, nobody knows. So today it's important to worship God. Also to dance a Cortez is fair and blessed.

Puc-Bulum Thunder God

One day a man died, but he was not accepted by God, because he did not dance or worship. He was sent back to Earth to do all these things to serve his community.

This story was learned from my father in Coban, Guatemala—my father knew how to live the Mayan way of life. He could play the Cortez flute, the drum, and do part of the *Morros* Dance.

Gods of the Mayas

The Ke'kchi and Mopan Mayas in southern Belize are direct descendants of Mayas that go back at least 4000 years in history. Ancient Mayan civilization was characterized by tremendous achievements in architecture, arts, mathematics, astronomy, writing, and religion. These Mayas engaged in a variety of scientific agricultural practices, including the ridge-field system.

Maya King

Like their achievements in agriculture and science, the ancient Mayas practiced a superb religion. They used incense in their religious activities and ceremonies. We Mayas believe that the mind and soul of quality men and women travel towards heavenly bodies to communicate with the God *Asab Shalab*, at the dawn of special days to offer ceremonies for special spiritual concerns. The sacred tree of the Mayas is the copal because we extract the resin called *pom* from it to use in the rituals and ceremonies. The *naba* or bark is also used. *Pom* and *naba* are burned in a clay incense burner; during the collection period the tree is tapped with a knife at the cardinal points. From East to West and from North to South, it is believed that the good spirits are stationed for the service of the Mayas.

Maya people regard the Moon in the form of a woman, the Sun in the form of a male, and the Eastern Morning Star as the son. The symbols of three heavenly beings represent the Creator of the entire universe, the great mighty spirit, the God of all Gods. Mayas believe that in every material the spirit of the living Creator exists. It is a living force.

Water has its special role in the Mayas' spiritual, isolated, secret cave. We mix fresh cave water with water from the sea. When collection is finalized the ceremony begins. The Maya shamans—*ilma* in Mopan or *ilonel* in Ke'kchi—invoke the Creator in the name of the lower Gods, for peace, health, abundant harvest, and for many good things in the daily lives of the Mayas. Mayas communicate and invoke these Gods, namely *Ka'na, Ka'cuas, Santil Wan Koha*. These are the first three Gods of the first maintenance.

Ka'cua Shucaneb, Ka'na Sayeb, Ka'na Etsamnot, Ka'na Coy, Ka'cua Bolonko, Ku'cua Shucub Tyuk, Ka'cua Che'ta'ka, Ka'na Betru, and *Ka'cua Yashtunbak* are the Gods the Mayas invoke at special ceremonies.

CHAK THE RAIN GOD...

Yum Kax, the corn god

IXCHEL

Goddess of childbirth, weaving, and healing

42

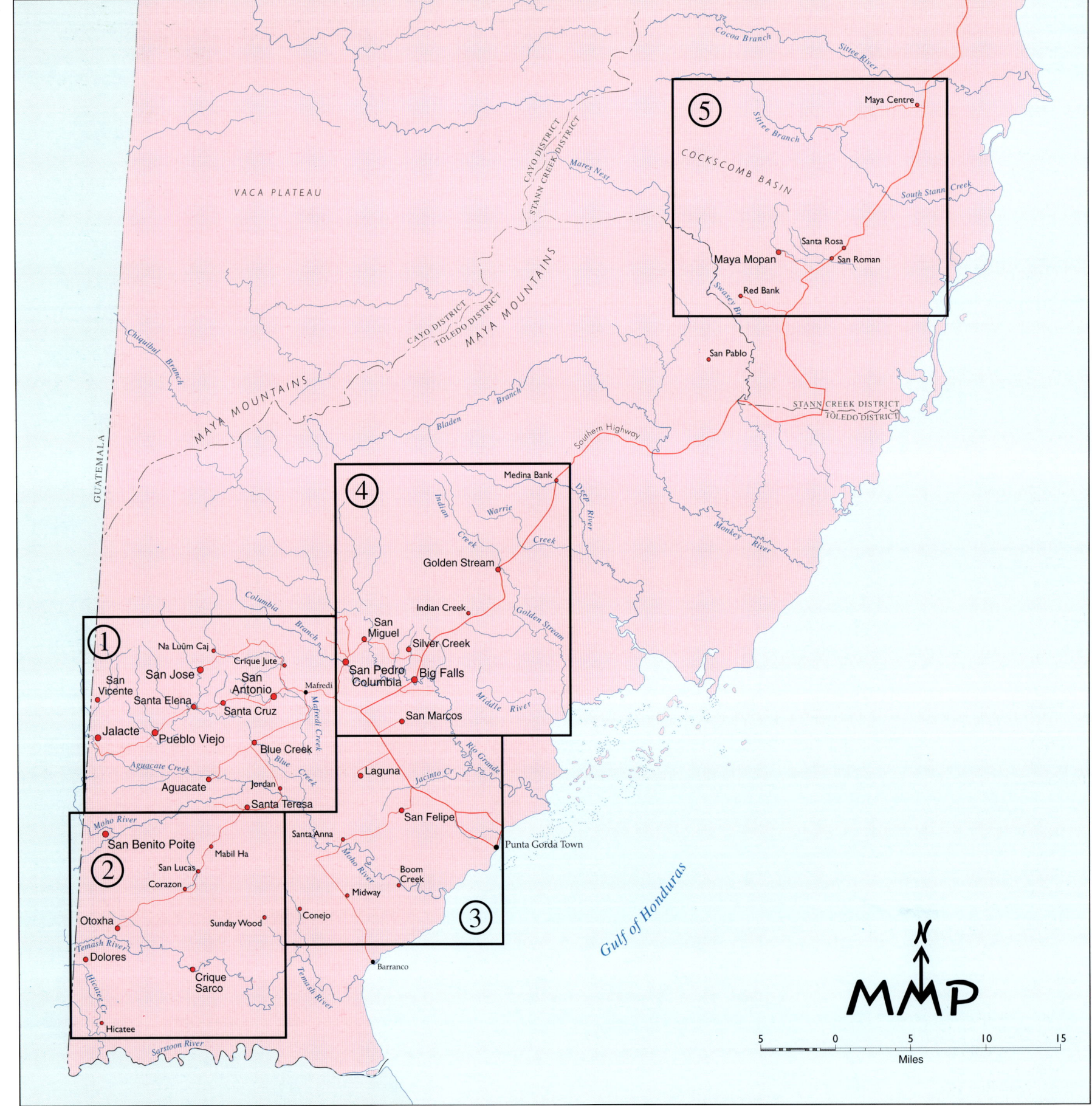

Village Maps

Village Groupings

	page
Region 1:	
San Antonio	44
Santa Cruz	47
San Jose	49
Santa Elena /Pueblo Viejo	50
Aguacate	52
Santa Teresa	55
Blue Creek /Jordan	57
Crique Jute	58
Na Luûm Caj	60
San Vicente	63
Jalacte	64
Region 2:	
San Benito Poite	67
Hicatee /Dolores	69
Crique Sarco	70
Otoxha	73
Sunday Wood	74
Mabil Ha	76
San Lucas	79
Corazon	81
Region 3:	
Laguna	82
Conejo	85
Midway	86
Boom Creek	88
Santa Anna	91
San Felipe	93
Region 4:	
San Pedro Columbia	95
San Marcos	96
San Miguel	99
Indian Creek	100
Big Falls	103
Silver Creek	104
Golden Stream	107
Medina Bank	109
Region 5:	
Maya Centre	110
Red Bank /Maya Mopan	113
Santa Rosa /San Roman	114

Symbols for All Village Maps

- RIVERS
- ROADS
- HOUSES
- WATERFALLS
- CAVES
- HILLS
- MOUNTAINS
- HISTORICAL AND SACRED PLACES
- FIREWOOD, MILPA AND WAHMIL
- DRINKING WATER
- HEALTH CLINICS
- TRADITIONAL HEALERS
- MARKETS
- CHURCHES
- COMMUNITY OFFICES
- GOVERNMENT HOUSE OR Offices
- GUEST HOUSE OR Rooms for RENT.
- HOUSE ANIMALS
- HUNTING
- FISHING
- FOOD PLANTS
- MEDICINAL PLANTS
- FOREST PRODUCTS
- ECONOMIC ACTIVITY
- ARTS and Crafts
- GAME AREAS
- OUTSIDE PROBLEMS
- HIGHLAND FOREST
- MATAMBRE
- BROKEN RIDGE
- SWAMPS
- GRASSLAND
- CITRUS
- PINE RIDGE
- PASTURE
- HIGHWAYS
- PATH/TRAILS
- STREAM
- CREEKS
- SCHOOL
- BIG AND IMPORTANT RIVERS
- LOGGING

San Antonio
Population 954

The Mayas have always inhabited the Yucatán, Guatemala, and Belize. The Mayas in the past lived wherever they wanted to live. However, as time caught up with them, they had to build a village to live together for a long time. San Antonio village was begun around 1850 by José Paquil and several others who were suffering under the military in Guatemala. Their land there was sold to foreigners. They were not paid or compensated in any way or given medical attention. Mayas were used to secure the Guatemalan border with the British, even though the border had nothing to do with us.

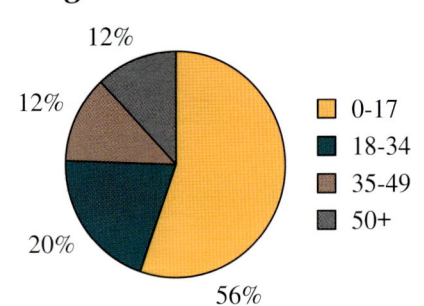

Mr. Paquil and his friends escaped at night to avoid the military. They first settled in Pueblo Viejo, then moved to San Antonio. Few people went back to San Luis, Petén, Guatemala. The new villagers went to San Luis secretly to get their Patron Saint, San Antonio, along with the church bells that are still seen in San Antonio at the Catholic Church. These bells have withstood two fires. Now they are safe in a beautiful stone church built by Father William Urlich, S.J., in the 1940s, with stones transported from the surrounding areas of San Antonio village by the indigenous Mopan Maya. The stones were brought on their shoulders or on their bare backs, tied with the Maya traditional tree bark on their heads.

The founding fathers of the village held celebrations every month marking their true beliefs and sacrifices with the intention of asking God to give them abundance in their harvest of the small areas cultivated.

Now San Antonio is the largest of all Maya settlements and is almost a town in size. It has several modern conveniences. The main attractions are the Catholic stone church, waterfall, ecotourism guest houses, and many shops. San Antonio has a safe water system.

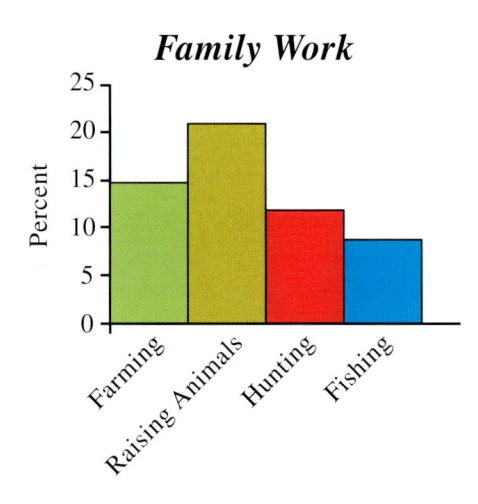

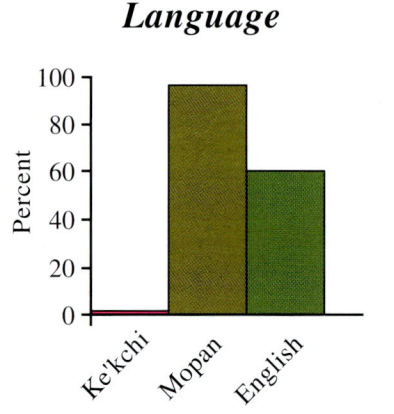

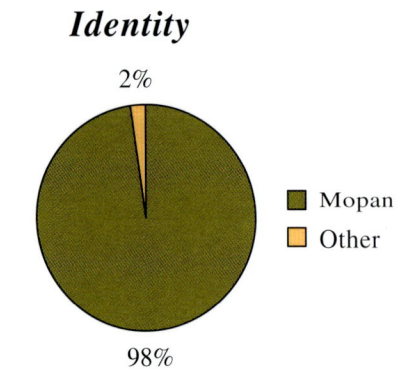

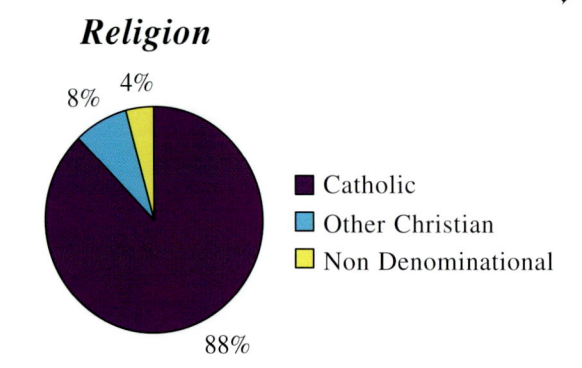

Age Distribution
- 0-17: 56%
- 18-34: 20%
- 35-49: 12%
- 50+: 12%

Family Work
- Farming: ~15%
- Raising Animals: ~21%
- Hunting: ~12%
- Fishing: ~9%

Language
- Ke'kchi: ~1%
- Mopan: ~97%
- English: ~60%

Identity
- Mopan: 98%
- Other: 2%

Religion
- Catholic: 88%
- Other Christian: 8%
- Non Denominational: 4%

Region 1

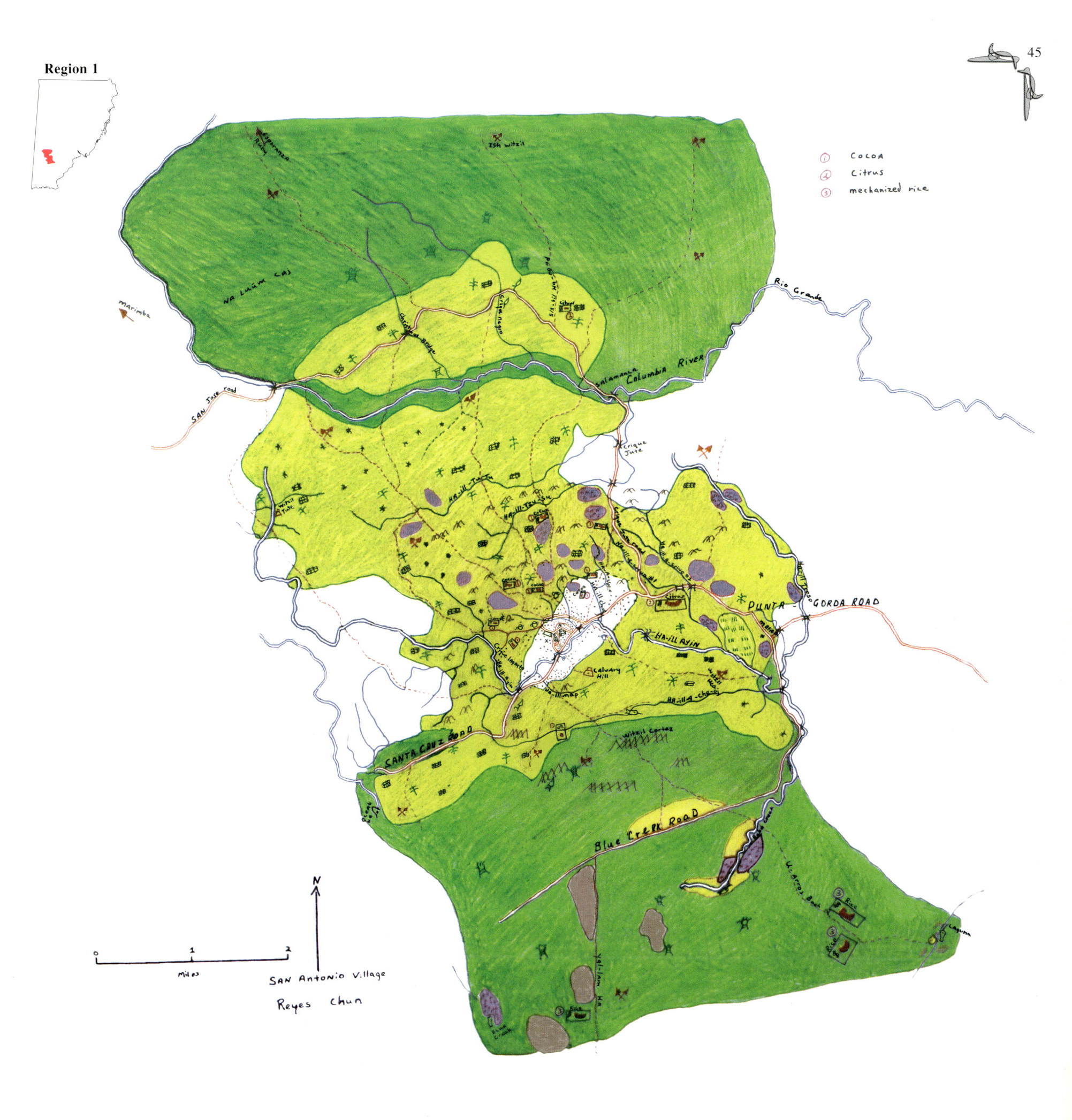

45

① Cocoa
② Citrus
③ mechanized rice

San Antonio Village
Reyes Chun

SANTA CRUZ VILLAGE
JUAN TEUL

Region 1

① Rice, Corn
② Beans

Santa Cruz

Population 347

Age Distribution

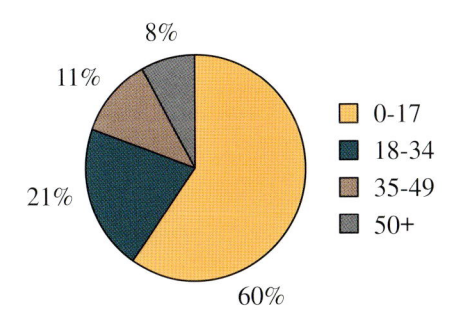

- 0-17: 60%
- 18-34: 21%
- 35-49: 11%
- 50+: 8%

Identity

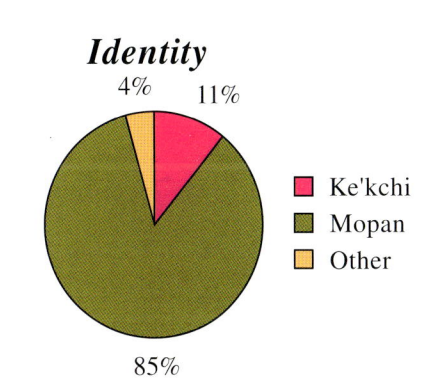

- Ke'kchi: 11%
- Mopan: 85%
- Other: 4%

Religion

- Catholic: 31%
- Other Christian: 55%
- Non Denominational: 14%

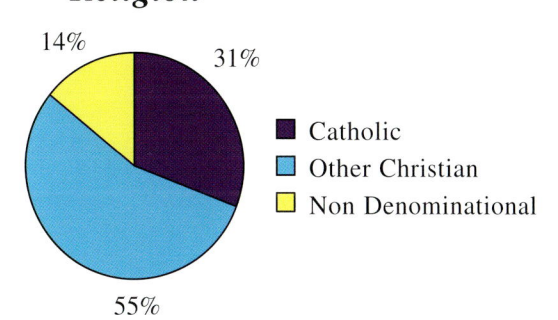

Santa Cruz village was first an *alkilo*, meaning that people lived in the forests far from each other in no particular order. In 1950, Santiago Canti, Benito Canti, Susano Canti, Lazaro Pop, and Thomas Sho encouraged people to begin a village. As people were associated with the Catholic religion, they named the village Holy Cross or Santa Cruz. A cross or crucifix was placed in the church and an *alcalde* or village magistrate was elected. The village feast is celebrated on May 3 traditionally. A cornmill was built in 1995.

Santa Cruz is one of the villages with the most religious denominations (Mennonites, Protestants, Church of Christ, and Baptists) scrambling for souls and competing with the established Catholic church. This village does not seem to increase in population because many people of this village migrated to Golden Stream village to begin it, and they also helped establish San Roman in the Stann Creek District.

Santa Cruz is a typical Maya village. It is situated next to the Maya ruin of Uch Ben Cah, giving it the appeal and aura of the ancient Maya civilization. Moreover, this village boasts two waterfalls, one within the village and one outside it.

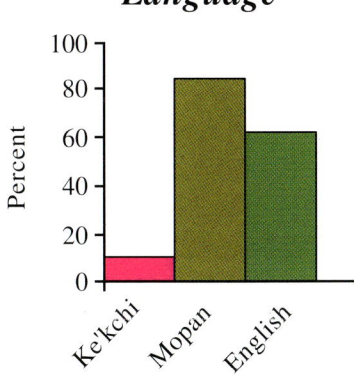

Family Work

- Farming: 18%
- Raising Animals: 18%
- Hunting: ~9%
- Fishing: 18%

Language

- Ke'kchi: ~10%
- Mopan: ~85%
- English: ~62%

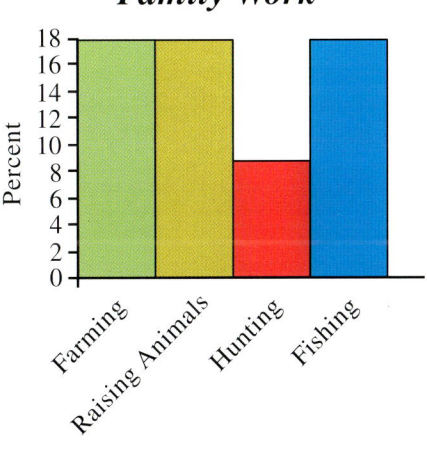

Region 1

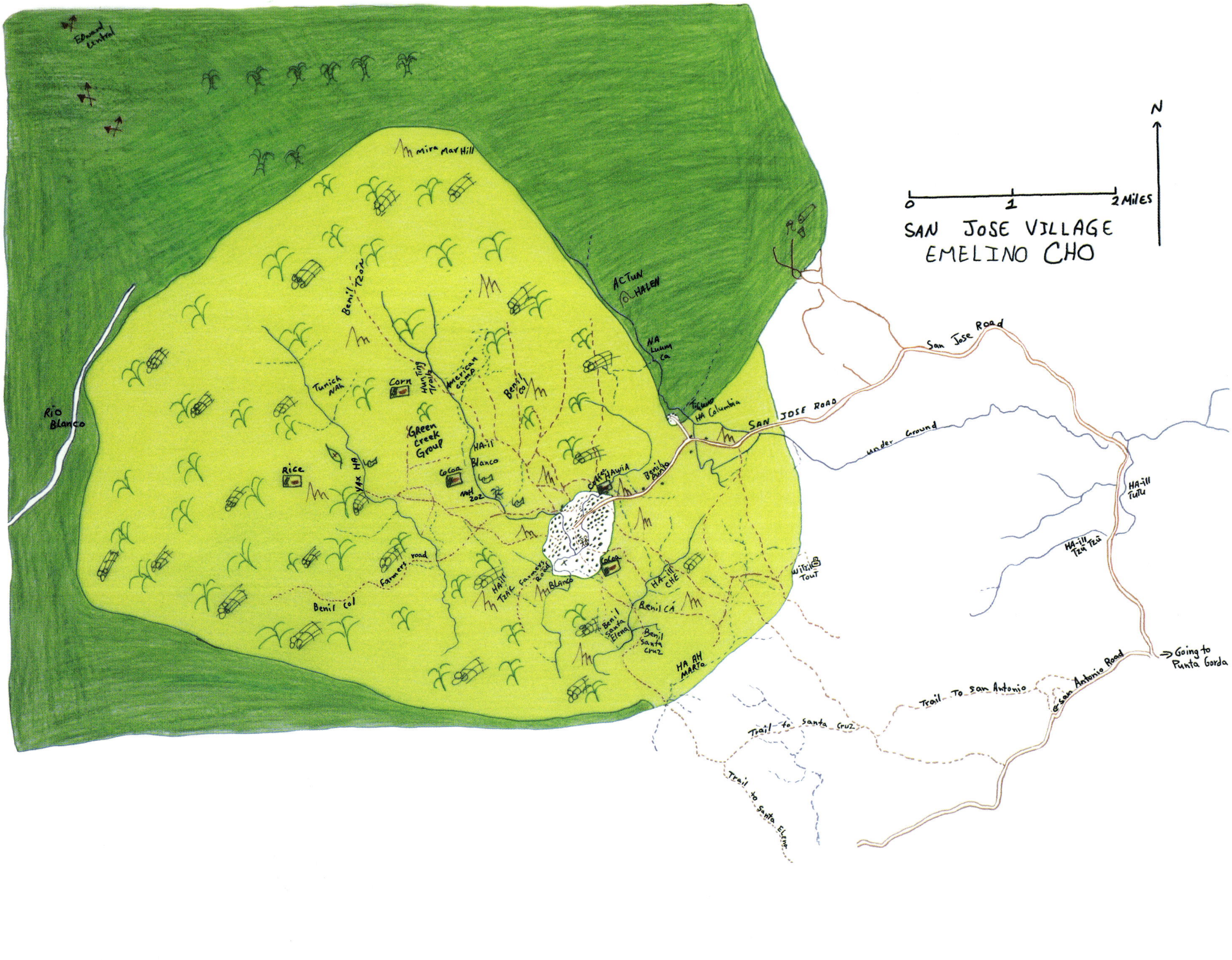
SAN JOSE VILLAGE
EMELINO CHO
N
0
1
2 MILES
Edward Central
Mira Mar Hill
ACTUN HALEN
NA LUUM CA
Tunich NAH
Corn
Hunting Trails
American camp
Benil Col
Green creek Group
HA-il Blanco
Rice
YAX HA
Cocoa
NAH ZOZ
HAWIA
Benil Punta
HA Columbia
SAN JOSE ROAD
San Jose Road
Under Ground
HA-ill Tutu
HA-ill Tzu Tzu
Cocoa
HA-ill CHE
Benil CA
Benil Santa Elena
Benil Santa Cruz
HA AH MARTA
Farmers road
Benil Col
Rio Blanco
Trail To San Antonio
San Antonio Road
Going to Punta Gorda
Trail to Santa Cruz
Trail to Santa Elena

San Jose

Population 685

No one used to live around the junction of the Hawia and Blanco rivers. This place was far in the jungle, fit only for wild animals and hunters, and later on, loggers and *chicleros* looking for the sap of the *sapodilla* trees. Martin Shal, Santiago Tzub, and Sebastian Ico were the founding fathers of San Jose village. The village came about when people from San Antonio and those in the *alkilos* (living in the jungle by themselves) yearned for a new village. Public meetings were held; a Catholic church was built. The village was named San Jose in 1954 after the feast of Saint Joseph; the village feast day is March 19. Traditionally, this date is celebrated with a three-day feast of eating *caldos* and dancing to marimba and harp music. By 1996, even after hundreds of people migrated to other districts in Belize, this village has a population of 685. It has modern school buildings, a huge community center, tourist guest houses, and three soccer teams. This village has produced several Maya teachers. It has good agricultural soil. Its cash crops and products are cacao, corn, beans, vegetables, pig-rearing, basket-weaving, and palm seeds. The people are pro-environment and believe in organic farming.

People in this village grow vegetables to sell in Punta Gorda Town. They grow corn in abundance to sell to other villages. San Jose boasts being the nearest village to the famous quartz ridge area, and of the most unique, rich, biodiverse tropical rainforest areas in Central America. The village has a guest house, several cornmills, a community telephone, a waterfall, and a cave.

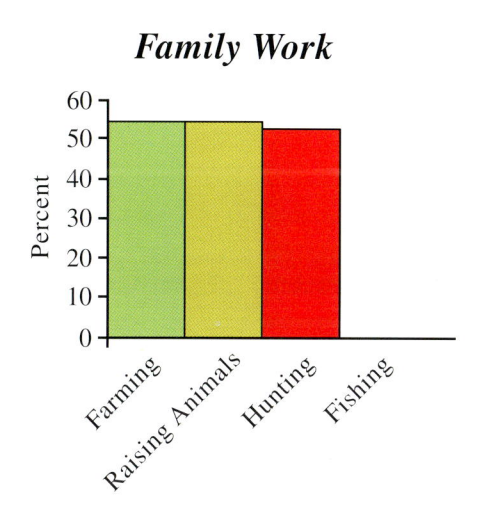

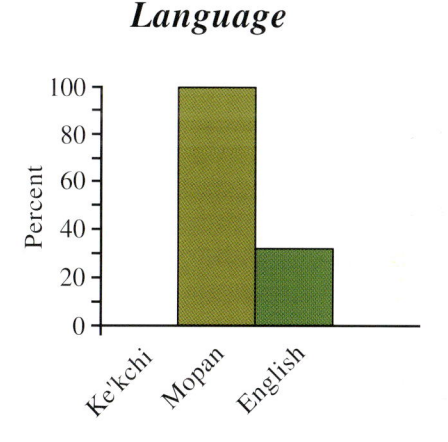

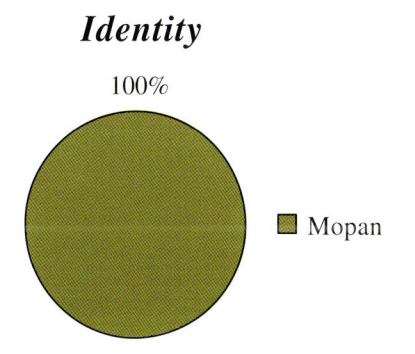

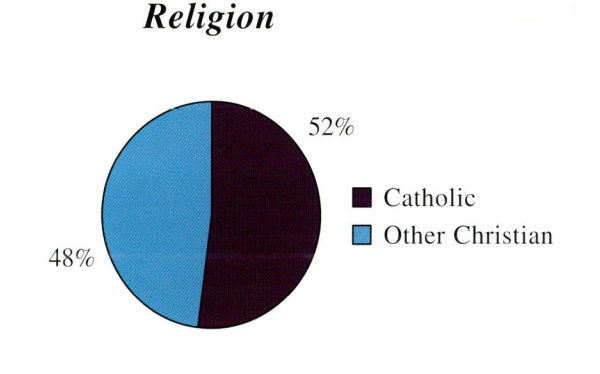

Age Distribution

- 0-17: 56%
- 18-34: 26%
- 35-49: 13%
- 50+: 5%

Family Work

- Farming: ~54%
- Raising Animals: ~54%
- Hunting: ~52%
- Fishing: 0%

Language

- Ke'kchi: 0%
- Mopan: 100%
- English: ~32%

Identity

- Mopan: 100%

Religion

- Catholic: 52%
- Other Christian: 48%

Santa Elena
Population 156

Enriquez Choc, Martin Choc, and Marto Choc, attracted by the beautiful waterfall, an abundance of wildlife, and the rich loamy soil of the area, moved with their families to begin the new settlement that is now called Santa Elena. The founding fathers first called this settlement Rio Blanco after the crystal-clear river that bordered their *alkilo* (scattered Maya houses in the forest). As more families from San Antonio came into the new community, a statue of Santa Elena was brought to Rio Blanco to be the saint of the villagers. The village name was changed to honor the Catholic saint.

As the village population grew, an *alcalde* was elected to look after the affairs of the villagers. The Rio Blanco Indian Reservation of some 940 acres was granted to the villagers. A primary school was built with the aid of the community, the Catholic mission, and the government of Belize. Later more religious denominations came scrambling for souls. To decrease time spent in food preparation, an electric corn-mill was set up, giving women more time to work on their crafts.

Population increase and the settlement of Santa Cruz created a land problem. Recently villagers from Santa Elena and Santa Cruz decided to use their beautiful waterfall to attract a limited number of tourists to their communities. The Rio Blanco National Park around the Rio Blanco Fall was created and a small guest house erected in Santa Elena. Ecotourism seems to be the future source of income for the people of Santa Elena.

Family Work

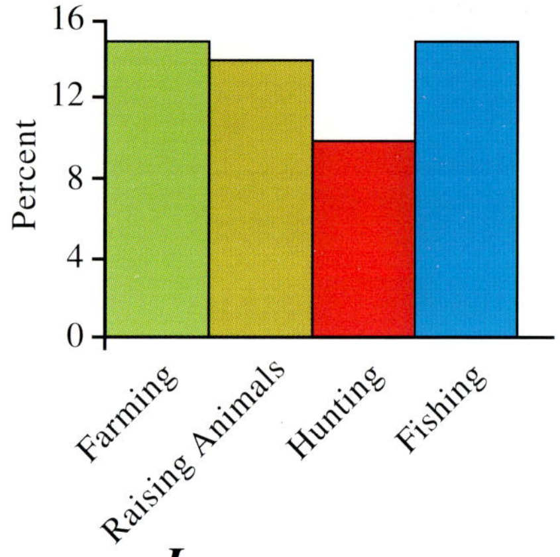

Language

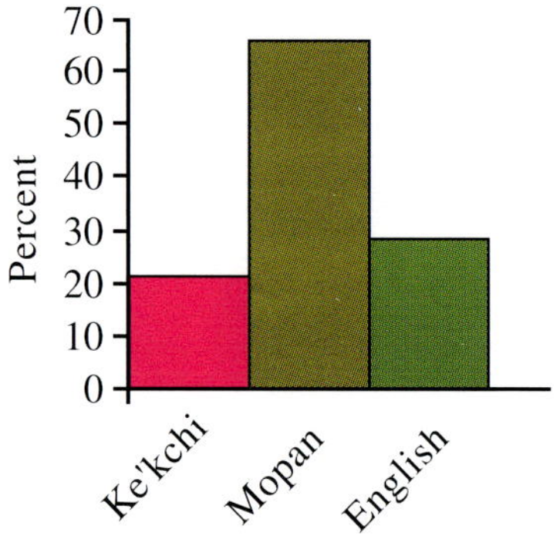

Age Distribution
- 0-17: 60%
- 18-34: 21%
- 35-49: 11%
- 50+: 8%

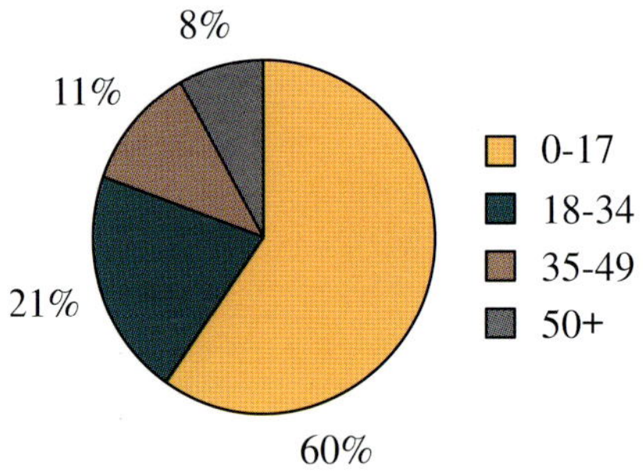

Identity
- Ke'kchi: 3%
- Mopan: 95%
- Other: 2%

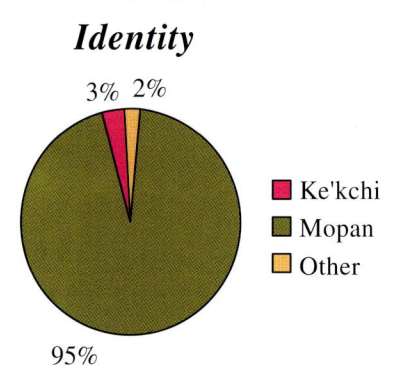

Religion
- Catholic: 28%
- Other Christian: 64%
- Non Denominational: 8%

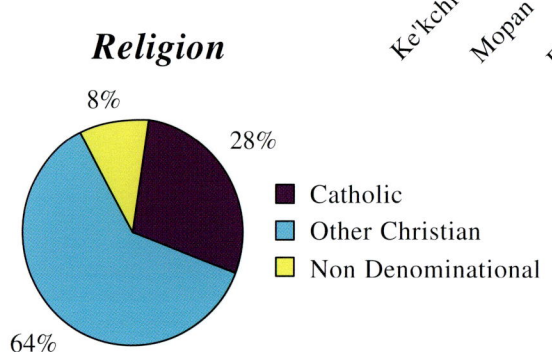

Pueblo Viejo
Population 542

Pueblo Viejo is a Spanish name given by the villagers, translated as "Old Town." It was the first village to be founded in southern Belize, about seven miles from the border of what is now Guatemala. The date the village began is unknown. The people who founded the village were returning to the area from San Luis, Petén in Guatemala and they are pure Mayas. When Miguel Coc, born in 1911, first visited Pueblo Viejo, no one was found in the village, but he could see one house post left standing.

They went back to San Luis and stole a deer mask, clothing, a statue and a marimba, and then left San Luis.

The main food of the villagers is traditionally corn, which they produce with their hands and machetes. After a period of time they learned how to plant beans and rice from a man. Diego Villanueva is a famous man to the villagers for teaching about the planting of beans and rice. One day, as related by Miguel Coc, they went to a field and the boss said that the workers were to eat rice for lunch. They said, "Oh, what is rice?" because no one had seen it. At lunch time they saw that rice resembles a worm. But when everyone tasted rice they said, "Oh, that is nice!" Together the villagers cooperate to see how the village can grow.

Age Distribution
- 0-17: 62%
- 18-34: 20%
- 35-49: 12%
- 50+: 6%

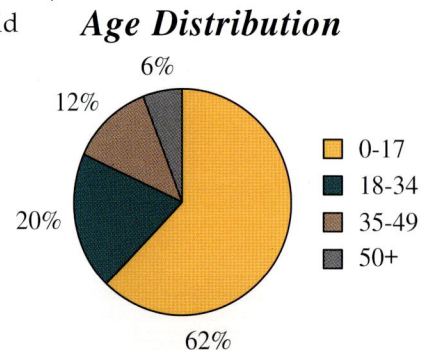

Identity
- Ke'kchi: 14%
- Mopan: 86%

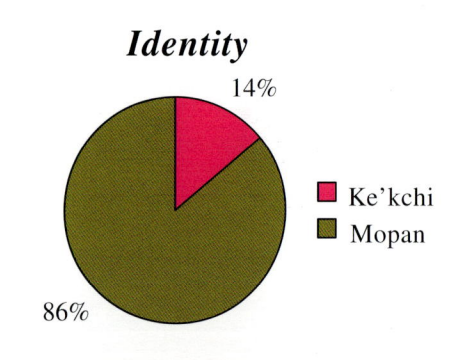

51

Region 1

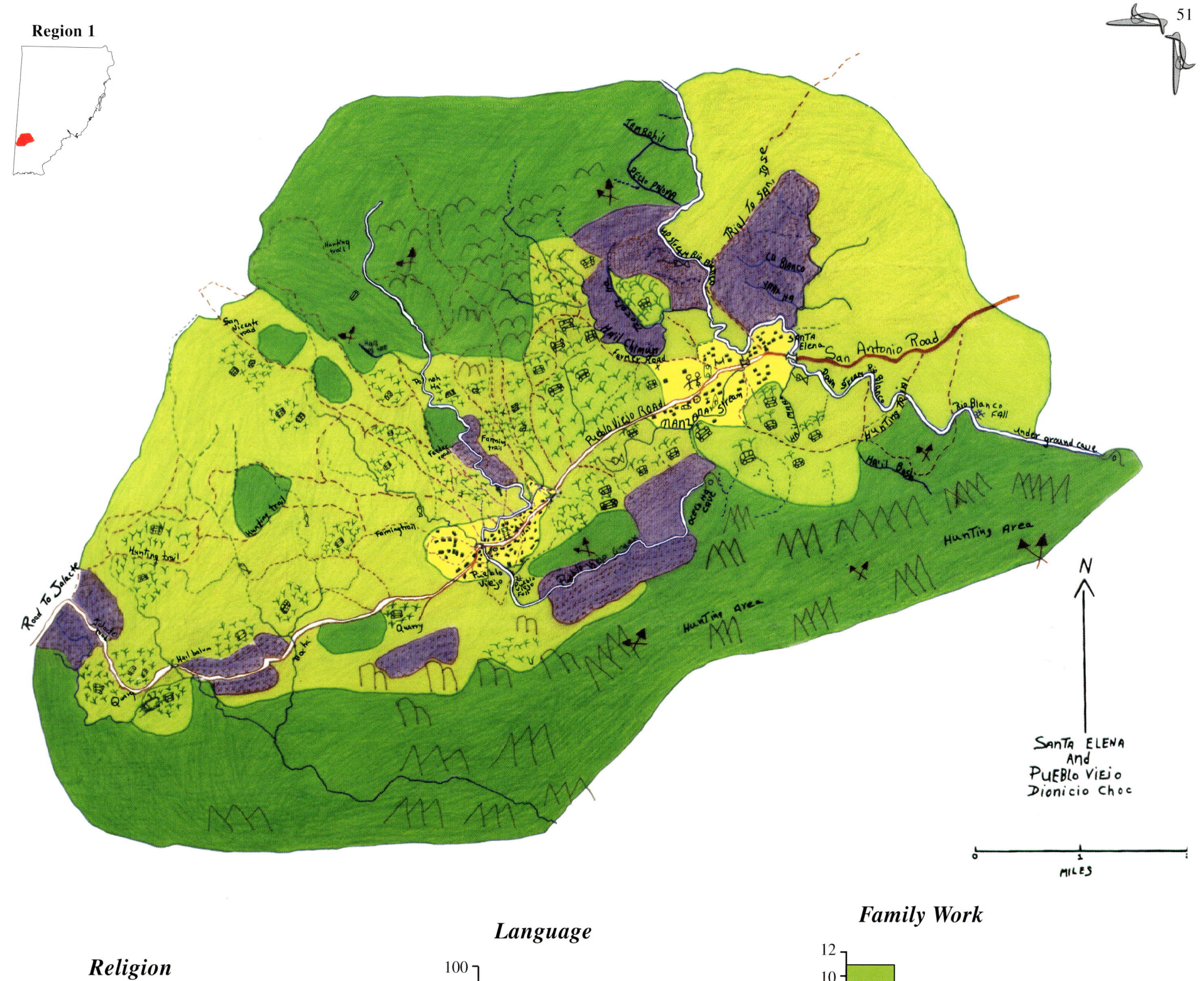

SANTA ELENA
And
PUEBLO VIEJO
Dionicio Choc

Religion

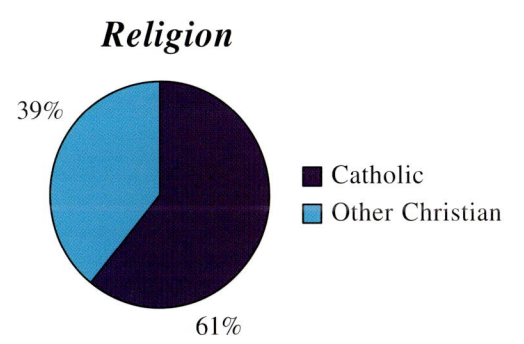

- Catholic: 61%
- Other Christian: 39%

Language

Ke'kchi	Mopan	English

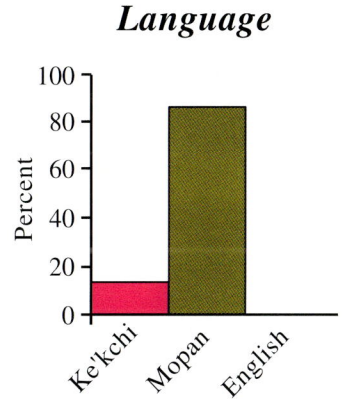

Family Work

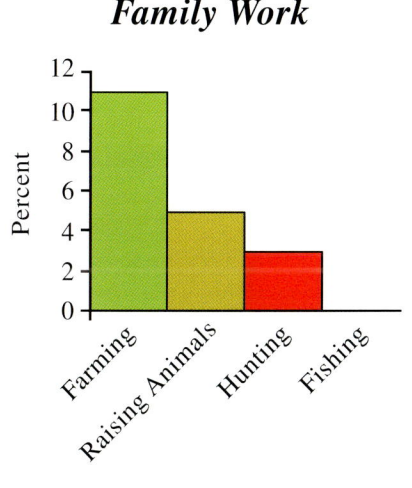

Farming, Raising Animals, Hunting, Fishing

Aguacate

Population 296

This is mostly a Ke'kchi village, the oldest and most traditional in Toledo. People from this village have been instrumental in beginning other villages in the Toledo District. They are very progressive. Many have completed high school and one has gone to university; they have a village phone, a health center, and a few churches. The people are friendly.

About one hundred years ago, the village was called Moho River Aguacate. Most people came from Guatemala and a few came from Pueblo Viejo to be the first settlers of Aguacate village. During those days the indigenous people in Guatemala were slaves; many escaped and returned to Toledo seeking survival.

The word *Aguacate* means "avocado" in Spanish, but it is not known exactly why they named the place Aguacate. Maybe it once had a lot of avocado trees.

In the old days, people traveled in dorys on the Aguacate River and the Moho River. It took them a week of paddling to go from Aguacate to Punta Gorda Town. Then in the late seventies the road was built, and after that the community center, the health post, and a concrete Catholic church. The village of Aguacate is progressing and improving and the people are friendly.

Family Work

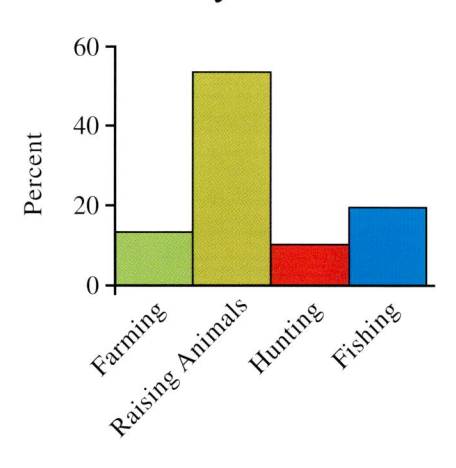

- Farming
- Raising Animals
- Hunting
- Fishing

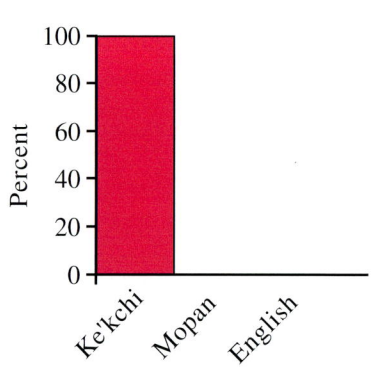

Age Distribution

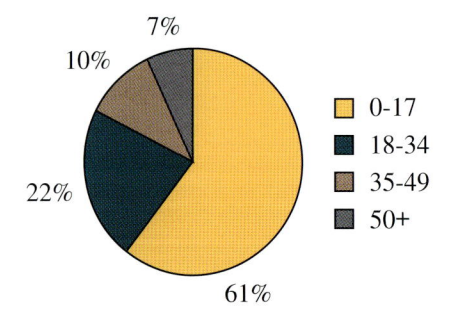

- 0-17: 61%
- 18-34: 22%
- 35-49: 10%
- 50+: 7%

Language

- Ke'kchi: 100%
- Mopan: 0%
- English: 0%

Identity

- Ke'kchi: 99%
- Other: 1%

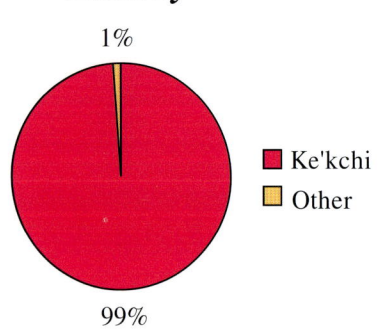

Religion

- Catholic: 59%
- Other Christian: 41%

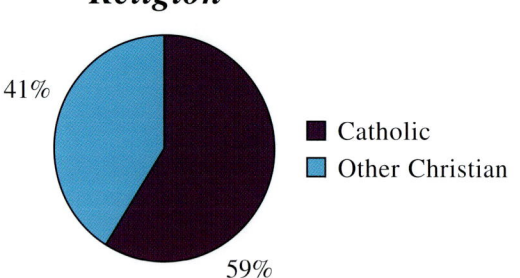

Region 1

53

Road to Blue Creek

Jalacte Creek
Aguacate River
Farmers Road
Hunting Trails
Pekil'Ha
Trail To Santa Theresa
Moho River
San Benito Poite Trail
Monkey Falls
Otonha Creek

N

0 1 2 miles

Aguacate Village
Domingo Cal

Region 1

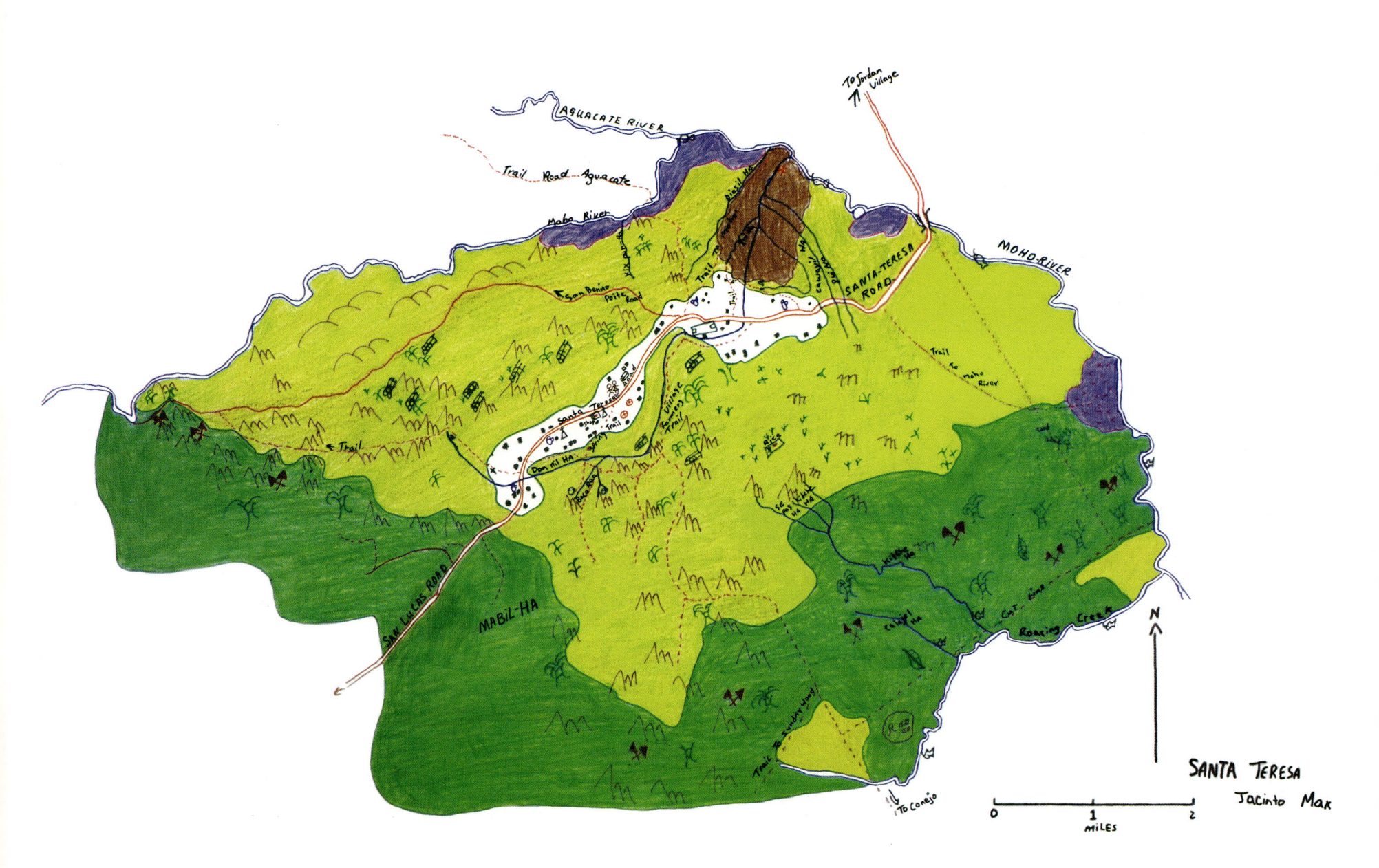

SANTA TERESA
Jacinto Mak

Santa Teresa

Population 269

In 1933, Domingo Cucul, Jose Pec, Santiago Pop, and Francisco Bo settled in this place known as Hinchosonnes. They had migrated from Dolores Sarstoon village and a place known as Machacon Moho River. After these people settled, others came in.

In 1943, trees and houses were destroyed by a great hurricane. The Catholic Church building with a statue inside named Santa Teresa was destroyed too. However, upon realizing that their statue was destroyed, the people desired to reestablish there and named it Santa Teresa. In our native Ke'kchi language, the local name we use for our village is Se-Pan. *Pan* means bread in Spanish.

When people founded this village, there was no road. They used a small trail alongside Santa Teresa Creek, meeting the trail at Moho River. These people then used a dory in the Moho River to travel to Punta Gorda Town. They took three days to go and three days to come back, for a total of six days paddling.

Mr. Wilkins used to buy pigs in those days and sold them in Punta Gorda Town Market. One day he was traveling in his dory with a woman and her child. He had brought some bread for sale. On the way up the Moho River, his dory turned over. The woman and her child and Mr. Wilkins could not swim and died. All the bread was destroyed too. This is why the people named their village Se-Pan. This village has easy access to waterfalls, caves and hiking in the jungles. It is a good place to go fishing on the Moho River.

Family Work

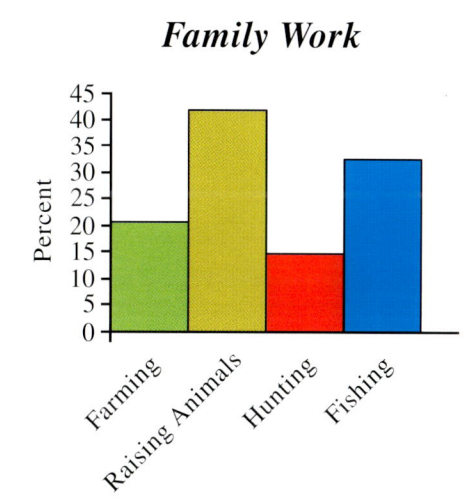

- Farming: ~20%
- Raising Animals: ~42%
- Hunting: ~15%
- Fishing: ~32%

Language

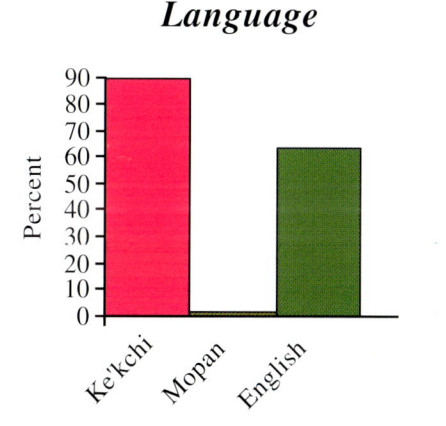

- Ke'kchi: ~90%
- Mopan: ~1%
- English: ~63%

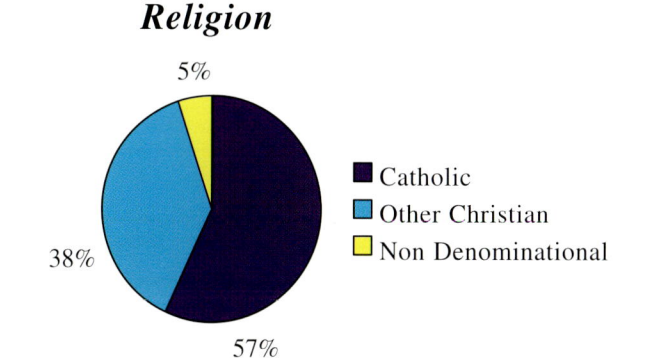

Age Distribution

- 0-17: 62%
- 18-34: 23%
- 35-49: 8%
- 50+: 7%

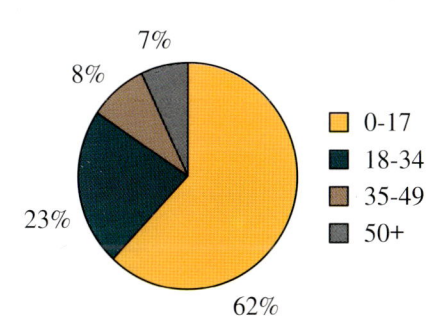

Identity

- Ke'kchi: 99%
- Other: 1%

Religion

- Catholic: 57%
- Other Christian: 38%
- Non Denominational: 5%

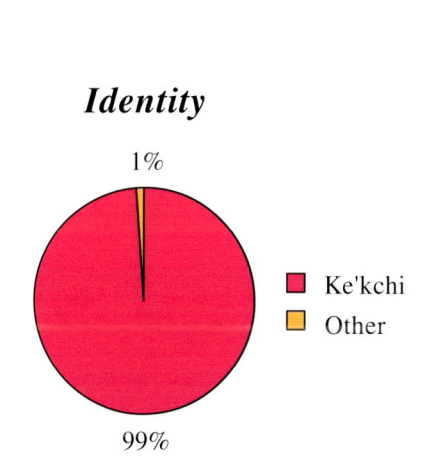

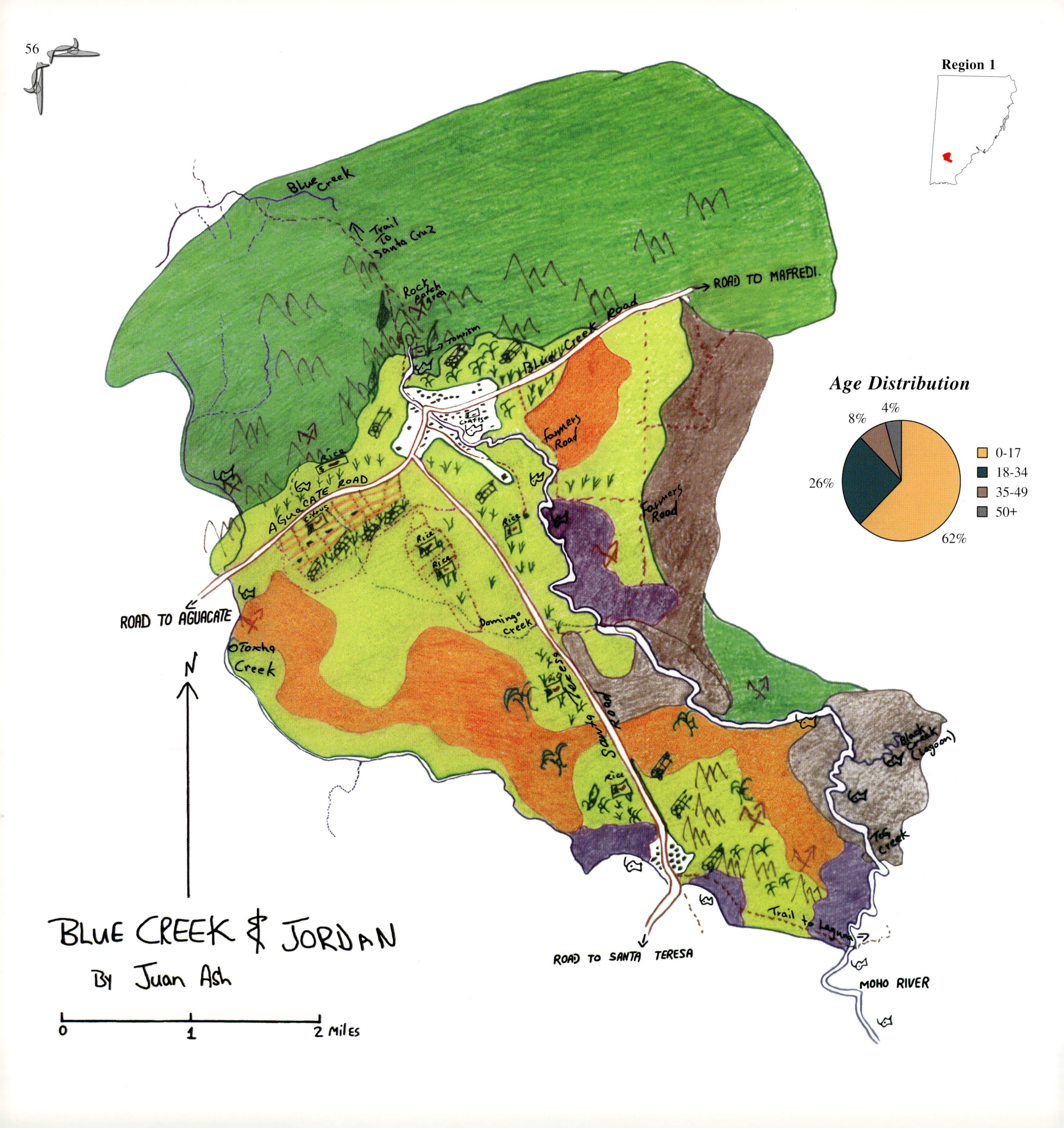

BLUE CREEK & JORDAN
By Juan Ash

Region 1

Age Distribution
- 0-17: 62%
- 18-34: 26%
- 35-49: 8%
- 50+: 4%

Blue Creek
Population 226

From 1925 to 1950, few families lived in Rio Blanco. During the year 1950 a few families came from Aguacate and San Antonio. Around that time the people decided to change the village name. They named the place Blue Creek because of the beauty of the river and hills. Clear water was abundant for washing and fishing; there were hillsides for hunting; and fertile soil for plantations.

Today people in Blue Creek speak both Mopan and Ke'kchi Maya because of the earlier settlers. Long ago Rio Blanco was a reservation. But a foreigner bought the area surrounding Blue Creek Cave. The Toledo Rural Development Project (TRDP) was established in 1980 to develop 150 acres of land behind Blue Creek. This is a beautiful area.

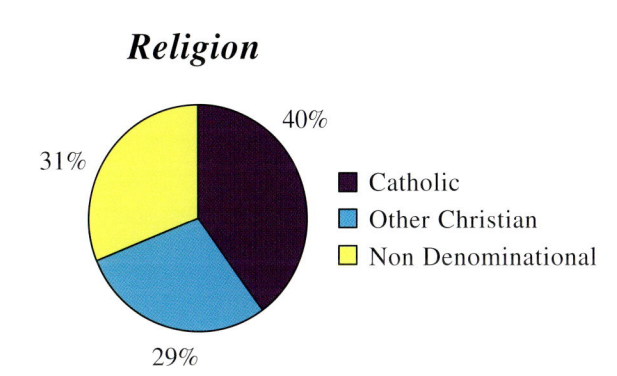

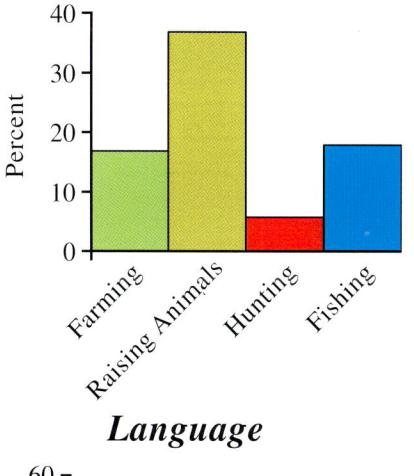

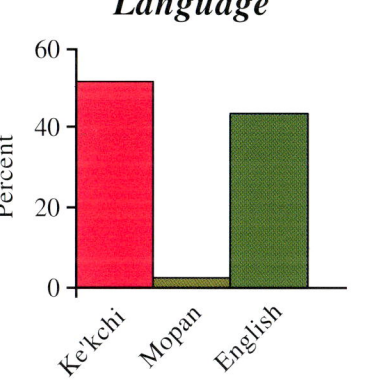

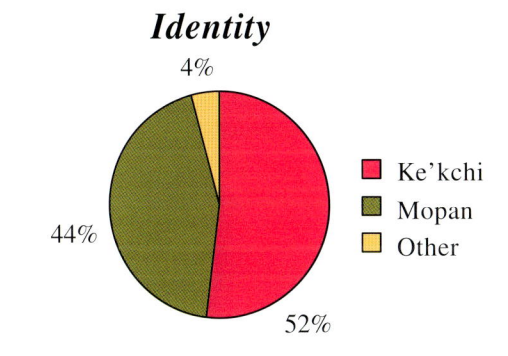

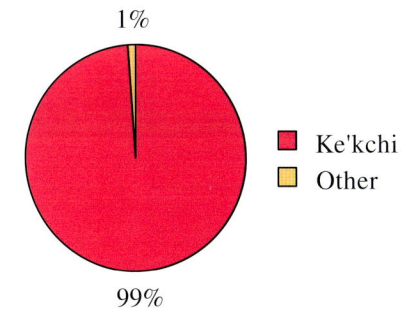

Identity
- Ke'kchi: 52%
- Mopan: 44%
- Other: 4%

Religion
- Catholic: 40%
- Other Christian: 29%
- Non Denominational: 31%

Family Work
Farming, Raising Animals, Hunting, Fishing

Language
Ke'kchi, Mopan, English

Jordan
Population 70

Jordan village was settled in February 1980. Two families came from Laguna, headed by Jose Teul and Domingo Pop. They sought more fertile land for agriculture. At the time the place was called Pooc [Ke'kchi], because there were many plum trees near the riverside. Two years later more families moved in. Finally the road was built. One day the previous Prime Minister George Price visited the place and named it Jordan village because of the river. The village was improved and cleaned up in 1990. The Mennonite Church was built, and then a school and water vat. Since then Jordan village has been permanently settled.

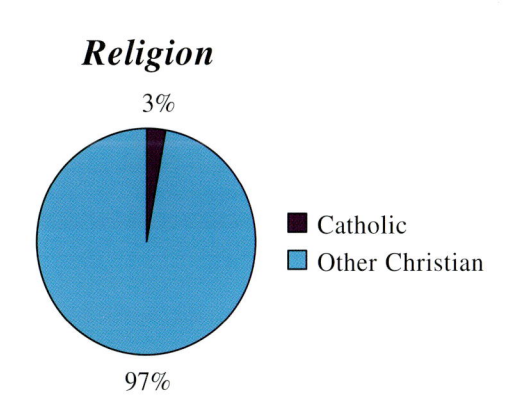

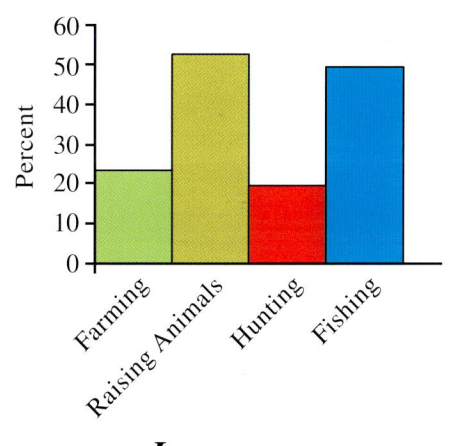

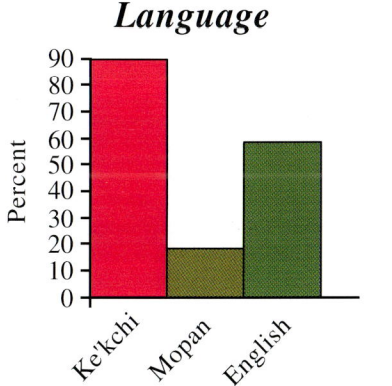

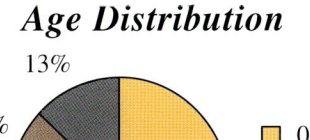

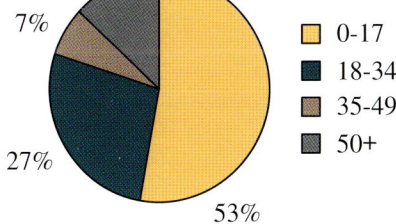

Identity
- Ke'kchi: 99%
- Other: 1%

Age Distribution
- 0-17: 53%
- 18-34: 27%
- 35-49: 7%
- 50+: 13%

Religion
- Catholic: 3%
- Other Christian: 97%

Family Work
Farming, Raising Animals, Hunting, Fishing

Language
Ke'kchi, Mopan, English

Crique Jute

Population 118

The villagers of Crique Jute were originally from San Antonio, Toledo, and some from Petén, Guatemala. It is uncertain why these people moved. They first settled in the village of Pueblo Viejo and then moved to San Antonio. It is possible people moved here from San Antonio because it was within easy reach of the plantations and the forests.

Enriquez Pop and his wife were the first to found the place in 1932 and named it Crique Jute. The name was chosen because *jute* (meaning snail) were found in that river and still are today. During that time there was no road or school. There were only seven families.

Others have lately come to settle here because of better land for farming. In 1955 mahogany cutters came and jobs were available felling logs with axes. In the 1960s, a small road was built by Phillips Oil Company to search for oil next to Caracol Hill, which is a Maya ruin. The road also began to improve. Later the Forestry Department established a camp at Salamanca, one mile from Crique Jute, at the edge of the forest.

In 1961 the population began to increase and they considered the need for a village leader. Around this time the government began transporting children to San Antonio village for education.

Today in Crique Jute a slow change is happening due to roads, a community center, hand pumps for water, and a school. In 1985 a community center was built and in 1991 a government primary school. Now the village Women's Group has a cornmill project. Some parents struggle for a better life for their children in the future, and to make a better Crique Jute. The *alcalde* seeks land security for his village.

The village has grown to 35 families. Five religions came in: Roman Catholics, Nazarenes, Mennonites, Adventists, and Evangelists. The presence of the British Army camp [now closed] at Salamanca near Crique Jute offered job opportunities and exposed the villagers to different ways of living. Gurkha [east Indian] children are found in Crique Jute.

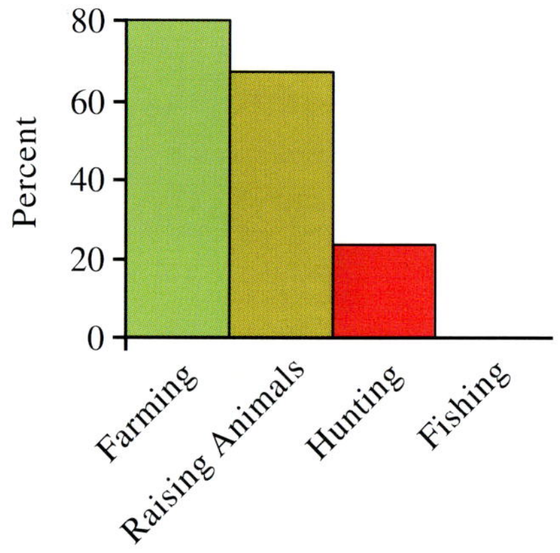

Age Distribution

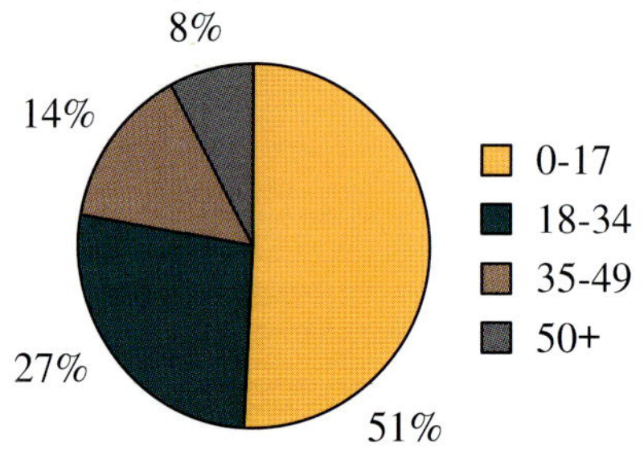

- 0-17: 51%
- 18-34: 27%
- 35-49: 14%
- 50+: 8%

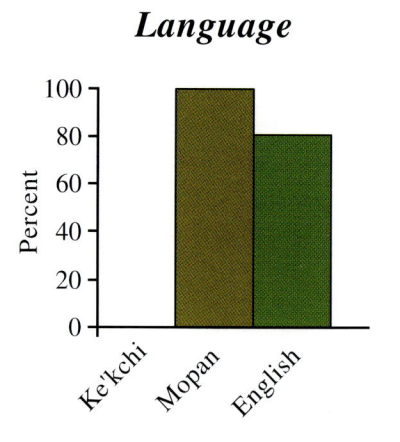

Identity

- Mopan: 100%

Family Work

- Farming: ~80%
- Raising Animals: ~68%
- Hunting: ~23%
- Fishing: 0%

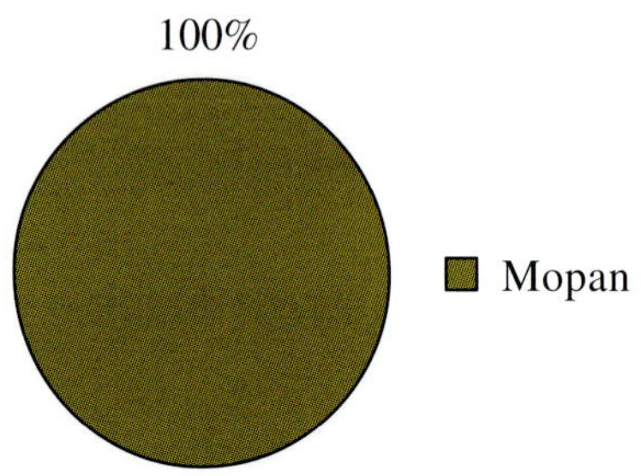

Religion

- Catholic: 57%
- Other Christian: 43%

Language

- Ke'kchi: 0%
- Mopan: 100%
- English: ~80%

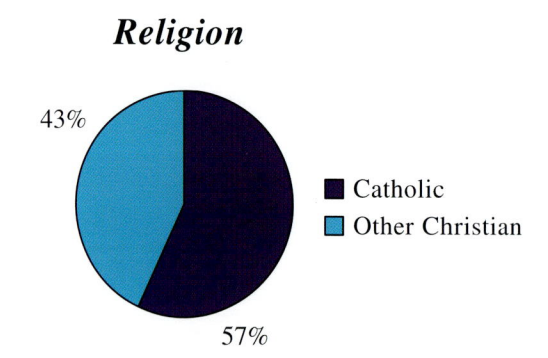

Region 1

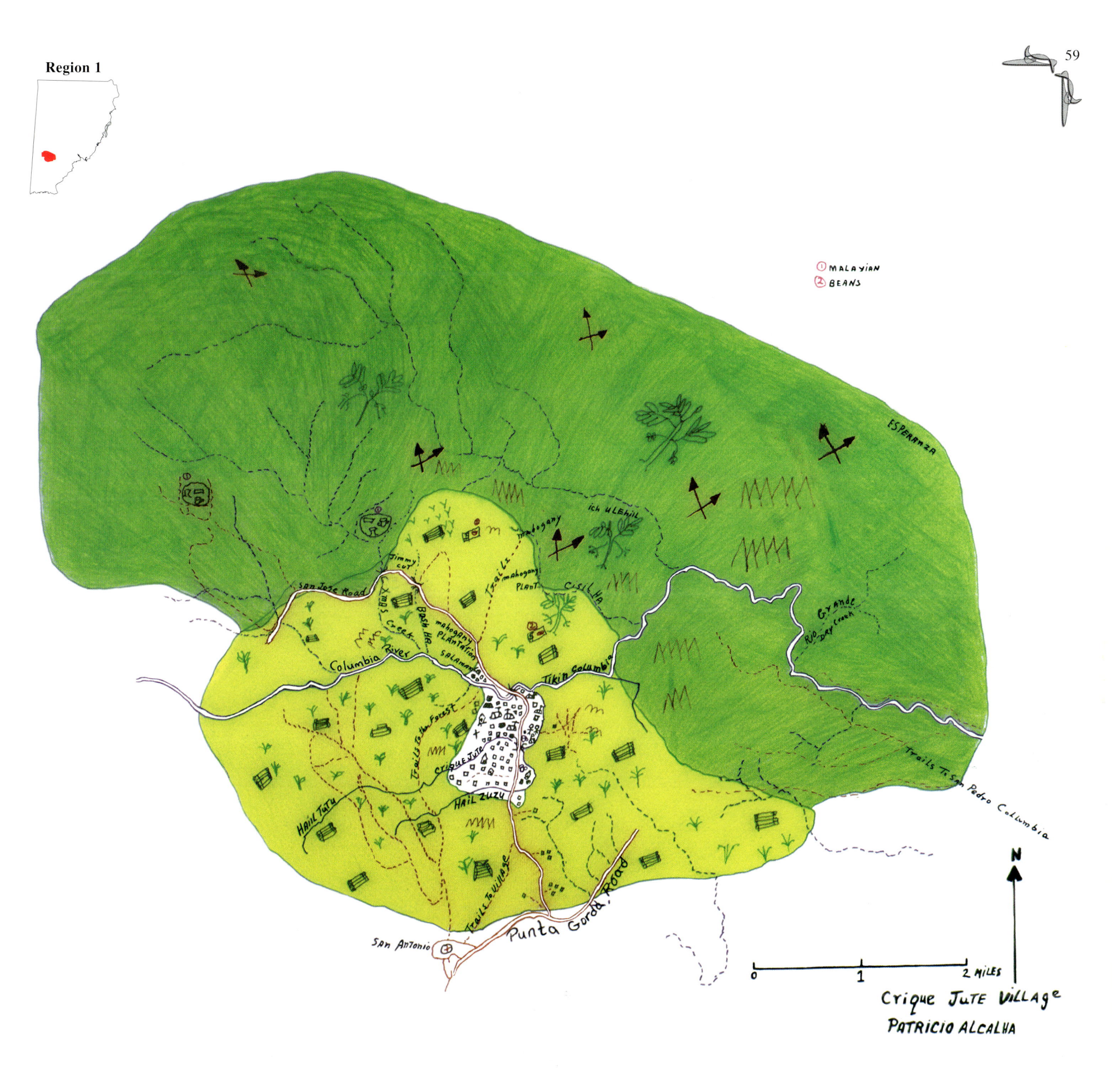

59

① MALAYIAN
② BEANS

Crique Jute Village
PATRICIO ALCALHA

Na Luûm Caj

Population 125

Na Luûm Caj was founded in June of 1986 by seven Mopan families from San Antonio. The concept of a model village, similar to a homestead, was conceived by young progressive Mopan farmers who called themselves the Cedar Farmers Group (CFC). This group, consisting of fifty members, and encouraged by the Toledo Maya Cultural Council, applied for 2,500 acres of land within the Jimmy Cut area bordering the Columbia River Forest Reserve. Each CFC member was allotted by the government a 50-acre parcel to lease and a house lot within an area set aside for a village site.

The village site was well surveyed and planned according to modern needs. Seven families from among the fifty members moved from San Antonio to begin the settlement they named Na Luûm Caj. These settlers were made up of Pablo Oh, Antonio Sho, Emeterio Sho, Clemente Sho, Juan Cal, Cyriaco Coh, and Lucio Sho. Various rules were put out to govern the village affairs. An *alcalde* was selected and a school built with the assistance of the British High Commission. Modern cement house walls were built for each family through self-help and funds from the International Rescue Committee's Quick Impact Project(UNICEF).

Pigs were not allowed in the village and each family was requested to build outdoor toilet facilities. A twenty-five-yard area is to be left untouched along streams, and each family must clean their lot. Unfortunately, the population remains stagnant. No more families from the Cedar Farmers Group are moving in. In fact, some of the members are giving up their 50-acre block. The concept of a homestead is not working and the village still resembles an *alkilo* (a style of Maya community in which the houses are situated at a distance from each other).

Na Luûm Caj, Mother Earth Village, is a good example of Mayan hesitance in adopting farming methods that are not traditional. Many are moving back into communal land practices, giving up their leased plots.

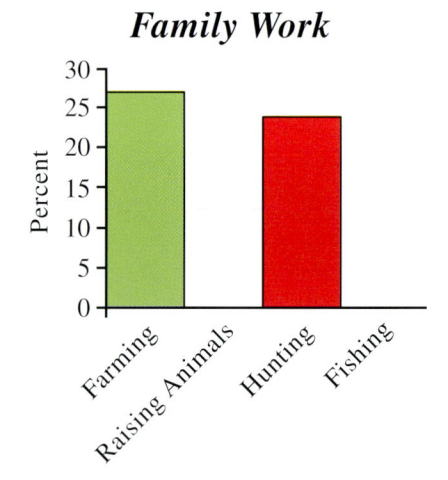

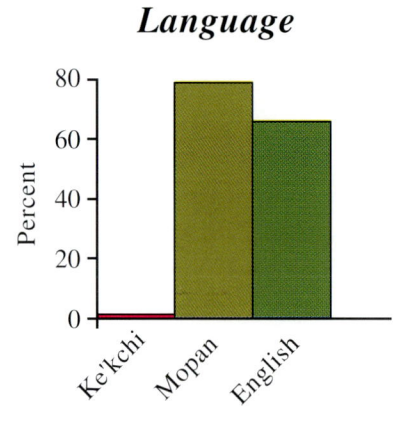

Age Distribution

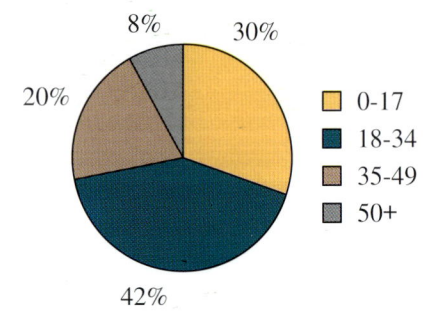

- 0-17: 30%
- 18-34: 42%
- 35-49: 20%
- 50+: 8%

Identity

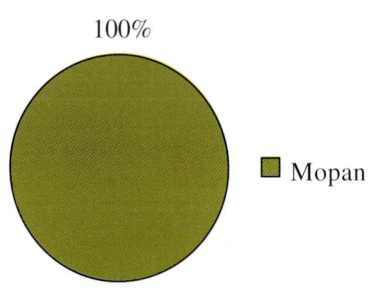

- Mopan: 100%

Religion

- Catholic: 46%
- Other Christian: 52%
- Non Denominational: 2%

Family Work

- Farming: ~27%
- Raising Animals: 0
- Hunting: ~24%
- Fishing: 0

Language

- Ke'kchi: ~1%
- Mopan: ~79%
- English: ~66%

Region 1

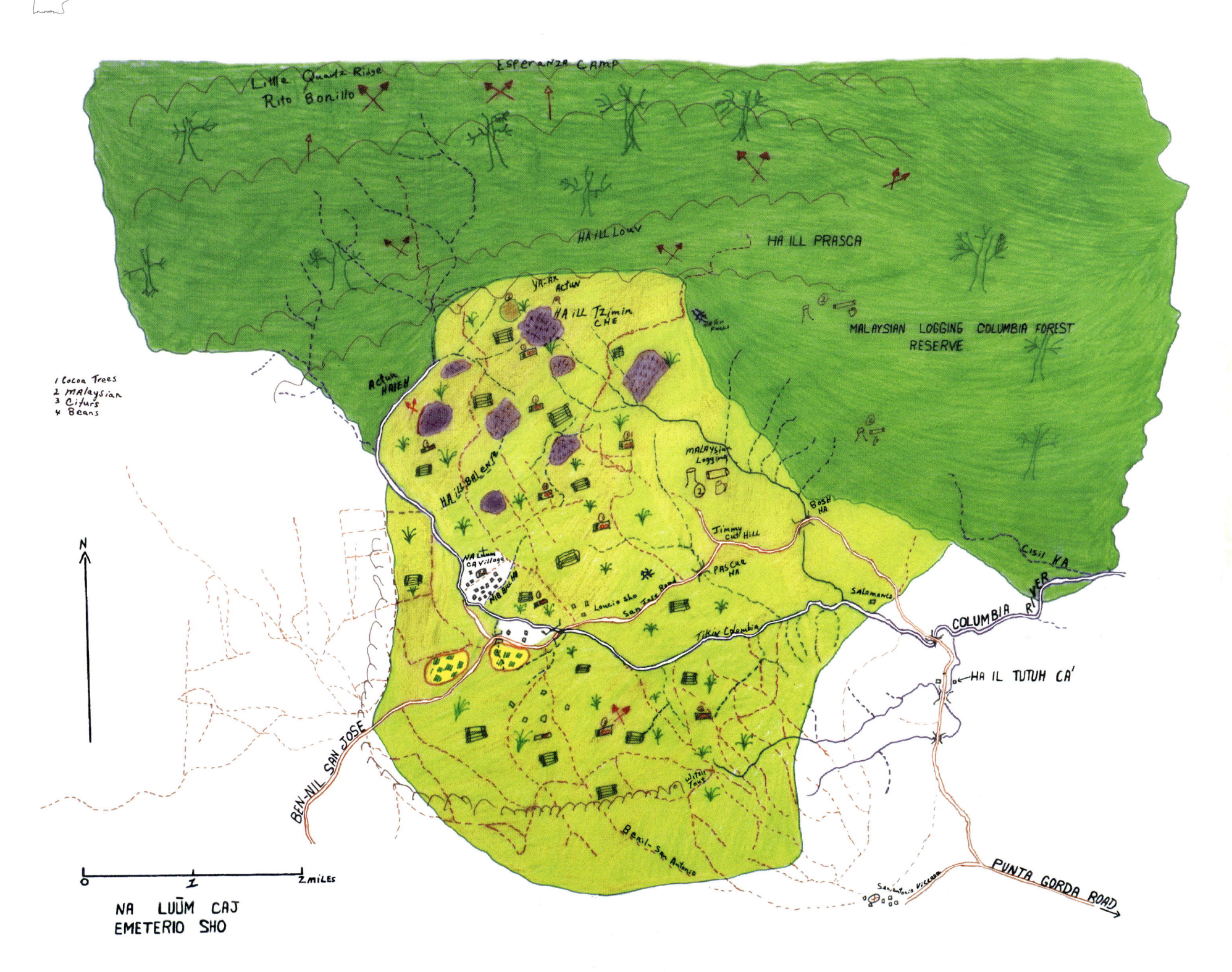

61

NA LUŪM CAJ
EMETERIO SHO

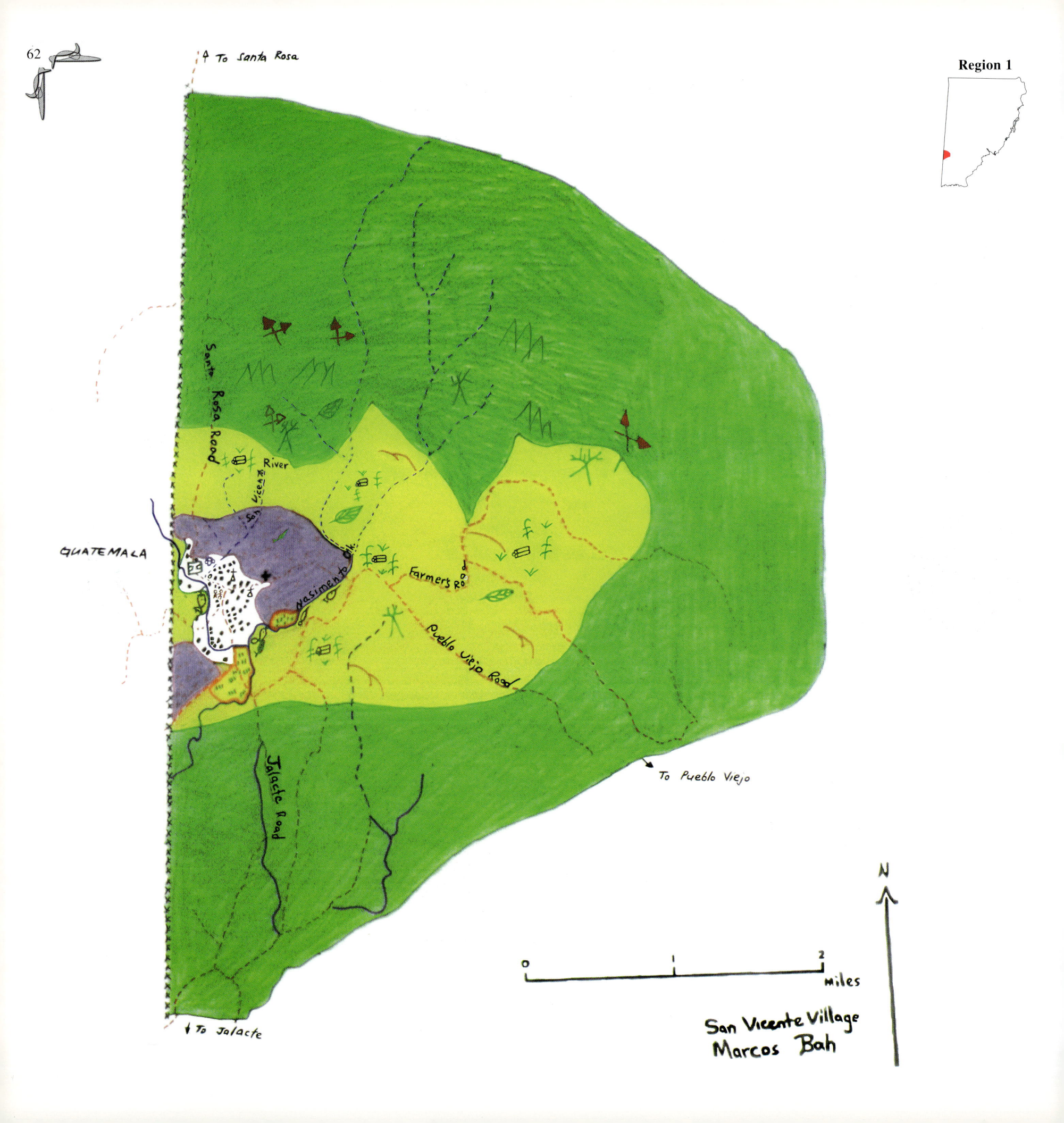

San Vicente Village
Marcos Bah

San Vicente

Population 318

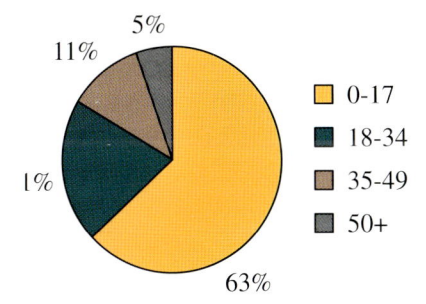

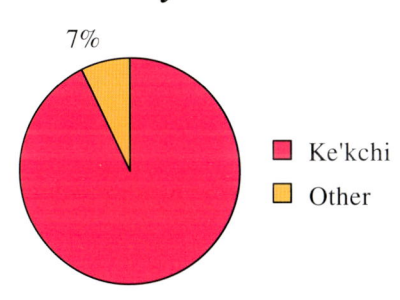

Age Distribution

- 0-17: 63%
- 18-34: 21%
- 35-49: 11%
- 50+: 5%

Identity

- Ke'kchi: 93%
- Other: 7%

This is a unique village. It came about because of the need for better agricultural land. Mayas from several villages including some from Guatemala built San Vicente despite strong objection from the Belizean government. The people permanently established themselves in 1986. For the first time an all-weather road is now being built to connect the village with the rest of Toledo.

In this village, the people do not use much government assistance but provide community services through private enterprise and their own initiative. One such example is a cornmill operated by Marcos Chen.

This village is isolated and tries to preserve its culture. The Spanish name of the village comes from San Vicente, a Catholic saint.

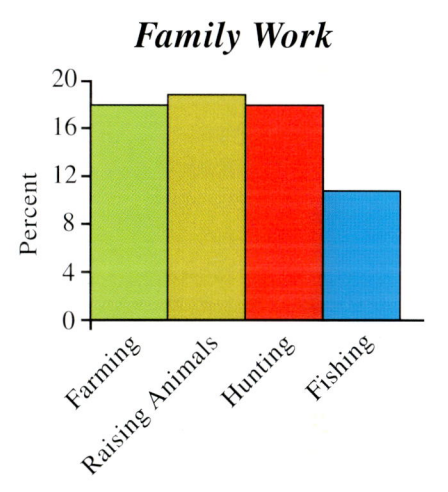

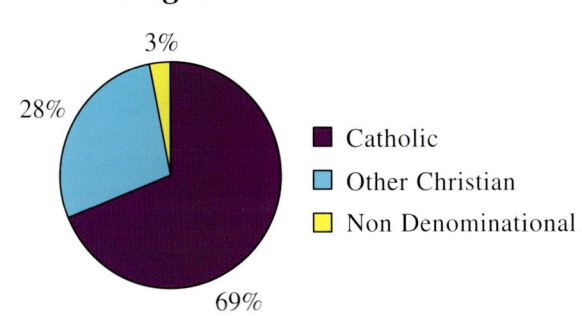

Family Work

Farming, Raising Animals, Hunting, Fishing

Religion

- Catholic: 69%
- Other Christian: 28%
- Non Denominational: 3%

Language

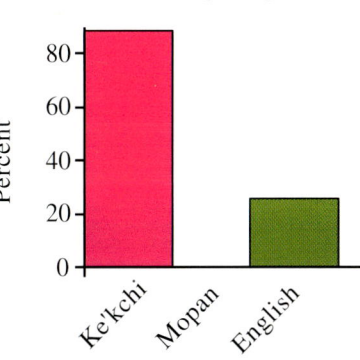

Ke'kchi, Mopan, English

Jalacte

Population 502

Jalacte is a good example of the Mayas having no concept of boundaries, all this land was Mayan land. Jalacte village was founded in the year 1972 by Joaquin Cal, Juan Pop, and one Doroteo whose title is unknown. The people who founded the new village had been living in what is now Guatemala. Spying around the new-found area, the settlers were surprised to see along the river, beautiful palm trees called *jalacte* in the Ke'kchi language. The settlers began clearing bush for rice fields and also in preparation for building their houses.

During preparation for the new settlement, the people were found on Belize soil by British forces and intimidated as trespassers. The new settlers were asked to go back to Guatemala, as they were not wanted on Belize soil. The new settlers were confused because they could not understand whether they were sitting on Belize soil, Guatemalan soil or Maya soil. During the initial settlement there were only three families. Making a serious decision, the new settlers heard about the current premier of Belize, the Hon. George Cadle Price. Joaquin Cal and the late Juan Pop then decided that they should meet Mr. Price and discuss their problem with him. Mr. Cal and Mr. Pop traveled to Belmopan through Guatemala and met Mr. Price in his Belmopan office. They were told that Mr. Price himself would visit the area. The two leaders returned to their new settlement and granted permission for the settlers to stay and establish their village.

Today Jalacte is a picturesque village lying on a hilly area surrounded by the beautiful Jalacte River. Jalacte now has a telephone system and two schools. Law and order is kept within the village by an elected *alcalde*. Jalacte village can be reached by bus, which runs on Mondays, Wednesdays, and Saturdays.

Jalacte is now occupied by approximately 80 families. The inhabitants are mostly Ke'kchi.

Jalacte is one of the most prosperous villages in the southwestern area of Toledo. However, their prosperity comes about at the expense of their soil, which is now depleted. The land around this village is being used to satisfy the demands of the Guatemalan market for beans and corn. This village has closer commercial ties with Guatemala than Belize because of its proximity to Guatemala and the problem of transportation and market outlets in the rest of Belize.

Age Distribution

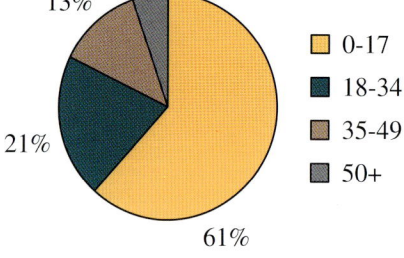

- 0-17: 61%
- 18-34: 21%
- 35-49: 13%
- 50+: 5%

Language

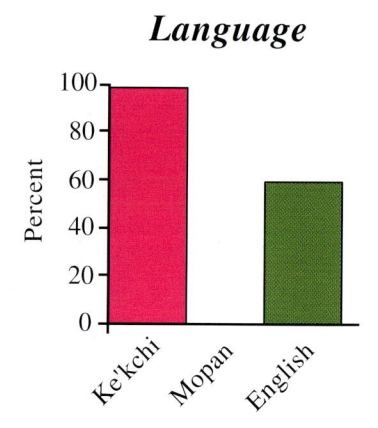

- Ke'kchi: ~99%
- Mopan: 0%
- English: ~59%

Identity

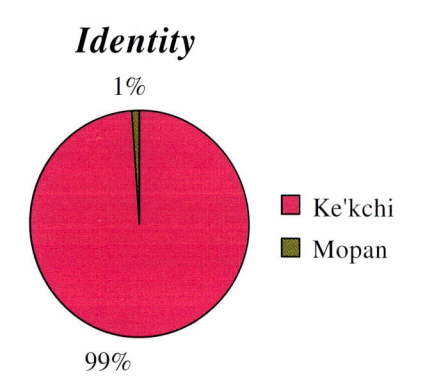

- Ke'kchi: 99%
- Mopan: 1%

Religion

- Catholic: 71%
- Other Christian: 29%

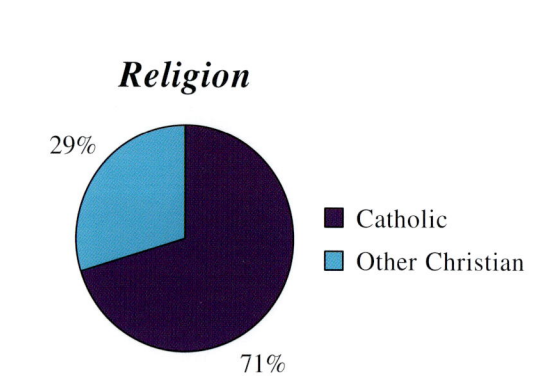

Family Work

- Farming: 16%
- Raising Animals: 17%
- Hunting: 15%
- Fishing: 16%

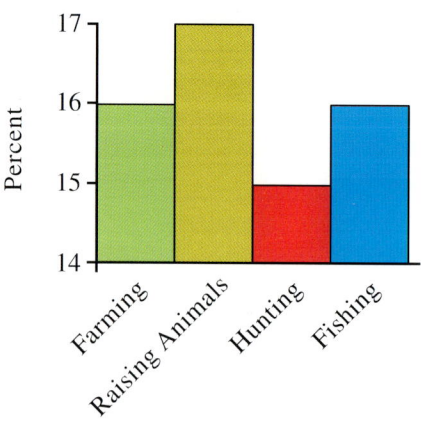

65

Region 1

① BEANS
② CORN

Guatemala

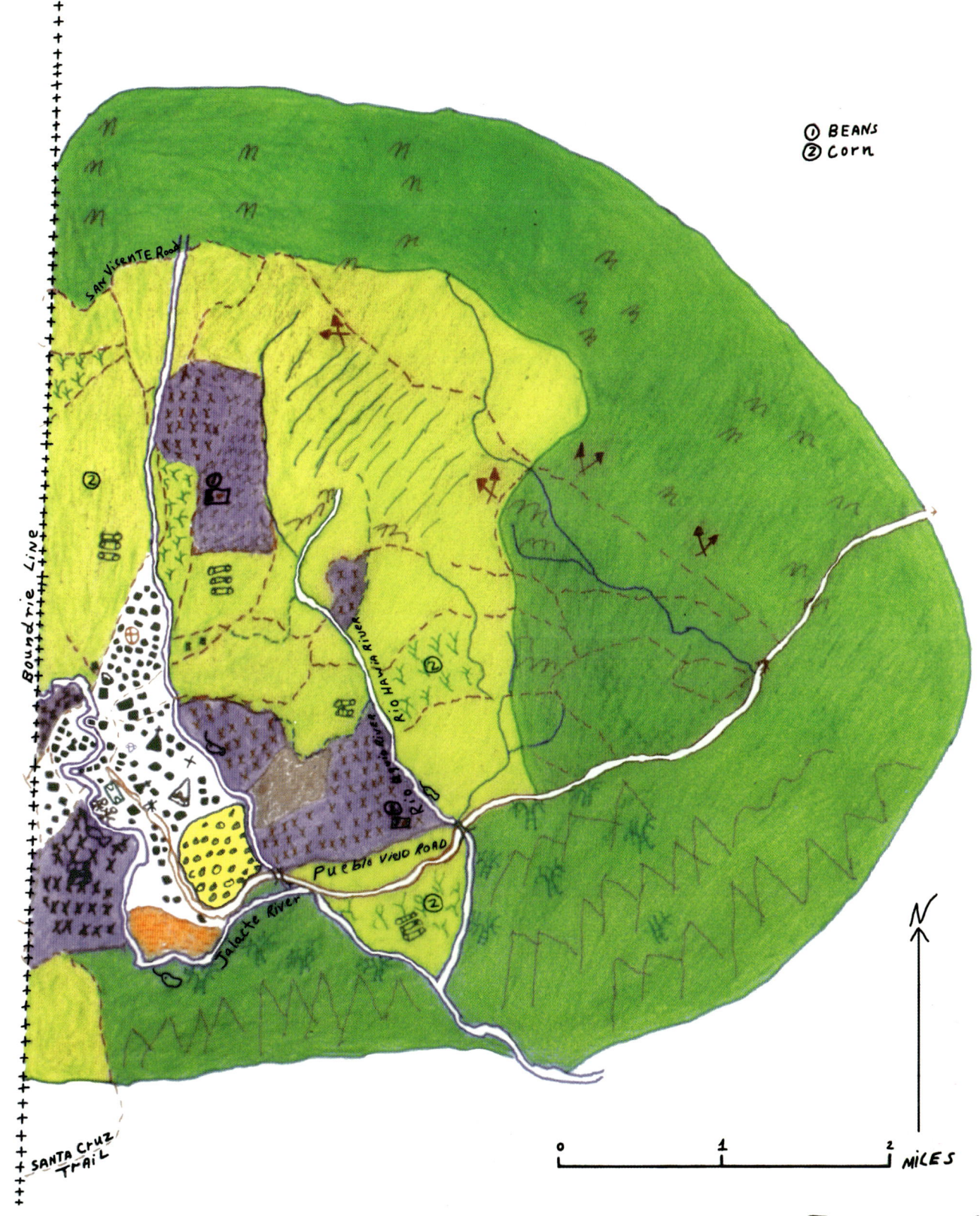

Boundrie Line
San Visente Road
Rio Hawia River
Rio Blanco River
Pueblo Viejo Road
Jalacte River
Santa Cruz Trail

N

0   1   2 MILES

JALACTE VILLAGE
RICARDO CUCUL

SAN BENITO POITE VILLAGE
SEBASTIAN TECK

San Benito Poite

Population 417

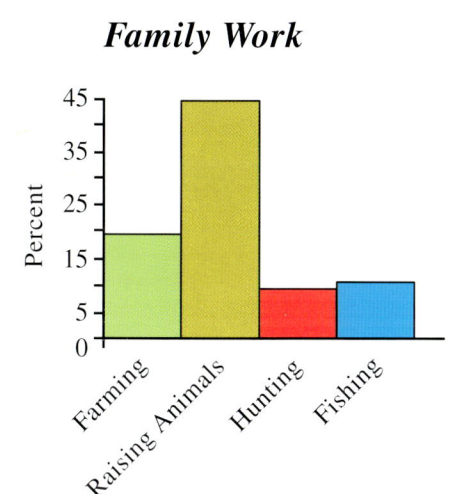

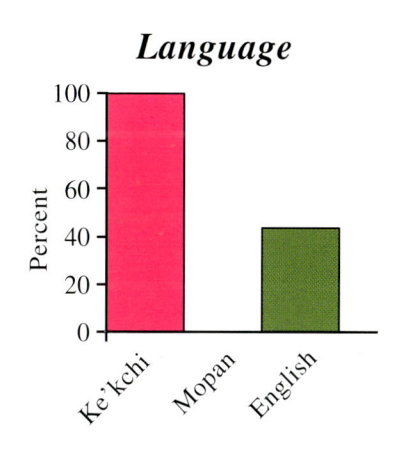

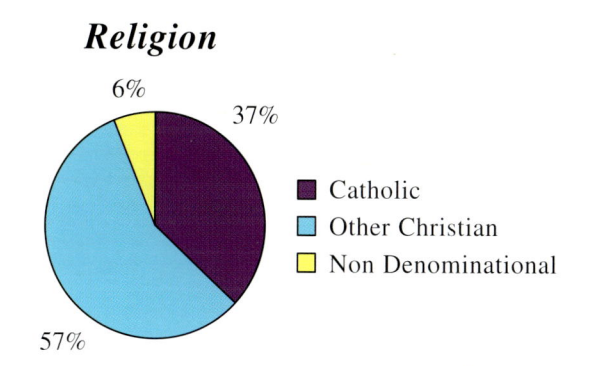

Family Work

Language

Religion

- Catholic 37%
- Other Christian 57%
- Non Denominational 6%

Identity

- Ke'kchi 100%

Age Distribution

- 0-17: 66%
- 18-34: 22%
- 35-49: 8%
- 50+: 4%

Pedro Makin, Antonio Makin, Marcos Shal, Victor Makin, and Santiago Cal went on a hunting expedition and fell in love with the rich soil of the area presently called San Benito Poite. In January of 1963, the above men cleared and planted their first crop and then moved from Otoxha to their new plantations to settle during harvest time. The site was chosen because of its proximity to Guatemala, where the villagers can sell their produce if it is too difficult to reach Punta Gorda Town. Their main products are corn, beans, rice, and pigs.

As the settlement increased in population, the villagers selected their *alcalde*. The first person to become the *alcalde* of San Benito Poite was Victor Makin, who agitated for a primary school and a road to transport their produce to Punta Gorda Town. Prior to the election of an *alcalde*, the small settlement was overseen by two village policemen selected by the founding members; they served between 1963 and 1974. Charles Wright (British) and Vicente Choco, the area representatives at that time, assisted in getting the *alcalde* recognized by the government of Belize. Through the assistance of Raleigh International and the British High Commission, a decent building with concrete floors was constructed to serve as a primary school. Two students attempted to pursue high school education but did not complete it.

A major attempt was made to connect San Benito Poite with an all-weather road for vehicular traffic but stopped halfway. There is high hope that the road will be completed soon.

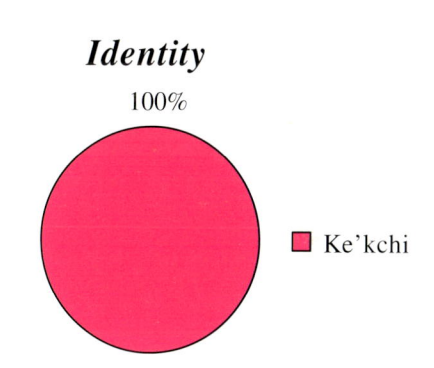

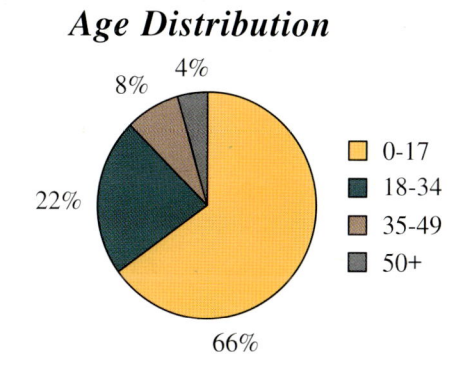

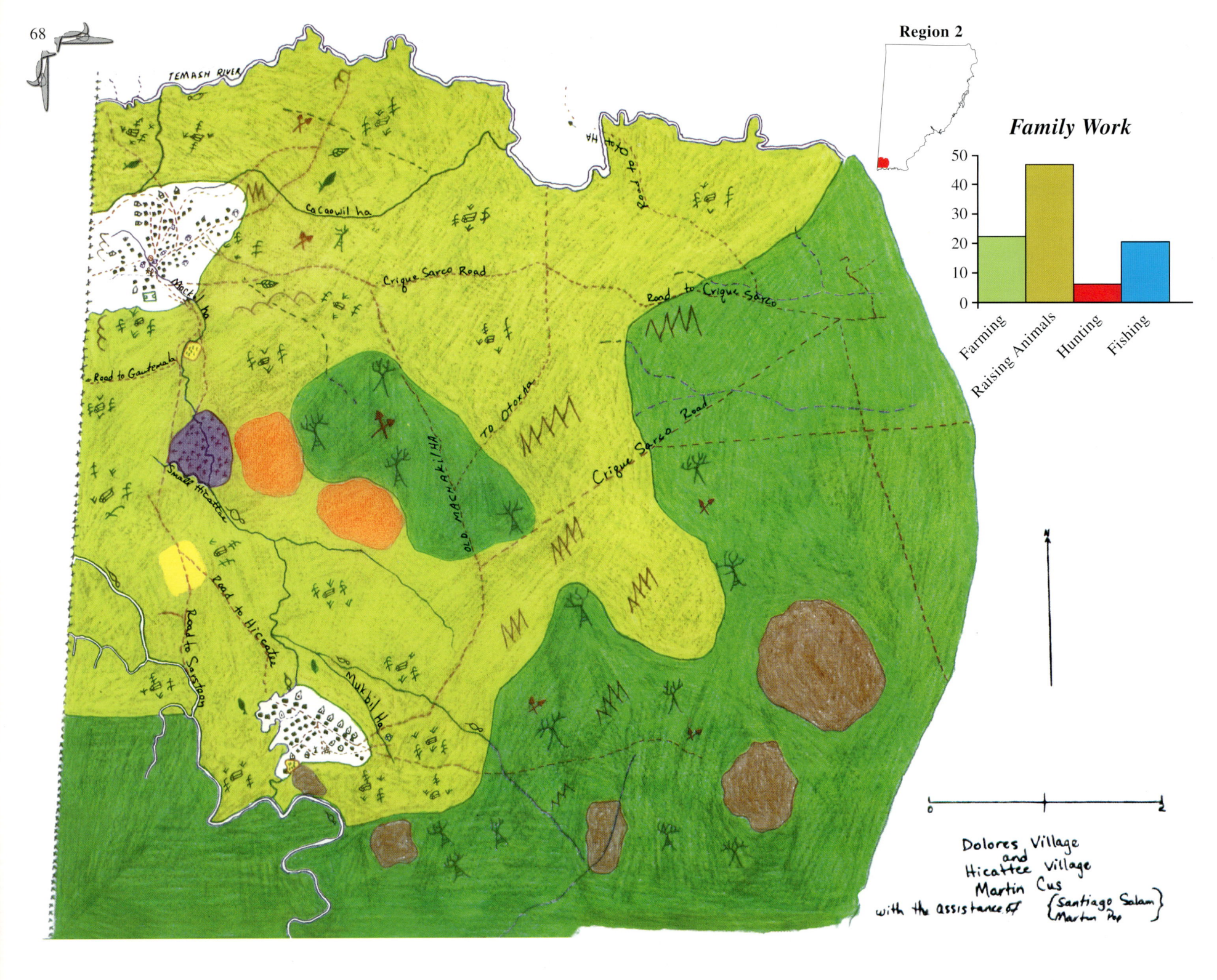

68

Region 2

Family Work

- Farming
- Raising Animals
- Hunting
- Fishing

Map labels: Temash River, Cacaowil ha, Crique Sarco Road, Road to Crique Sarco, Mach ki ha, Road to Guatemala, Small Hicattee, Old Mach Aki Ha, To Otoxha, Crique Sarco Road, Road to Hiccatee, Road to Sarstoon, Mukbil Ha

Dolores Village and Hicattee Village
Martin Cus with the assistance of (Santiago Salam, Martin Pop)

Graphs on this page represent Dolores

Age Distribution
- 0-17: 62%
- 18-34: 24%
- 35-49: 10%
- 50+: 4%

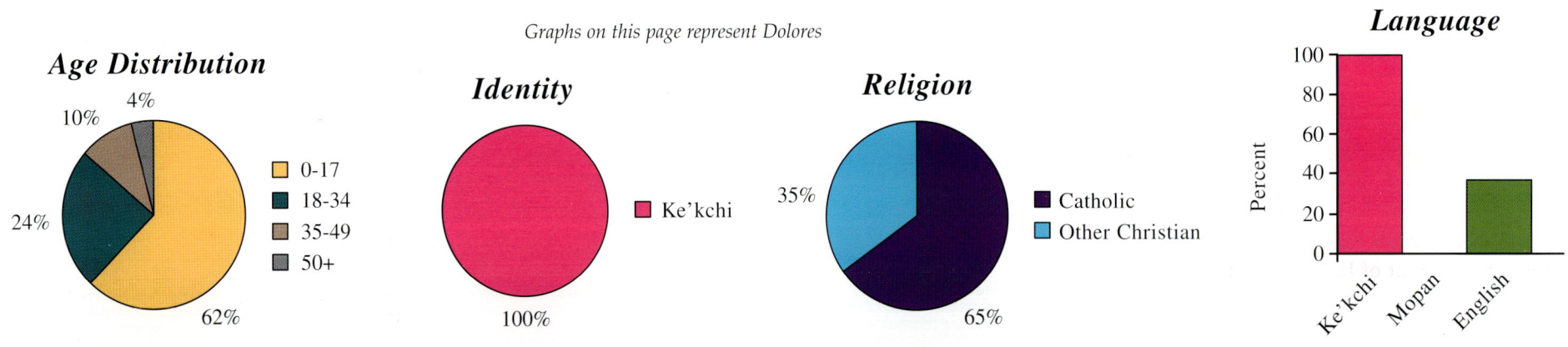

Identity
- Ke'kchi: 100%

Religion
- Catholic: 65%
- Other Christian: 35%

Language
- Ke'kchi
- Mopan
- English

Dolores

Population 298

Dolores is located six miles from San Pedro Sarstoon, Guatemala. In the beginning, the people living in this present-day village (Dolores) stayed at San Pedro Sarstoon for more than ten years. Their work site was two hours' walk into the jungle. Their farm of that time produced cacao, coffee, nutmeg, and mahogany.

In 1929, they had a long, dry summer. The creeks went dry and the wells where they drew drinking water also went dry. This made them move from their settlement.

They settled down about six miles from their previous settlement. They brought along with them the statues of San Pedro and Santa Dolores. They settled close to an operating company known at that time as the Cramer Estate, which produced cacao and coffee. The people asked the manager of the company to be allowed to farm nearby and work for the company. The manager, Mr. Cramer, liked this idea so he willingly agreed.

In 1930, twenty-five houses were built and the people began farming. In early October that year, after the corn harvest, the company began to set up a mill to dry cacao and coffee. They built a cement floor on which to dry the cacao beans and coffee grains. In 1932, the elders of the village, Santiago Ke, Quakin Bo, Manuel Chok, Juan Salam, and Jose Ixim, suggested that a name be given to their new settlement. They agreed to this name, Santa Dolores, after the name of one of their saints. The statue of this saint could still be found in their church. The creek's name became Maquil Ha because of the remains of the mill that can still be found at the creek where the church, school, and health post are located today.

The Cramer company did not succeed because Mr. Cramer worked for five years then went to his country to visit but did not return. Another English man took over the company, by the name of Fred Finn, but eventually the work just slowed down and the people remained on the land where Dolores village is now located. At Dolores, remains of the cacao trees can still be found in two separate locations. One plantation can still be seen on the trail going to Temash Crique Sarco. The other ten acres of cacao are located in the westward direction along the *kix pec* (sharp-edged rock) road.

Today, there are sixty families living in Dolores. They have a church, health post, *cabildo* (courthouse), and school. A road goes to Dolores, beginning in Otoxha; it was cleared by a bulldozer in 1993. The local income is from corn, pigs, and pepper.

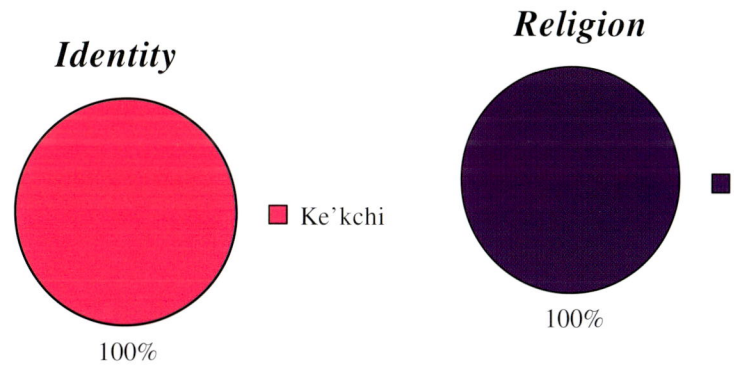

Hicatee

Population 177

Age Distribution

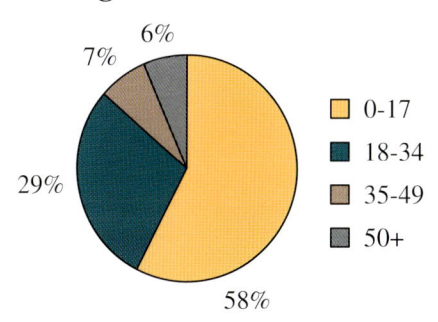

- 0-17: 58%
- 18-34: 29%
- 35-49: 7%
- 50+: 6%

This village is located next to Hicatee Creek in the Toledo District. It is a new village. The people came from Machakilha, Guatemala, in 1925. Most Maya never updated their identification papers as they moved freely across the Belize-Guatemala border to keep up with their roots. The people decided to move to this area because Machakilha is too far from everything—no road, no communications, no shops to get necessary items, and difficult to sell their produce. Hicatee is comprised of all Ke'kchi Mayas.

An incident in Hicatee concerning land problems occurred on February 23, 1997, when a contingent of Belize Defence Force soldiers with orders from the Cabinet arrived there checking peoples' identification, harvesting their crops, and asking people to leave. People left without creating difficulty.

No time was given to the village for them to harvest their crops. Therefore they left without any possibility of harvesting, after investing months in preparing their plantation. The "fault" of the people of Hicatee is that they are Ke'kchi Mayas. No chance for negotiation was given.

The human rights of people must be honored. The Rights of Children, of which Belize is a signatory, has been violated because Belizean children were moved to Guatemala soil from Belize. If we are not safeguarding the rights of children, whose rights are we protecting?

Identity

- Ke'kchi: 100%

Religion

- Catholic: 100%

Family Work

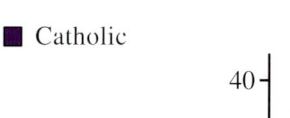

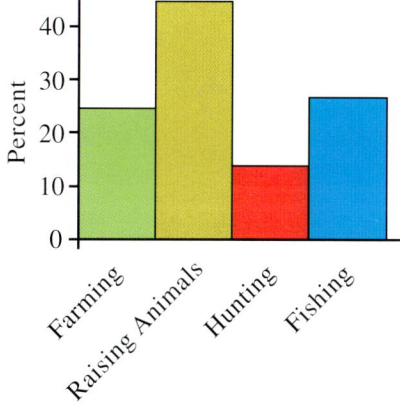

- Farming: ~25%
- Raising Animals: ~45%
- Hunting: ~14%
- Fishing: ~27%

Language

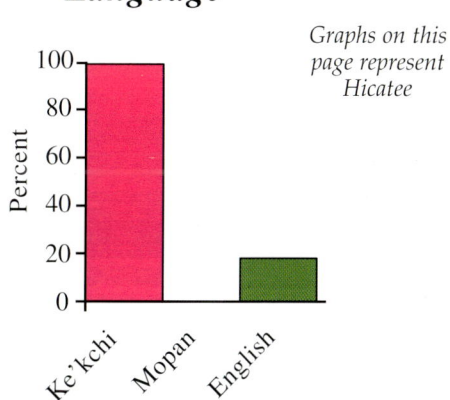

- Ke'kchi: 100%
- Mopan: 0%
- English: ~18%

Graphs on this page represent Hicatee

Crique Sarco
Population 224

Manuel Baki and Marcos Cho began this village. The place was popular among hunters and fishermen, enhanced by the beauty and splendor of the Temash River as it finds its way to the Caribbean Sea. This village became the stepping stone for people visiting the remote villages in Toledo.

The river is the food basket of the village. It is also a way of transportation; the doctors, magistrates, Catholic missionaries, and adventurers used this river to reach their destination.

On hunting trips many years ago, our old grandfathers came from parts of Poptun, Guatemala. They first came to a village by the name of Dolores, but after staying there for many years they discovered the place of Crique Sarco. After three days of hunting, they found a river and called it Temash River, and then a creek they called Crique Sarco. Then they returned to Dolores. Two of the men involved were Manuel Baki and Andres Cho. Later cutting bush for *milpa* the same two men came together and worked near Crique Sarco. When it was time to plant they started to make houses, and when they finished they stayed.

They worked together and other people came in little by little. As they saw and knew about the place, more and more people came to the village and stayed. When the people of the village saw that the village was growing, they thought about an elected *alcalde*. After being recognized in Punta Gorda by the District Officer, they decided to have a school. Then finally they went to a priest and talked to a Catholic mission, and the mission decided to operate a school built by the villagers. The priest and the government sent in a teacher, who worked out so well that the people elected the teacher as secretary for the village. This worked well for the village. But the village they left behind was the non-*alcalde* village of Dolores. Now it is the village of Crique Sarco that takes care of Dolores.

Any work that comes to Crique Sarco or Dolores comes to this village. It is the *alcalde* of Crique Sarco who rules the other village. All work, like building a school or *cabildo* building is done together.

Every three months the priest comes to the village and the *alcalde* gives him a report. Finally a Spanish family moved into the village, headed by Leoncio Canelo, and he knew how to read and write in Spanish. The village elected him to be a secretary. And from there the people have children in the school.

Finally the villagers needed medical help because of overwhelming sickness. The people of the village wrote to the Governor General in Belize City to ask for help. Owen Luis from England came to help with all the sickness. He worked for many years and brought other doctors in as well. Mr. Luis also brought a radio to the village to contact Punta Gorda.

The government then sent in another person to watch the village, Mr. Charles Wright, who was the person to do soil tests on the land. Things were going well, so a clinic was established. A nurse came to the village to serve the people. When the time came, the villagers thought about asking for a police station, then it was done.

Finally, the people encouraged the nurse, the teacher, and the police to work together. Their idea is to live in good peace, and teachers are trying their best to teach. Today the younger generation keeps changing their way of life. Some of the young people are leaving school and doing well, some are passing the B.N.S.E. (Belize National Selection Exam). We have some going to college and some are graduates from high school.

Age Distribution
- 0-17: 51%
- 18-34: 33%
- 35-49: 12%
- 50+: 4%

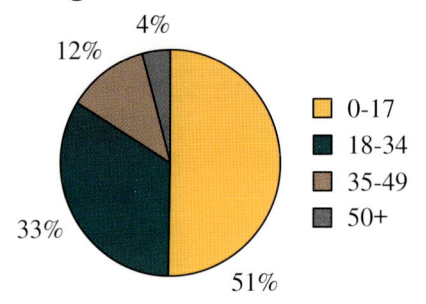

Identity
- Ke'kchi: 100%

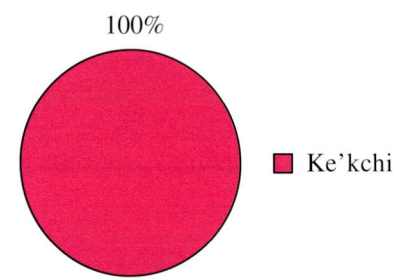

Religion
- Catholic: 69%
- Other Christian: 31%

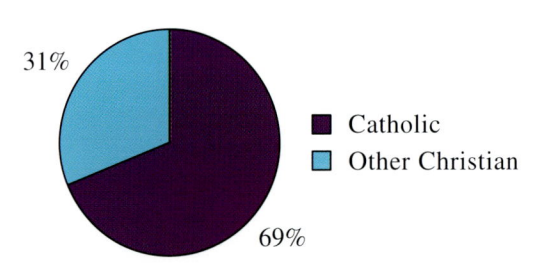

Family Work
- Farming: ~21%
- Raising Animals: ~21%
- Hunting: ~16%
- Fishing: ~19%

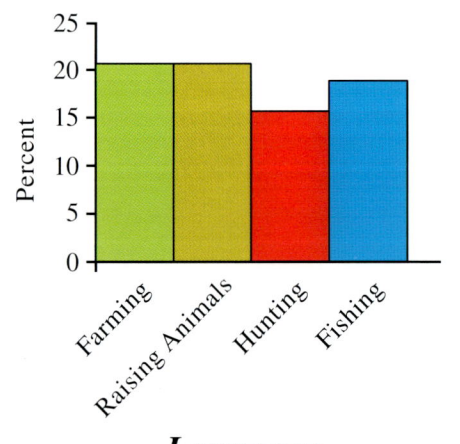

Language
- Ke'kchi: 100%
- Mopan: 0%
- English: ~75%

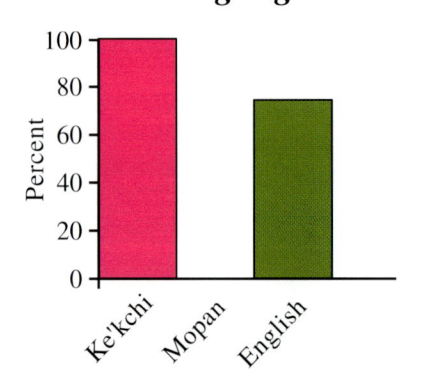

Region 2

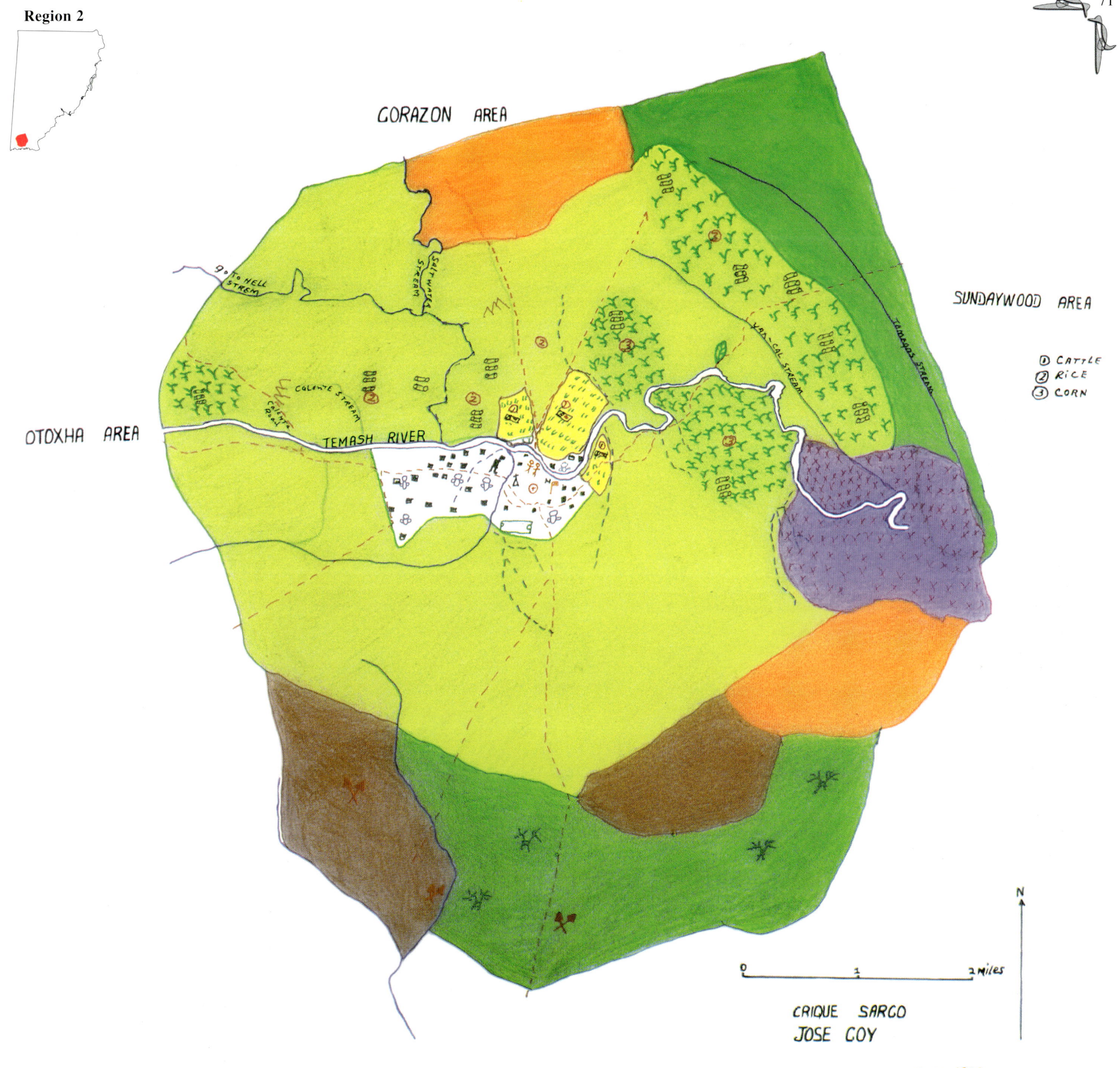

71

GORAZON AREA

OTOXHA AREA

SUNDAYWOOD AREA

- ① CATTLE
- ② RICE
- ③ CORN

go to HELL STREM

Saltwater Stream

Colente Stream

TEMASH RIVER

Yax-Cal Stream

Teboado Stream

N

0 1 2 Miles

CRIQUE SARCO
JOSE COY

25-7-1996

72

Guatemala

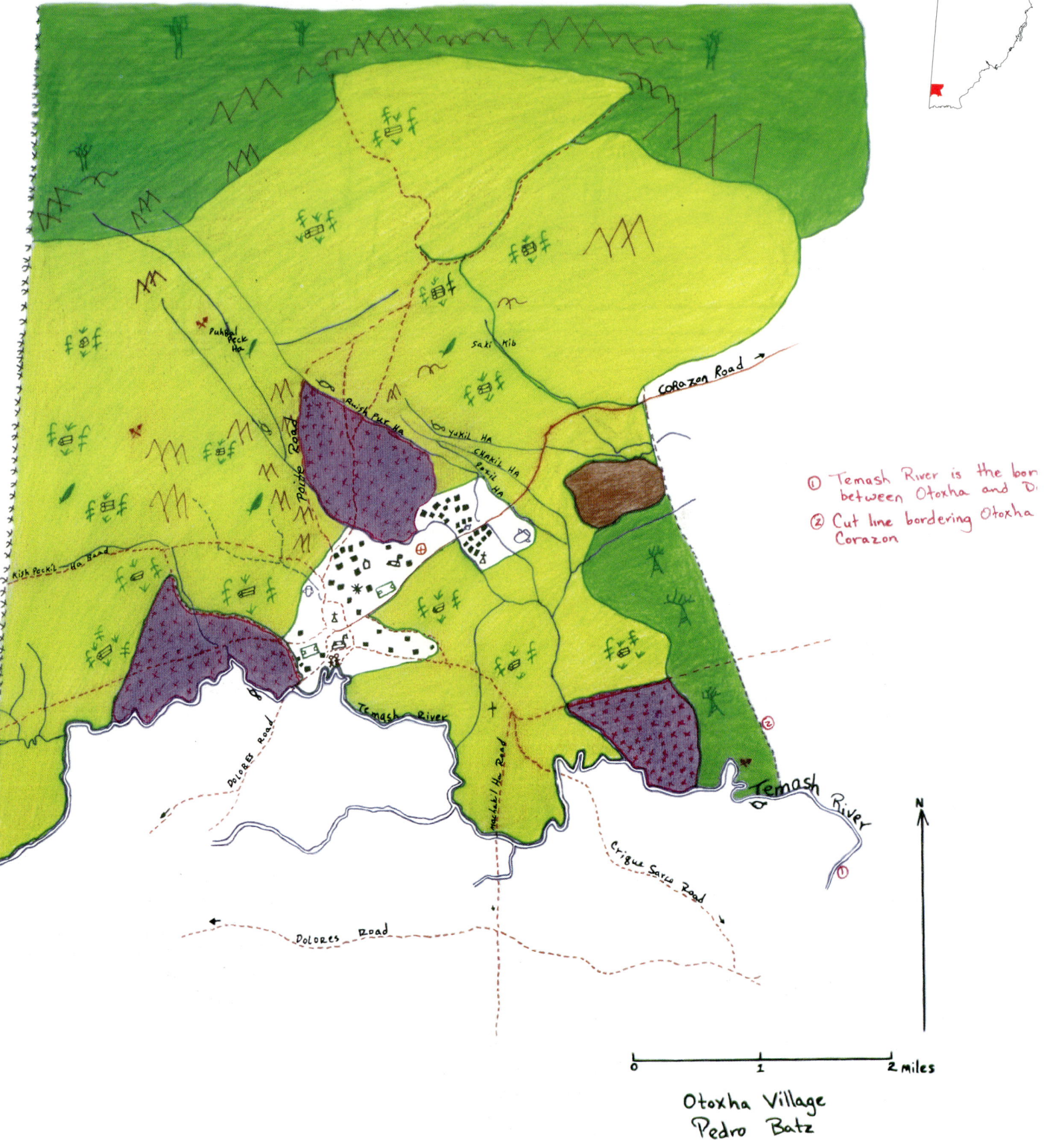

Region 2

① Temash River is the border between Otoxha and D...
② Cut line bordering Otoxha Corazon

Corazon Road

Puhbal Peck Ha
Puish Pur Ha
Saki Kib
Boyukil Ha
Chakil Ha
Pasil Ha
Poile Road
Kish Pockil Ha Road
Dolores Road
Mahlub Ha Road
Temash River
Crique Sarco Road
Dolores Road

N

0   1   2 miles

Otoxha Village
Pedro Batz

Otoxha
Population 231

The village of Otoxha began as people made an effort to live together by the Otoxha River in 1924. It is claimed that Lucas Chub, Marcos Shack, Pedro Tzub, Santos Ahal, and Manuel Cal were the first settlers of Otoxha. They named their new settlement *Kôtoxha* (winding stream); however, because of the different pronunciation of the Maya word, it is spelled as Otoxha. This village began because there is good soil for farming and a gentle river for fishing. People gladly lived together and burned incense before planting corn, and the soil yielded plenty.

Otoxha is an offshoot of the Dolores Estate. Ke'kchi Mayas working for Bernard Cramer in the production of cacao, nutmeg, allspice, plantain, and bananas found themselves jobless when overseas shipping became irregular. The Ke'kchi Mayas then moved to such settlements as Graham Creek, Crique Sarco, and Otoxha.

An *alcalde* system was put in place. In the year 1953 the overseas experts were proved wanting. Their experts' demonstration plot produced less than the plot cultivated under the traditional *milpa* system. This was proved on the day of Queen Elizabeth II's coronation, when some 500 Mayas were gathered to celebrate the coronation event in Otoxha. The harvest was made on the same day.

In 1992 Otoxha was linked to other villages by a dirt road passable only during the dry season.

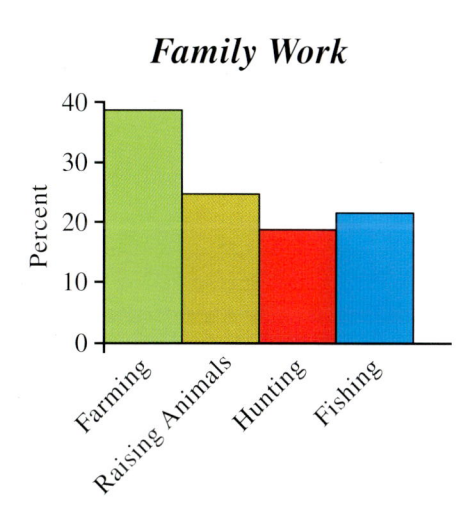

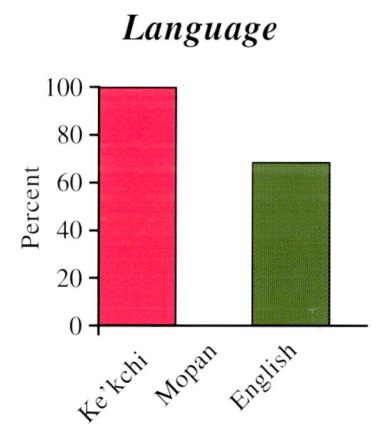

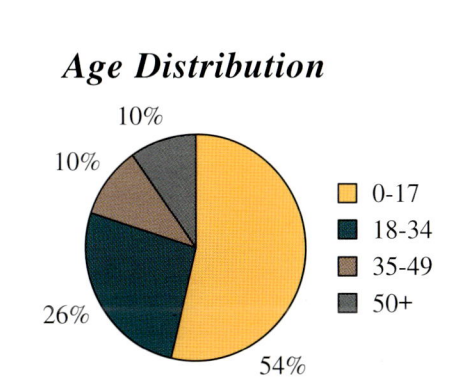

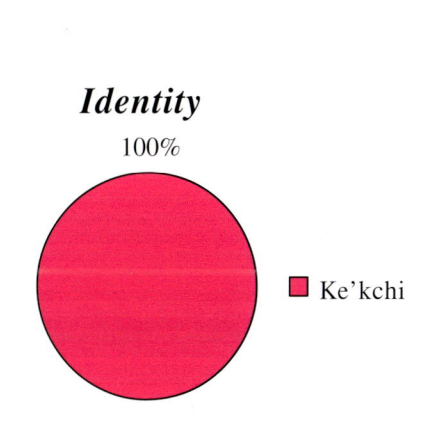

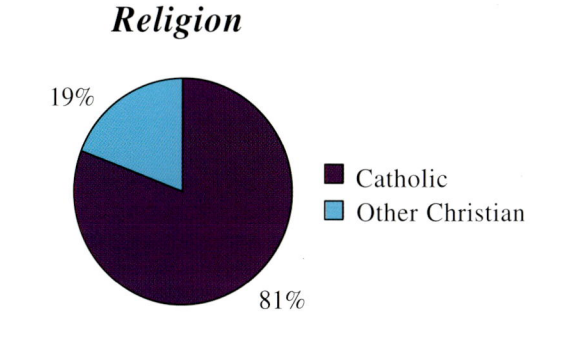

Family Work
- Farming
- Raising Animals
- Hunting
- Fishing

Language
- Ke'kchi: 100%
- Mopan: 0%
- English: ~68%

Age Distribution
- 0-17: 54%
- 18-34: 26%
- 35-49: 10%
- 50+: 10%

Identity
- Ke'kchi: 100%

Religion
- Catholic: 81%
- Other Christian: 19%

Sunday Wood
Population 116

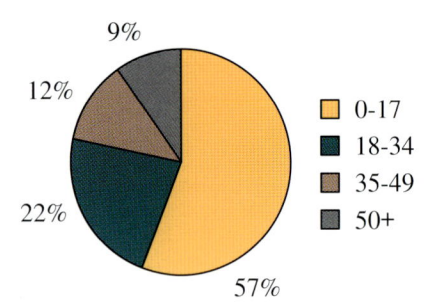

Age Distribution

- 0-17: 57%
- 18-34: 22%
- 35-49: 12%
- 50+: 9%

Identity

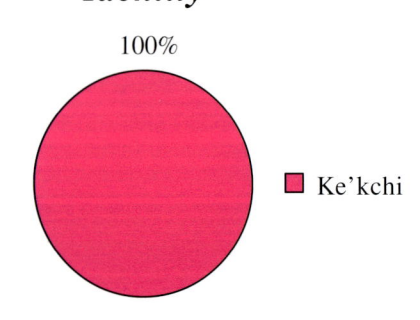

- Ke'kchi: 100%

Religion

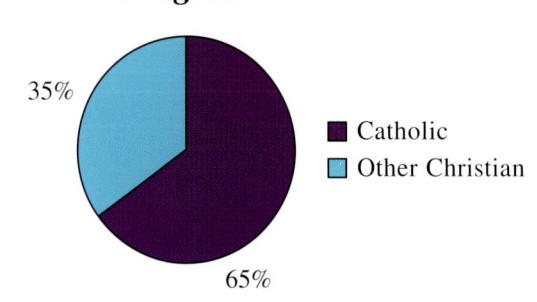

- Catholic: 65%
- Other Christian: 35%

Family Work

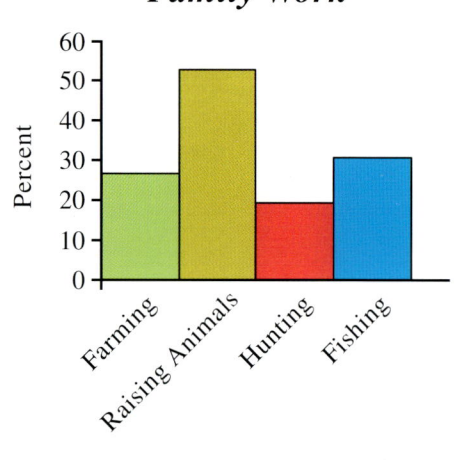

- Farming: ~27%
- Raising Animals: ~53%
- Hunting: ~19%
- Fishing: ~30%

Language

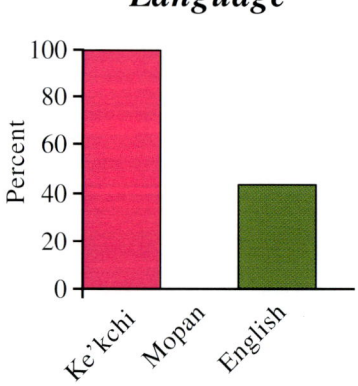

- Ke'kchi: 100%
- Mopan: 0
- English: ~44%

Sunday Wood is located in the lowland area of the Toledo District. A group of Ke'kchi Maya migrated from San Lucas to look for fertile land in the year 1983. They moved to this area to do farming. In the same year Francisco Tush, the *alcalde* in San Lucas village, requested to move to the new area that is now known as Sunday Wood village.

The request was granted. The settlers cut down places to make their *milpa*, where they grow their food and raise animals to earn their living. The village of Sunday Wood is now approximately 14 years old[1997]. There is no road to the village. People mainly use the Temash River and Sunday Wood Creek to transport their produce to Punta Gorda Town.

In 1994 the government of Belize granted a logging concession to the Malaysian-backed Atlantic International to cut logs around the village without consultation with the people. Logging currently continues.

Region 2

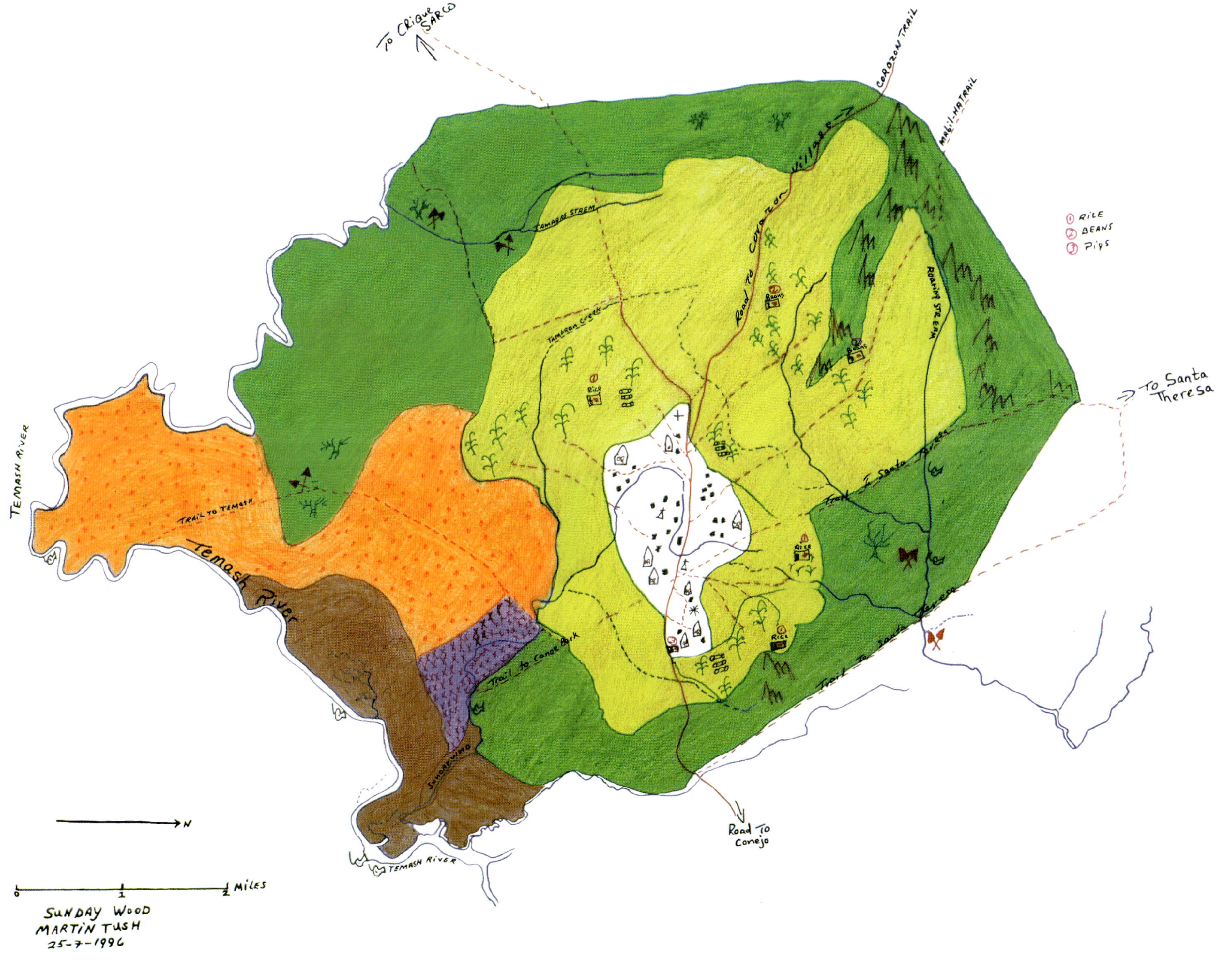
TO CRIQUE SARCO
COROZON TRAIL
MABIL-HA TRAIL
Road To Corozon Village
TAMAGRE STREM
Tambran Creek
ROARING STREAM
① RICE
② BEANS
③ PIGS
Rice
Beans
To Santa Theresa
Trail To Santa Teresa
Trail To Santa Teresa
TEMASH RIVER
TRAIL TO TEMASH
Temash River
Trail to Canoe Park
SUNDAY WOOD
TEMASH RIVER
Road To Conejo
N
0
1
2 MILES
SUNDAY WOOD
MARTIN TUSH
25-7-1996

Mabil Ha

Population 130

Family Work

This small village is one of the beauties of the deep south. It was formed in the late 1970s. It is still small, but its beauty is enhanced not only by the hills and the people, but the majestic beauty of the *Mabil Ha* (creek of round stones). People work together; they are cooperative and traditional.

Mabil Ha is comprised of two groups of settlers. One group settled along the old Mabil Ha road and the other by the new road. The old Mabil Ha group is predominantly Mennonite, and the new group is mostly Catholic.

In January of 1997, Marion Tulsey established a sawmill next to the village to extract logs from a concession given to him by the government of Belize, thus adversely affecting the livelihood of the people. Tulsey's concession is seriously controversial because it is on Maya ancestral land that is currently a Maya reservation. The road to this area is in a bad state because it is neglected by the government and abused by logging trucks—all contributing to the poverty of the area.

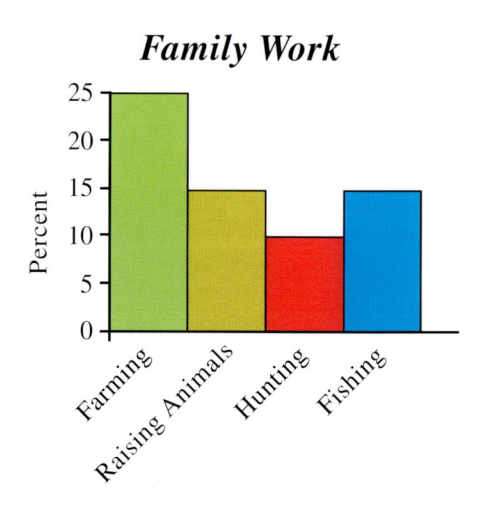

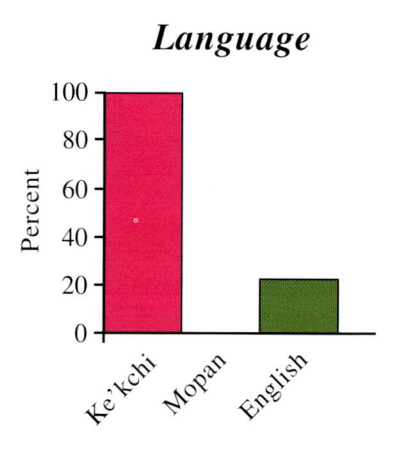

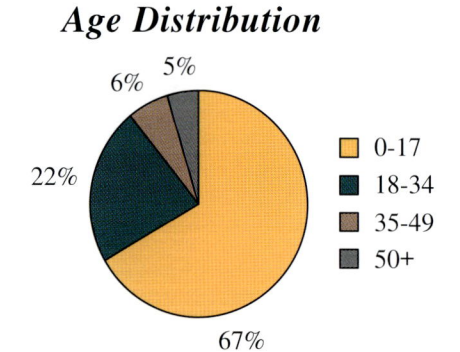

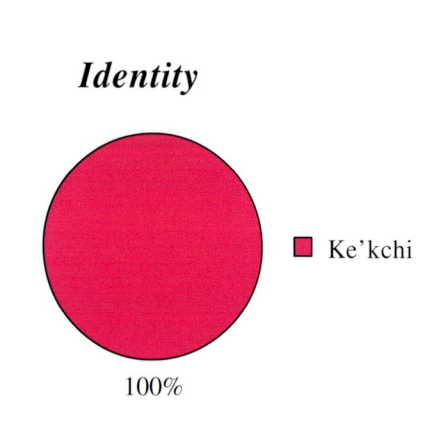

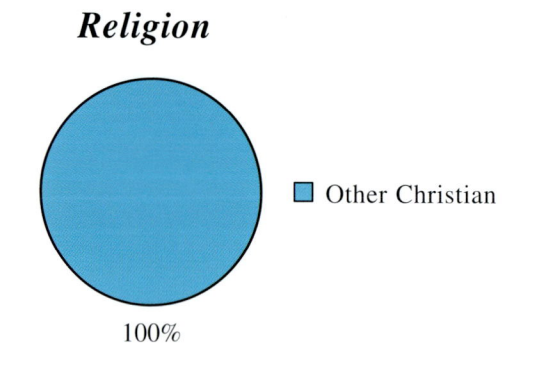

Language

Age Distribution

- 0-17: 67%
- 18-34: 22%
- 35-49: 6%
- 50+: 5%

Identity

Ke'kchi 100%

Religion

Other Christian 100%

Region 2

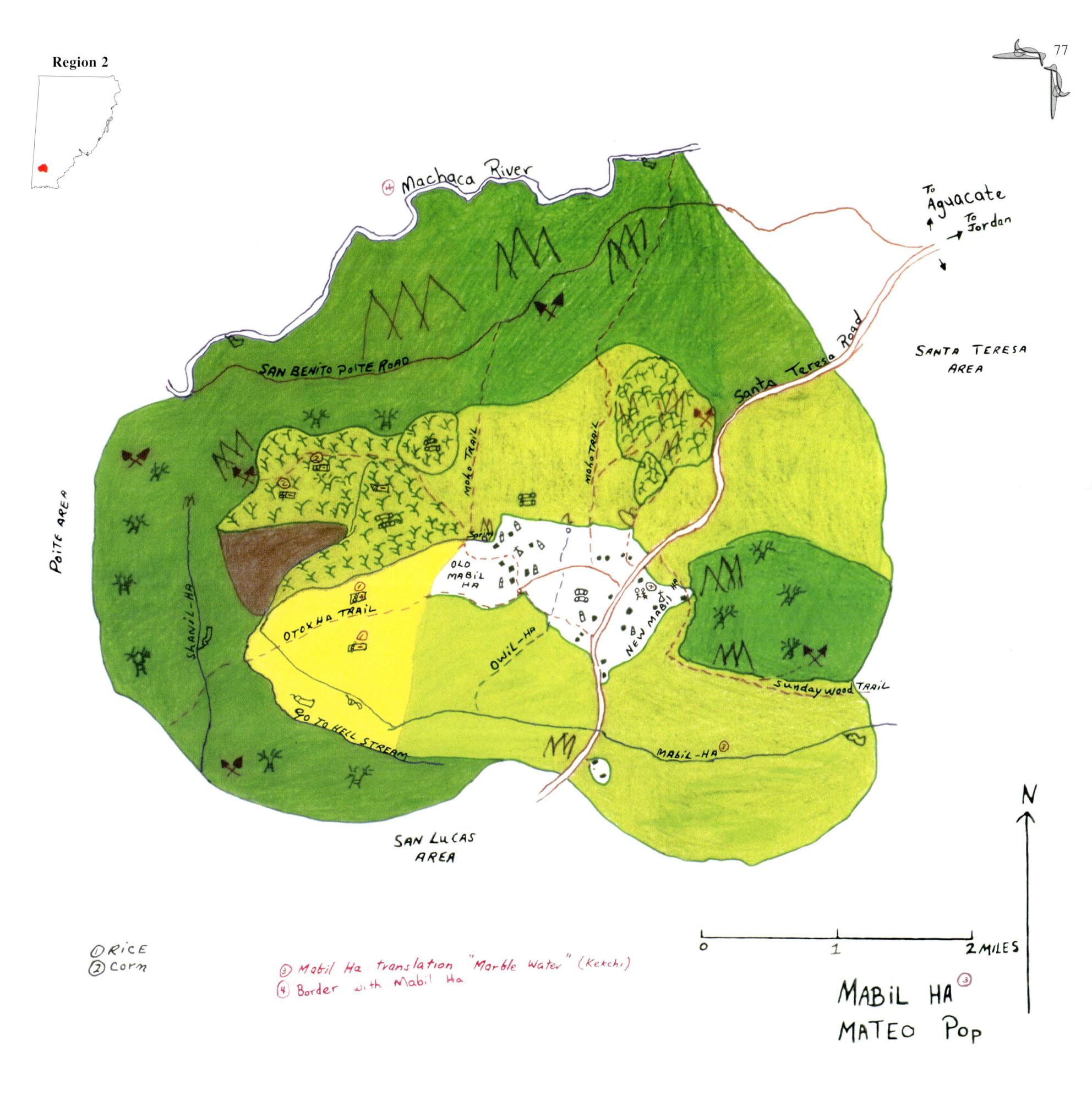

77

Machaca River

To Aguacate
To Jordan

Santa Teresa Area

San Benito Poite Road

Santa Teresa Road

Poite Area

Skanil-Ha

Molo Trail

Molo Trail

Spring

Old Mabil Ha

Otoxha Trail

Owil-Ha

New Mabil Ha

Sunday Wood Trail

Go to Hell Stream

Mabil-Ha ③

San Lucas Area

N

0 1 2 MILES

① Rice
② Corn
③ Mabil Ha translation "Marble Water" (Kekchi)
④ Border with Mabil Ha

MABIL HA ③
MATEO POP

78

Region 2

To Mabil Ha

Sundaywood Road

Cotohel Crk

To Corazon

Cotohel Creek

Sundaywood Road

Salawat Creek

N

0 1 2 Miles

San Lucas Village
Juan Bo

San Lucas

Population 121

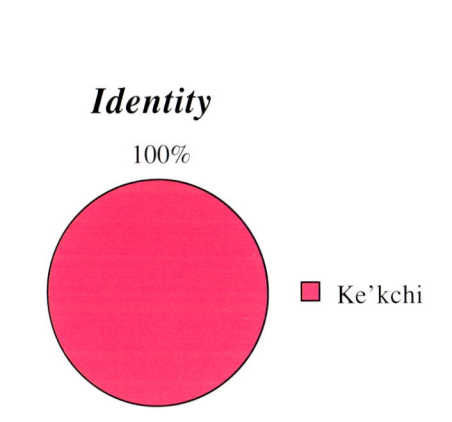

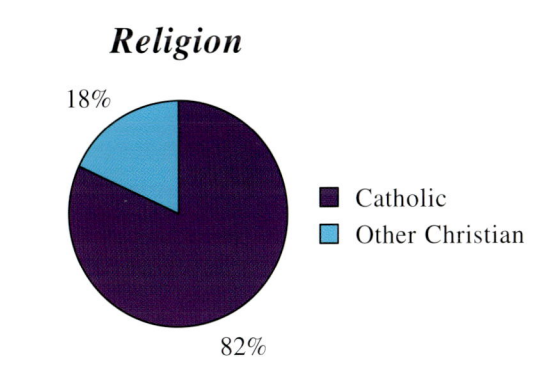

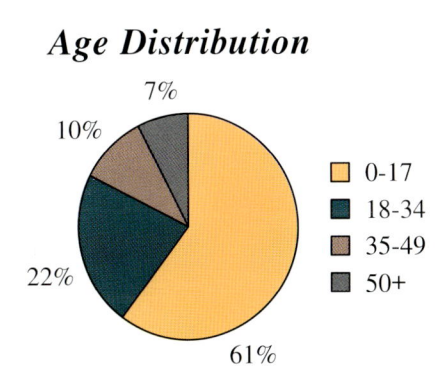

Identity

- Ke'kchi: 100%

Religion

- Catholic: 82%
- Other Christian: 18%

Family Work

Percent by category:
- Farming: ~24
- Raising Animals: ~54
- Hunting: ~23
- Fishing: ~21

Age Distribution

- 0-17: 61%
- 18-34: 22%
- 35-49: 10%
- 50+: 7%

Language

Percent:
- Ke'kchi: ~100
- Mopan: 0
- English: ~27

This village was founded by Domingo Acte and Sebastian Tush. After settling they had a consultation. They came up with an idea to buy a statue. So they bought it and put it in the church. The statue is named Saint Luke. That is why this village is called San Lucas. That was between the years 1955 to 1960.

The old people who founded this village are all dead or have gone to other villages, but the young generation keeps this village alive.

This village is small and traditional. San Lucas is now bordered by two logging companies: Toledo Atlantic International (Malaysian) and Marion Tulsey (Belizean).

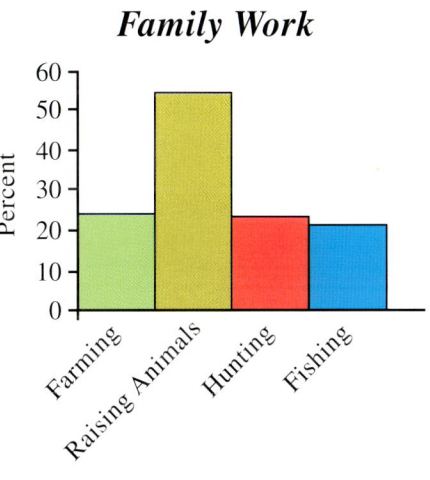

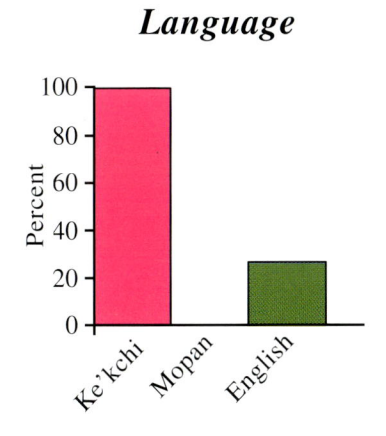

Corazon Village
Crus Cal.

Region 2

Corazon

Population 140

Pedero Makin, who once lived in Otoxha, began the village of Corazon because his farm was too far from Otoxha. He informed Mr. D.F. Cruz, District Officer for Toledo, of his intentions. Mr. Cruz agreed and the letter of approval was finally written that gave a green light to this new settlement.

The village began in January of 1976. It lies between the villages of San Lucas and Otoxha. Mr. Makin dedicated the village as Corazon after the Patron Saint Corazon.

The two Maya villages of San Lucas and Otoxha did not like the idea of people forming a village in Corazon. They were informed by the District Officer that the people of the new settlement were given permission to develop the land. Land use in Corazon is more likely to be the same as other villages. People must pay the government for the usage of the land.

The *alcalde* system is an ongoing tradition in the villages. The *alcalde* is the main person considered to be in charge of any new settler wanting to enter the village — he can say yes or no. He will also give permission to the person to develop the high bush, since all the *wahmil* lands are occupied.

Lands are given to the son of the family, and traditionally on to the grandchildren. It is in this way the people pass on their land.

A land survey was carried out in Corazon approximately ten years ago, but the acreage is not known. When a problem arises between the villages, there are times when the people of one village continue to work in another village's area. These types of problems are dealt with by the *alcaldes*.

Non-Maya people in many cases would want to settle among the Mayas. They would find out from the *alcalde* if he can admit them to the settlement. Most Mayas in rural areas do not allow this to happen without permission. They would just file a report against anyone entering without permission from the *alcalde*.

As in the case of the hungry land settler, the Maya people are anxious to have land secure and properly demarcated and that non-Mayas should not settle among them, because the lands they use are for themselves and their children. The Mayas are concerned with the growth in population and the limited work area they have. Expansion of the reservation is badly needed in most cases. A secured land for the Maya would allow the Maya to just move for their survival when land is available. These needs can be addressed only in the security of a communal land system.

Long ago, a Western priest in the land of the Maya began his mission work by visiting a Maya. He visited on a regular basis, and the Maya became his friend and finally allowed the priest to have a way to preach the good news. He began to sing praises and the Maya began to dance when they heard him singing. For the Maya children it was a joke. The Westerner did not bother about the children's behavior; he continued his mission and later converted some Maya people.

Maya people in the olden days did not use metal as a tool. The tools used were flint and the bones of animals hunted. The skin and bones are useful to the Maya.

Language

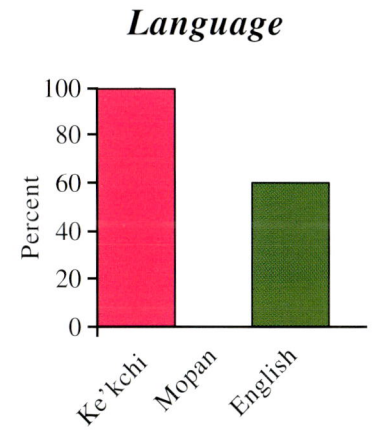

- Ke'kchi: 100%
- Mopan: 0%
- English: ~60%

Family Work

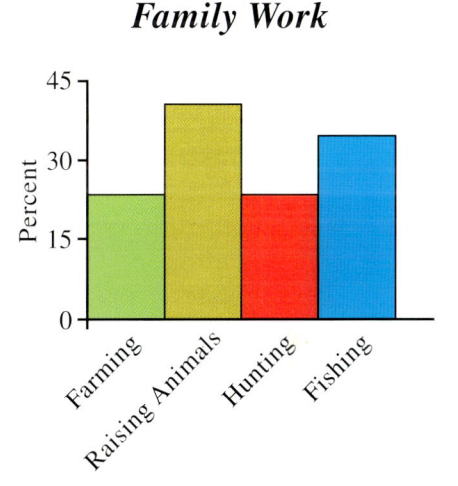

- Farming: ~23%
- Raising Animals: ~41%
- Hunting: ~23%
- Fishing: ~35%

Religion

- Catholic: 76%
- Other Christian: 24%

Age Distribution

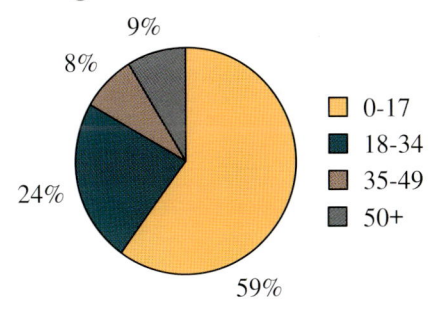

- 0-17: 59%
- 18-34: 24%
- 35-49: 8%
- 50+: 9%

Identity

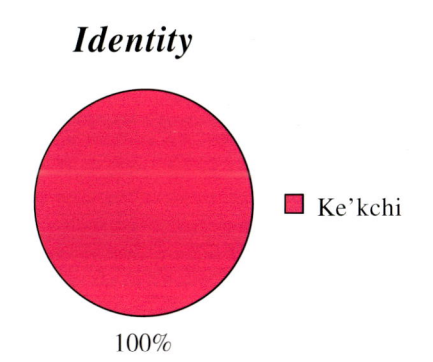

- Ke'kchi: 100%

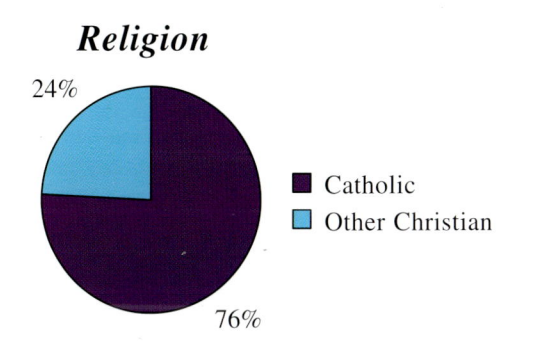

Laguna
Population 247

Age Distribution
- 0-17: 58%
- 18-34: 21%
- 35-49: 11%
- 50+: 10%

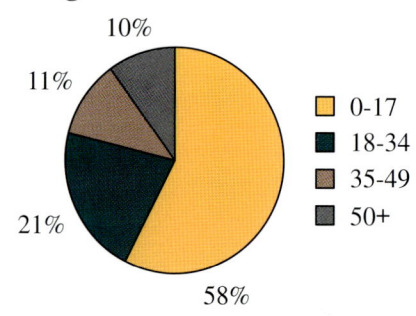

Identity
- Ke'kchi: 100%

Religion
- Catholic: 11%
- Other Christian: 88%
- Non Denominational: 1%

Language
- Ke'kchi: ~95%
- Mopan: ~5%
- English: ~65%

Family Work
- Farming: ~22%
- Raising Animals: ~52%
- Hunting: ~10%
- Fishing: ~22%

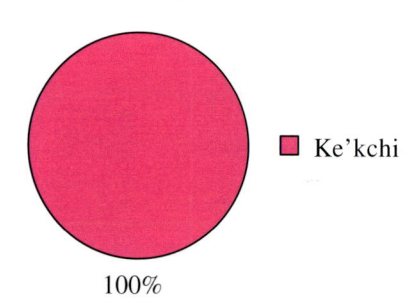

In 1959, Francisco Shal, Vicente Coc, and Petrona Choc began the village of Laguna. They left San Miguel village to avoid getting embroiled in a conflict between San Miguel village and San Pedro Columbia village. Some pigs were damaging crops. The new settlement was located near a lagoon from which it derived its name—Laguna.

More and more families from different villages came to join the founding families and thus the need to elect an *alcalde* arose. The children from Laguna had to attend primary school at the dump area called the San Isidro Primary School, some six miles from home. However, in 1976 a primary school was built in Laguna by Christian missionaries; it was later taken over by the government of Belize.

In an attempt to better the living conditions of the people in Laguna, the community, with the assistance of Peace Corps Volunteers, constructed in 1989, an overhead water system powered and supplied by a spring coming from the hill near the village.

A small village museum was opened to attract tourism but later folded. In 1990 a guest house was built and plans are underway for the creation of a national park surrounding the often-visited lagoon.

Laguna is noted for being the first Ke'kchi village to have a hand-operated telephone, the first to have a non-Catholic primary school, and the first to produce a non-Catholic pastor in the person of Pedro Shol. Laguna can also be considered the first village to get the best rocked road to the Southern Highway.

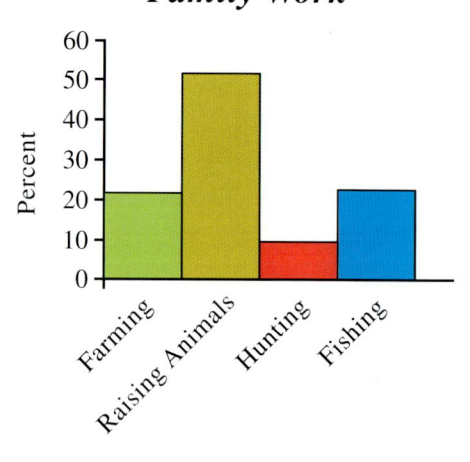

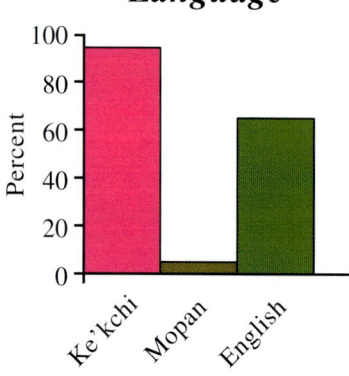

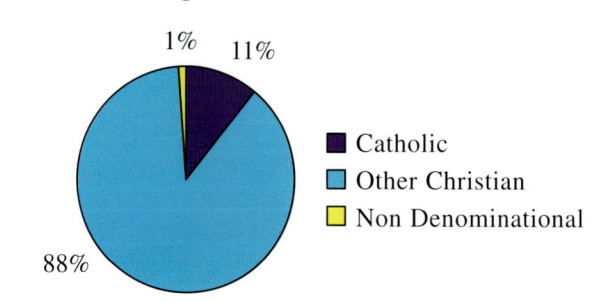

Region 3

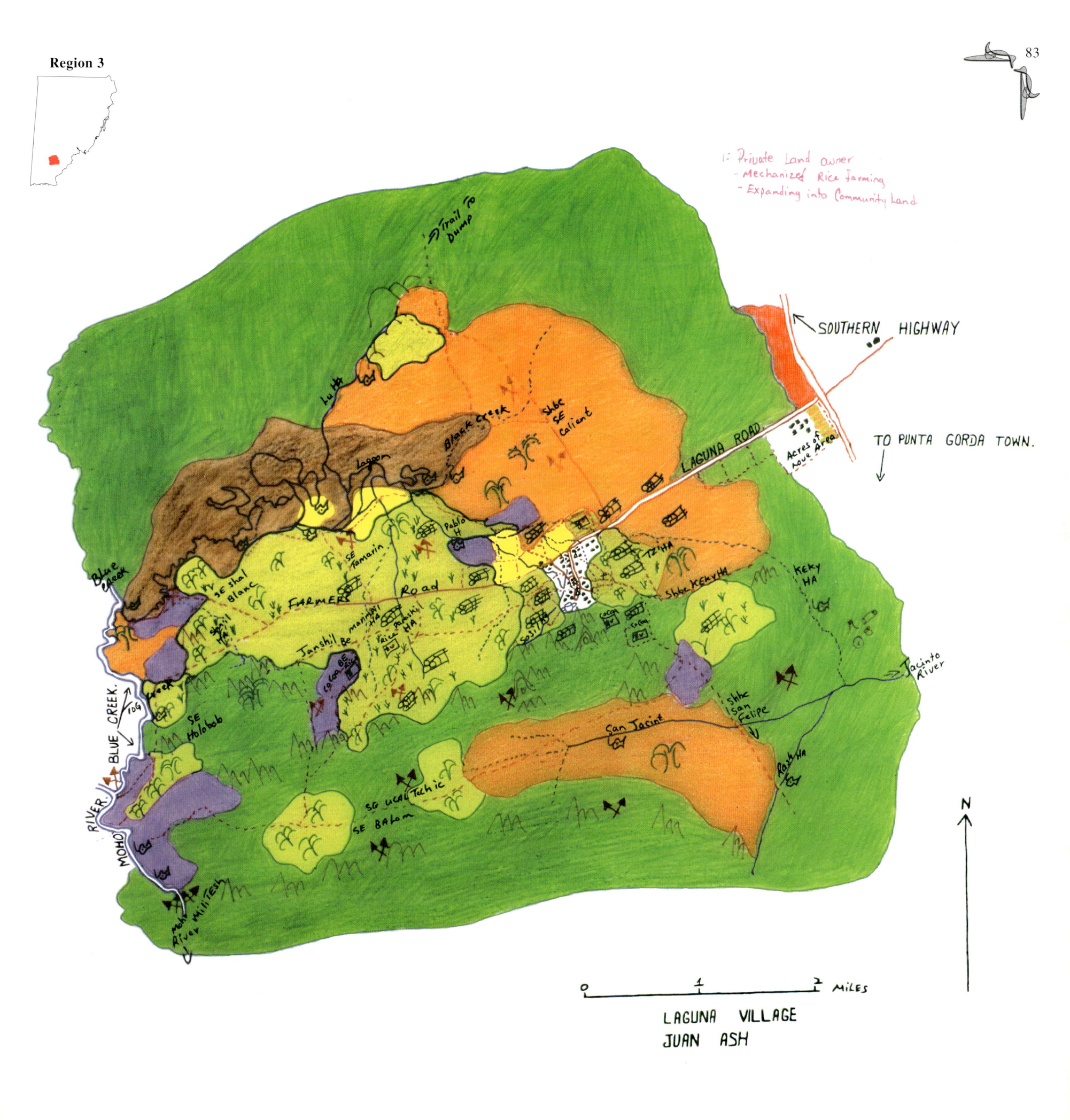

83

1: Private Land owner
- Mechanized Rice farming
- Expanding into Community Land

LAGUNA VILLAGE
JUAN ASH

CONEJO VILLAGE
MARTIN TUSH
MATILDO MAKIN

Region 3

① Rice
② Malaysian Company

Conejo

Population 95

The village of Conejo is approximately 90 years old. It was founded in 1907 by Jose Makin. He did his hunting in the area prior to its settlement. The village is comprised of Ke'kchi Maya who engage in the production of pigs, corn, and rice to earn their living. In 1950 the village sprang from one household family to twenty-two household families.

Conejo is only accessible by road in the dry weather. In 1991 a road was pushed to link Conejo with the rest of the southernmost villages, with the intent to put in an all-weather road. It was unsuccessful due to changes in the government's policy and decision-making process. Lack of bridges and culverts is the main setback to the reality of the road.

In 1992 a combination church/state-run school was established to serve the community, taking into consideration the high illiteracy rate that existed here. The school presently has an enrollment of about 31 students, with two teachers.

Conejo has no other departmental buildings to enhance the development of this remote village. The community has practiced Catholicism more widely than other villages in the district.

The people of Conejo rely on the rich resources of the old Temash River for survival as subsistence for hunting and fishing.

The Ke'kchi Maya community is run by an *alcalde*.

Family Work

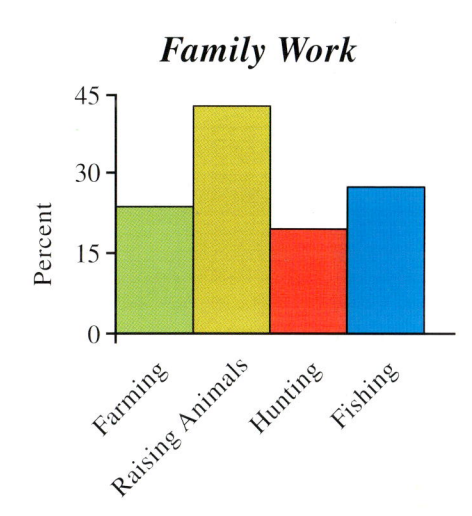

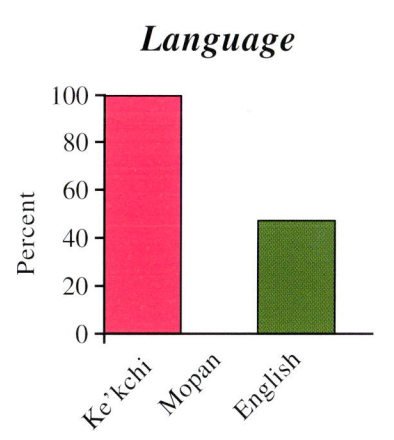

Age Distribution

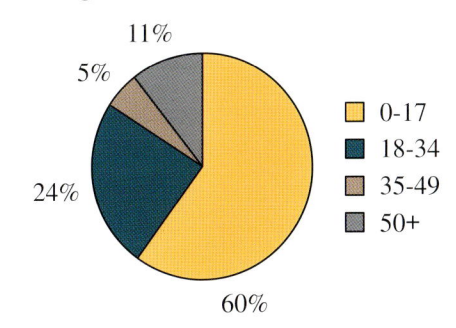

- 0-17: 60%
- 18-34: 24%
- 35-49: 5%
- 50+: 11%

Language

Identity

Ke'kchi 100%

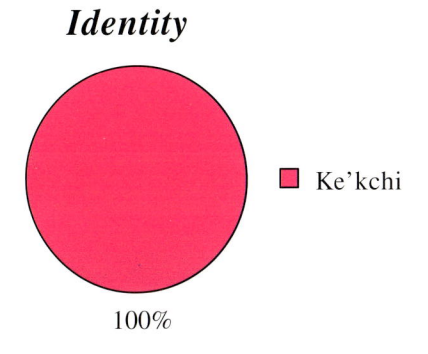

Religion

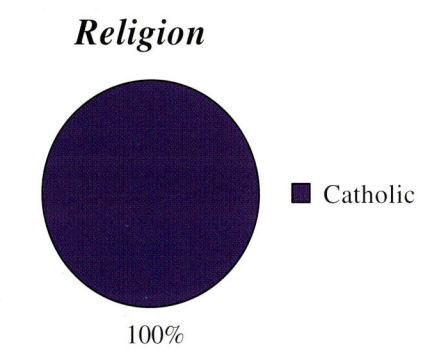

Catholic 100%

Midway

Population 90

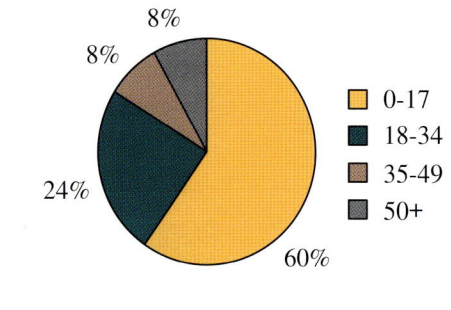

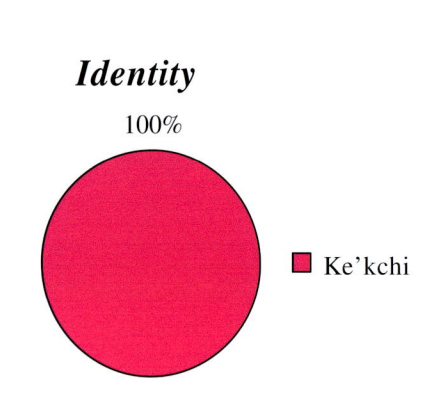

Identity
- Ke'kchi: 100%

Age Distribution
- 0-17: 60%
- 18-34: 24%
- 35-49: 8%
- 50+: 8%

Religion
- Catholic: 34%
- Other Christian: 66%

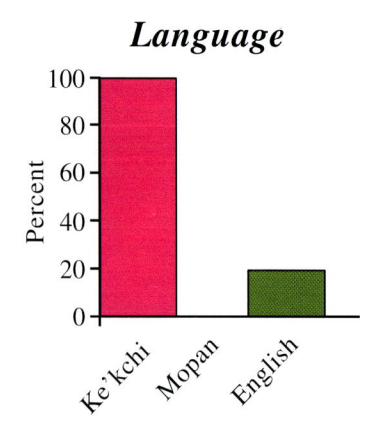

Language
- Ke'kchi: 100%
- Mopan: 0%
- English: ~20%

Family Work
- Farming: ~40%
- Raising Animals: ~30%
- Hunting: ~50%
- Fishing: ~33%

Midway village was founded in 1992 by Nathaniel Cayetano and Sebastian Shol. It was named Midway because the area was used as a resting place for people travelling to more remote areas. Midway is exactly what the term means. In early January 1992 they started clearing brush for their plantations of ground food. This Ke'kchi village is equidistant from Barranco and Santa Anna villages, and it is halfway between the villages that have rocked road and those that are reached by means of foot trails.

The settlement is very recent and thus working toward establishing a primary school and an *alcalde* system. The Catholic church is assisting in establishing a primary school. This settlement is considered an *"alkilo"*—houses built apart or in *milpa*.

Most people here originated from San Benito Poite and Conejo.

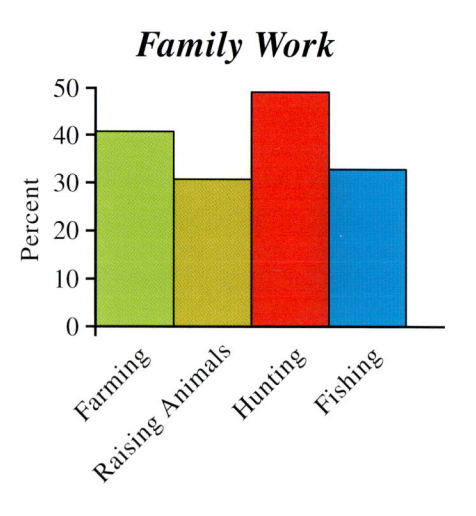

Region 3

87

1 Malasian Logging.
2 Malaysian Logging.

MIDWAY VILLAGE
SEBASTIAN TUSH

0   1   2 Miles

Boom Creek

Population 136

Boom Creek village is located about three miles below the village of Santa Anna, along the banks of the Moho River. Boom Creek got its name from a boom cable suspended across the river to retain logs. This is a stopping point to check the logs before their final journey to the sea.

During the time when the settlement was just beginning to develop, loggers were cutting wood. After the log extraction was over, a few people came down from Santa Anna.

Mayas working with the loggers remained where the logging camp was located. Here they built houses. Boom Creek at present is made up of twenty-one families—eight Mestizo families, and thirteen families of mostly Ke'kchi-speaking people. The oldest Ke'kchi people at this village are Jose Bo and Jose Coc. Boom Creek has a private missionary school called Iglesia de Dios. The private school was built because of the distance for the children to attend school in Santa Anna village.

The independent school was built through the effort of the people that began in 1995. The missionary in charge is Mr. Robert Dickens and this year, 1997, the new concrete building is complete. It will accommodate growth of the school in the future.

At this school the parents must contribute twenty-five dollars [US$12] for each child per year. This has to be paid by September.

For the last five years, Boom Creek people mostly travel by river to Punta Gorda Town. In early April 1994 a road was cleared from Punta Gorda Town to Boom Creek village that can be used during dry weather but is impossible during the rainy season, when a dory on the river is necessary to reach the village.

The occupations of families are local wood extraction, fishing, and seeking employment in Punta Gorda Town. Most Ke'kchi grow rice and corn for home use.

Boom Creek is a typical example of Mayas being exploited by missionaries, who have increased in numbers recently. Bobby Dickens, local missionary, said, "I don't want to hear anything about these Malaysians, because they are some of the best people I've met," as he produced a check for BZ$125 [US$63] which he said the company had committed to the school.

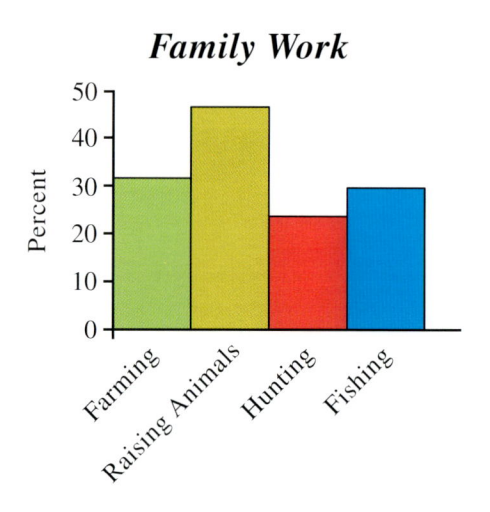

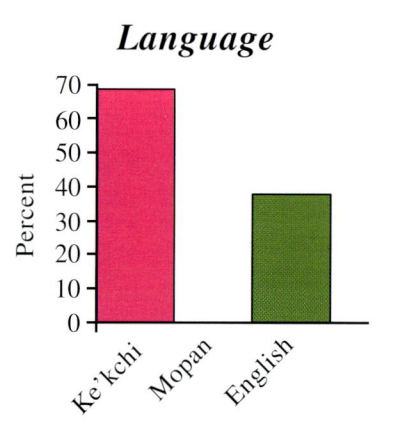

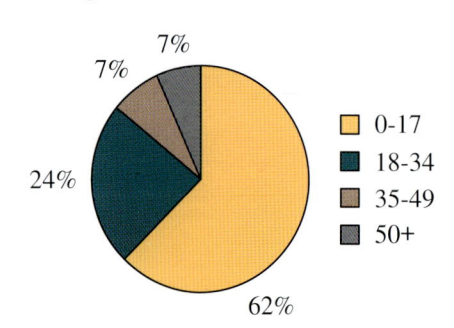

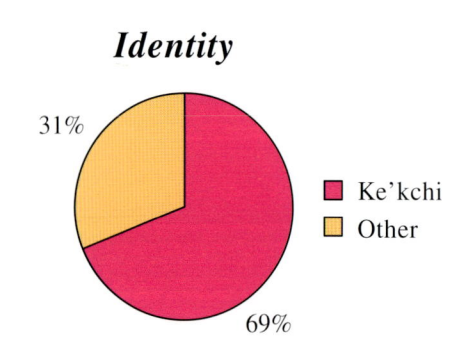

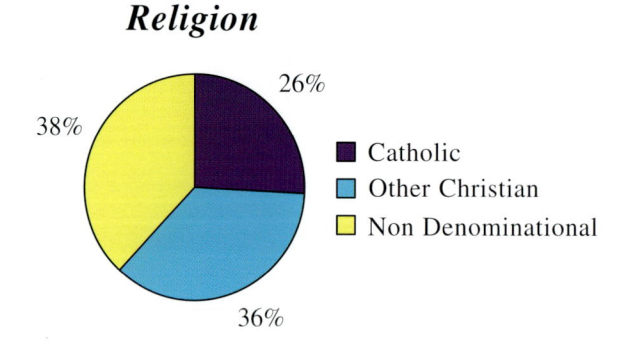

Family Work

Language

Age Distribution
- 0-17: 62%
- 18-34: 24%
- 35-49: 7%
- 50+: 7%

Identity
- Ke'kchi: 69%
- Other: 31%

Religion
- Catholic: 26%
- Other Christian: 36%
- Non Denominational: 38%

Region 3

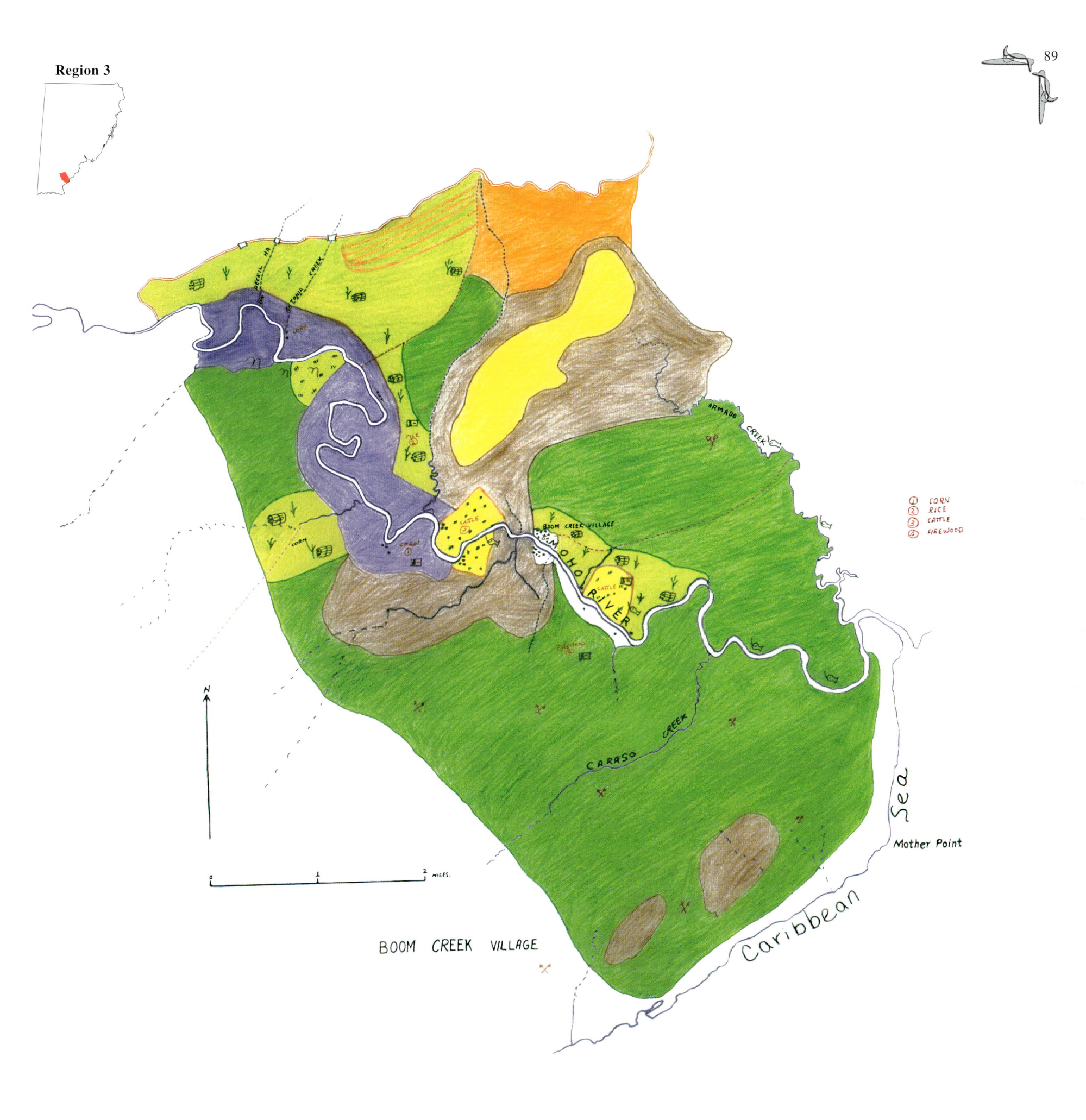

1. CORN
2. RICE
3. CATTLE
4. FIREWOOD

BOOM CREEK VILLAGE

Caribbean Sea

Mother Point

90

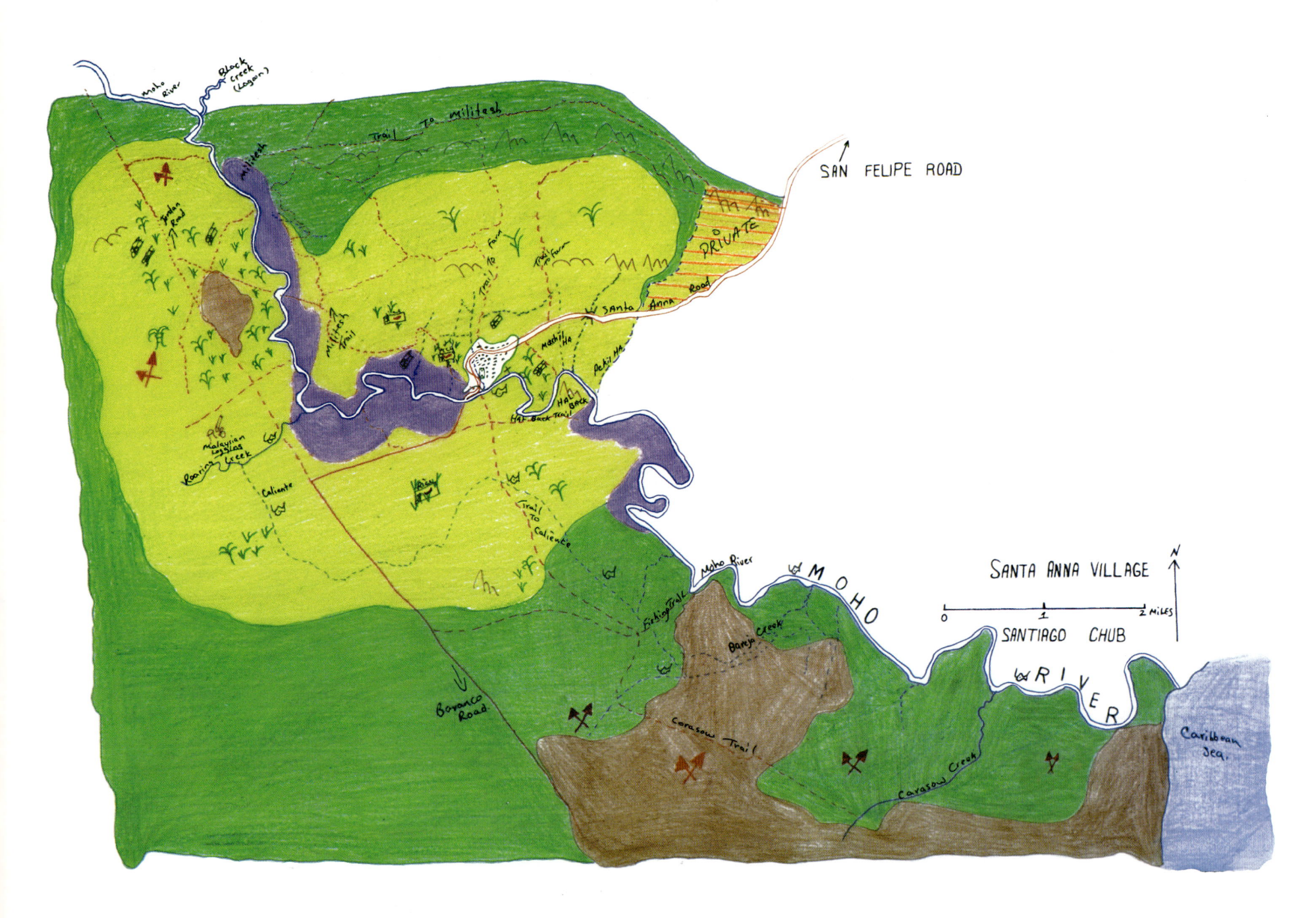

Region 3

Santa Anna

Population 185

Santa Anna is a small village of thirty-four houses by the bank of the crystal-clear, wide, lazy Moho River. This village loves this village because its river banks are full of iguanas sunning themselves and its fishes love to bite. Agriculturally the villagers do mechanized rice and corn plantations on a small scale.

Santa Anna village got started in 1973 by four families: Choc, Rash, Velize, and Itch. In January these four families made their *milpas* where they planned to build their homes. One year later five families from San Felipe came to live in Santa Anna and settled by the river. These nine families held their first meeting. During the meeting they all agreed to elect an *alcalde* to serve as their leader.

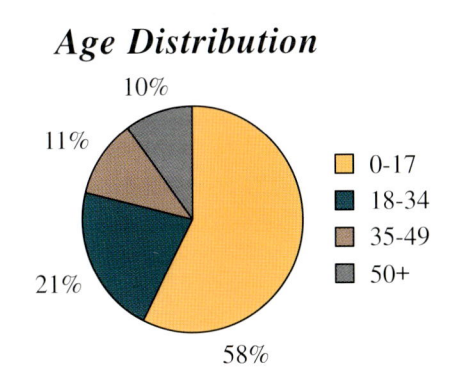

In 1975 they elected Mr. Coy as their first *alcalde*. During his first year they built a school. Thomas Enrique and the nine families held their second meeting. The purpose of the meeting was to name the village and school. During the meeting Mr. Enrique said, "The school should be named after me, because I am the first teacher and whenever I die my name may continue." Therefore the school was named St. Thomas R.C. School. Secondly, Mr. Enrique named the village Santa Anna because there is one village in the northern district named Santa Anna and there must be a second one. The people added Moho River so that it can be easily located. Today it is known as Santa Anna, Moho River.

At that time the road reached the village, which caused more people to come to Santa Anna to live.

The first church that was built was called Christian Church. Eventually the people became more religious and built two churches, Pentecostal and Baptist.

Today there are forty families living in Santa Anna. The main language is Ke'kchi. Santa Anna is developing quickly. Under the previous government administration a new school was built in 1991, and a community center, corn mill, and water tanks in 1992.

Some students from primary school are continuing their studies to a secondary and tertiary level of education, while others have joined the Belize Defence Force.

The people in Santa Anna are now improving their standard of living. They are also enjoying life with the new supply of electricity. In the future more improvement and expansion are expected to occur.

The beauty of Santa Anna is the Moho River, where our fellow Belizeans in and out of the Toledo District enjoy swimming and boating.

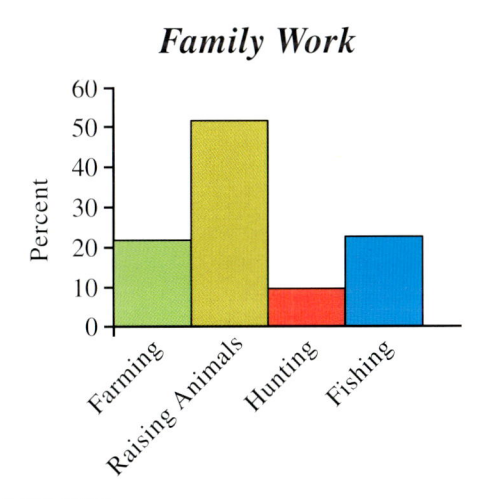

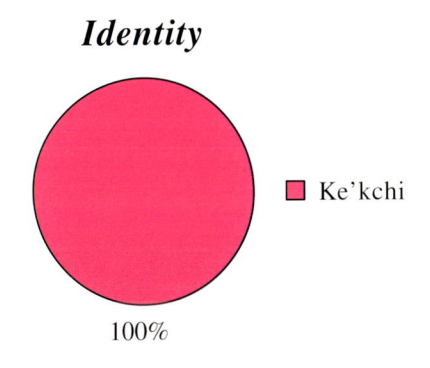

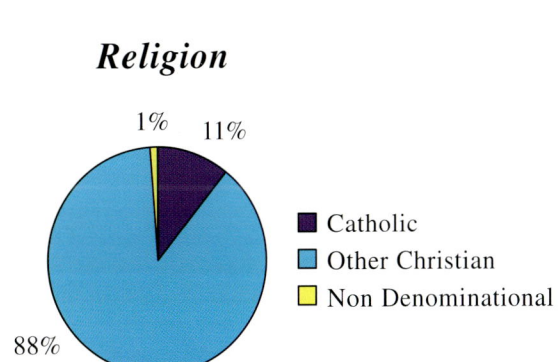

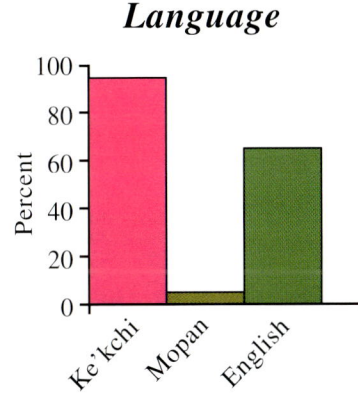

Age Distribution
- 0-17: 58%
- 18-34: 21%
- 35-49: 11%
- 50+: 10%

Identity
- Ke'kchi: 100%

Religion
- Catholic: 11%
- Other Christian: 88%
- Non Denominational: 1%

Family Work
- Farming: ~22%
- Raising Animals: ~52%
- Hunting: ~10%
- Fishing: ~23%

Language
- Ke'kchi: ~95%
- Mopan: ~5%
- English: ~65%

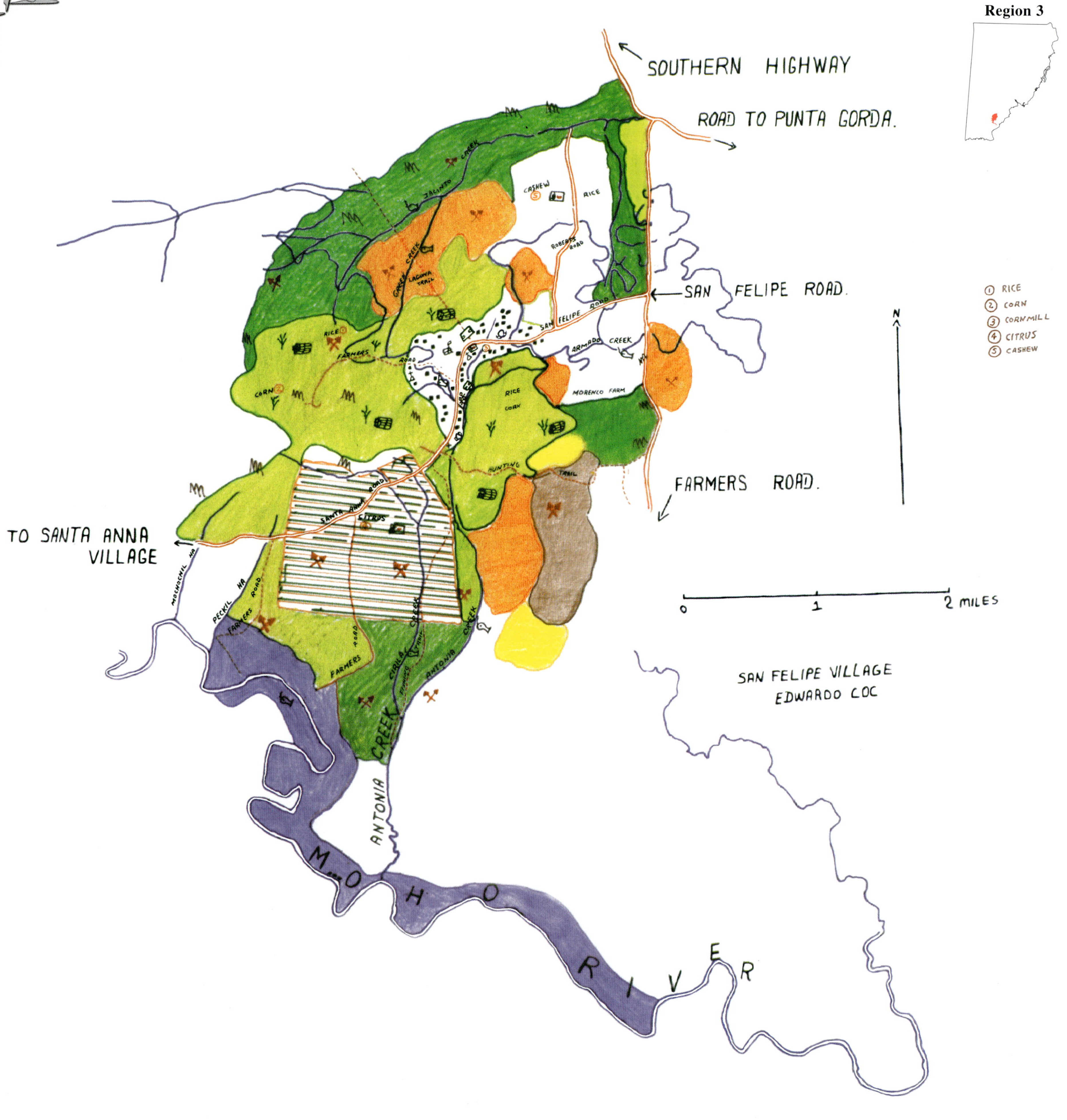
Region 3
SOUTHERN HIGHWAY
ROAD TO PUNTA GORDA.
SAN FELIPE ROAD.
FARMERS ROAD.
TO SANTA ANNA VILLAGE
N
0 1 2 MILES
① RICE
② CORN
③ CORNMILL
④ CITRUS
⑤ CASHEW
CASHEW
RICE
ROBERTS ROAD
JACINTO CREEK
LAGUNA TRAIL
FARMERS ROAD
SAN FELIPE ROAD
ARMADO CREEK
MORENCO FARM
HUNTING TRAIL
SANTA ANNA ROAD
CITRUS
ANTONIA CREEK
MOHO RIVER
SAN FELIPE VILLAGE
EDWARDO COC

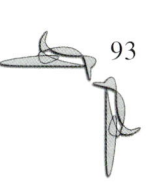

Age Distribution

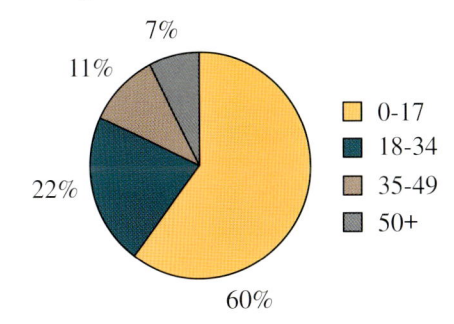

- 0-17: 60%
- 18-34: 22%
- 35-49: 11%
- 50+: 7%

Identity

- Ke'kchi: 89%
- Mopan: 11%

Religion

- Catholic: 7%
- Other Christian: 87%
- Non Denominational: 6%

San Felipe

Population 218

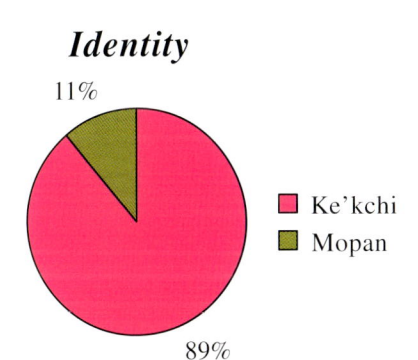

The desire for cash propelled Jose Tush and family to move from Rio Blanco and establish a settlement closer to Punta Gorda Town. Upon arriving at a small stream he once scouted, Jose Tush found a single house being occupied by Felipe Pinto. Mr. Pinto claimed to have a lease on a few acres but agreed to let Tush and family settle outside of his lease. The new arrivals decided to name their new village San Felipe. The founding of San Felipe occurred in 1960.

Within a period of five years, more and more families from other Ke'kchi villages came. The villagers then elected an *alcalde* who began agitating for a reservation, a school, and a road. The premier of Belize granted them rights to a piece of land for communal use. Since the grant was made only verbally, San Felipe has been sandwiched by foreign companies doing agricultural development. Presently the villagers of San Felipe have no more communal land and are forced to cultivate hillsides or travel to the Moho River to plant their *matambre*.

In 1991, San Felipe was provided with a community center, then a concrete primary school building, water pumps, and electricity. The villagers are very much economically depressed and landless. There is an unending feud between San Felipe and Santa Anna over land. Villagers of San Felipe have allowed foreign companies to purchase land around their village in the hope of opportunities which have not materialized. Having given up their own land to foreigners, they are now encroaching on land used by the villagers of Santa Anna. San Felipe is a typical example of a village taken for a ride by the promises of private ownership of land and the lures of inviting foreign investors.

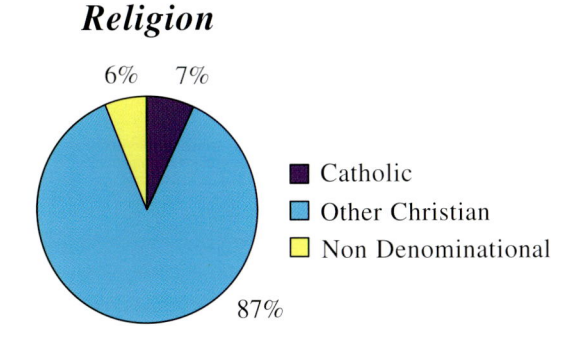

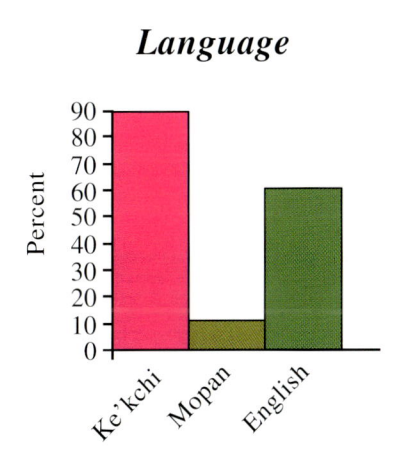

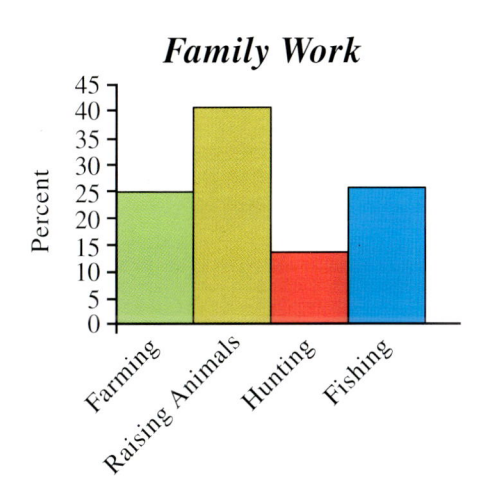

Language

(Ke'kchi ~90%, Mopan ~11%, English ~61%)

Family Work

(Farming ~25%, Raising Animals ~41%, Hunting ~14%, Fishing ~26%)

94

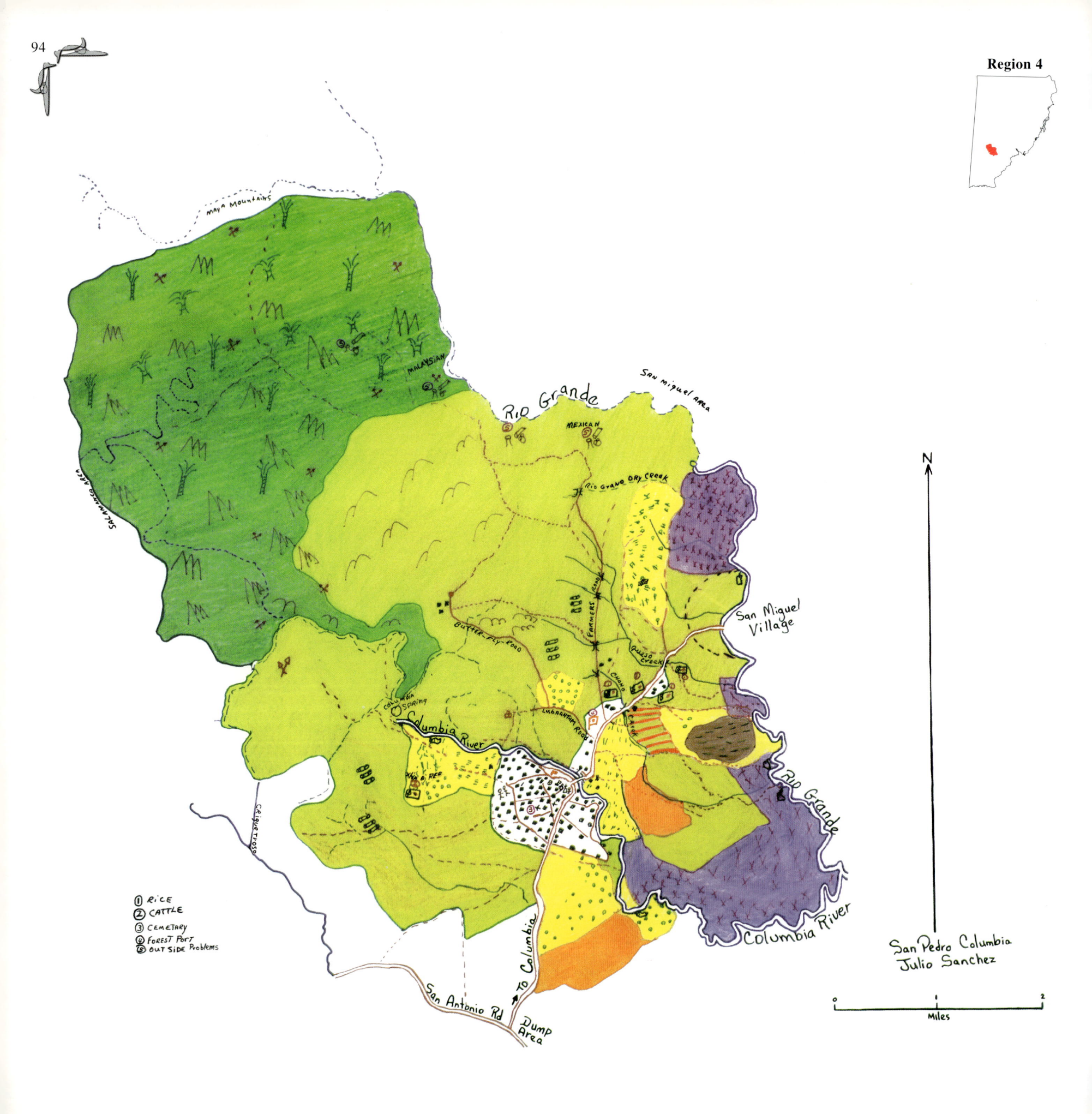

Region 4

① RICE
② CATTLE
③ CEMETARY
④ FOREST PORT
⑤ OUT SIDE PROBLEMS

San Pedro Columbia
Julio Sanchez

San Pedro Columbia

Population 717

The first group of people who settled and brought about the birth of a southern village known today as San Pedro Columbia were originally from San Luis, Petén, Guatemala.

In the year 1850, during the rule of Ubico's leadership in Guatemala, fifty families ran away under the cover of night from the cruel treatment, civil war, and repression of the Guatemalan government.

These families entered Belize, then known as British Honduras, by way of a new but already developing village known today as Pueblo Viejo; by following a small trail they passed through the village of San Antonio and continued to move eastward. These people carried along with them the statues of saints — Santo Domingo, San Pedro, and Santo Concepcion. They decided to settle near a creek known as Cacao Creek. Here they began to develop the area but after ten years were forced to leave their new settlement because of water contamination and disease. They moved from Cacao Creek to San Pedro Columbia, home to Ke'kchi and Mopan Mayas and small numbers of people from other ethnic extraction like Mestizo and Creole. Proof of these people originally settling in Cacao can be seen. They have their cemetery there. Before settling in San Pedro Columbia they stayed at Gallina Creek for three years, building their houses on hilltops. They began to cultivate the land and plant banana in 1930. In 1935 their crops were destroyed by huge clouds of grasshoppers.

After three years in Gallina Creek, hunters tracking game came across a huge river. How overjoyed they must have been. They quickly moved close to the river and at last began to develop a permanent village known today as San Pedro Columbia. A few years later, a land colonial right was passed out where a portion of land was taken for reservation.

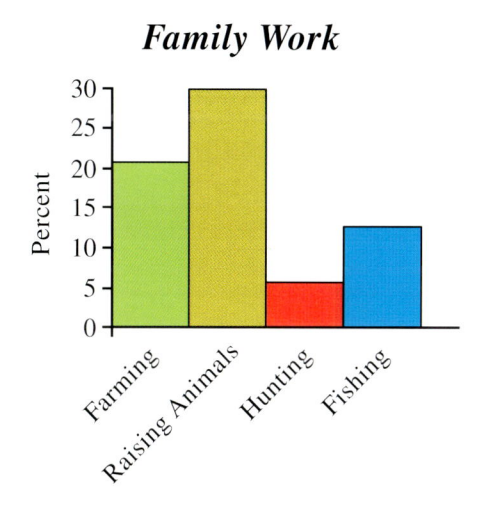

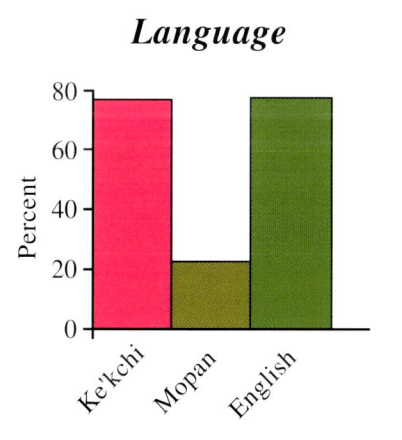

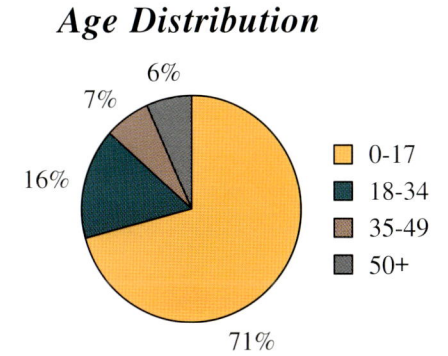

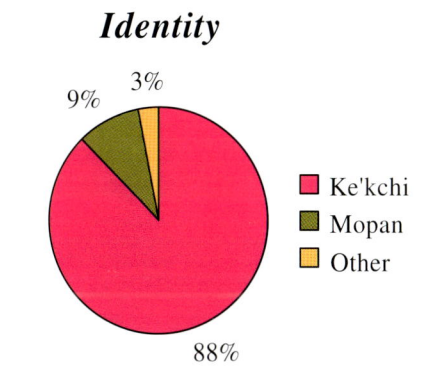

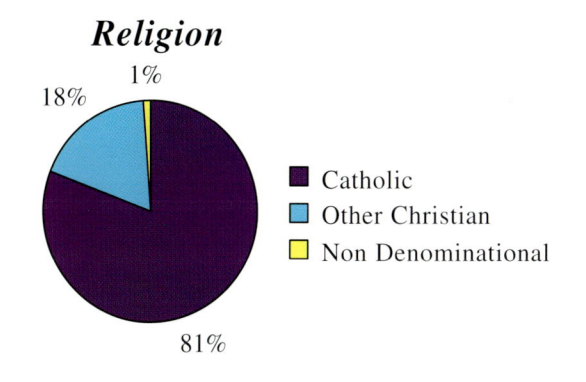

Family Work

Language

Age Distribution
- 0-17: 71%
- 18-34: 16%
- 35-49: 7%
- 50+: 6%

Identity
- Ke'kchi: 88%
- Mopan: 9%
- Other: 3%

Religion
- Catholic: 81%
- Other Christian: 18%
- Non Denominational: 1%

San Marcos

Population 328

Identity

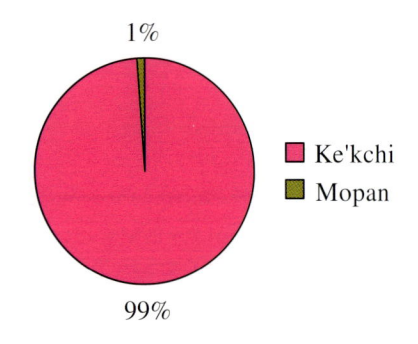

- Ke'kchi 99%
- Mopan 1%

Religion

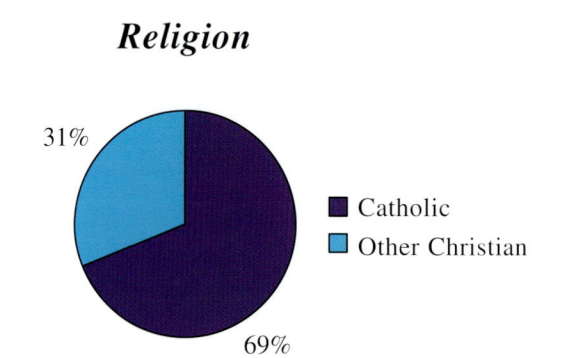

- Catholic 69%
- Other Christian 31%

Age Distribution

- 0-17: 64%
- 18-34: ()%
- 35-49: 9%
- 50+: 7%

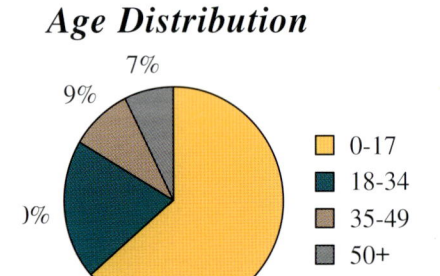

Beginning in 1975, Santos Muku, Camilo Rash, and Luciano Muku and their three families made their plantation and came to settle in this place.

The three families once lived on private property owned by a person in the dump area. Therefore the families were tired of living on private land. Their intention was to form a new village. The new settlement was established and as the years went by, more and more families came and lived in it. However, many of the first settlers were Guatemalans. It happened that the Ke'kchi people in Guatemala left for the country of Belize gradually. Today, the majority of the people in San Marcos are from Guatemala.

During the year 1981 the new Catholic church and school were built. So the people decided to name the place San Marcos village.

Language

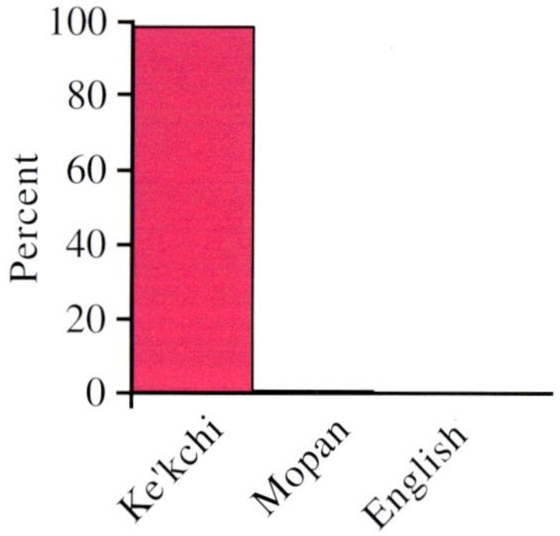

(Bar chart: Ke'kchi ~100%, Mopan 0, English 0)

Family Work

(Bar chart: Farming ~17%, Raising Animals ~46%, Hunting ~10%, Fishing ~16%)

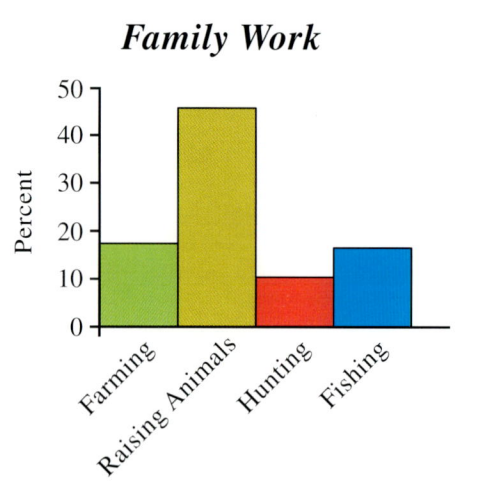

Region 4

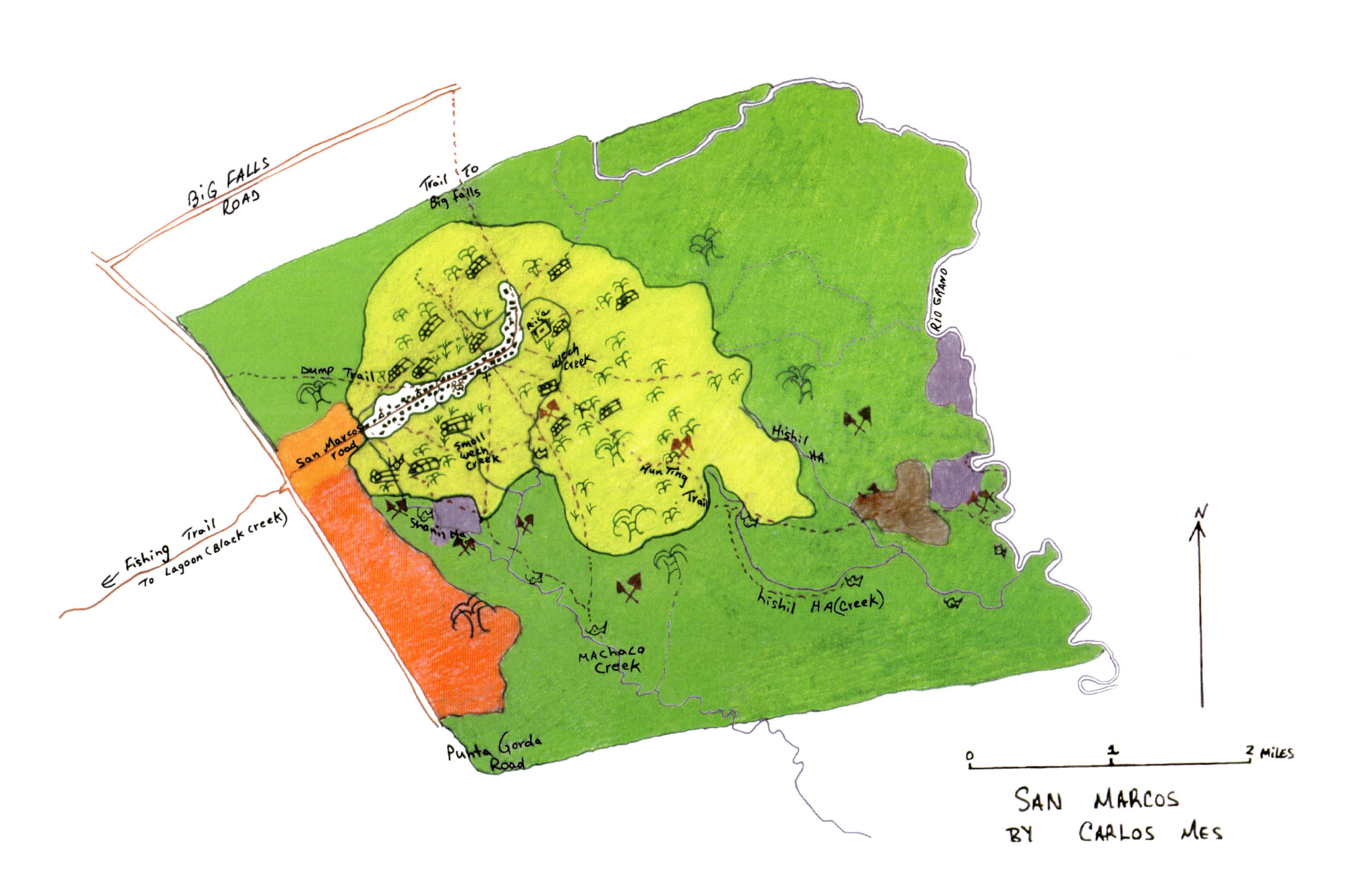

97

SAN MARCOS
BY CARLOS MES

98

Region 4

① Malaysian Logging
② Beans
③ Cattle

SAN MIGUEL VILLAGE
SABASTIAN CHOCO

San Miguel
Population 382

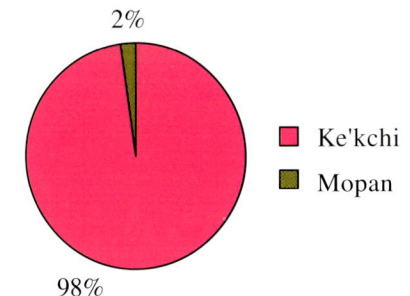

In the year 1950 a group of people migrated from a small village known as Santa Teresa. They moved from this village because of the poor fertility of the soil. Moving eastward, they found fertile soil. Here they decided to settle but first asked the people of San Pedro Columbia to give them some land. They were given 150 acres. These settlers crossed the Columbia River to select their site. They brought along with them the statue of St. Michael, from which the village name is derived. This statue can still be seen in the church of San Miguel village. The people began to develop and cultivate the land; they built thatch houses and slowly the settlement developed into a small village known today as San Miguel village.

Fifteen years later a few families decided to move a little further from the main settlement. They moved northward and settled about four miles from the village of San Miguel. This small village is known today as Silver Creek village. Today most people from these two small villages live on reservations. A few people have leased land.

Age Distribution
- 0-17: 58%
- 18-34: 26%
- 35-49: 8%
- 50+: 8%

Identity
- Ke'kchi: 98%
- Mopan: 2%

Religion
- Catholic: 73%
- Other Christian: 27%

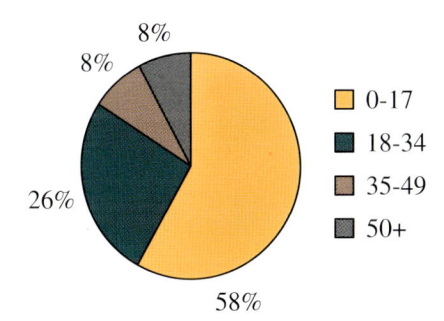

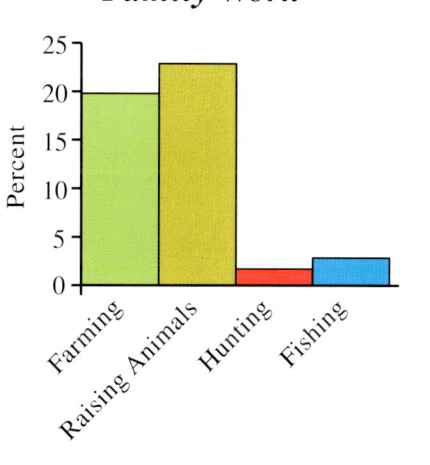

Family Work
- Farming: ~20%
- Raising Animals: ~23%
- Hunting: ~2%
- Fishing: ~3%

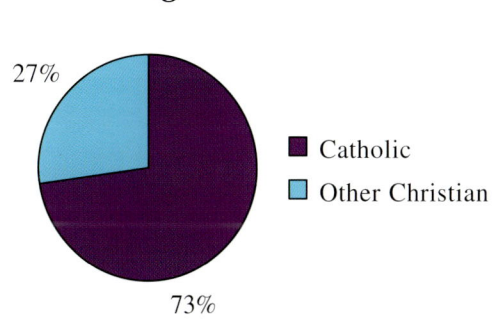

Language
- Ke'kchi: 100%
- Mopan: 0%
- English: ~55%

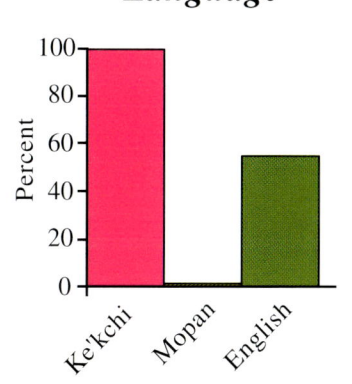

Indian Creek

Population 447

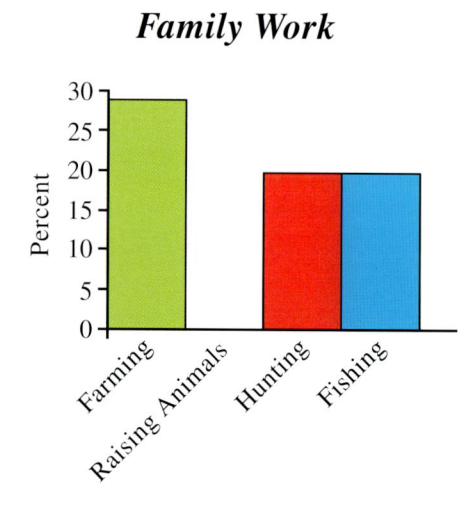

Martin Rash and Augustin Chub, originally of Laguna village, were the first to settle in Indian Creek. They came in search of better land for *milpa* and better hunting and fishing areas. The village was recognized as a community in 1969 when the government began to push the Southern Highway through to link the Toledo District with the rest of the nation. The people asked the government to secure their land. In 1974 the government sold a huge parcel of land to Whitney's Company with the promise of economic development by the company. The village grew. A few people have parceled lease land from the government and there will soon be no space for expansion. The people still rely on *milpa*. Jobs are scarce.

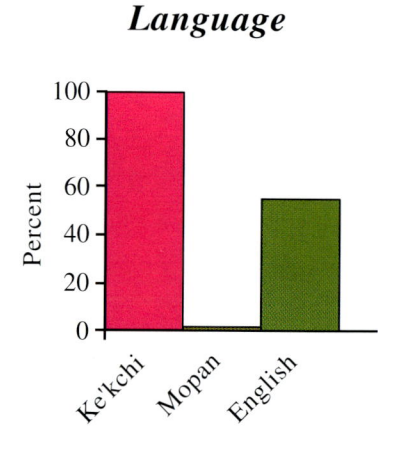

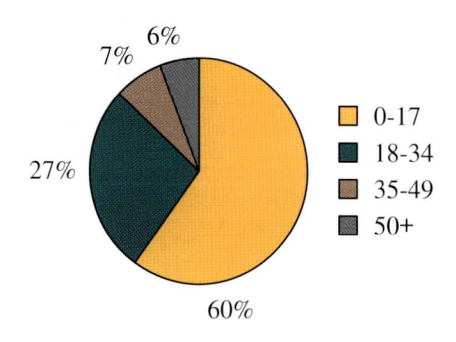

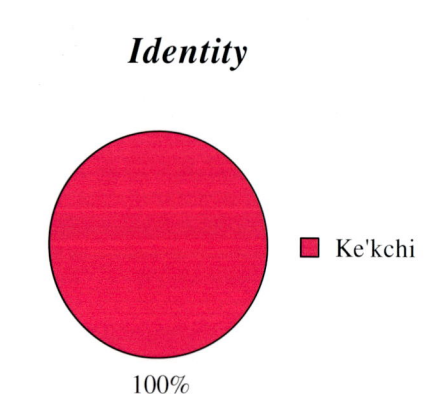

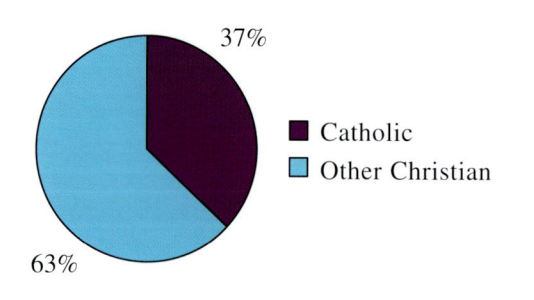

Family Work (bar chart, Percent): Farming ~29, Raising Animals 0, Hunting ~20, Fishing ~20

Language (bar chart, Percent): Ke'kchi 100, Mopan 0, English ~55

Age Distribution (pie chart): 0–17: 60%, 18–34: 27%, 35–49: 7%, 50+: 6%

Identity (pie chart): Ke'kchi 100%

Religion (pie chart): Catholic 37%, Other Christian 63%

Region 4

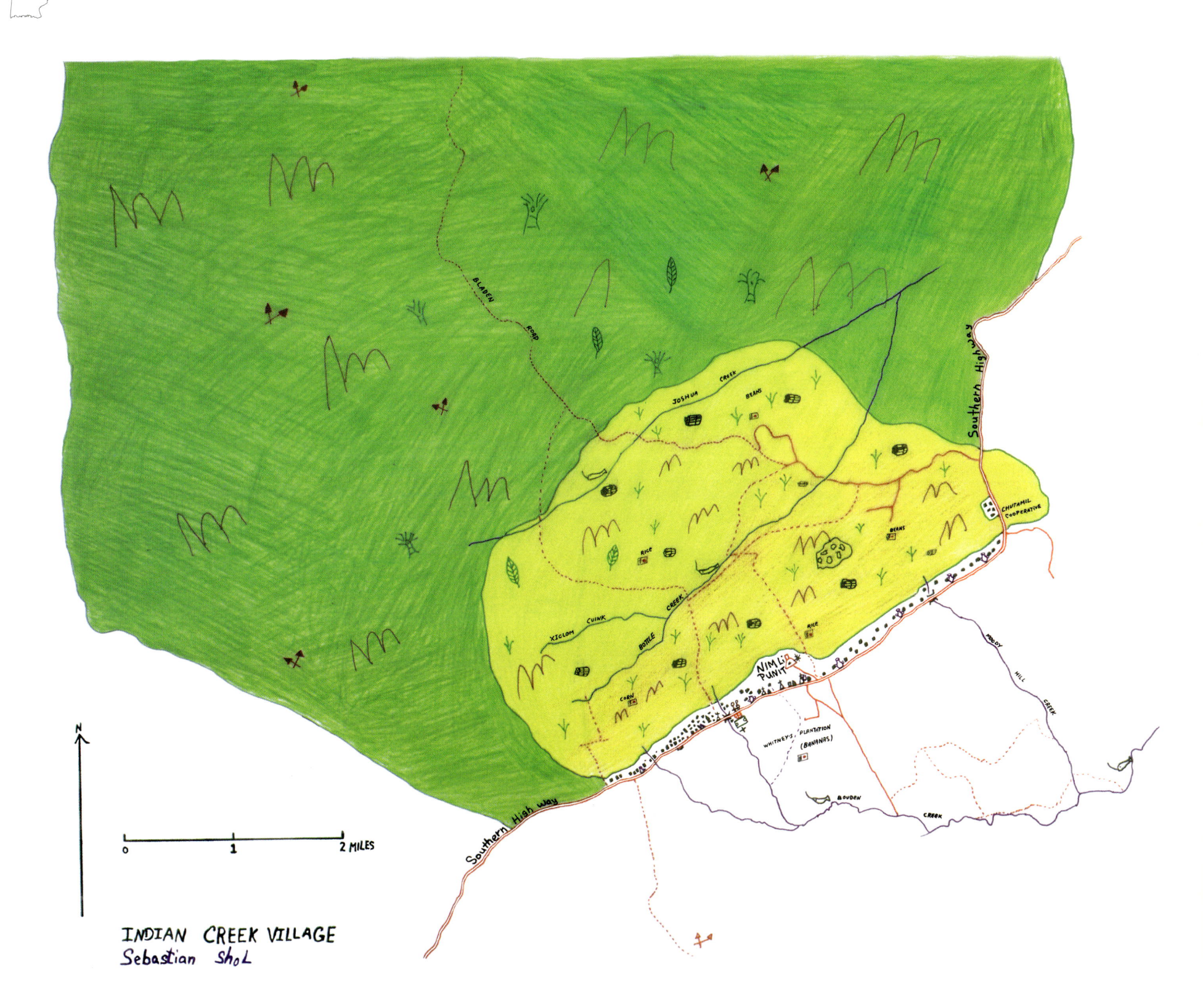

101

INDIAN CREEK VILLAGE
Sebastian Shol

Big Falls
Domingo Pau

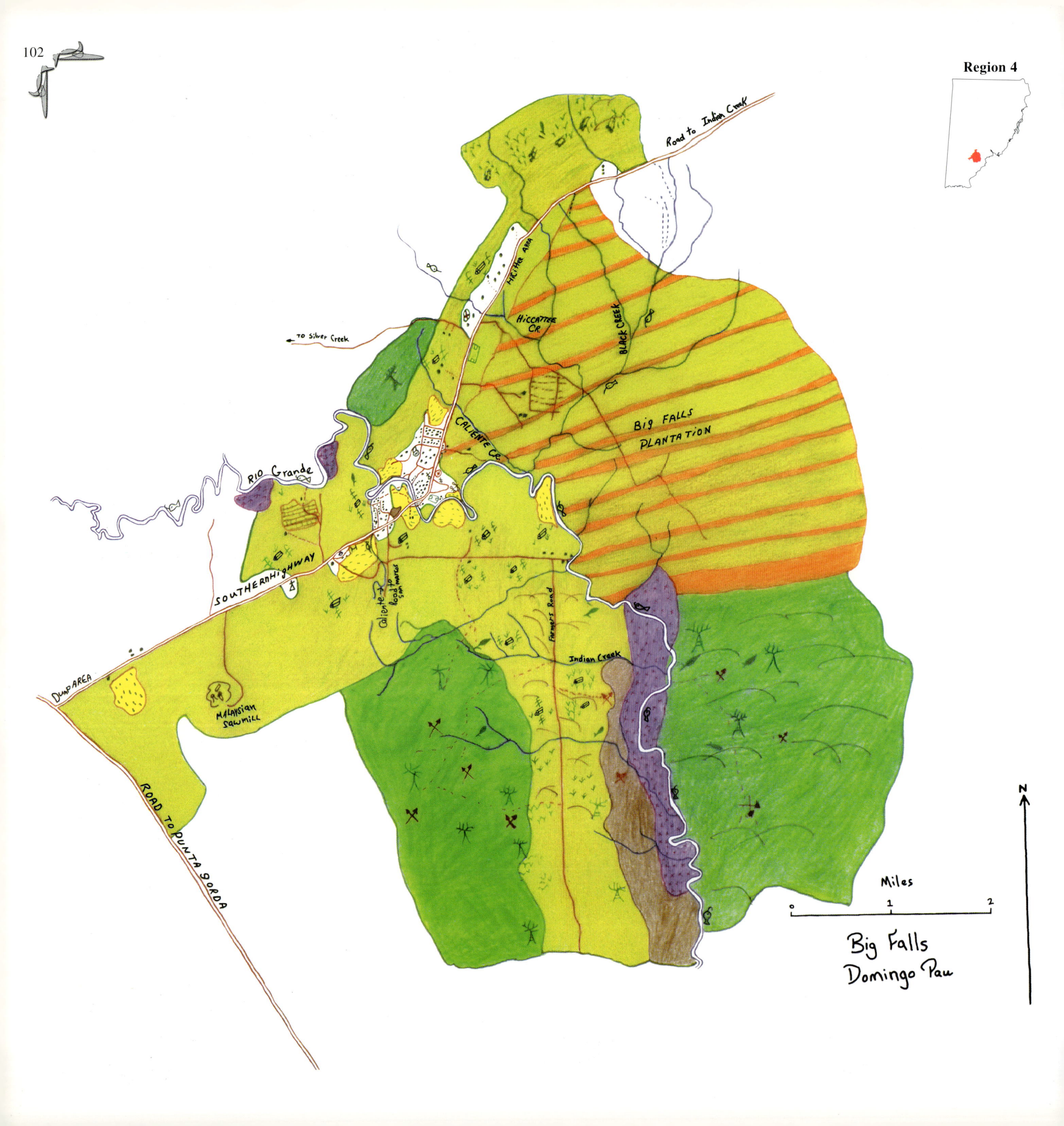

Region 4

Big Falls

Population 604

Big Falls got its name from the rapid waterfalls of the Rio Grande. The largest of the falls is situated almost directly under the new ferro-concrete bridge located in the heart of the village.

The settlement of Big Falls began in the early 1920s with people of Hispanic descent who migrated from Honduras. Surnames like Palma, Aleman, Hernández, Martínez, and Calíz were the first to settle here. In 1963 Mr. Owen Lewis, a British citizen working for the colonial government as Indian Liaison Officer, brought the first Maya Ke'kchi families to Big Falls. These Ke'kchis were brought from Crique Sarco to work for Mr. Lewis on his newly acquired block of land. Names like Domingo Chen, John Baki, Santiago Coy, and Santiago Tut were among the first to have arrived. Thereafter other Ke'kchi families followed, mostly from Crique Sarco and some from Santa Teresa. In the early 1970s Maya Mopans from San Jose came to live at Big Falls.

Today Big Falls has a population of some 600 people comprised of various ethnic groups such as Mopans, Ke'kchis, East Indians, Mestizos, Creoles, and Garifunas. All co-exist in harmony and are working together for a better future for their children. From a collection of small *milpa* farms on private land to a semi-industrial community, Big Falls is well on its way to becoming the next town in the Toledo District.

Big Falls is approximately eighteen miles from Punta Gorda Town, situated along the Southern Highway. It is divided by the Rio Grande and spanned by a bridge built in 1991 to replace a low wooden bridge built in 1967. The wooden bridge was often referred to as a dry-weather bridge because during the rainy season it was usually submerged under eight to ten feet of flood water, halting the flow of traffic for up to three weeks.

The Belize Marketing Board, established on 24 September 1979, is also called Big Falls Rice Mill. It is a semi-governmental establishment that buys all rice from local farmers and resells it to all Belizeans as polished rice. Big Falls Plantation Limited was established in 1985 and presently owns more than 2,500 acres of productive citrus trees. This company has plans to construct its own processing plant. There are four large citrus farms in Big Falls.

There are three petrol stations, two variety stores, several mini-grocery shops, three restaurants, two guest houses, and four bars with billiards.

Big Falls primary school in recent years has been a school to reckon with when it comes to academic performance by its students. The first school was built on the property of Julio Caliz in the late 1950s. It was later moved to the dump area some four miles away in 1961 and is now called San Isidro Roman Catholic School. This school caters to both Laguna and Big Falls villages. In 1982 the first concrete classroom building was erected in Big Falls, and in 1994 an extension was built of two additional buildings to accommodate the 395 children enrolled.

A health education center was built in 1986. This center is managed by a rural health nurse, Sister Marian Joseph. It also serves as a clinic to assist villagers with basic medical needs.

A community center was built by the government in 1973. Today this building serves as village meeting place, recreation hall, and as *cabildo* (courtroom).

There is a functioning *alcalde* system, village executive council, and a parent-teachers association. The *alcalde* takes care of all judicial matters within his authority, and the village council chairman looks after administrative and infrastructural affairs of the village.

The future of Big Falls may well lie in ecotourism after examining its potential socio-economic development. It is easily accessible by water and land. Ancient Mayan temples are just minutes away. The tropical rainforest, if managed properly, the Rio Grande, and the two hot springs are all natural attractions. The Mayan culture is surely an asset and can be used to develop the community. In spite of all this there is a need to recapture what may have been lost and to promote our cultural way of life with particular attention given to our land and environment.

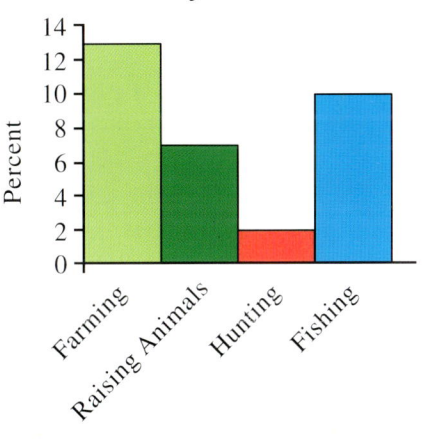

Age Distribution

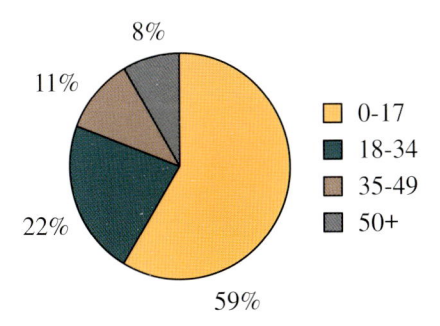

- 0-17: 59%
- 18-34: 22%
- 35-49: 11%
- 50+: 8%

Identity

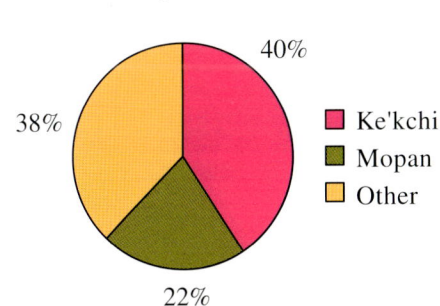

- Ke'kchi: 40%
- Mopan: 22%
- Other: 38%

Religion

- Catholic: 75%
- Other Christian: 25%

Family Work

- Farming: 13%
- Raising Animals: 7%
- Hunting: 2%
- Fishing: 10%

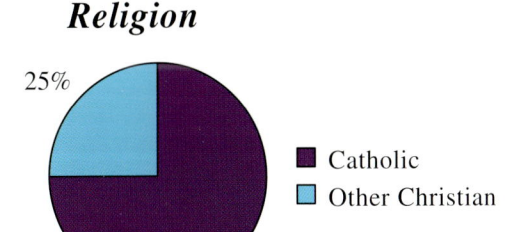

Language

- Ke'kchi: ~75%
- Mopan: ~39%
- English: ~68%

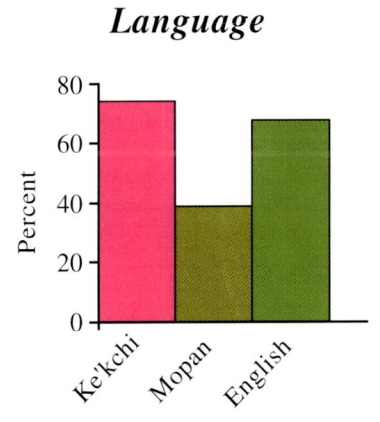

Silver Creek

Population 267

Age Distribution
- 0-17: 59%
- 18-34: 25%
- 35-49: 9%
- 50+: 7%

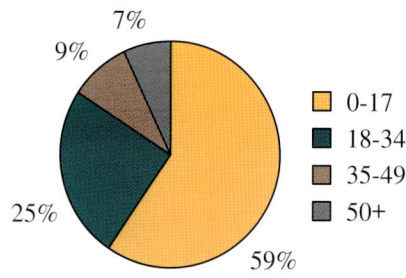

Identity
- Ke'kchi: 99%
- Mopan: 1%

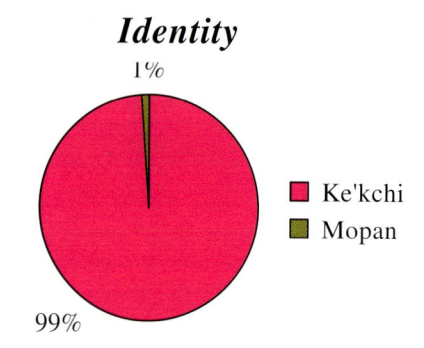

Religion
- Catholic: 86%
- Other Christian: 14%

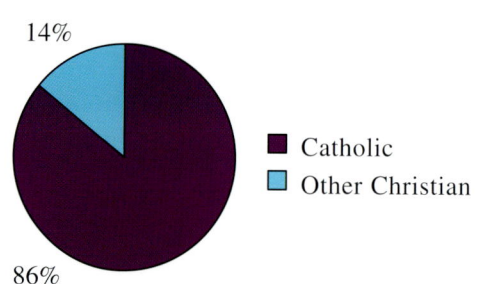

Language
- Ke'kchi: ~100%
- Mopan: ~8%
- English: ~78%

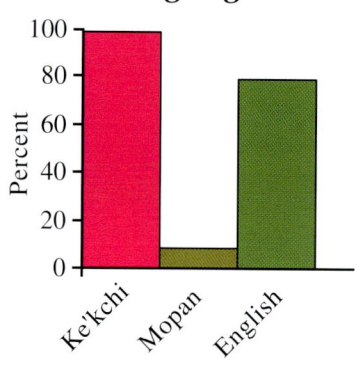

Family Work
- Farming: ~20%
- Raising Animals: ~48%
- Hunting: ~7%
- Fishing: ~15%

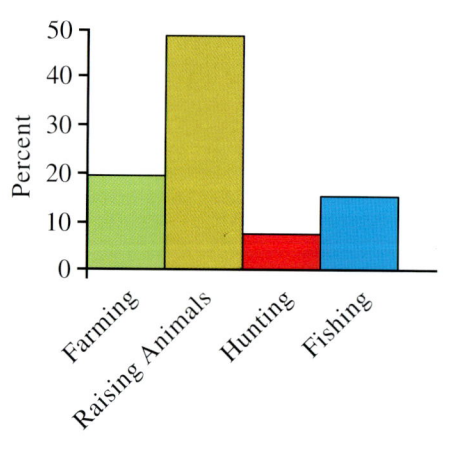

In 1969 fourteen Ke'kchi Maya men from San Miguel came to work the fresh virgin rainforest, headed by Lorenzo Sam. They were all equipped with machetes, files, axes, water, and bags of food to serve them for a week. All men initially chopped three acres each for rice. The villagers saw that this was a good area for farming, hunting, and living.

In 1970 there were heavy discussions among the men and women about forming a new village. The area where the first rice field was planted was called *wapinol* by some Spanish people who had a ranch north of the village. Wapinol is a common wild fruit tree that grows along the side of a living creek.

In 1971 the first family to live in Silver Creek was that of Jose Choco. He lived in a thatched-roof house where rice was stored. He came between April and May during the planting season. Then a few days later Lorenzo Sam's crew came from San Miguel village. They immigrated due to better farming land closer to the newly built Southern Highway. Corn, rice, beans, and ground food grow best in the area. Mr. Sam headed the village, because he was a former chairperson for four years in San Miguel. After some time there were discussions about the village name. Mr. Sam said, "I named the village Silver Creek because in this area we harvested good crops and we can have a good living here. The land is very rich and similar to silver."

Until 1974, Lorenzo. Sam served as the first *alcalde*. The *alcalde* system was officially launched with the assistance of local political representative Alejandro Vernon. The area representative began opening the Southern Highway to Silver Creek. The *alcalde* made local rules to govern the village and set meetings for development. The traditional culture is rich, including the Cortez Dance, making pottery, embroidery, and other art work. The village was awarded first prize for being the cleanest village by having regular *fajina* (a clean-up program).

In October 1974 the local political representative, Vicente Choco, completed the road connection from Silver Creek to San Miguel with a proper graveled road. The village *alcalde* Lorenzo Sam, area representative Vicente Choco, and Harry Gomez, land officer of Punta Gorda Town, officially filed a statement that the local border between San Miguel and Silver Creek is Go-To-Hell Creek.

In 1975 the Roman Catholic primary school was built at a cost of BZ$1,600 [US$800] by a priest, Fr. John Cull S.J. After that, the *alcalde* requested a meeting house—*cabildo* (*popol*)—which cost BZ$350 [US$175]. The *alcalde* also requested a water supply but was unsuccessful.

In November 1992 the Saving Animals, Vegetation, and Environment (SAVE) youth group was founded by student Martin Choco. It included fifteen high school boys. The objective is to assist in community development, and the group has been very active from its start.

In 1993 the Sajil Cholexil Women's Group was founded by some young and elderly women. The women's group corn-mill was requested by the Ke'kchi council and presently operates for the benefit of the village.

In 1995 the Baptist church was founded by Vicente Teul.

Finally, the people here are very friendly and instrumental in hosting village meetings. The people include bush doctors, teachers, police, soldiers, students, health workers, drivers, and farmers.

Region 4

105

① Beans

SAN MIGUEL ROAD

RIO GRANDE RIVER

Rio Grande River

SOUTHERN HIGHWAY

Champion Road

Farmer's Road

Go To Hell Creek

Nicaragua Creek

→ To Indian Creek

Parlor Road

Rogers Lane

Silver Creek

Southern Highway

N

0   1   2 MILES

SILVER CREEK VILLAGE
EVERISCIO COH

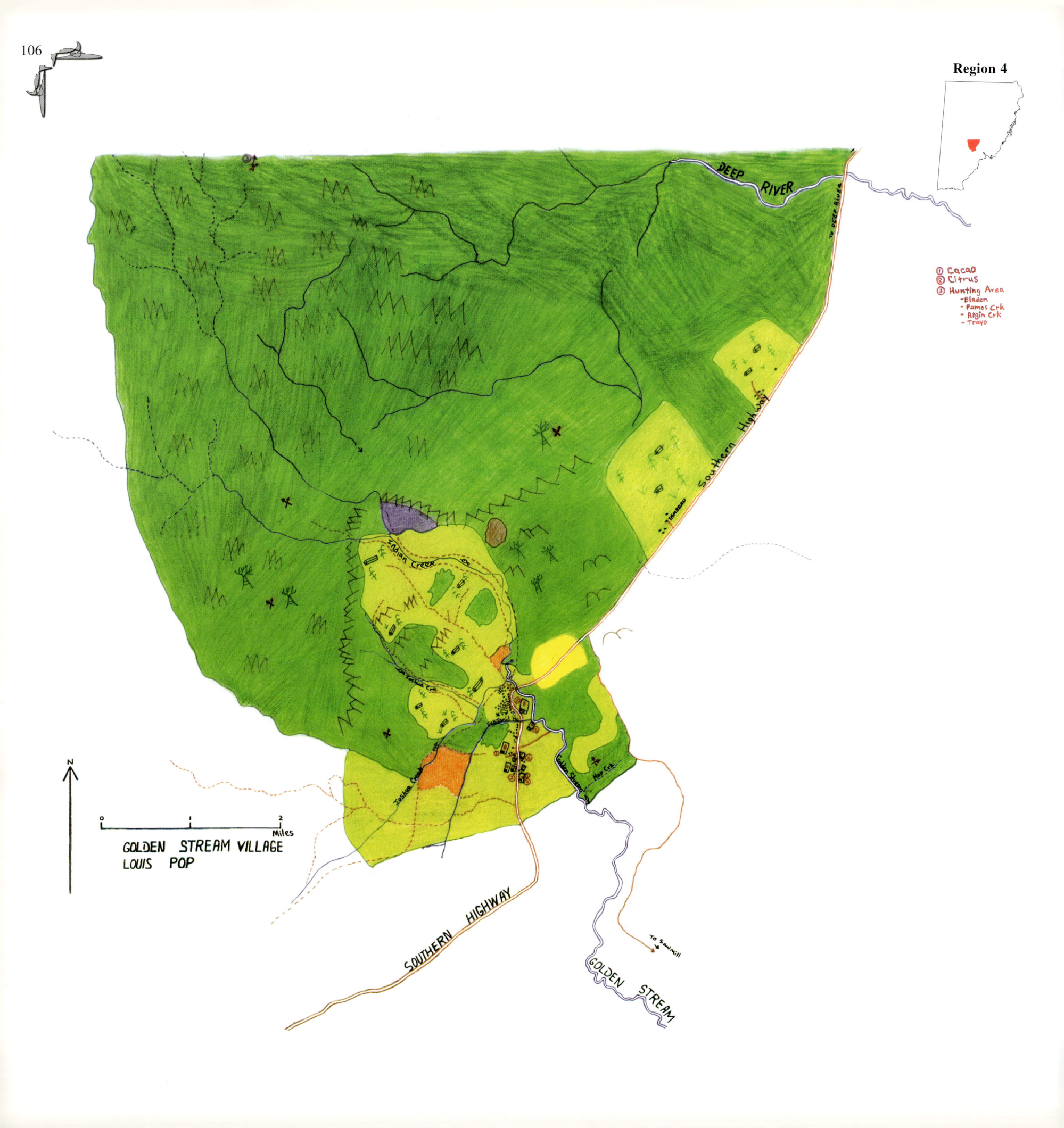

GOLDEN STREAM VILLAGE
LOUIS POP

Region 4

1. Cacao
2. Citrus
3. Hunting Area
   - Bladen
   - Pamos Crk
   - Argin Crk
   - Trayo

Golden Stream

Population 304

This village began in 1970 with a few families; in 1985 more families came from Pueblo Viejo and Santa Cruz, making a total of twenty-two families. The *alcalde* of Indian Creek had jurisdiction over this village for almost a year, but the people got tired of giving free labor to Indian Creek. Instead the people formed a Village Council. Then in 1986 they elected their own *alcalde*. People began lobbying the government for a school building in 1994. With the help of the village people and the government, a school was built in February 1996. The name Golden Stream is given to the village because it is situated next to the golden, crystal-clear stream known by that name. This river is well-known for its natural pools north of the village.

This village has one of the most dynamic women's groups; its members sell embroidery and carving made of slate from the river.

Not only do Golden Stream people enjoy this beautiful stream, but people all over the country of Belize and international tourists enjoy swimming in the river. The river does not run dry in the dry season. So it has been remembered and never forgotten.

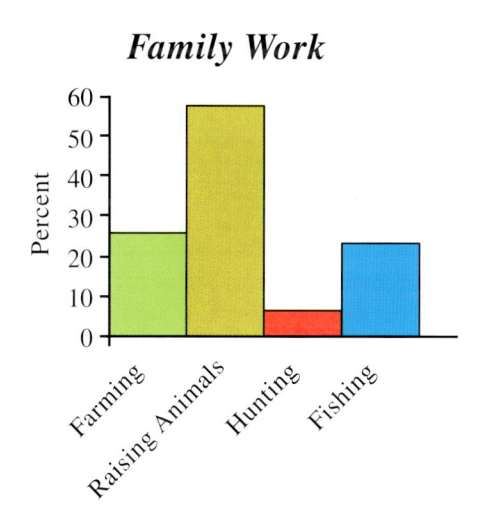

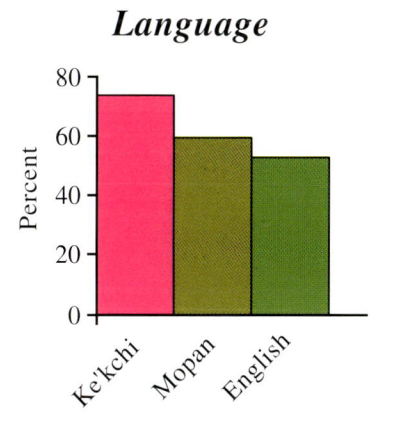

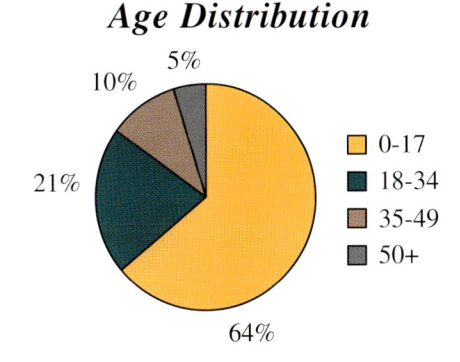

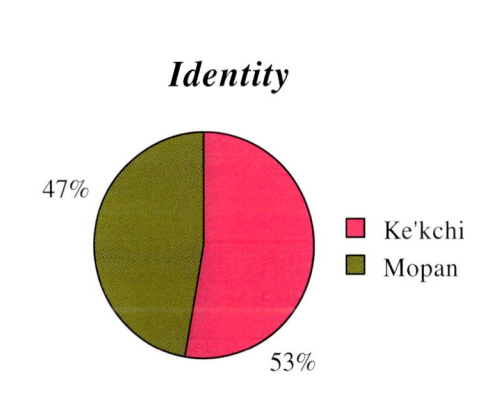

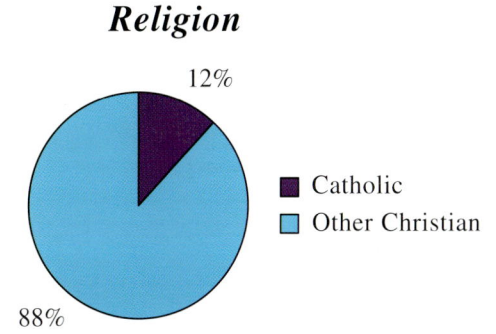

Family Work

- Farming: ~26%
- Raising Animals: ~58%
- Hunting: ~6%
- Fishing: ~23%

Language

- Ke'kchi: ~74%
- Mopan: ~60%
- English: ~53%

Age Distribution

- 0-17: 64%
- 18-34: 21%
- 35-49: 10%
- 50+: 5%

Identity

- Ke'kchi: 53%
- Mopan: 47%

Religion

- Catholic: 12%
- Other Christian: 88%

108

Region 4

1: Logging
 - Charles Seller
2: Logging
 - Genus

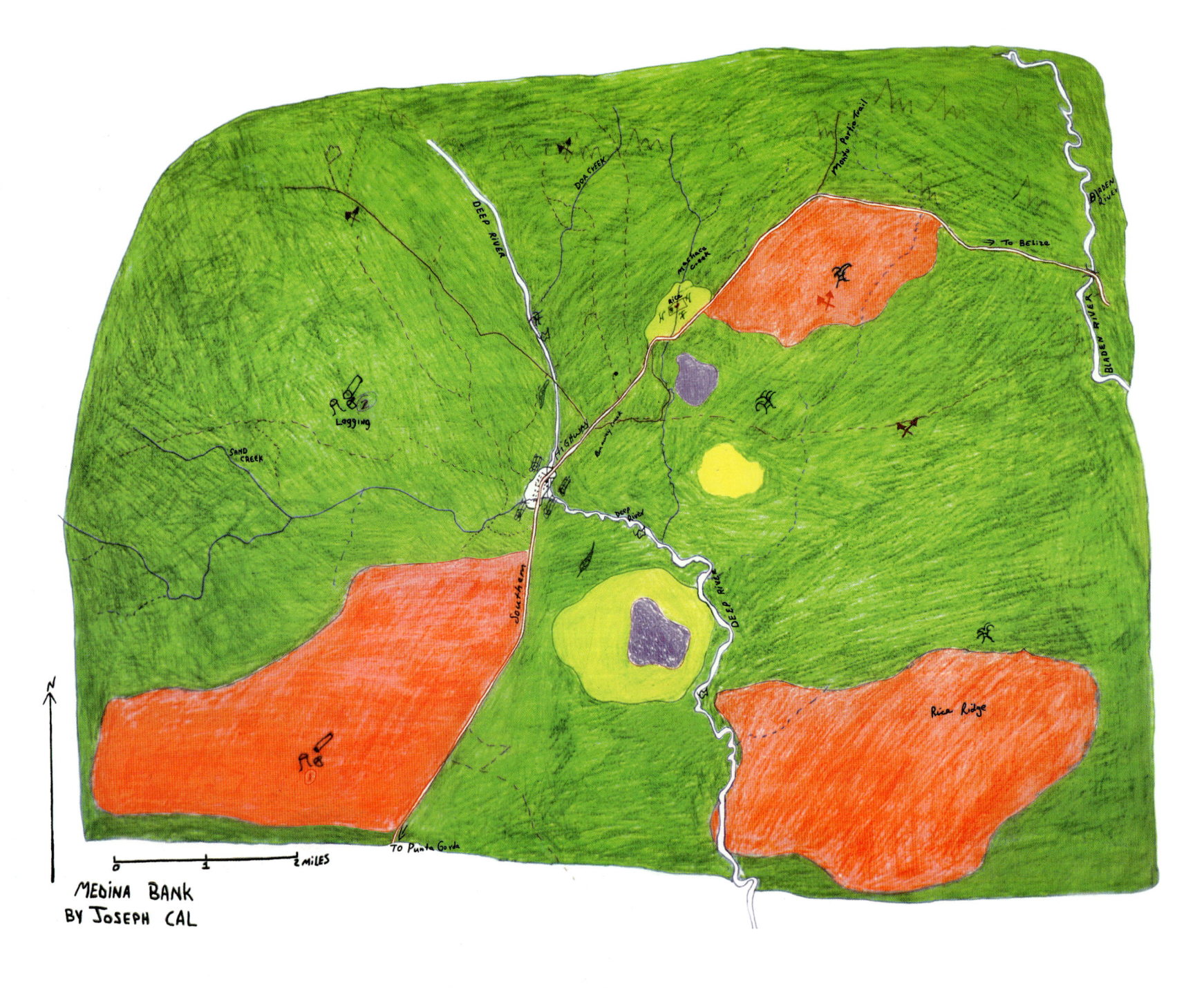

MEDINA BANK
BY JOSEPH CAL

Medina Bank

Population 188

Age Distribution

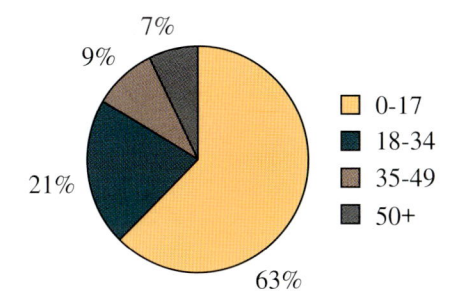

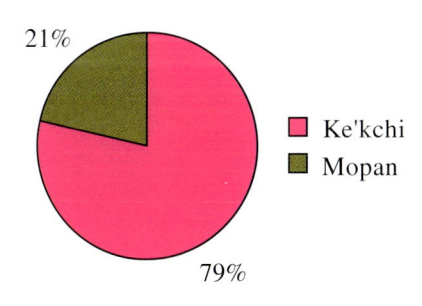

- 0-17: 63%
- 18-34: 21%
- 35-49: 9%
- 50+: 7%

Identity

- Ke'kchi: 79%
- Mopan: 21%

Religion

- Catholic: 38%
- Other Christian: 62%

Language

- Ke'kchi: ~72%
- Mopan: ~21%
- English: ~26%

Family Work

- Farming: ~19%
- Raising Animals: 0%
- Hunting: ~10%
- Fishing: ~12%

Medina Bank village is located along the Deep River area. Nearby there is fresh spring water for drinking. Having a shower and swimming is very enjoyable in the cool, clean river.

Medina Bank is a respectful and new small village near the Southern Highway. It is very easy to find at any time. This village was founded by Joseph Cal and sons in 1989. The nations are Ke'kchi and Mopan. Within the village is a government school, a Baptist church, and a Catholic church, which was our plan in 1989. The village is small and new and they just got a primary school. The people are either Catholics or Seventh Day Adventists.

The people's survival is by what we call the *milpa* system, which has been practiced by the indigenous people from the very beginning. The crops are corn, rice, and beans. Ground foods are yam, *yampi*, and potato, and the fruit trees are mango, avocado, soursop, rose-apple, plum, grapefruit, *crabu*, papaya, *mami*, orange, and calabash and cacao. Plantains and bananas are also found. One concern the village has is land, as there is no room for them to do their *milpa*.

Marketing is one of our major problems with most of our produce except for rice, because it has a market. In the past five years we have learned more and more about what we need in the future, especially land and marketing.

How can we benefit in the future? First we are looking forward to the amount of land to be a reserve in the forest. Our basic plan is to own the amount of land we need. Our protected area will be among our lands, as we are looking to benefit our children in the future. A feeder road is also necessary for the people to access our farms and our protected or conservation area. The feeder road was almost opened by Charles Seller; it only needs a little work to be complete.

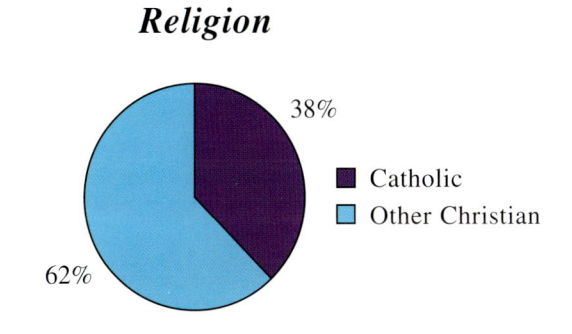

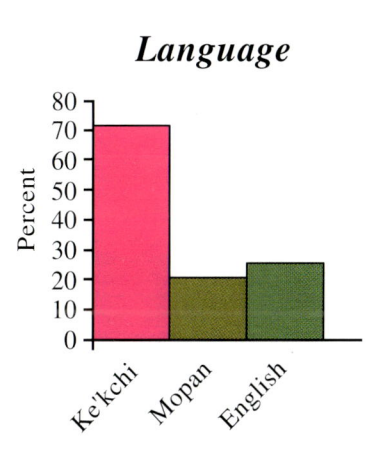

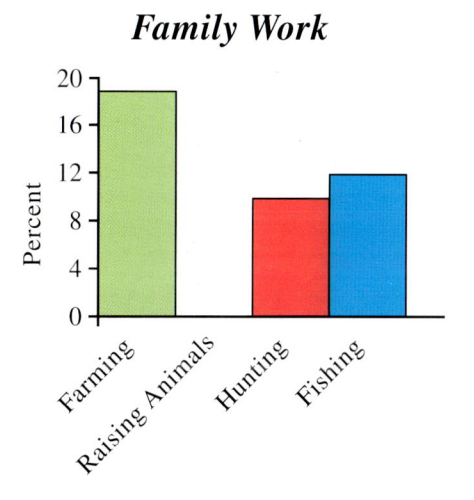

Maya Centre *Population 84*

Maya Centre village, located some fourteen miles from the Southern Highway's beginning in the Stann Creek District, is populated mostly by Mopan Mayas. This is a Mayan village that has proven itself progressive in this district.

Maya Centre village started when a group of families decided to break away from Maya Mopan. Some of their primary reasons for leaving were lack of access to the Southern Highway, no access to education, and produce from agriculture could not make it to local markets. However, there was already a disagreement between the settlement of Alabama and the settlement of Maya Mopan (of which Elogio Sho was the village council chairman), and one villager got killed, so the chairman decided then we could not stay there.

On December 26, 1975, a few family heads left in search of land and reached the Sittee River area. They were told that they could not stay and returned to Cabbage Hall Creek and decided that this was the place they were looking for. They then started making camps for their families. On January 2, 1976, family members began settling down and establishing themselves. They started farming, building a church, and building a school in late 1976. The government has not fully recognized the school and cannot provide a teacher. Ernesto Saqui, a high-school graduate, has started teaching voluntarily.

At the end of 1976, Donald Ho, the owner of the land that we settled on, came and informed us. Chairman Elogio Sho took the matter to the Prime Minister and demanded that the land be made available to the newcomers. The newcomers began farming on what is now the access road to the Jaguar Preserve.

In 1977, one family decided to leave again and went to settle down in the Cockscomb area, known as "Quam Bank." Three or four families followed and settled in Cockscomb. The struggle continues for land and recognition. In 1989, land was granted to us. It was 1,000 acres, with 50 acres blocked for the village site. In late 1982 and mid-1983, our chairman (E. Sho) became political and religious and began doing activities in his own way, causing the village to split. In 1984, there was a change of government and his party lost.

In 1985, the villagers called for a B1-election, as their needs were not being met. Ernesto Saqui was then elected to replace Elogio Sho. This was a turning point in the life of the village of Maya Centre. In late 1985, we began asking for a school, a football field was put in place, and streets were constructed. In 1986–87, a health post was constructed through a grant from Kirathimmo International. Two justices of the peace were also sworn in, Ignacio Rop and Ernesto Saqui. We requested the government to block land for individuals. In 1988, land was blocked off into thirty blocks. Village lots were also blocked. Around this time, a community was being erected. In 1989, there was a change of government again, but new development continues. A feeder road was completed, and farmers were encouraged to apply for their parcel of land and the electrification of the village.

Around this time, the primary school was removed and housed in Georgetown village. We decided that this was not in our best interest and resisted the removal of our school. Our school at this point was not producing good students. In 1993, our church-state system of education needed a change and villagers requested our own villager to be the principal of our school. Liberato Saqui filled the post. Despite all the difficulties in our school, we were able to produce good students from 1977 that graduated from high school up to the university level.

In 1994, the program of the village was being fulfilled. The new school was completed, donated to the village by the International Rescue Committee's Quick Impact Project (UNICEF). A water system was also put in place. The International Rescue Committee helped in the project. Most of the villagers at the end of 1994 were all into cash crops, such as citrus. Telephone service was also installed. Tourism was introduced.

The Saqui, Sho, Bolon, and Pop families are the people who have contributed significantly to the development of Maya Centre village. The current village chairman, who is also park director for Cockscomb Basin Wildlife Sanctuary, is Mr. Ernesto Saqui. He has been the village chairman since 1985.

Since the establishment of a protected area in the Cockscomb Basin, families were forcibly removed. In 1984 a law was passed prohibiting hunting, fishing, and farming there. Most of these people went back to where they originally came from and decided to stay in Maya Centre. Groups began to organize themselves since 1987, through the efforts of the village council, the health team, the Maya Centre Water Board, the Parent-Teachers Association, and the Maya Centre Women's Group.

Since 1987, tourism has been very much alive. This has opened up avenues for entrepreneurs to start their own businesses, individually or in groups. The Maya Centre Women's Group established a craft center at the entrance to the Jaguar Preserve. This has also encouraged home industry. Certain individuals erected cabañas, hotels, campgrounds, and restaurants, while some prefer to be professional tour guides.

All of the founding people living in Maya Centre were originally from San Antonio, Toledo. People work together and they are happy to have what currently exists here. I would like to take this opportunity to thank all those individuals who have helped and supported me, especially the villagers of Maya Centre. I am happy to be a part of you all and together we shall move forward.

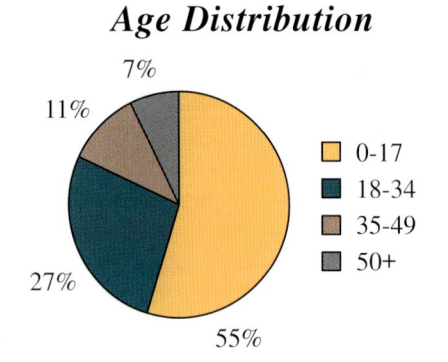

Age Distribution

- 0-17: 55%
- 18-34: 27%
- 35-49: 11%
- 50+: 7%

Region 5

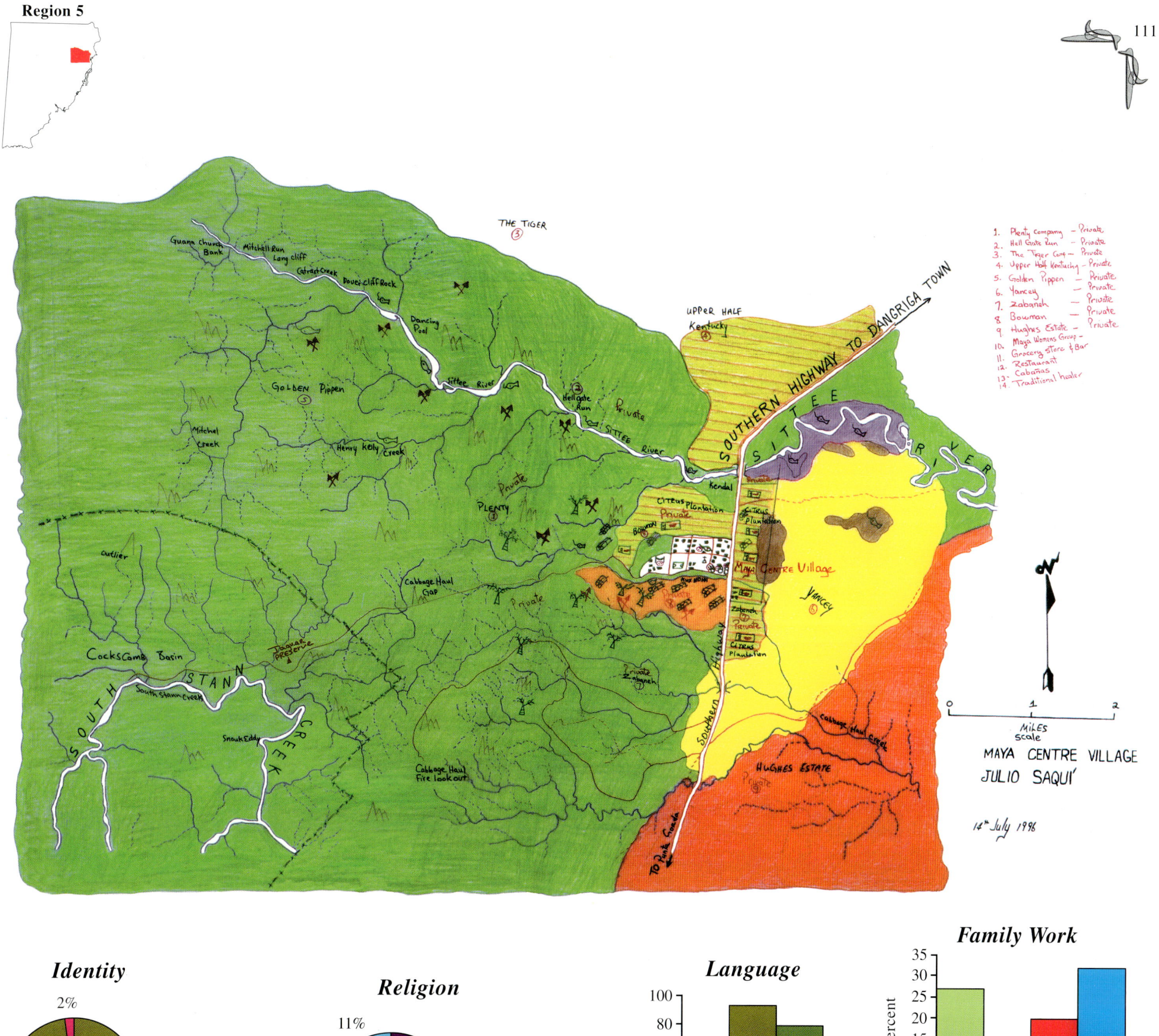

111

Map Legend

1. Plenty Company — Private
2. Hell Gate Run — Private
3. The Tiger Cry — Private
4. Upper Half Kentucky — Private
5. Golden Pippen — Private
6. Yancey — Private
7. Zabaneh — Private
8. Bowman — Private
9. Hughes Estate — Private
10. Maya Womens Group
11. Grocery Store & Bar
12. Restaurant
13. Cabañas
14. Traditional healer

MAYA CENTRE VILLAGE
JULIO SAQUI
14th July 1998

Identity
- Ke'kchi: 2%
- Mopan: 98%

Religion
- Catholic: 89%
- Other Christian: 11%

Language
(Ke'kchi, Mopan, English)

Family Work
(Farming, Raising Animals, Hunting, Fishing)

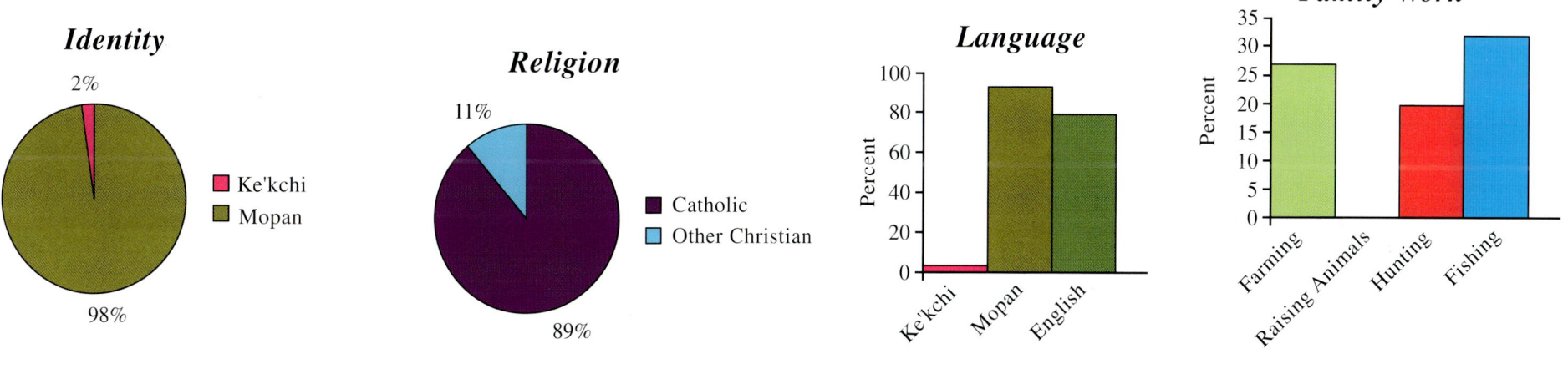

112

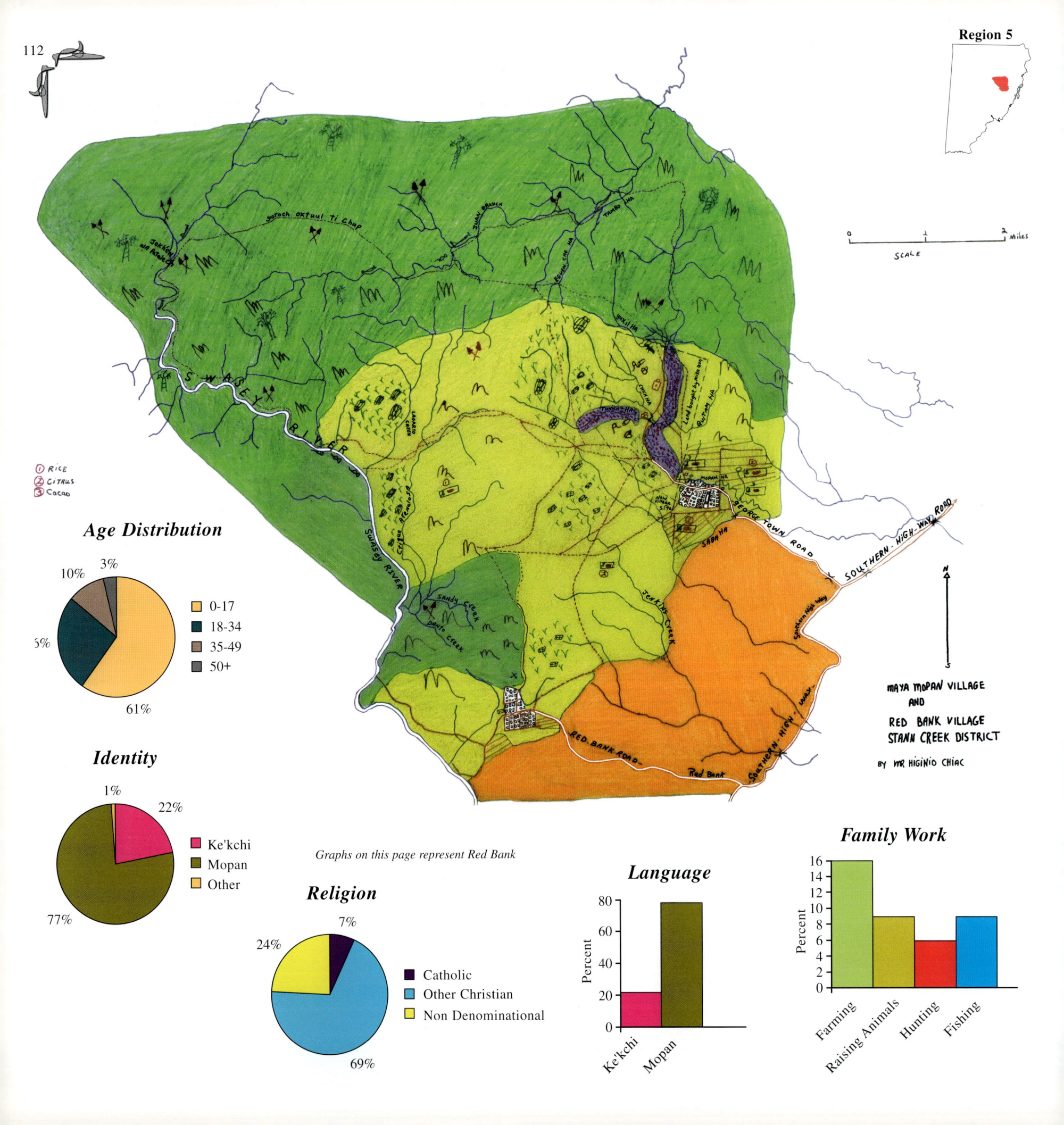

Region 5

① RICE
② CITRUS
③ CACAO

MAYA MOPAN VILLAGE
AND
RED BANK VILLAGE
STANN CREEK DISTRICT

BY MR HIGINIO CHIAC

Age Distribution

- 0-17: 61%
- 18-34: 5%
- 35-49: 10%
- 50+: 3%

Identity

- Ke'kchi: 22%
- Mopan: 77%
- Other: 1%

Graphs on this page represent Red Bank

Religion

- Catholic: 7%
- Other Christian: 69%
- Non Denominational: 24%

Language

Ke'kchi ~20%, Mopan ~80%

Family Work

Farming 16%, Raising Animals 9%, Hunting 6%, Fishing 9%

Red Bank

Population 176

Red Bank village was established on January 10, 1982, with only six families. It was developed along creeks and rivers where the soil is fertile. The banks of the river are high and the soil is a reddish color, giving Red Bank its name. It has historically been considered a place of beauty and a site for finding gold, which attracted many people. Later on, areas along the river became private land where banana industries were established.

Since 1982 the population has grown rapidly. Most of the people do farming and some work at the nearby industries. At present there are one hundred families consisting of Mopan and Ke'kchi Mayas. The Ke'kchi Mayas were refugees brought into the village by the government in 1992; they were in the Chiquibul area and are originally from Guatemala. Their migration to Belize was a result of ill treatment by the government of Guatemala. The people of Red Bank were not informed by the government and had no advance knowledge of the Ke'kchi arrival in the village. The cultural differences caused a conflict among the established Mopan people, but as time progressed the people of Red Bank and the Ke'kchi refugees agreed to cooperate and unite for the better development of the village.

Today there is a lot system in Red Bank where all of the villagers have surveyed lots. About 75 percent of the villagers have farmland; however, not all farmlands are fertile enough to grow staple food such as maize and beans, hence *milpa* is still practiced. Cash crops such as citrus are grown on a limited scale.

Tourism has accelerated since March of 1997 when it was publicized that the adjacent rainforest is the home of the endangered scarlet macaw, especially in the months of October through March. On May 27, 1997, the Scarlet Macaws Conservation Project was launched with a grant of BZ$150,000 [US$75,000] from the Global Environmental Facility. This grant also helps the women's group.

Age Distribution

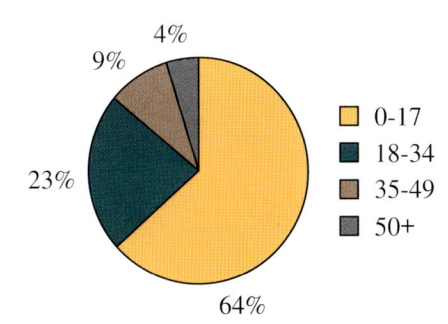

- 0-17: 64%
- 18-34: 23%
- 35-49: 9%
- 50+: 4%

Identity

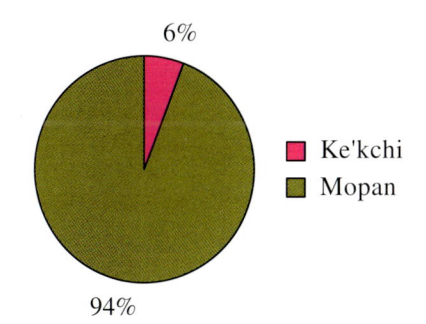

- Ke'kchi: 6%
- Mopan: 94%

Maya Mopan

Population 247

The village of Maya Mopan was established in 1975 by Elogio Sho, who came from San Antonio, Toledo District. The reason Mr. Sho moved out of Toledo was to find good land for farming. First, he had to negotiate with the government for land. He was very successful getting the land where the village is now. Mr. Sho called it by the name Maya Mopan, because all the settlers came from San Antonio, San Jose, and other surrounding Mopan villages in the Toledo District. He was also successful negotiating with the government for the village farmland, school, and church. At that time, the villagers started to do their *milpa* farming and pig raising, rice planting, and *matambre* along Alabama Creek northwest of the village. Maya Mopan is blessed with rich soil, Maya ruins, waterfalls, and high forest where the villagers do their hunting and live happily. At present, the village has gone into citrus and cacao farming. In 1984, an American missionary by the name of John Cullen came to the village of Maya Mopan and asked the people to join his church so that he could help them with their daily needs. He also requested 300 acres of land from the government, saying that it will be for the village, and asked the villagers to donate labor to plant fifty acres of citrus, so one day it will benefit the village. He also promised electricity and a hospital. The village gave him free labor but in the end John Cullen never kept his promises. In 1996, a man named Mike Dunken moved in and started to work the same land where the villagers gave their free labor for the citrus plantation. When the village council chairman asked Mr. Dunken if he knew what he was doing, Mr. Dunken said that he bought the land from John Cullen, and nobody can stop him from working it.

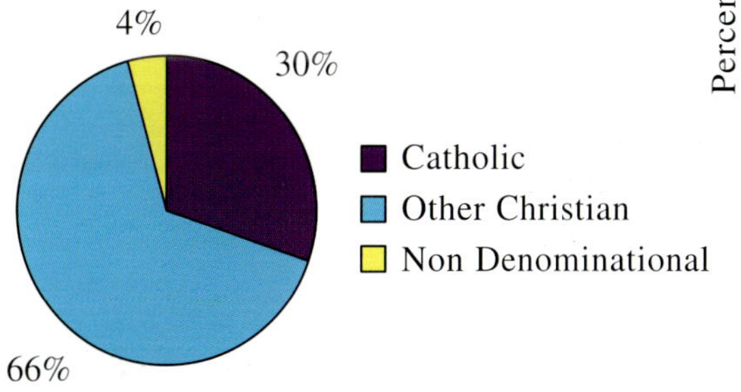

Graphs on this page represent Maya Mopan

Religion

- Catholic: 30%
- Other Christian: 66%
- Non Denominational: 4%

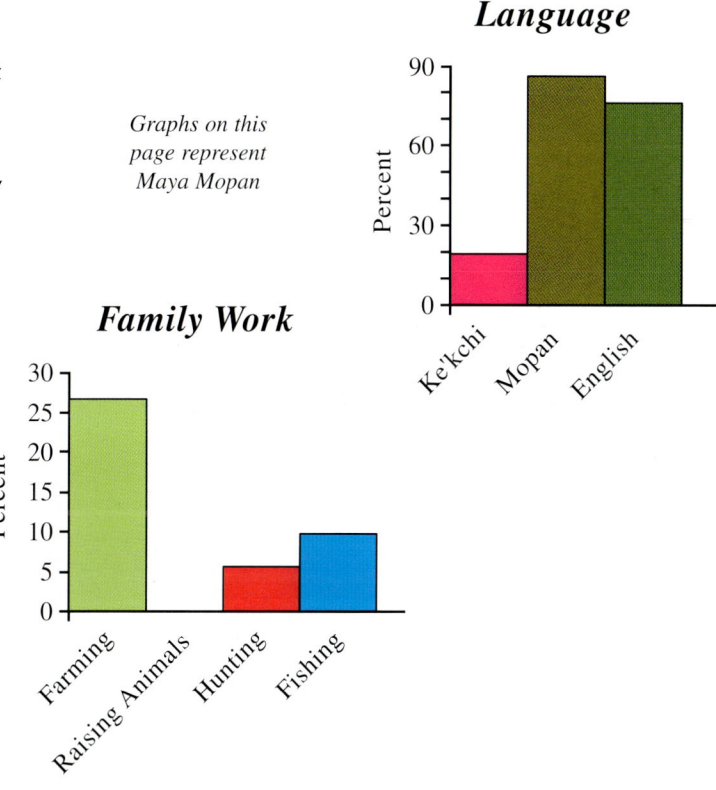

Family Work

- Farming: ~27%
- Raising Animals: 0%
- Hunting: ~6%
- Fishing: ~10%

Language

- Ke'kchi: ~18%
- Mopan: ~87%
- English: ~77%

San Roman

Population 275

Founded in June 1975 by Edilberto Canti and Jose Ical, the village had only five families by the end of the first year. At that time the settlement was named Waha Leaf. Dissatisfied with this name, Mr. Canti and the other settlers fought to change it. The one and only denomination existing at that time, the Catholic parish, helped fight to get the name of the settlement changed. After seven years of lobbying, the government finally agreed in 1982 to have the settlement name changed from Waha Leaf to its present name, San Roman village.

The traditional systems are farming, *milpa,* slash and burn, and planting of corn, beans, rice, and ground food. The traditional food is *caldo* made of corn tortillas and chicken. The traditional music is that of the marimba.

In 1988 a cacao cooperative was formed. It was founded by Edilberto Canti and funded by help from Progress Ltd, a non-governmental organization that helped ten farmers plant twenty acres of cacao.

In 1993 another cooperative was formed—a citrus cooperative again funded by Progress Ltd, which helped ten farmers plant some thirty acres of citrus and build a cement cooperative house measuring 24 x 35 feet. San Roman's present population stands at a figure of 275. It has two churches, Catholic and Baptist. There are two hand pumps for healthy drinking water, a community telephone, a health center, three shops, three school buses, and three private vehicles. The village of San Roman consists of pure Maya Indian people and three Jamaican families.

Santa Rosa

Population 157

In the year 1972, my father had some family problems so he decided to get out and look for bountiful soil in the southern Stann Creek region. There he started to farm. But before the year was finished, word came to him that the land he was working was private land. But soon, more people came from Toledo, just as my father is from the district of Toledo. Then the people were told that the land was not available to establish the village or farmland, so they came together and held a meeting to discuss where and how to find a piece of land. They went to Belmopan to ask for a piece of land from the government. They made more than one trip. At last they were appointed to a place called Pepper Camp, where they could farm as much as they wanted, on permanent trees. So they gathered the rest of the families and came to settle here. And that's how Santa Rosa village was founded in the year 1974. Of the twelve families that started the village, only four of them are still here.

Graphs shown represent Santa Rosa

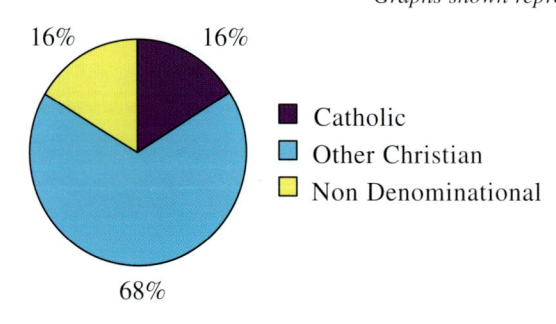

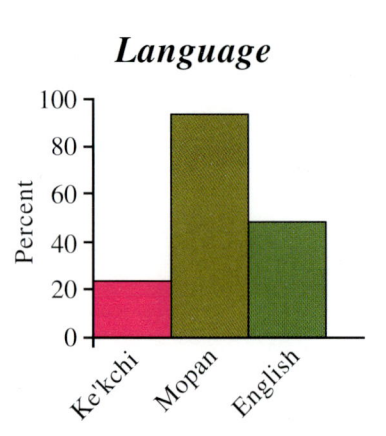

Age Distribution

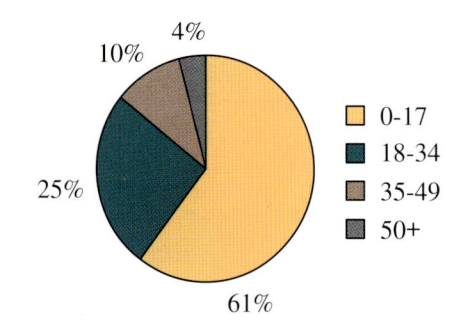

- 0-17: 61%
- 18-34: 25%
- 35-49: 10%
- 50+: 4%

Identity

- Ke'kchi: 5%
- Mopan: 95%

Religion

- Catholic: 16%
- Other Christian: 68%
- Non Denominational: 16%

Language

- Ke'kchi: ~23%
- Mopan: ~94%
- English: ~48%

Region 5

115

Santa Rosa
San Roman
MARCOS SHAL

Family Work

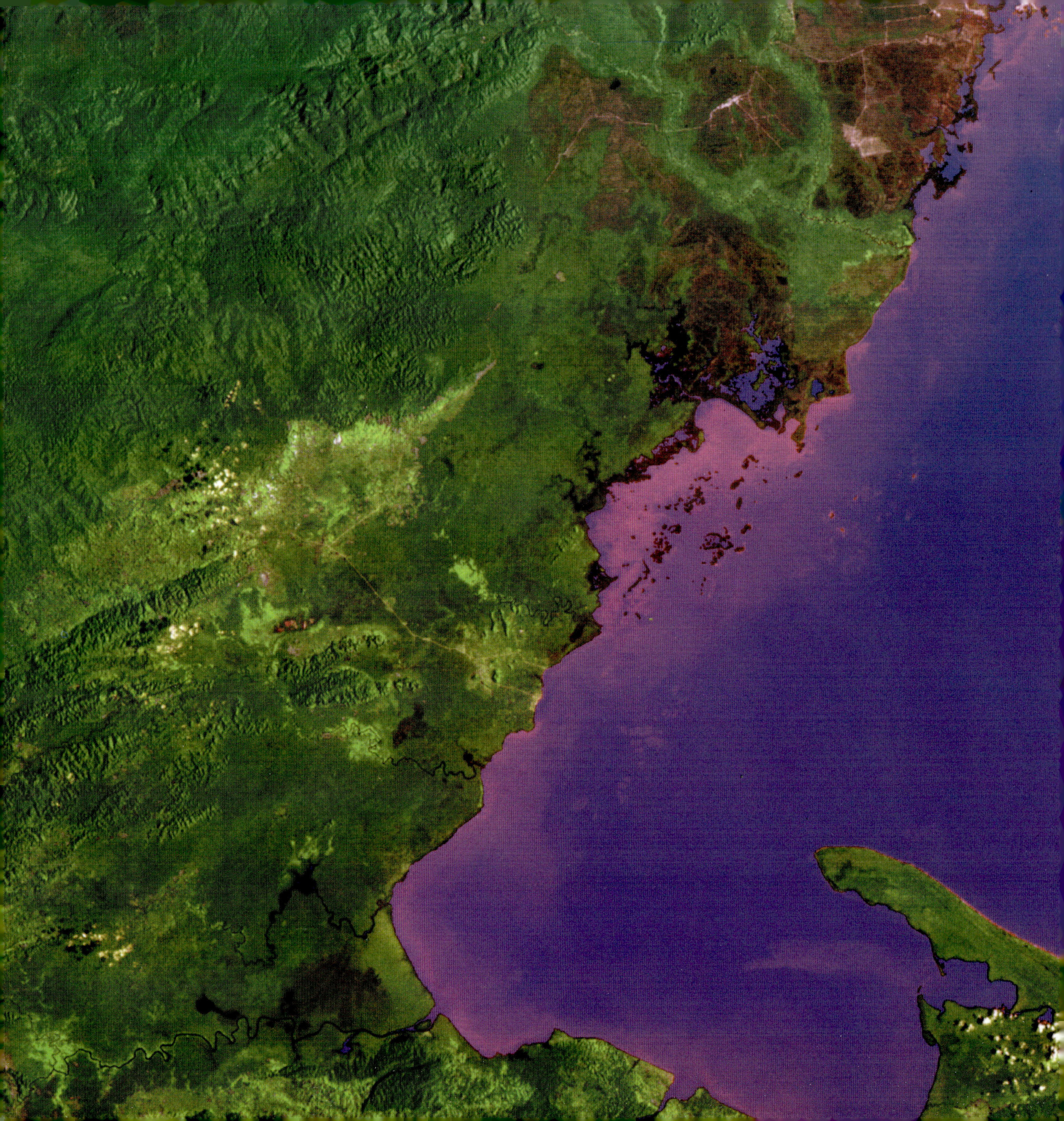

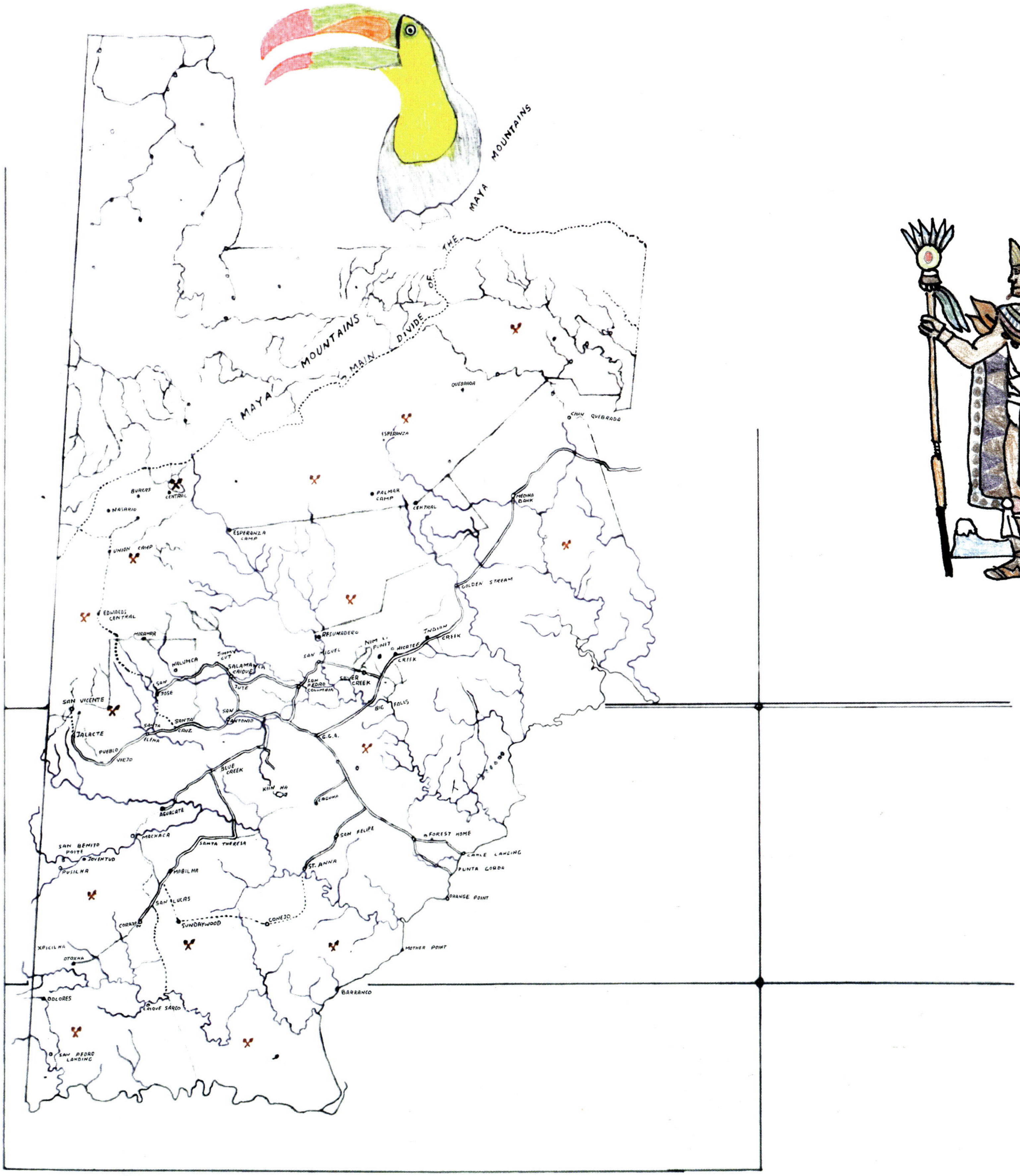

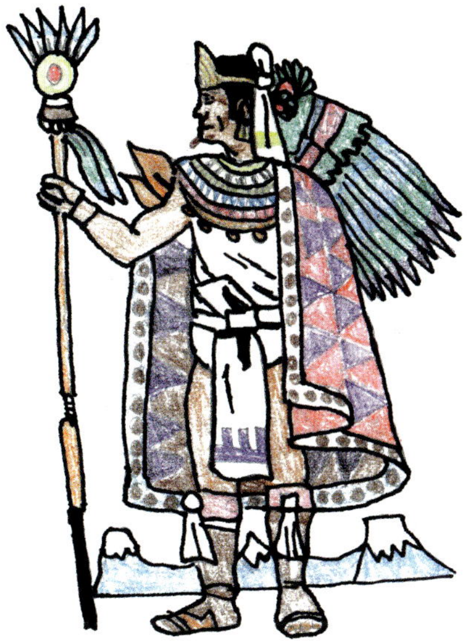

MMP

Community Services

Legend

- School
- Store
- Electricity
- Alcalde
- Arts & Crafts
- Medical Services
- Telephone
- Cornmill
- Government Office
- Bus Services

- Lakes
- Islands
- River
- Marsh
- Reefs
- Creek
- 800m Elev
- Population 0-199
- Small Road
- 600m Elev
- Population 200-399
- Large Road
- 400m Elev
- Population 400+
- District Border
- 200m Elev
- Non Maya Population
- International Border
- Foot Trail

Miles: 5 0 5 10 15

Community Services

As with every society, Maya villages have gone through changes. During the 1850s every Maya village was autonomous. It was self-sufficient. With the advent of education and transportation, villages accommodated themselves to these changes.

Several community services rose to satisfy the demands of expanding villages.

Each village has a village council charged with the responsibility of directing the growth of the community. Most villages now have a primary school, a community center, and an all-weather road. A few villages have community phones. A water supply system is found only in San Pedro Columbia and San Antonio. Health centers are found only in the villages of Santa Teresa, San Antonio, San Pedro Columbia, and Crique Sarco.

In the 1970s only the Catholic church was predominant in every village. Now almost every village has more than one religious denomination.

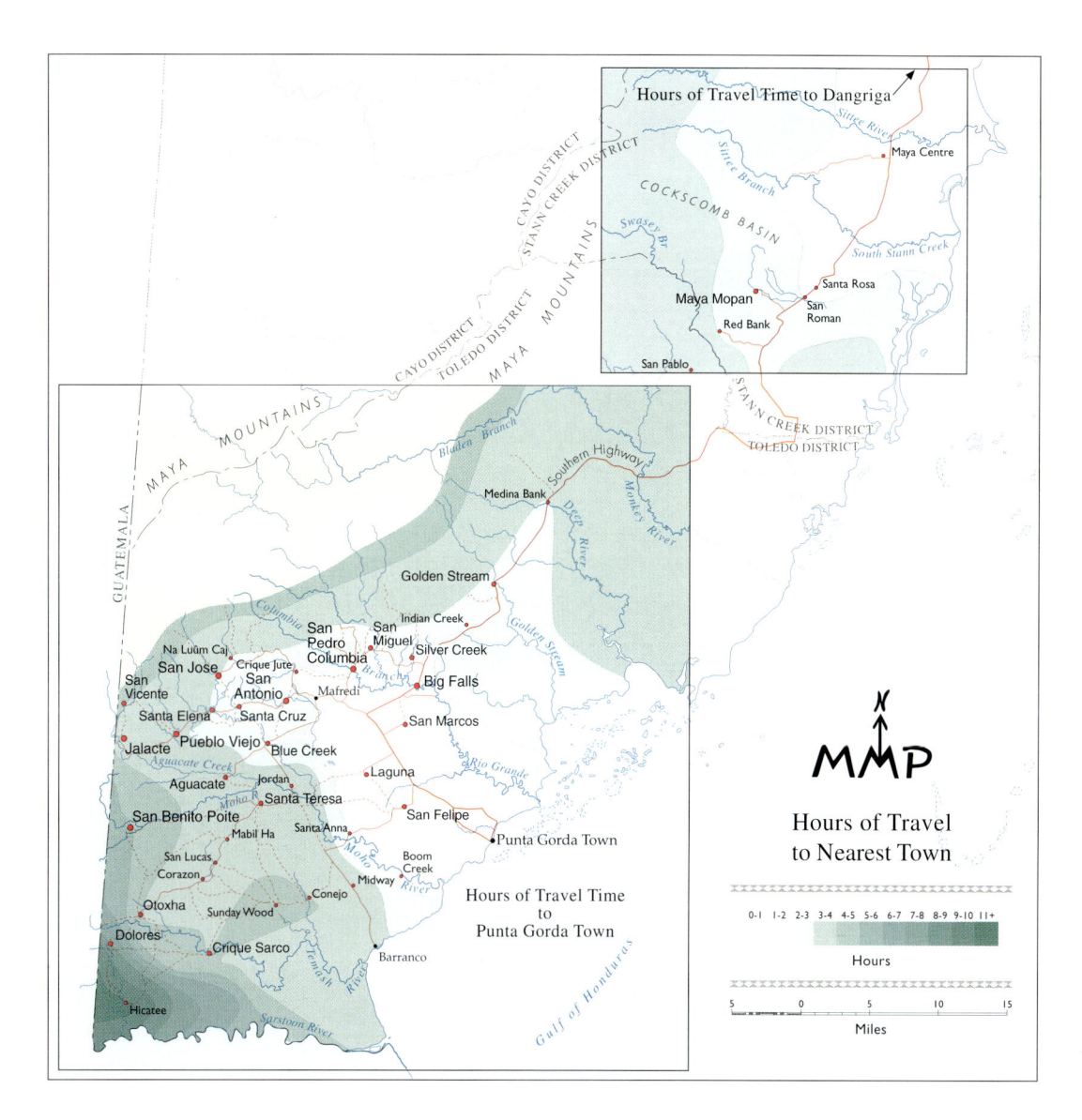

Modern Maya art

The Maya are gradually getting into ecotourism projects that bring many types of services for communities and tourists. This is a new venture for the Mayas.

Two major services needed are efficient widespread health services and secondary education. The only hospital in the region is remote for the people. They have to travel for several hours to Punta Gorda Town to see a doctor. Students have to attend high school away from their village. The only high school is situated in Punta Gorda Town.

In addition to this is the need for electricity in all villages. Rural electrification began taking place in the year 1993, and these services have been extended to Barranco, Santa Anna, Midway, San Felipe, Mafredi, San Pedro Columbia, and Big Falls. Expansion of rural electrification has been requested by rural citizens from the government of Belize and Belize Electric. However, no further development has occurred to date.

Tourism

In the early 1980s, tourism and ecotourism in southern Belize began to be encouraged. The Maya people formed groups to make available proper accommodations and resting places such as cabañas or *sha'an sho'yuk na* [Mopan] and *sursukil sha'nal cabl* [Ke'kchi], where inexpensive meals are prepared and rooms are available at a cheap rate. The Toledo Ecotourism Association has undertaken to create places at important sites where tourists can be accommodated in bird watching, sightseeing, enjoying waterfalls, caves, springs, ancient Maya monuments, and more.

Cohune Palm, tree of many uses. The leaves are used to thatch houses, the nuts for oil, and the heart of the tree for food (cohune cabbage).

Noh Sos Falls near San Antonio on the road to Santa Cruz—a popular picnic and recreation area.

The Maya began to adapt themselves to this new venture; more began to do work for tourist attractions; more and more places of importance are given priority for development.

Tourism has contributed financially to this venture. This has enabled both Maya ethnic groups to participate as tour guides, hotel owners, and food vendors; they also make embroidery, works of art, carvings, sculptures, weavings, baskets, *cuxtals*, bracelets of marking thread, clay products, pottery, and much more.

Tourism in Belize has generally contributed foreign earnings. Eventually Belize will be largely dependent on tourist income.

Tourism has called for greater availability of Maya arts and crafts, such as woven baskets.

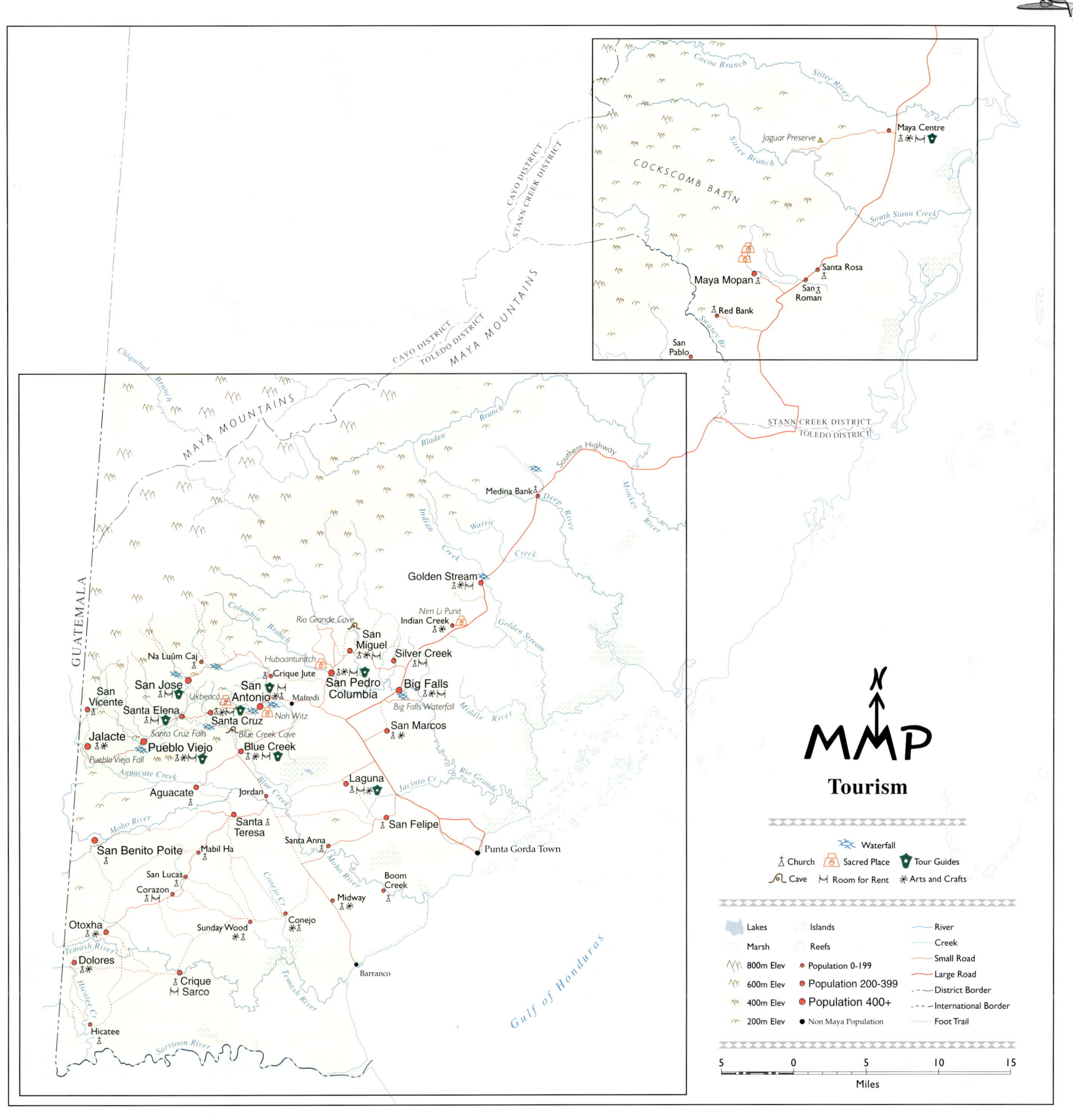

Tourism

Outside Problems

Maya leaders at the Atlantic Industries Ltd. sawmill outside Big Falls

The land tenure issue, with regard to Maya land rights, is the overarching problem, from which several other issues threatening Mayan existence originate. The two chief issues are the logging of Maya lands by foreign companies, and the negative social impacts of the paving of the Southern Highway. In addition to land-related problems, there are other social problems such as the ongoing threat to indigenous religion, the looting of Mayan ruins by foreigners, the high illiteracy rate among Mayas, and the general problem of access to political power.

Logging

Since 1995, the Toledo District has been doled out to seventeen different logging companies, both foreign and Belizean. None of them are Mayan. These concessions, granted by the government of Belize, disregard the uniqueness of these rainforests and were made without the participation of local Maya communities. The Toledo Atlantic International logging company, which has received the largest concession, is backed by a Malaysian company. They have licenses to log over 159,000 acres bordering seven Ke'kchi Mayan communities in the southern part of the Toledo District, directly affecting the streams where these people bathe and get their drinking water, and threatening their traditional hunting grounds. In addition, another Malaysian-backed company known as Atlantic Industries Limited has permission to log 24,000 acres of rainforest in the Columbia River Forest Reserve and the Maya Mountain Forest Reserve. Small as this concession may be, it is probably the most damaging in terms of environmental degradation and is directly threatening the existence of fifteen Maya communities bordering these reserves. For example, all of the streams passing through these communities originate in the areas designated for logging.

The Forest Department has said that all "social, economic, environmental, and ecological concerns have been addressed," but the lack of enforcement undermines the Forest Department's goals. Without any

Thomas Choco, Chair of the Ke'kchi Council of Belize, Estevan Assi, Chair of the Toledo Alcaldes Association, and Cayetano Ico, executive member of the TMCC, discuss the logging threat to Maya survival.

enforcement of the eighty-three rules outlined in the Columbia River Forest Management Plan, the work of the Forest Planning and Management Project in designing a model plan for the sustainable logging of the Columbia Forest Reserve is meaningless. For example, measures taken to control log extraction are not being carried out because there is rarely a Forest Department officer on site at the logging activity!

On November 16, 1995, a team of observers, representing the Toledo Maya Cultural Council (TMCC) and the Ke'kchi Council of Belize (KCB), walked to the Atlantic Industries logging site north of Jimmy Cut in the Columbia Forest Reserve, near the village of San Jose. On that day, bulldozers were expanding the logging road and log hunters were in the forest searching for specimens of hardwood to cut. According to the logging concession granted to the Atlantic Company, there should be absolutely no felling or removing of logs from this section of forest (#25 in the Columbia River Forest Management Plan) until the year 2007, but area clearing by bulldozers and construction of sawmill facilities have already begun. The observers counted eleven large trees within a two-mile area that had been cut without Forest Department approval. None of the logs or stumps displayed the required marks of the Forest Department or the Atlantic Company.

As long as the Forest Department is significantly understaffed, enforcement of rules will continue to be a major obstacle to sustainable forestry in Belize. For example, revenues and taxes from cut logs will probably never be fully collected by the government. The Atlantic Company has already broken several of the concession laws. Why should we trust that they will pay all of their taxes? The people of Belize should not be fooled into thinking that the logging concessions must be allowed in order to raise funds for our country. We will lose the precious national heritage that can only increase in value over the years. A company that disregards the guidelines set up for sustainability does not deserve to manage the area.

The protection of rainforests will not only benefit the Maya, but Belize and the world as well. The Columbia River Forest

Maya leaders outside the Atlantic Industries sawmill near Big Falls

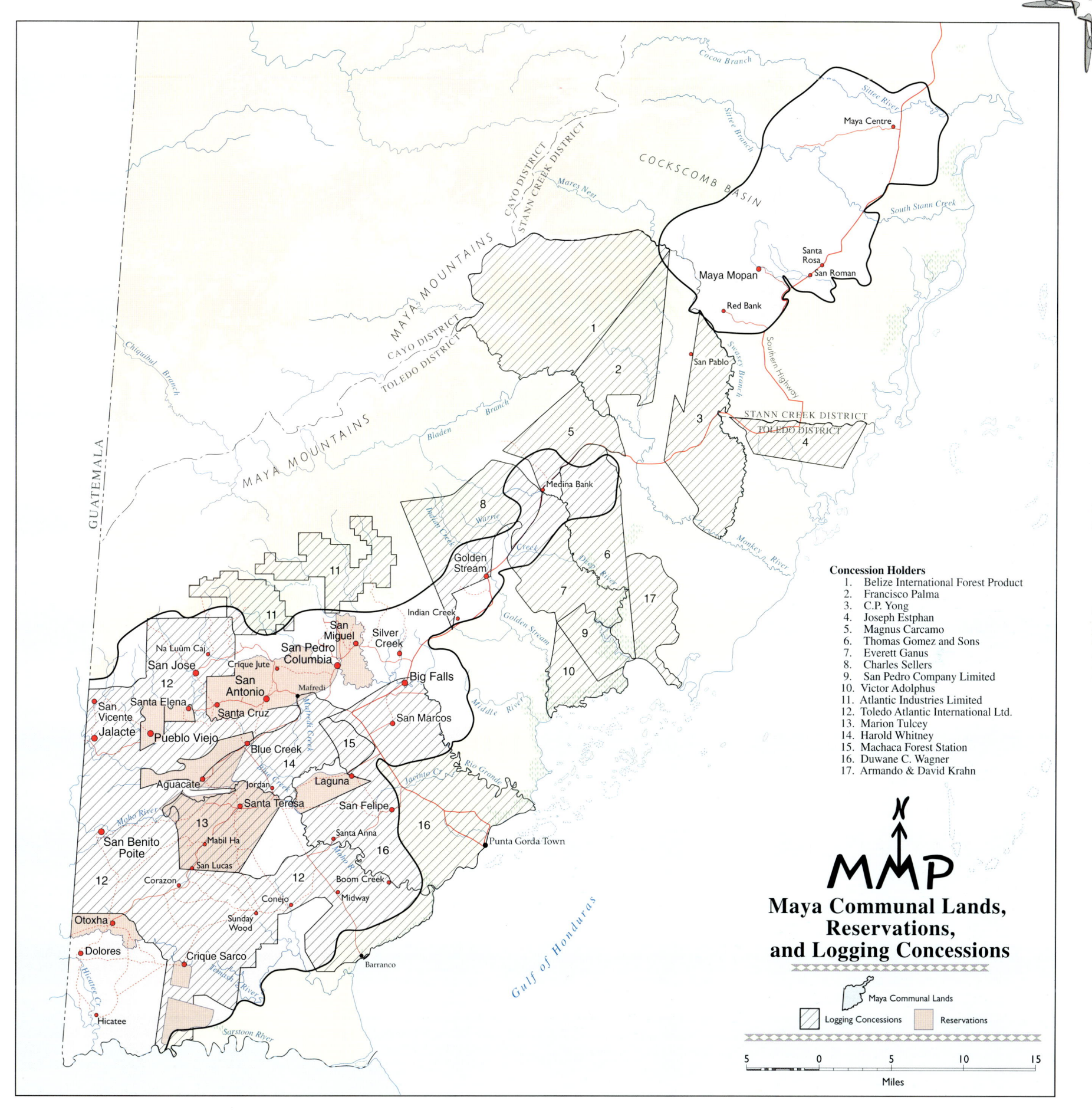

Maya Communal Lands, Reservations, and Logging Concessions

Concession Holders
1. Belize International Forest Product
2. Francisco Palma
3. C.P. Yong
4. Joseph Estphan
5. Magnus Carcamo
6. Thomas Gomez and Sons
7. Everett Ganus
8. Charles Sellers
9. San Pedro Company Limited
10. Victor Adolphus
11. Atlantic Industries Limited
12. Toledo Atlantic International Ltd.
13. Marion Tulcey
14. Harold Whitney
15. Machaca Forest Station
16. Duwane C. Wagner
17. Armando & David Krahn

Legend:
- Maya Communal Lands
- Logging Concessions
- Reservations

Atlantic Industries establishing a sawmill in the Columbia River Forest Reserve next to San Jose village, November 1995

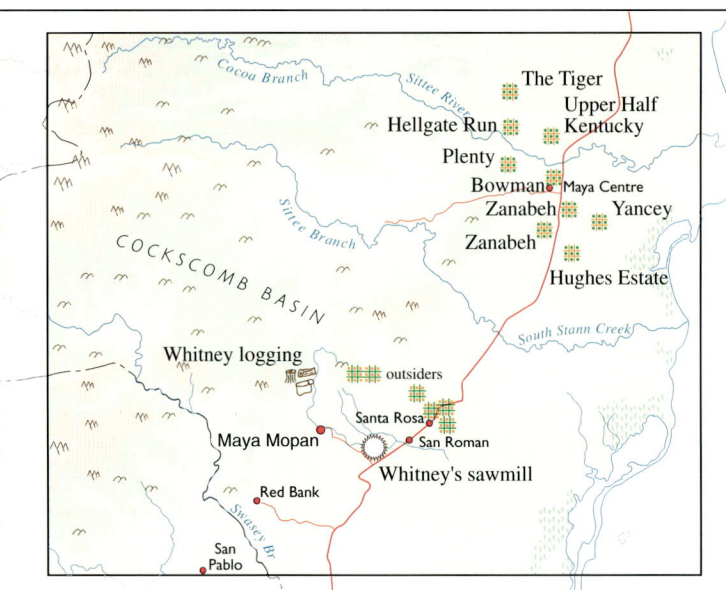

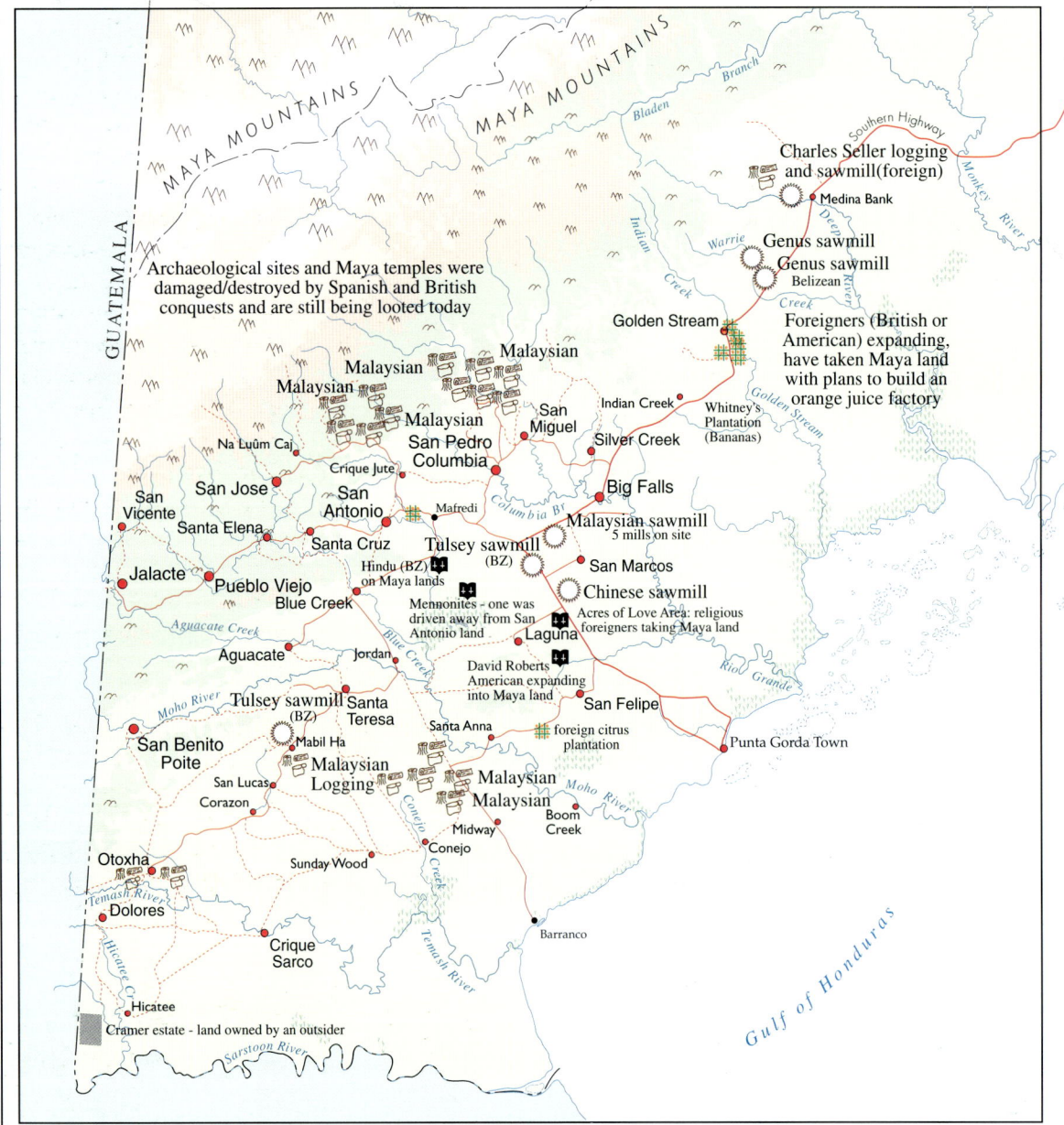

Outside Threats to Maya Lands

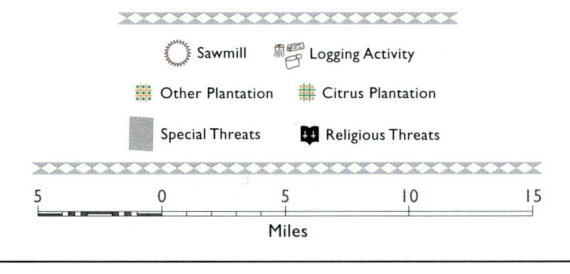

Legend:
- Sawmill
- Logging Activity
- Other Plantation
- Citrus Plantation
- Special Threats
- Religious Threats

Scale: 5 0 5 10 15 Miles

Cockscomb Basin inset (locations):
- The Tiger
- Upper Half Kentucky
- Hellgate Run
- Plenty
- Bowman
- Maya Centre
- Zanabeh
- Yancey
- Zanabeh
- Hughes Estate
- Whitney logging
- outsiders
- Santa Rosa
- Maya Mopan
- San Roman
- Whitney's sawmill
- Red Bank
- San Pablo

Main map locations and notes:

- Charles Seller logging and sawmill (foreign) — Medina Bank
- Genus sawmill
- Genus sawmill (Belizean)
- Golden Stream
- Foreigners (British or American) expanding, have taken Maya land with plans to build an orange juice factory
- Archaeological sites and Maya temples were damaged/destroyed by Spanish and British conquests and are still being looted today
- Malaysian (multiple)
- San Miguel
- Indian Creek
- Whitney's Plantation (Bananas)
- Silver Creek
- Na Luûm Caj
- Crique Jute
- San Pedro Columbia
- San Jose
- San Antonio
- Mafredi
- Big Falls
- Malaysian sawmill — 5 mills on site
- San Vicente
- Santa Elena
- Santa Cruz
- Tulsey sawmill (BZ)
- San Marcos
- Jalacte
- Pueblo Viejo
- Blue Creek
- Hindu (BZ) on Maya lands
- Chinese sawmill
- Mennonites - one was driven away from San Antonio land
- Acres of Love Area: religious foreigners taking Maya land
- Laguna
- Aguacate
- Jordan
- David Roberts American expanding into Maya land
- San Felipe
- Tulsey sawmill (BZ)
- Santa Teresa
- San Benito Poite
- Mabil Ha
- Santa Anna
- foreign citrus plantation
- Punta Gorda Town
- San Lucas
- Corazon
- Malaysian Logging
- Malaysian
- Midway
- Conejo
- Boom Creek
- Otoxha
- Sunday Wood
- Dolores
- Crique Sarco
- Barranco
- Hicatee
- Cramer estate - land owned by an outsider

Rivers/features: Sarstoon River, Temash River, Moho River, Rio Grande, Deep River, Bladen Branch, Monkey River, Maya Mountains, Guatemala, Gulf of Honduras, Stann Creek District / Toledo District

MMP

Reserve has an invaluable ecological significance. Located in the northwestern corner of the Toledo District, it borders Guatemala to the west, Chiquibul National Park and Bladen Nature Reserve to the north, the Maya Mountains Forest Reserve to the east, and several Mayan Indian communities and Reservations to the south (see Map of Sanctuaries, Reserves, and Parks, page 126). In 1993, Conservation International conducted a biological assessment of the Columbia River Forest Reserve and concluded that "protection of these forests is a high conservation priority for the country." The scientists stated that "we can say without any hesitation that the evergreen forests of this area are of great national and international importance as a reservoir of biological diversity. Our studies strongly indicate that the most species-rich plant and animal communities in Belize occur in the Columbia River Forest Reserve." Botanists documented diverse local flora that may surpass 1,500 species, which represents a high percentage of all plant species in the country. Several plant species identified are unique to this area, including fifteen species not previously seen in Belize. A recently described tree and a mountain palm are known only in this area and in Alta Verapaz, Guatemala.

Over 224 bird species were recorded, including 43 wintering bird species from Eastern North America. According to the survey, one bird is of special concern: "the Keel-billed Motmot needs special concern because deforestation can directly threaten its geographical and ecological range. It is also worth noting that thirty-five species found are rare in the country." The biological team also found three previously unrecorded species of frogs, indicating the unique qualities of this particular forest. Additionally, the reserve is "a critically important watershed that traps and recycles the heavy rainfall that is so critical to the productivity of agricultural lands [in Toledo]. The removal of forest cover ... will undoubtedly have strong and lasting impacts on the rural economy of southern Belize."

The logging practices we have observed threaten this fragile ecological balance. In contrast, the Maya system of agriculture has proven to be more environmentally friendly. Mayan farming methods use local plants to supply nutrients to the soil and help stop erosion all year round. This is crucial in an area that receives 180 inches of rainfall every year. In addition, we are moving towards a more intensive form of sustainable agriculture by promoting the planting of permanent crops such as cacao and citrus. The transition, though, will take time. Logging the Columbia River Forest Reserve will not enhance our goal of sustainable agriculture. Although some farmers have *milpas* near the Forest Reserve, they do not represent a threat to the existence of the rainforest compared to the intensive logging operations to be carried out by the Malaysians.

Julian Cho, Santiago Coh, Santos Coc, Estevan Assi, and Juan Choc inside the Atlantic Industries Ltd. sawmill, Big Falls

The Southern Highway

The logging situation we are confronting is not an isolated issue. All of the same questions about environmental justice are posed by the upgrading of the Southern Highway. Paving this road will be a blessing and a curse to the people of Toledo. It will bring much revenue to the district and tie in this "forgotten district" with the rest of the nation. This area is the last frontier to be exploited for mineral, marine, and agricultural resources, and it is a potential haven for government and private enterprises to expand their profits. However, the incorporation of Toledo into the rest of the country may further disadvantage indigenous communities. The Maya are the poorest people of the nation, unable to tap into the benefits of increased commerce. The land tenure question, regarding the control of the land on which we live, must be resolved before the highway is completed. We want to make it clear up front that we are not against development. But neither do we support development which would have lasting negative impacts on the social structure of the local people. The Maya are unprepared for mass development projects because of their lack of education, health services, transportation between villages, and political voice. The road is not being paved to benefit the indigenous community, but the wealthiest people of the nation. Imagine what could happen with the arrival of rich investors looking for land to buy or sell if they are allowed a free hand in the vicinity of the Maya communities.

Heavy equipment in the Columbia River Forest Reserve, November 1995

The principle of stewardship over our natural resources, which makes Maya agriculture superior to logging, would inevitably be undermined by the "mine-and-run" philosophy of land speculators.

As people concerned with the fate of the environment and social justice, we must ask ourselves: who stands to benefit from the upgrading of this road? The answer can be found by examining the interests of those who are pushing the project. Consultation of the Mayas has been minimal, and the flow of information has been essentially one-directional. This is true even with our supposed participation in the Environmental, Social, Technical Assistance Program (ESTAP), created by the government of Belize and the Inter-American Development Bank (IDB). Representatives from local communities were invited to sit on the steering committee, but their voices are consistently ignored. This superficial representation frustrates community leaders, as government plans hatched up in Belmopan are implemented on Mayan lands. Clearly, those who stand to gain the most are the large commercially-exporting banana and citrus companies who would love to expand their fields in the south, and will do so if given the opportunity, regardless of what local people say.

Other Problems

The Mayas of Toledo are faced with numerous, severe socio-economic and political problems. The educational system is woefully inadequate, and consequently the illiteracy rate of the Mayas is the highest in the country. The Mayas are often called the "poorest of the poor" in Belize, with government statistics indicating that the average annual family income is only US $600 per year. Basic social infrastructure, including health care, transportation services, and communication services, is sorely underdeveloped. To compound these problems, the Mayas lack a means to redress their grievances, as we have absolutely no political representation in the government of Belize and are treated as the "forgotten people" of our own country.

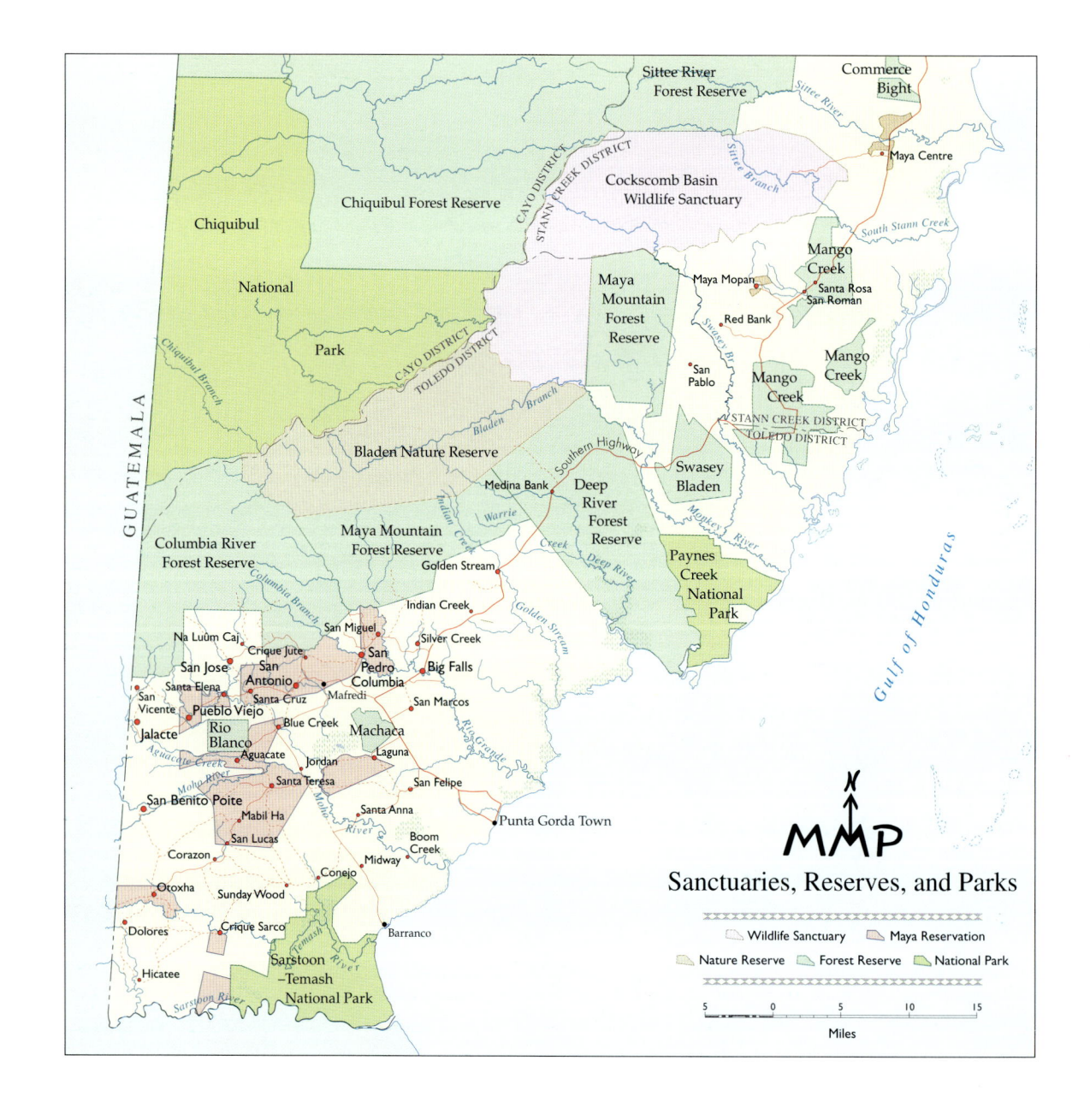

Maya Land Use and Outside Threats

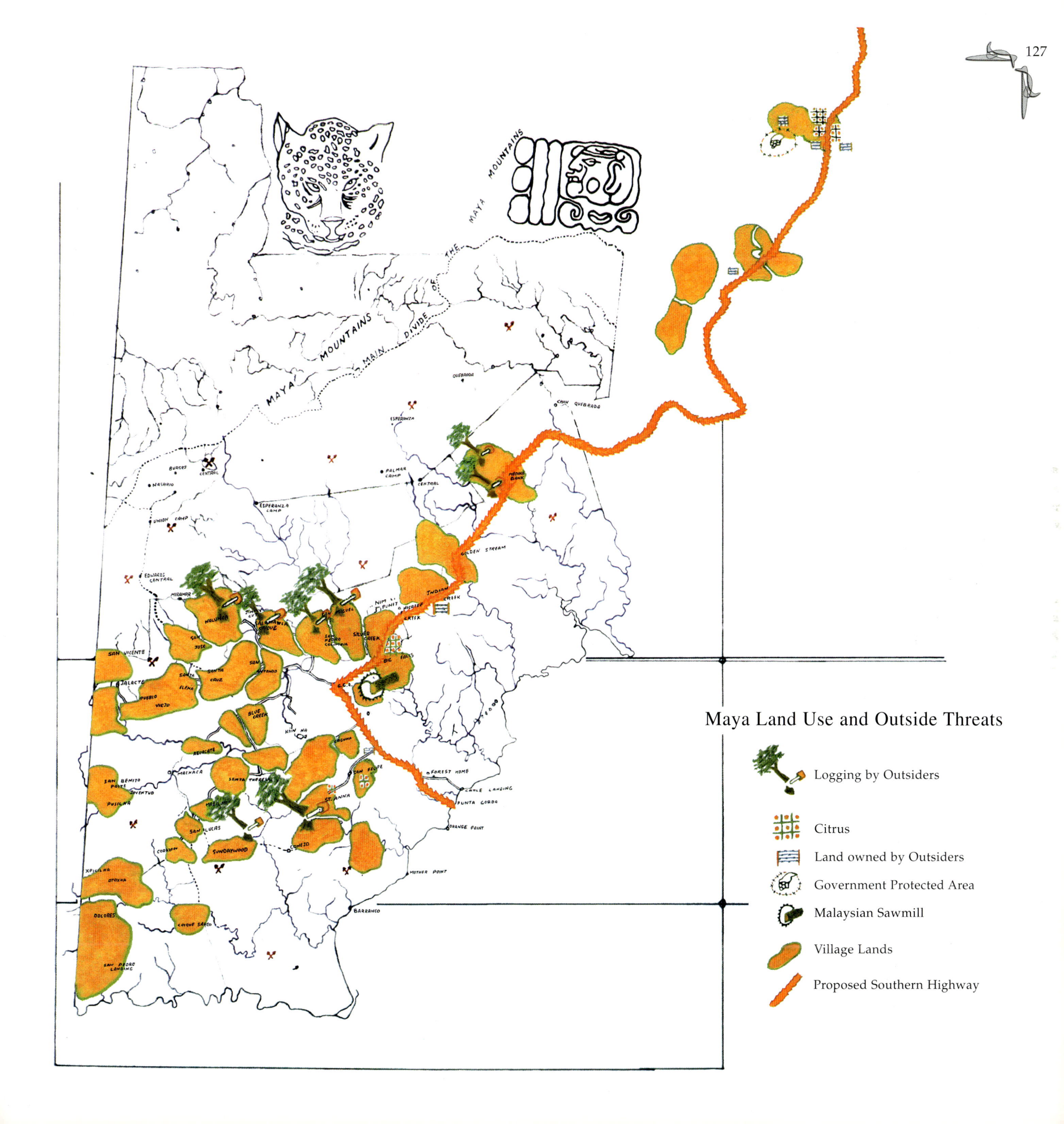

- Logging by Outsiders
- Citrus
- Land owned by Outsiders
- Government Protected Area
- Malaysian Sawmill
- Village Lands
- Proposed Southern Highway

Special Topics

Hipolita Ico with nephew

Carmela Salam of San Antonio with necklaces

Women's Groups

In most villages in the Toledo District, women contribute significantly to the growth and improvement of entrepreneurship that relates to development. In the district, Mayan women are active in selecting the type of venture they choose to pursue. In all Mayan villages, women group together to establish some type of development. Projects are drafted through the assistance of NGOs involved. These projects undertake to build centers for a cornmill, rice huller, arts and crafts, pottery, weaving, carving, thread making, and calabash preparation, just to mention a few. The women are very successful in the search for funding.

Production is well on its way in many of the activities mentioned. Recently a craft center was erected in Punta Gorda Town to house productions from various Maya villages for market. This center serves as a main outlet for these products. The Fajina Craft Center has opened for the marketing of baskets, clay pots, bracelets made out of thread, beads, embroidery, clay earrings, and other crafts made by the women's groups in the villages. The Fajina Center is funded by donor agencies.

Maya women work hard to keep their households clean and also work along with their husbands in the plantations. Although a man maintains the family financially, the woman has a very important role to play. When the man is out working for money she ensures that everything goes well in the family. They work along with other women communally for the benefit of the village. They are serious, happy, and approachable in their homes.

San Antonio Women's Group

In San Antonio they have five women's groups. The only group interviewed here was the Tiger Women's Group.

Miss Teodora Castellano is the Chairlady. She has forty-six members. Due to rain, only twenty-three were present for the interview. Within the group, they decided to build a craft shop where they could market their products. The size of the land for the building is 14 x 20 yards. They also want to open a small restaurant, they said.

I interviewed the women who make the baskets, clay pots, calendar-days, and calendar-months. Some create toucan pictures on cloth. According to Miss Teodora Castellano, she would like to see more development.

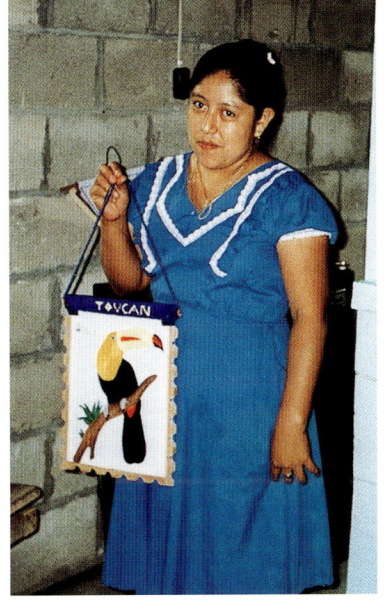

Women's group meeting to discuss how women can benefit from the International Farmers Aid for Development program

Felicima Coc from Crique Jute with embroidered art

The first conversation was with Miss Ambrosia Bol from Crique Jute, who was embroidering a picture of a jaguar on cloth. She said she did not do it all day, just half-time. She will sell it for BZ$40 [US$20]. She learned this skill with the group.

Miss Felicima Coc of Crique Jute was making a toucan picture on cloth. How did she learn? She also said from the group. She just does it part time, not all day. According to her, it takes three weeks to make one of the pictures. She will sell it for BZ$20 [US$10].

San Antonio Women's Group

Miss Jacinta Choc spoke about baskets. She said she gets the *jipijapa* from the bush and boils it, which is a lot of work. She sits down to weave. She said it takes two weeks to make one basket, not working all day. She also said she did it part-time, depending on the size of basket. A big one sells for BZ$85 [US$42.50].

Miss Amelia Coc works on clay pots. She makes them from clay collected from the river or creek banks. It's a special clay, she said. She can make clay pots big and small as well as bracelets. She sells a small pot for BZ$5 [US$3.50].

Miss Prudencia Coc, from San Antonio, works on embroidery. She learned it from her mother when she was young so she could do her own embroidery work, but she also sews for sale. She is member of a group. She does it part-time also. An embroidered blouse costs BZ$45 [US$22.50].

Antonia Pop and Claudia Saqui in the office of the Maya Centre Women's Group

Miss Maria Oh, Crique Jute, works on placemats to set dishes on a table. She makes them out of straw. Tourists buy them for BZ$5 [US$2.50] each. She said she works part-time and it takes one week to make one placemat.

Miss Adela Bolon of San Antonio makes belts and waist straps. She weaves them and it takes time. One belt takes two weeks. One woman's belt costs BZ$5 [US$2.50] or more depending on the size. She learned this craft from the group.

Miss Angela Chun from San Antonio makes Mayan calendars. She does not know what it means. She learned from Donatila Chun. One calendar costs BZ$20 [US$10]. She also works on them part-time.

Miss Felicima Coc from San Antonio makes baskets from *bay'l* [Ke'kchi] or *buyul* [Mopan] obtained in the forest. Her husband also works on baskets. It takes him one week to make one, part-time. It sells for BZ$20 [US$10], depending on the size.

Miss Clara Cum makes clay pots with a special clay mix. It takes one week to mold. She works for her use only. She sells a pot when it is ordered by someone. Depending on the size, a big one costs BZ$30 [US$25].

Miss Teodora was interviewed with the long dress she has used from the time she was engaged. It is the way the Mayas used to dress. It's very respectful to wear a long dress, she said. She would like to see the younger generation use a long dress instead

Victoria Coh from San Antonio with a basket

of the modern style. But she said they have an excuse: the long dress costs more, is heavy to wash, and takes more time to sew. Today some of the younger girls use pants, she said. She did not like to see it. She would prefer the longer dress. Everybody agrees on this.

The members of the San Antonio Tiger Women's Group were very proud to be interviewed and pleased to explain how they strive to improve their group.

We support the development and increased involvement of women leaders in

Celestina Pop with carving

Maya woman with an embroidered calendar

our movement to preserve our land, culture, and resources. Although women are nominated, they often decline to become leaders. We have identified the following obstacles to the meaningful integration of women:

• Women do not have the same access to education and often lack literacy required for leadership.

• Women lack the experience of what role an organization plays in achieving goals.

• Women are not exposed in their daily life experience to villages outside Toledo.

• Women's husbands do not always support their efforts to become involved.

• Women often lack skills that would make it possible for them to market their arts and crafts effectively.

Maya Centre Women's Group

Celestina Pop and Ophelia Pop of Maya Centre

Anna Bolon, Josepha Cho, Dora Pau, and Rufina Bolon of Maya Centre

Recommendations

1) Women leaders should be trained to speak for the benefit of their group or community.

2) The woman leader's family and community should support her so she can dedicate herself to attend all available training, workshops, and conferences, after which she will come back to the community to share what she experienced and learned.

3) Efforts to find funding locally and/or internationally should include women's activities and technical assistance for women's involvement. Women should participate in raising money for these activities.

4) In order to promote better leadership skills among group members and to make women leaders available to partake in community development, we support family spacing.

5) The promotion and marketing of women's arts and crafts will be assisted through the development of brochures with pictures and prices of high-quality items for sale, to be issued both locally and internationally.

6) In July of 1997 the Maya women came together to begin a Maya women's organization. The association would serve as a platform for women's development needs. Pulcheria Teul has been organizing the women to become active and to assert their voices in the development of Toledo.

Ophelia Pop and Ramona Pop at the cornmill in Maya Centre. The cornmill has liberated women from much food production work. Now there is time to diversify women's labor.

Maya Youth

Mayan youth and teenagers find many ways of using their leisure time productively. Some of these ways are education, work, and recreation.

Education: Some young Mayans get opportunities for a higher level of education beyond primary level. These young people are considered elites in their villages. Usually in these rural communities, older people encourage them and help students to try their best. In society they are supposed to show more responsibility and discipline.

Boy Scouts, San Jose village, July 1996

Domigo Pau of Big Falls and Juan Ash of Laguna

Work: Maya teenagers who don't get an opportunity for higher studies usually find jobs such as masonry and carpentry. These people are also respected for helping to construct and develop the community. Other youths who don't find jobs simply help their parents in the fields and at home.

Recreation: Both studying and working young people engage in recreation. After coming from school or work, youngsters find ways to relax and have fun such as playing ball (football, basketball, or volleyball), swimming, talking to friends, or reading and drawing. By doing this young people develop themselves both physically and mentally, and become conscious of the outer world, which prevents them from getting into using drugs (smoking and drinking) and also helps them keep out of trouble.

We support the participation of youth in culture, traditional ways of life, and preservation of our land and resources. In some villages youth have undertaken activities like gardening, painting the school, starting a library, fund-raising for projects like a cement block-making machine, and getting involved with farming, poultry, and pig raising. In many villages, however, there are no activities for the youth, and some villages have only sports as an activity.

Some young people have one parent missing while growing up and have no role model to look up to. There is no one to put them to work. They are forgetting their culture. For example, they refuse to speak their language and are ashamed of their clothing style and music. Education is a problem because the only high school is in Punta Gorda Town, which is far from many villages, and it does not teach our children about Maya culture and language.

We see education as necessary to preserve our culture. So it is mandatory to help our youths understand the importance of Maya culture.

Members of Saving Animals, Vegetation, and Environment (SAVE), Silver Creek

Recommendations

1) Establishment of a high school in San Antonio or San Pedro Columbia. This high school will teach languages (English, Mopan, and Ke'kchi), mathematics, vocational and technical courses, as well as arts and crafts.

2) Establishment of long-term income-producing activities in the villages other than agriculture, such as small factories to press jams from local fruits.

3) Land must be made available for the use of young people.

4) Training and education for youth in youth dynamics.

Cooperatives

In the early 1970s a business known as the Southern Bee Keeper Cooperative, in San Antonio, began producing honey for the export market. Production of honey was expanded and many more members were registered to this viable project in other villages like San Pedro Columbia, San Miguel, Santa Cruz, and Santa Elena. Honey production began to decline in 1985 because of some type of mismanagement. Very little production is taking place at present.

Another obstacle to honey production is the swarming of the "killer bees" or African bees in Belize. Very little is done about this problem. It has set back honey production.

San Pedro Columbia Rice Grower Cooperative began operation in 1965 and has expanded into mechanized farming. This cooperative worked well for nearly fifteen years but began to decline in 1985. This cooperative does not exist any longer.

Rio Grande Cooperative is the only operating cooperative in the village of San Miguel. Its members produce mechanized rice and their product is sold to the Marketing Board in Belize. This cooperative is operating to date.

Recommendations

1) Cooperatives should operate according to a plan that includes by-laws, with proper management to keep up its activities.

2) Leaders need training to properly direct the activities. They must be strong, with the full cooperation of the villagers. Leaders must consult with villages for their ideas, and not use a village's name without consent of the people.

3) Cooperatives should be organized to share profits and activities among villagers, not among a family. The proceeds should benefit the entire village.

4) If a cooperative does not succeed the first time, the people should let others form a new group to try again.

5 When funding is received to form a cooperative, or a loan is made, the money must be spent wisely and properly.

6) Members of the group should be willing to work voluntarily sometimes.

Economic Activities to Further Maya Development

The Mayas of Toledo mostly depend on agriculture for their economy and growth. Industrial development is a negative notion among the Maya people. In the past the Maya people depended mostly on trading their produce with neighboring Maya communities. It was not until the latter part of the 1800s that trading changed course. People of the other ethnic groups began arriving in Maya communities to purchase domestic animals such as swine and other commodities such as rice and beans.

In the late 1950s there was a tremendous change in the economic development of the Maya people. The production of paddy grains became abundant due to the introduction of mechanized farming. Many of the Maya people could not finance such mechanized work. So they continued the traditional way of living.

A chief advantage of modern life among the Maya is the educational system. Until the beginning of the 1900s the Maya people lacked a formal educational system. At first, only a minority of the Maya people attended primary school, while the majority continued to survive on farm produce. Most Maya young people today have attended and are attending grade schools, but there is need for the introduction of industrial economic activities among the Maya people for a better way of life and for the educated youths to do their part.

The economic activities to develop ourselves as Maya people need to be improved in order to improve ourselves. There is a need for a Maya market—a general Maya market where farm produce can be sold locally and beyond.

The economic activities now available for us include farming (rice, cacao, beans, corn, citrus), raising animals, self-employment in ecotourism and arts and crafts, teaching, and timber industry. Prosperity in agriculture and livestock is inhibited by lack of markets locally and abroad, and low prices. Few Maya have the education necessary to become teachers, and many people lack the experience and training to earn sufficient income in self-employment. Timber industry jobs are presently very limited and unsatisfactory because the Maya do not yet have the resources and training to develop their own sawmills, and thus must work for foreign companies who do not respect the environment or our culture.

Recommendations

1) Creation of an agricultural board that will speak on behalf of Maya farmers; such a board would negotiate for good prices and develop new markets within Belize and internationally.

2) Establishment of a Maya high school in Toledo.

3) Further development of cooperatives, including women's groups.

4) Development of sustainable, Indian-owned logging.

5) Creation of a Maya Development Fund to finance new economic activities and provide funds for necessary training.

6) Identification of ways for the Maya community to be more self-sufficient, for example, to grow our own cotton for our cloth.

7) Investigation of possibilities for the development of industry in the villages.

Education

People in Maya land are taking advantage of Belize's education system, beginning in the primary schools for about eight years, starting about the age of five or older, depending on test scores of the Belize National Selection Examination (BNSE). The selection takes place according to the percentile a student earns, and the percentile rate changes annually based on agreements made in board meetings and standardization of the level of education needed to compete with other institutions in Belize.

In secondary education, a student will do a specialized subject, and math, language, science, agriculture, industrial arts, social studies, dairy science, home economics, scripture, and physical education.

In the second, third, and fourth form at high school a student can choose the department and the field he or she will pursue for the three years' course. This allows the student to pursue further studies if successful in the three years' course.

Upon graduation, the student can enter a tertiary-level institution where one can major in any field. This will enable the student to earn an associate degree in the field. This is not the final journey in education; further studies can be undertaken when finance is not a problem. The length of the course offered at the tertiary level is two school years.

Without education we Maya people will not be able to challenge other people who are educated. We must be able to educate ourselves. Currently, the only high school in Toledo is in Punta Gorda. It has few Indian teachers and it is hard for our children to maintain their culture. Youth from many villages must travel far to attend school, and their parents must pay to board them there during the week. Few people can afford this. Without parents there, it is more likely that our children will get involved with drugs and alcohol.

More Mayas go to high school each year but very few have an associate degree.

Night class literacy program in Maya Centre

Serpent god

Because so few economic activities occur among the Maya, they will continue to lag behind in providing good education for their children. The Mayas have been demanding that a high school be established in the vicinity of the villages, but this is still a dream. For the time being, they have to travel to the biggest town in Toledo District, Punta Gorda Town, far from home, to get a secondary education.

Recommendations

1) Establishment of a high school that is built in a central Maya community, staffed with Indian teachers and administrators, with at least partial funding from the central government.

2) In school and at home, our youth should be encouraged to keep to the same traditional Maya culture, and to remain proud of their Maya style of dress and language. Children who have an education should share their knowledge with their village community.

3) Both parents and children should be encouraged to get an education.

4) Programs discouraging Maya youth from drinking, smoking, and using drugs should be supported.

Health

Many Maya villages, especially the most remote ones, lack health facilities. Even the few villages with health facilities lack personnel and adequate supplies. Transportation for health care is difficult and expensive, and may be impossible for emergencies.

Recommendations

1) Funds should be sought for the Toledo Maya Cultural Council to study health care needs in our communities, so that the problem can be effectively addressed.

2) Our traditional Maya healers should be involved in providing health care in all the villages.

3) Government should be encouraged to commit funds to Maya health care needs.

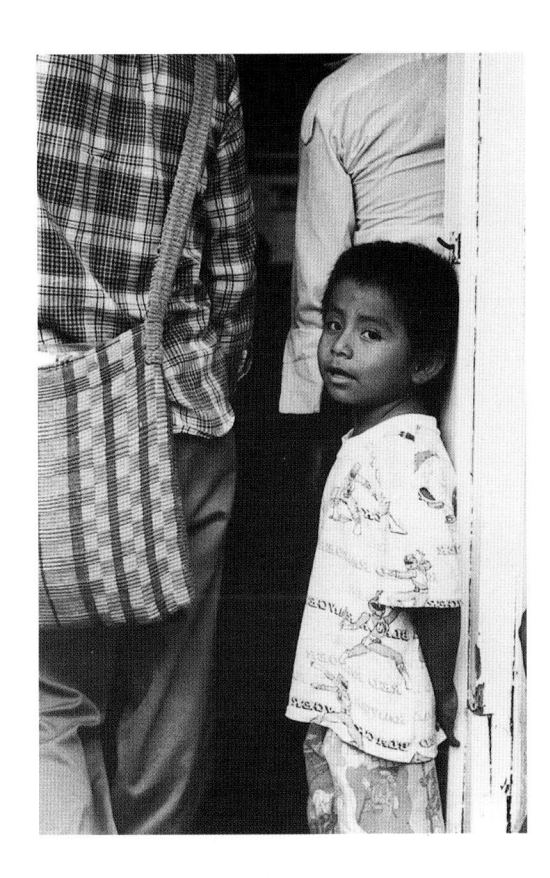

Community Government

Maya communities are governed today by our traditional system. Every village elects an *alcalde*, who serves for two years and provides services like a mayor and judge. The government of Belize has tried to convince the Maya to abandon the *alcalde* system, and has instituted by legislative action a system of elected party officials (called village chairmen) in each village. We are committed to maintaining and strengthening our traditional system of government so that we can preserve our culture. In fact, the traditional system among the indigenous peoples of Toledo is Belize's only such system.

Recommendations

1) Parents and teachers must teach and encourage respect for our traditional system among the young people. They must participate in the *fajina* (village cleaning)—*sah'-calebal* [Mopan] or *ak'ink* [Ke'kchi]—.when called by the *alcalde*, as all villagers must.

2) The *alcaldes* chosen must be able to work for the entire village, with time to attend workshops and other project meetings.

3) The Alcaldes Association should seek funding so the Chairman of the Association and other *alcaldes* can more effectively represent the Maya people of Toledo by attending meetings and advocating with government.

Cultural Preservation

Many, many years ago, the early Indians held many beliefs and practices, but as they were passed on from one generation to the next, some were forgotten or no longer used. Some of these beliefs and cultural practices are listed below.

Housing: The ancient Indians built houses of thatched roofs similar to the ones built by modern-day Indians. Making this type of house is not very complicated; it is simple but requires hard labor. The leaves used for thatching these houses are the abundant cohune leaves. These leaves are chopped down and left to dry a couple of weeks before the house thatching, depending on the climate.

Farming: To cultivate the land and harvest crops for food, the Indians use a system of slash-and-burn. This is done by chopping a couple of acres of land and then leaving it to dry for a few weeks before burning. Then whatever type of crop is needed is planted. Planting rice is different from planting corn. Most corn planting in rural areas uses the *milpa* system.

Food: The main dish eaten by today's Indian people is *caldo*—*ca'iutzlu* [Mopan] or *tialinbie* [Ke'kchi]— and corn tortillas with hot pepper. *Caldo* is a watery type of meat cooking. Pig and chicken meat are usually used. For tortillas, the corn is ground into fine *masa*, then it is baked over fire in a circular, flat shape.

Mobil Health Clinic in San Pedro Columbia

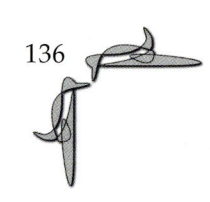

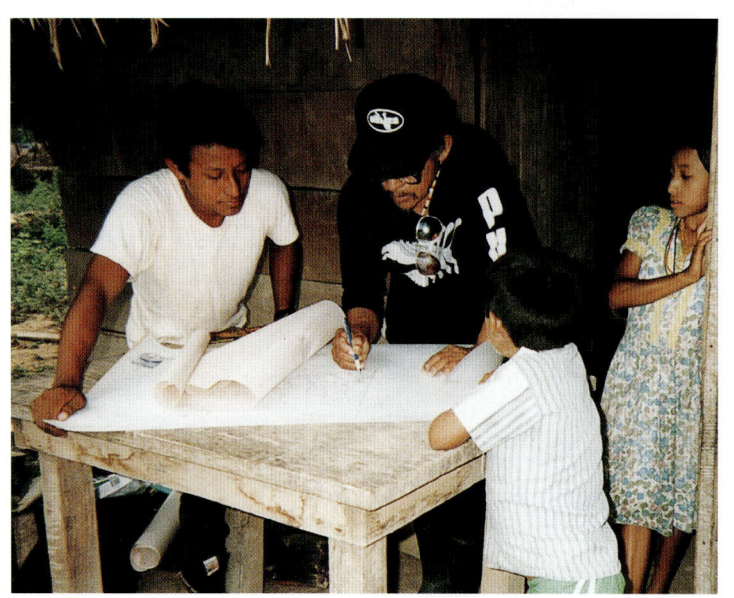

Basilio Ah (cartographer) studies the map produced by village researcher Juan Bo of San Lucas.

Diego Bol (administrator to the mapping project and advisor to the TMCC) working with Cayetano Ico (TMCC treasurer) and Leonardo Acal (founding father of TMCC), compiling information from the survey work.

TMCC accountant Crecensio Cho manages the books for the atlas project.

Julian Cho leading an atlas planning discussion in San Antonio

The Making of the MAYA ATLAS

Community-Based Cartography

The *Maya Atlas* you hold in your hands was conceived, researched, mapped and written by people from thatched-roof villages in the tropical forest southeast of the Maya Mountains. The atlas documents the land and life of 42 Maya communities located in Toledo and Stann Creek Districts, southern Belize. The 36 Maya communities in Toledo District and 6 in Stann Creek District worked together to produce the materials for their atlas. People from these villages designed and voted on the map symbols and colors, drew the maps, carried out the household surveys and analyzed the results, took the photographs, interviewed the elders, wrote the text, voted on the contents and layout, designed the cover, reviewed and edited the maps and text, and helped raise the funds to finance and co-publish the atlas. All of this was done with little or no map-making experience.

It took one year to produce the *Maya Atlas* from the first community mapping workshop (June 12-18, 1996) to the last community review and edit of the completed pages (June 2-18, 1997). Much of the atlas work was done according to the agricultural cycle. First the corn was planted, then the maps and surveys were worked on until the corn was ready to harvest.

The *Maya Atlas* is the first community-made atlas. All other atlases are made by professional mapmakers who most often live and work far from the places on the pages. This atlas is made by people who live in the maps, in the text, in the photographs. The task was to create a way that people who live in their geography could make maps of it; that is, to make their geography visible and accessible. Every people in the world has developed a capacity to gather, analyze, and communicate geographic information about places in culturally appropriate ways. This information is in a people's language, in the names they give to physical features and to cultural places, in the experience of using the land, and in the stories and meanings they invent to provide an explanation of how things came to be.

To transfer geographic information such as this from the culture of a people to a map is challenging because professional cartographers don't usually understand the people's culture, and the people usually don't have professional cartographers.

When our UC Berkeley GeoMap group first met with Maya leaders to explore making a map of Maya land use, we reached the obvious conclusion that it would be much easier to teach Maya people to be cartographers and researchers, than it would be to

Martin Chen (TMCC executive) recording Mayan stories as related by Pedro Batz

teach our cartographers and researchers, to be Maya. We agreed to collaborate on developing a community-based cartography. The main work for the *Maya Atlas* collaborators would be to invent — piece by piece — a methodological bridge between the Maya and Berkeley for the two-way transfer of knowledge, technology, and understanding.

The community-based cartography that we used was developed from five inflexible requirements:

1) The entire process must be **transparent**, that is, understood by Maya villagers and Berkeley student researchers, by Maya and Berkeley cartographers, by the editors and publishers, and by the atlas users.

2) It must be **bi-technological**, that is, both the Maya and Berkeley cartographers must be able to do some of each other's work.

3) It must be **democratic**, that is, participatory, collaborative, and representative.

4) It must be economically and technologically **appropriate**, that is, affordable, do-able, teachable, and accessible.

5) It must be **accurate**, that is, culturally, cartographically, and geographically the atlas must be the best possible.

Because we had no chart ourselves to follow to make these maps, early on we made a decision that always got us across uncharted territory: put the problem requiring a solution before all the collaborators and don't accept a short cut. Looking back over what has been accomplished in such a short time, what we now call a methodology is really but a string of solutions we developed together as we set out to map Maya land and life.

Together we found a way to merge the geography in Maya lands and culture to the geography shown in the pages of the *Maya Atlas* by way of linking the workshops that invented and taught community-based cartography to handmade colored-pencil maps, tape recorders, disposable cameras and Global Positioning System receivers used in Maya communities in Maya lands, to Nikon N-90 cameras and a Nikon slide scanner, Mac 8200 and Power Computing 225 computers, and Zip and Jaz drives, and Quark and PhotoShop software used in Berkeley, to Mac 3400 laptops and Sharp computer projectors used to return to Maya lands to review and edit the atlas with the collaborators.

If it were possible to enlarge each of the village maps to 1:1, that is, to the same scale as the real place, and lay them out over southern Belize, then each map should closely match the geography underneath, and, fitted together like pieces of a jigsaw puzzle, all of the maps should closely portray actual Maya lands and land use.

TMCC executives after the launching of the Maya Mapping Project in April 1996, San Antonio

Maya Workshops and Mapping

In 1995, the leadership of the Toledo Maya Cultural Council and the Toledo Alcaldes Association decided to seek assistance making a map of Maya land use as a means of demonstrating the Mayas' historic rights to their lands and resources. Their decision was prompted by the government of Belize's claims that the Maya peoples were squatters and immigrants on Crown Lands, and that they had no communal, historic, or indigenous land rights; therefore, the government of Belize was free to grant logging, toxic waste dumping, and road-building concessions on what the Maya people said was their land.

The TMCC and TAA received initial funding from the MacArthur and Inter-American foundations. The Indian Law Resource Center in Washington, D.C., advised TMCC to ask Mac Chapin at Native Lands and Bernard Nietschmann at UC Berkeley's GeoMap to collaborate on the mapping project.

On April 8, 1996, at the Indian Law Resource Center office in Washington, D.C., a meeting was held to discuss how best to go ahead with the mapping project. At this meeting were Julian Cho (TMCC), Santiago Coh (TAA); Curtis Berkey, Steve Tullberg, and Armstrong Wiggins (ILRC); Mac Chapin and Bill Threlkeld (Native Lands); and Bernard Nietschmann and Charles Tambiah (GeoMap, UC Berkeley). Julian Cho and Santiago Coh said it was critical to begin the project immediately because people in the communities demanded a response from their leadership to the Malaysian logging. It was agreed to hold a planning meeting at the end of the month in San Antonio, Toledo District. Mac Chapin informed the group that Native Lands had a pre-existing obligation to assist an indigenous mapping project in Bolivia, and that his group could help on the Maya project afterwards.

Agreement was made to collaborate on the Maya Mapping Project (MMP). The TMCC and TAA would be responsible for organization and logistics in the Maya communities, the ILRC would be responsible for communications and fund-raising, and GeoMap would be responsible for workshop training and mapmaking.

Three principles were forged at this meeting that guided successful collaboration on the Maya Mapping Project: 1) no top-heavy control — maintain equal sharing of responsibility and open communication; 2) no bureaucracies — keep it personal, respectful and at the same scale (TMCC, TAA, ILRC, and GeoMap are all small, and small works well with small, but big would not work well with small, for example USAID and the TMCC); and 3) no prima donnas — this isn't about personal careers, agendas, elections or promotions; this is about something sacred, a people's land.

At a TMCC-hosted meeting in San Antonio, Toledo District, April 27-28, 1996, representatives from the UC Berkeley GeoMap team, Indian Law Resource Center, and the TMCC and TAA met to decide on what would be mapped and what would be produced. Instead of a single land use map, it was decided that an atlas would be more appropriate because it could include a more complete range of Maya contributions: maps, writings, photographs, interviews, drawings, and household survey results. A single-page land use map only shows a narrow aspect of an indigenous people's claim to a homeland, whereas an atlas could provide a powerful, stand-alone, full-spectrum testament to validate a people's historical claim to a territory, a Homeland.

Charles Tambiah of GeoMap explaining the role of community researchers to Simeon Coc (executive member of TMCC), San Antonio, April 1996.

Cartographer Basilio Ah of San Antonio and Armstrong Wiggins (Indian Law Resource Center) in San Antonio, April 1996

The meeting was led by Julian Cho (TMCC) and Santiago Coh (TAA). Domingo Choco translated between Mopan and Ke'kchi speakers.

The Maya Mapping Project and the *Maya Atlas* were designed to be an assessment of the natural and human resources of the Mayas' proposed homeland. To govern a Homeland it is necessary to know what is there to govern. Therefore, the Maya Mapping Project would map and inventory the Homeland communities and community lands. To do this every field would be mapped and every household would be surveyed with a questionnaire. People from each community would be trained to do the research.

At this meeting an itinerary was scheduled so that the first workshop would be held after the first corn planting; the subsequent community research could then be done during the rainy season when people would stay close to the village; and the second workshop would be held before the major weeding of the fields was necessary. The production schedule for this mapping work was ruled by the sun, rain, and corn.

It was decided that Deborah Schaaf, from the Indian Law Resource Center office in Helena, Montana, would be the lead counsel in the project, assisted by Lisa Shoman, an attorney in Belize City. Joël Wainwright,

Joël Wainwright (Fulbright Scholar), Armstrong Wiggins (ILRC), Deborah Schaaf (ILRC), and Charles Tambiah (GeoMap), San Antonio, April 1996

a Fulbright Scholar, would help with local logistics and assessment of government map coverage for the Toledo District. Dean Roches from SPEAR (Society for the Promotion of Education and Research) in Belize City would be responsible for administering the Maya Mapping Project funds.

Everyone had only six weeks to prepare for the first training workshop.

Preparations
May 1-June 11, 1996

It takes a huge amount of effort to organize and coordinate a community-based mapping project when most of the communities are distant, isolated, and without a telephone. Representatives from the TMCC visited each community to explain the Maya Mapping Project and to ask the communities to select two people to attend the workshops, usually the *alcalde* and another person who would be trained in cartography and household survey methods to be the village researcher.

Indian Law Resource Center offices in Washington, D.C., and Helena, Montana, coordinated communication and organization among all the collaborating groups. Many items for the mapping workshop were purchased in Belize City. Some necessary cartographic supplies had to be purchased in Berkeley.

From these early preparations we learned three important things: 1) maintaining communication is expensive; 2) organizing community participation is expensive; and 3) supplying a community-based mapping project is expensive.

During May and early June, GeoMap worked with TMCC to prepare a ten-page village survey questionnaire (2100 copies were made in Belize City). GeoMap also prepared 1:25,000 village basemaps from the 1:50,000 topographic series for southern Belize, and prepared and purchased materials to teach the essentials of mapmaking.

The TMCC facilitated the selection of village researchers from thirty-six Maya communities in Toledo and five communities in Stann Creek, along with seven coordinators, each of whom would be responsible for a region and approximately one-seventh of the total forty-one communities. (San Pablo, a sixth Maya community in Stann Creek District was settled in 1997)

Maya Mapping Project

Regional Coordinator Julian Cho

Village	Village Researcher
Crique Jute	Patricio Alcalha
Golden Stream	Luis Pop
Indian Creek	Sebastian Shol
Medina Bank	Joseph Cal
Na Luûm Caj	Emeterio Sho
San Jose	Emelino Cho

Regional Coordinator Domingo Choco

Village	Village Researcher
Corazon	Cruz Cal
Crique Sarco	Jose Coy
Dolores	Santiago Salam
Hicatee	Martin Pop
Mabil Ha	Mateo Pop
Otoxha	Pedro Batz
San Lucas	Juan Bo

Diego Bol opening the training workshop for community researchers at Machaca Outreach Center in June of 1996

Regional Coordinator Pio Coc

Village	Village Researcher
Santa Elena	Dionicio Choc
Pueblo Viejo	Venancio Coc
Jalacte	Ricardo Cucul
Santa Cruz	Juan Teul
San Vicente	Marcos Bah
San Antonio	Reyes Chun

Regional Coordinator Santos Coc

Village	Village Researcher
Aguacate	Domingo Cal
Blue Creek	Juan Ash
Jordan	Jacinto Max
Laguna	Juan Ash
San Marcos	Carlos Mes
Santa Teresa	Jacinto Max

Regional Coordinator Santiago Coh

Village	Village Researcher
Big Falls	Domingo Pau
San Pedro Columbia	Jose Teul
San Miguel	Sebastian Choco
Silver Creek	Everiscio Coh

Regional Coordinator Jose Salam

Village	Village Researcher
Conejo	Matildo Makin
Midway	Sebastian Tush
Boom Creek	Sebastian Tush
San Benito Poite	Sebastian Teck
San Felipe	Eduardo Coc
Santa Anna	Santiago Chub
Sunday Wood	Martin Tush

Regional Coordinator Julio Saqui

Village	Village Researcher
Maya Centre	Julio Saqui
Santa Rosa	Marcos Shal
San Roman	Marcos Shal
Maya Mopan	Higinio Chiac
Red Bank	Higinio Chiac

The First Mapping Workshop
June 12-18, 1996
Machaca Camp, Toledo District

The First Mapping Workshop was led by Julian Cho and Diego Bol (TMCC) and Santiago Coh (TAA). English was the main language used to teach in the workshops. Most Maya in southern Belize speak English as a second language to either Mopan or Ke'kchi. Mopan and Ke'kchi speakers use English to speak to each other. Oftentimes, however, it was necessary that cartographic concepts and methods be explained in Mopan and Ke'kchi for greater clarity. Several able people assisted in this. Domingo Choco again assisted in translating directly between Mopan and Ke'kchi.

Food preparation and cooking for the eighty participants was done by Teodora Castellano, Clara Bol, Sophia Cho, and Linadora Bol.

The UC Berkeley GeoMap team of Bernard Nietschmann, Charles Tambiah, Jennie Freeman, and Tim Norris led the training of village researchers from Mopan and Ke'kchi communities in Toledo and Stann Creek districts. The intensive seven-day workshop covered the basics in field mapping, including map projections, scale and scale transformations, coordinate systems, map reading, map design, data categorization and presentation in map-making with symbols and legends, portraying physical and cultural features, locating points and places in the field using compass and map, making transects and orientation with compass and map, and the use of cartographic tools. Additionally, training was given in how to carry out the survey. The training in survey questionnaires and field-mapping methods was taught by lectures, demonstrations, and hands-on exercises.

Workshop participants spent one day designing, selecting, and voting on some thirty Maya-made symbols to depict the physical, cultural, and historical features of their region, including types of landforms, vegetation, and land use found in the area. Conventional or Maya-invented symbols and colors were used as appropriate. Conventional symbols were selected for such things as roads and rivers; Maya symbols were selected for such things as caves, ruins, traditional healers, hunting grounds, traditional medicine areas, and waterfalls — all of which have strong cultural and territorial significance. All selected symbols were compiled onto one page, photocopied, colored appropriately, placed in a protective plastic sleeve, and a copy given to each village researcher so that everyone would follow the same system of symbolization.

The maps in the atlas are made with democratically selected legends, symbols, colors, and land use terms. Whereas professional cartography follows conventions of standardized map symbols, community-based cartography is different because map symbols are almost always designed and selected by "town meeting democracy."

Each village researcher was supplied with a complete mapping and census kit which included mapping materials, paper, a 1:25,000 base map for each village region, a map tube, a clipboard and questionnaires, compass, and a *cuxtal* (woven wool bag) with the MMP letters (Maya Mapping Project) to carry the mapping supplies. The bags were woven by women in several Maya communities.

Three people — Basilio Ah, Julio Sanchez, and Andres Coh — were selected by the TMCC to be trained as cartographers, and they received a full kit of professional cartographic equipment and a cartographer's backpack.

The village researchers and cartographers learned very quickly, in part because of the way they organized themselves into work groups. The GeoMap team had planned on teaching the researchers and cartographers as in a classroom in the United States, one person per

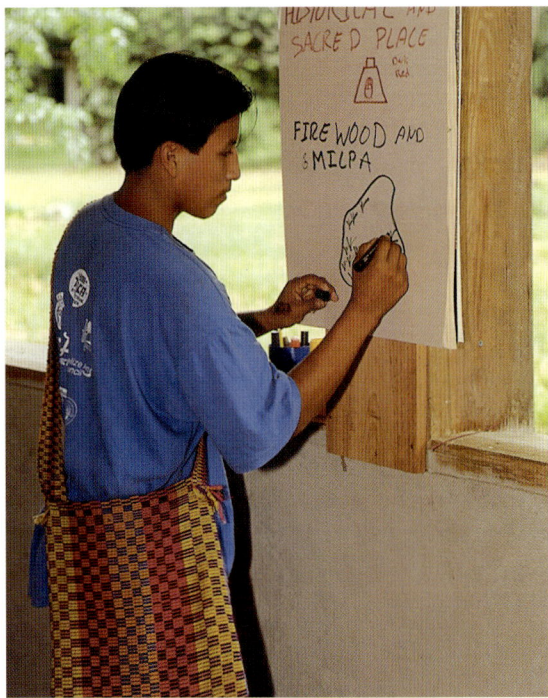

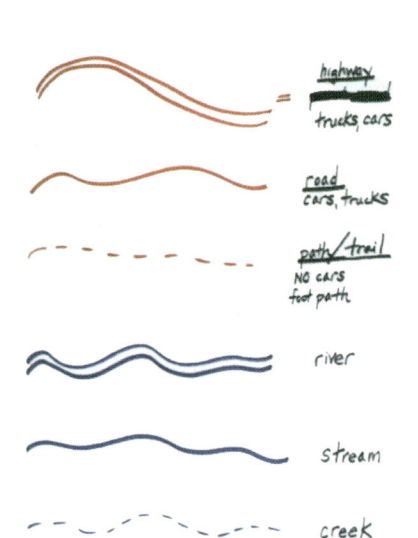

Domingo Pau of Big Falls designs a symbol for firewood and milpa

desk, each person responsible for doing the assignment alone. Instead, the Maya researchers and cartographers worked together on cartographic assignments, four to six to a desk, which meant that when any one person from the group understood the cartographic concept and methods, he would explain them in Mopan or Ke'kchi to the others at the table, who in this manner learned probably ten times faster than they would have working alone and only in English. This change was due to the initiative of the village researchers, and it was the single-most important reason for the remarkable success of participants in all the workshops. This led to an insight important for those who work in community-based mapping: adapt and invent, don't adopt and prevent.

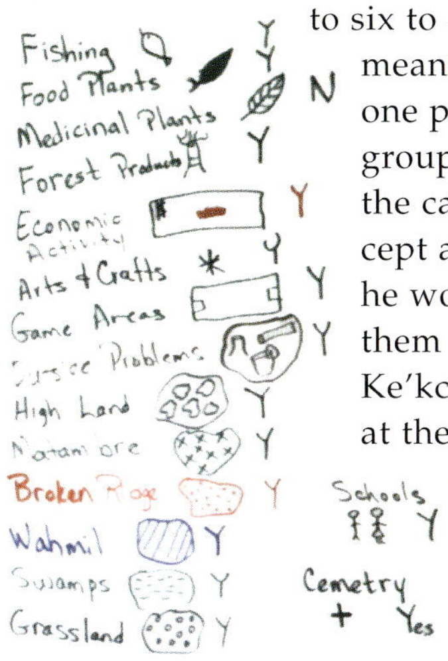

Videographer Widdicombe Schmidt assisted with logistics and used Hi-8 video to document the workshop.

Reyes Chun, village researcher for San Antonio, working on the community map

Training Workshop for the Research Coordinators
June 19-21, 1996
San Antonio, Toledo District

GeoMap's Charles Tambiah, Tim Norris, and Jennie Freeman, and Joël Wainwright met with the seven Maya Mapping Project coordinators to help them prepare for their tasks of assisting the village researchers. Their tasks were to solve any logistical problems, to ensure that the proper survey and mapping methods were being followed, and to see that each village researcher's work was as accurate and complete as possible. In addition, each coordinator was shown how to compile composite information from the questionnaires when they were complete, and to crosscheck the maps for consistency and accuracy. During this time the coordinators were taught how to use handheld GPS (Global Positioning System) units so that they could locate with a great deal of accuracy scores of points of latitude and longitude that could later be used to crosscheck locations on the village researchers' maps.

Training Workshop for the Maya Cartographers
June 22-25, 1996
San Antonio, Toledo District

Three members of the UC Berkeley GeoMap team met for four intensive days of advanced cartographic training for the three Maya cartographers: Basilio Ah, Julio Sanchez, Andres Coh. Included in the training were detailed exercises such as drawing technique, text placement and usage, and data representation techniques. The cartographers were also introduced to the concepts of computer cartography, and an intensive troubleshooting session on field cartography was held.

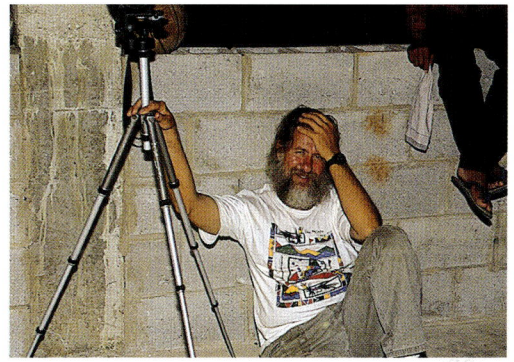

GeoMap videographer Widdicombe Schmidt after 40 hours of taping in three days

Community Mapping and Household Surveys
June 20–July 21, 1996
Toledo and Stann Creek Districts

Jacinto Max of Santa Teresa working in his community

The village researchers made 1:25,000 land use maps and conducted a questionnaire survey for each household in each community. The land use maps were made by overlaying 30 x 40-inch sheets of .005 inch single-side frosted mylar over same-size 1:25,000 maps enlarged from the D.O.S. 1:50,000 topographic map series. Land use locations, areas, and geographic extent used by people in the village were then mapped and crosschecked by on-the-ground field mapping and interview/questionnaires with members of each household. The Maya communities use an intricate system of names for their local lands which allows them to pinpoint, with a great deal of accuracy, areas where they farm, hunt, fish, collect medicinal and food plants and firewood, as well as where their culturally important caves and waterfalls are situated, and where their ancestral ruins are found. Most of this information is not found on Belize's 1:50,000 map series. This work was completed in four weeks in the larger communities such as San Antonio and San Pedro Columbia, and over less time in the smaller communities such as Sunday Wood and Silver Creek.

Tape recorders and 35mm cameras were distributed to people expert in different specializations so that they could photograph and record activities and descriptions for inclusion in the atlas.

The regional coordinators evaluated the village researchers' progress in completing the mapping and household surveys and helped solve problems such as convincing uncooperative families to participate, explaining that the mapping and surveys were for the Maya, not for the government, and keeping the work on track in the face of rain, flooded creeks, and rivers, often making for difficult communications in isolated areas.

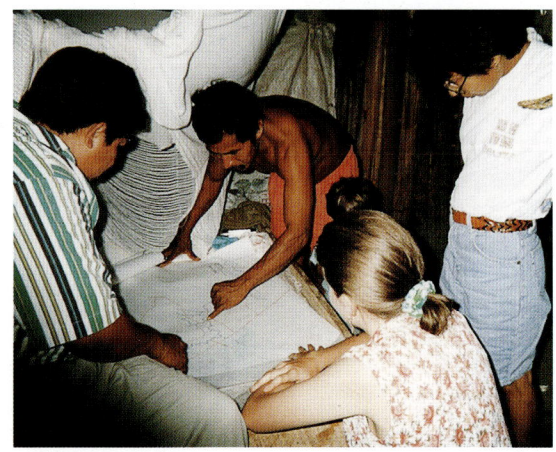

Jorge Cawich, Santiago Chub, Magdalena Cho, and Joanne Abbot (International Farmers Aid for Development)

The Second Mapping Workshop
July 22–30, 1996
Cockscomb Jaguar Reserve, Stann Creek District

The Second Mapping Workshop was led by Julian Cho and Diego Bol (TMCC), and Santiago Coh (TAA).

Food preparation and cooking were done by men and women in the community of Maya Centre, 7 kilometers down the often-muddy road. They were assisted by Clara Bol, Teodora Castellano, Sophia Cho, and Linadora Bol who also worked at the First Mapping Workshop.

This nine-day workshop focused on training the village researchers to rectify, conform, and transform their 1:25,000 maps for greater accuracy. Additional symbols and colors were selected and voted upon for land use and vegetation types. The village researchers were taught how to do a second draft and a final map using their 1:25,000 field map, redrafting it using an overlay sheet of .005-inch frosted mylar, permanent ink drafting pens, and colored pencils to fill in land use and land type categories. The UC Berkeley GeoMap team

Regino Cowo and Julio Sanchez compiling information collected by community researchers

taught and assisted during every stage of this workshop. By the end of the ninth day, every village map had been crosschecked, redrafted in ink and colors, and used to make several thematic 1:250,000 maps of Maya lands in the Toledo and Stann Creek Districts, such as land use and threats to Maya lands (destructive logging, orange tree plantations, and foreign-owned lands located within the Maya territory).

We had planned to reduce the completed

Martin Pop of Hicatee at Cockscomb

1:25,000 maps to 1:250,000 using "similar squares," that is, a process by which grids of different sizes are used to redraw maps

Jose Coy of Crique Sarco at the Cockscomb mapping workshop

to different scales. This is done by eye, square by square, line by line, sometimes with 300-400 squares per map. This method proved to be much too time-consuming and inaccurate.

As happened throughout the project, when a major problem came up, we held a meeting, described the problem, and asked for solutions. Invariably, someone would

Cartographers Basilio Ah, Julio Sanchez, and Andres Coh after the Cockscomb workshop

suggest a solution that not only got us past the problem, but it often was a totally new idea. In this situation, it was suggested that the problem was due to asking the Maya researchers and cartographers to divert their skills and labor from things they are now good at doing — drawing on traditional knowledge to draw maps — to something nobody is good at — the tedious and mind-numbing process of making maps at smaller scales by eye and pen. Instead, it was suggested that the map reduction problem was a technical problem that could be solved with technology (photography, xerography, and computer scanners). Therefore, the researchers' and cartographers' skills should be directed to making their maps better, not smaller. As a result, the workshop plan changed, the village researchers and cartographers were provided with new sheets of mylar and new sets of colored pens and pencils, and they were encouraged to use their skills and knowledge to make their maps better. And they did; this is why the maps in the *Maya Atlas* came to be colored and filled in with with more detail and accuracy. Another lesson in community-based mapping was learned: flexibility not rigidity produces solutions.

As with the first workshop, ILRC's Deborah Schaaf worked to keep transportation and communication flowing between the workshop participants and other places and people. Deborah Schaaf, along with ILRC colleague Jim Anaya and TMCC's attorney Lisa Shoman, gave a seminar to TMCC and TAA leaders on indigenous land rights and international and Belizean law.

UC Berkeley graduate Heidi Quante assisted by using Hi-8 video to document the second workshop and to interview Maya women.

Maya Cartographer Training and Making the Land Use Map
September, 1996 UC Berkeley

Maya cartographers Basilio Ah, Julio Sanchez, and Andres Coh came from Toledo to the University of California for two weeks to help complete the final stages of making the land use map and to work on other sheet maps for the *Maya Atlas*. The Maya cartographers received additional cartographic training from Dr. Cherie Semans, the Department of Geography's staff cartographer, and training in computer cartography from Don Bain, head of the Department's Computer Facility.

Working closely with the UC Berkeley GeoMap team of Charles Tambiah, Jennie Freeman, and Tim Norris, the Maya cartographers again went over the 1:25,000 village maps to crosscheck them for accuracy and

Basilio Ah lecturing to an upper-division geography course at UC Berkeley, September, 1996

completeness. These maps were then photographed using a Nikon N-90 with a special 60mm copy lens to produce fine-grain 35mm color transparencies. These transparencies (slides) were then placed into a Nikon LS-1000 Slide Scanner (2500 dpi) and the

Julio Sanchez lecturing at UC Berkeley.

images imported into a Mac computer, with back-up images stored on high-capacity 100MB Zip disks. With the images of the maps made by the village researchers on the computer hard drive, each image could then be reduced by a uniform scale reduction and

Jennie Freeman and Basilio Ah explore the San Pedro Columbia website.

put together (much like pieces of a puzzle) to produce the land use map, the first of several maps being made for the *Maya Atlas*. The Maya cartographers assisted at every stage of the computer work and made decisions on many atlas map questions and problems. The Maya cartographers gave four lectures to an advanced UC Berkeley conservation geography class on the Maya, land use, conservation and the making of the *Maya Atlas*.

Don Bain, the head of Geography Computing at UC Berkeley, gives computer training to the Maya cartographers Andres Coh and Julio Sanchez, with Tim Norris looking on.

To create the land use map, the UC Berkeley cartographers used all of the village maps (forty-one communities) to assemble by means of GeoMap computers the composite land use areas. Where there were small overlaps from village to village, the Maya cartographers — based on their on-the-ground familiarity with community lands — directed the Berkeley computer cartographers where to make the minor adjustments. Overall, each village map fit closely with neighboring village maps.

The final 20 x 30-inch high-quality land use map and smaller copies were completed at the end of November and sent to TMCC in Belize and the Indian Law Resource Center in Washington for inclusion in the Maya land rights case currently before Belize's Supreme Court.

GeoMap Computer Cartography and the Atlas,
February-July, 1997
Department of Geography, University of California, Berkeley

At the end of November 1996, all Maya Mapping Project funds had been spent. Some back salaries to the GeoMap group were unpaid. This did not come as a surprise. What was surprising was how long the MMP was able to continue by stretching out the funds. Work on the project slowed down and stopped. Charles Tambiah returned to work on his dissertation. Jennie Freeman began work on other projects. Tim Norris continued to work on a volunteer, part-time basis.

Running out of funding is a common hazard in community-based mapping projects. The more participatory, democratic, and collaborative a project is, the more it costs. Funding organizations will support expenses for mapping workshops and supplies but usually will not fund salaries, expensive equipment, overhead, and publishing costs. Therefore, it is very difficult for a community-mapping project to overcome funding limitations and to carry through with the original goals, which invariably involve using maps to assert rights to territory and resources. Because of funding limitations, what usually happens is the great enthusiasm from the workshops and all the work and hopes dissipate and are distilled into a couple hundred copies of one map. The Maya Mapping Project was developed not simply to make maps, but to use mapping to organize the communities, assess the natural and human resources,

Diego Bol, Tim Norris, Deborah Schaaf, and Madison Roswell discuss a satellite image of southern Belize in the GeoMap office, U.C. Berkeley.

Richard Grossinger, publisher of North Atlantic Books, discusses publishing plans.

provide the leadership with a blueprint for sustainable development, authenticate Maya land rights, promote a homeland, conserve one of Central America's most important centers of biodiversity, and to defend against and challenge the invasion of Maya lands by clearcut logging, citrus plantations, plans to site toxic waste disposal centers, and impending International Development Bank (IDB) loans to pave penetration roads.

So, when the money ran out at the end of 1996, we didn't just close up and let the MMP and *Maya Atlas* die. By this time the project had become very visible internationally and the story of the Maya *vs.* the Malaysian loggers had been prominently featured in newspapers and news magazines. The IDB loan to Belize to pave the Southern Highway was on hold because of the TMCC, ILRC, and the Maya Mapping Project.

Five things happened within the space of five weeks in February and March, 1997, to recharge the Maya Mapping Project and production of the *Maya Atlas*: 1) the Government of Luxembourg provided a grant of $100,000 to TMCC; 2) GeoMap hired two very talented cartographers, Madison Roswell and Steve Rose, to work with Tim Norris on the atlas; 3) money from the Pew Charitable Trusts was used by GeoMap to purchase the best computer equipment and software to produce professional-quality maps and layouts; 4) a leading alternative press, North Atlantic Books in Berkeley, agreed to publish the *Maya Atlas* under contractual conditions that are very favorable to the TMCC and TAA; and 5) the National Geographic Society provided a $25,000 grant to assist publication of the *Maya Atlas*.

During March through May, missing pieces of the atlas were sent by the Maya leaders and researchers by fax, mail, and DHL. GeoMap cartographers, assisted by volunteers Andrew Nystrum, Amy Moss, and Heidi Quante, worked late hours to enter the pages of text into computer files and layout.

Mr. Reginio leading the discussion about the Maya flag, San Antonio, June 1997

Returning the Atlas to Belize to Edit
June 2-18, 1997

The first draft of the atlas was ready by the end of May. Many parts of the text were still missing, but overall the atlas was 90 percent complete. It was time to bring it back to Belize so that the Maya could review and edit the text, maps, illustrations, and other graphics.

On June 2, 1997, the *Maya Atlas* was taken to Punta Gorda, Toledo District, Belize, by GeoMap cartographers Tim Norris, Madison Roswell, and Steve Rose. To display the atlas so that it could be reviewed and edited by its many authors, the GeoMap team brought two Mac 3400c laptops, an external Jaz drive with 1 GB disks, a Sharp computer SVGA projector, and a 6 x 8-foot semi-transparent white plastic screen.

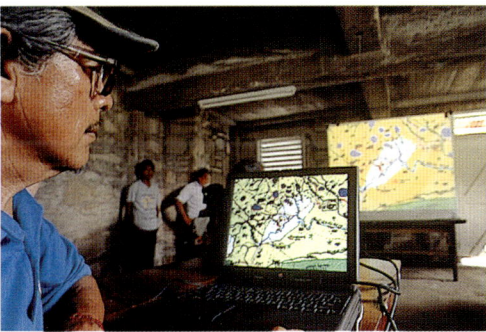

Basilio Ah checks the map of San Antonio in the basement of the church, San Antonio, June 1997.

Magdeleno Ah checks the village center of the San Antonio map, San Antonio, June 1997.

In Punta Gorda the next day, the GeoMap cartographers met with TMCC people in their office to brief them on the status of the atlas, and the many questions that remained concerning content, design and layout, and to discuss the logistics and location where the presentation would be made. During the next three days, TMCC organized the atlas meeting and helped bring the village researchers and regional coordinators from the very distant villages to San Antonio. The GeoMap cartographers worked with the Maya cartographers on major design issues and generated JPEGs (high quality computer images for easy display), in facing-page formats, for the presentation.

The atlas draft was reviewed by approximately 160 people including its 80 authors and contributors, and all the old and new *alcaldes* on Saturday, June 7, in the Mopan community of San Antonio. Among the participants were the village researchers, regional coordinators, cartographers, TMCC leaders, the TAA *alcaldes*, people from the Indian Law Resource Center, SPEAR, and the GeoMap cartographers. All discussion was translated into Mopan and Ke'kchi in order for all of the participants to understand the legal and practical issues involved with producing the *Maya Atlas*. Page by page the atlas was reviewed, missing information contributed, work assigned to complete village history sections, and colors, design and layout checked. The *Maya Atlas* may be the world's first democratically designed, written, and edited book.

Julian Cho explaining the cover of the draft copy of the atlas, San Antonio, June 1997

For the next eight days—June 9-17, the GeoMap team worked with Maya cartographers and researchers in Punta Gorda and San Antonio to add the missing pieces of information and double-check all existing material.

Reviewing the atlas, prior to publication in Berkeley, July 1997

Berkeley, July 1997

The entire month of July 1997 was spent in Berkeley getting the atlas ready for publication. Funds ran out again. The Lannan Foundation provided crucial funding to keep the work moving ahead to completion. Work days extended into work nights. Three cartographers sat at three computers working on the atlas while listening to rock and roll, country, jazz, reggae, and Punta Rock (Garifuna music from Belize). The result is what you hold before you now. The Maya of southern Belize offer it to you for your enlightenment and enjoyment.

The cartographers, both from Belize and GeoMap, hard at work, San Antonio, June, 1997

Ironing the Maya Flag before studio photographs

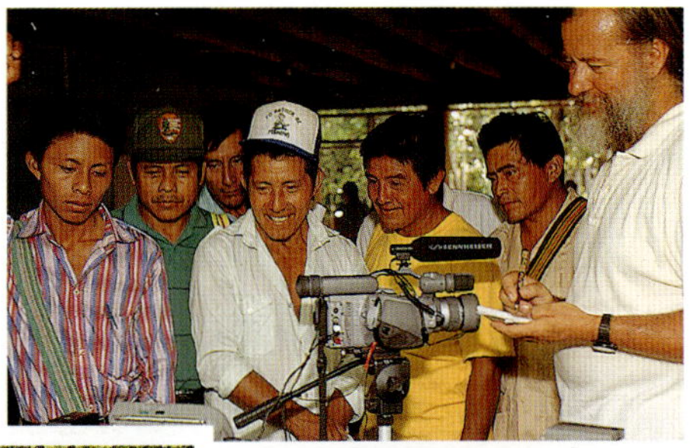
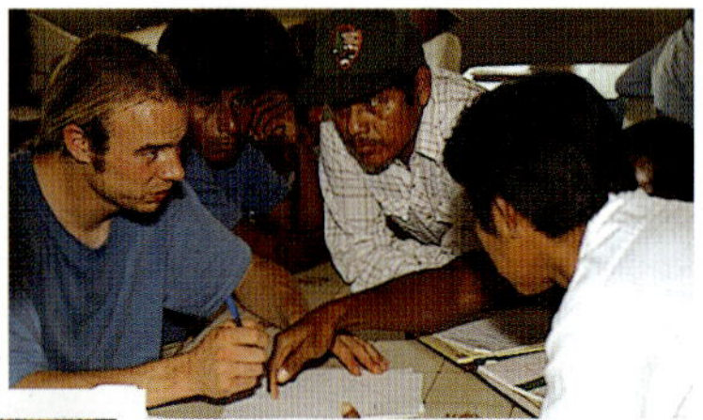
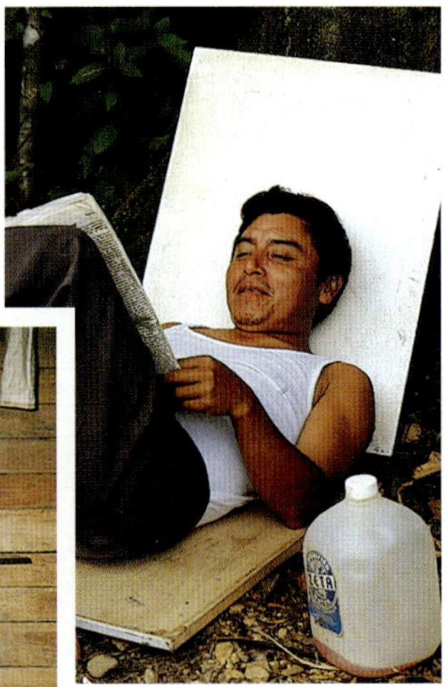
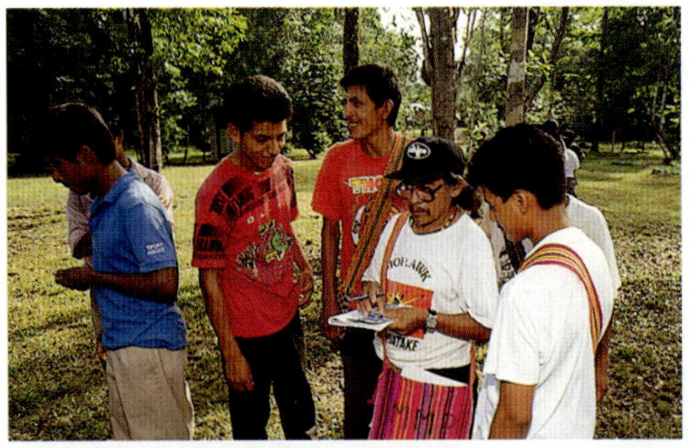
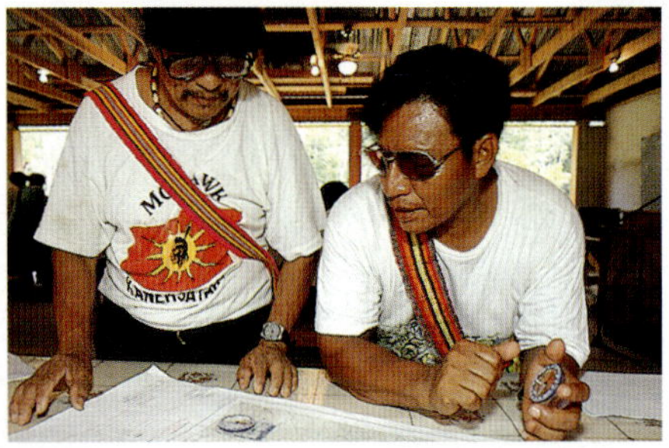
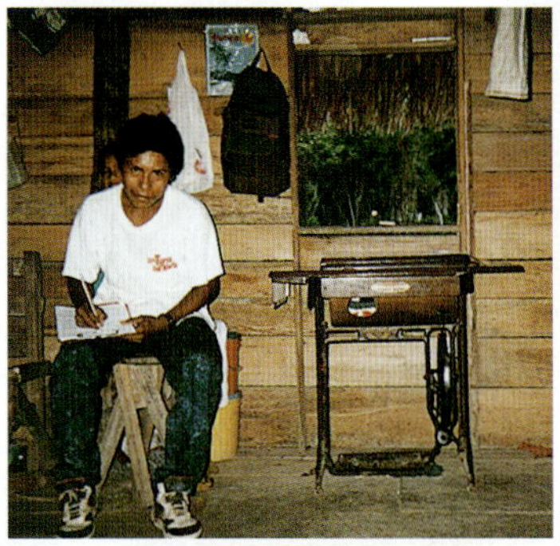
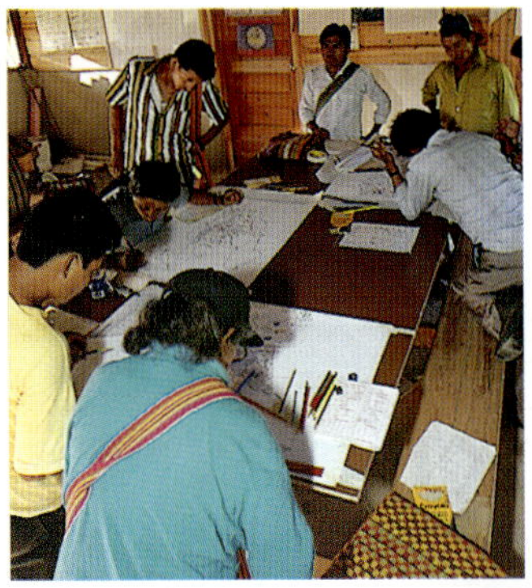
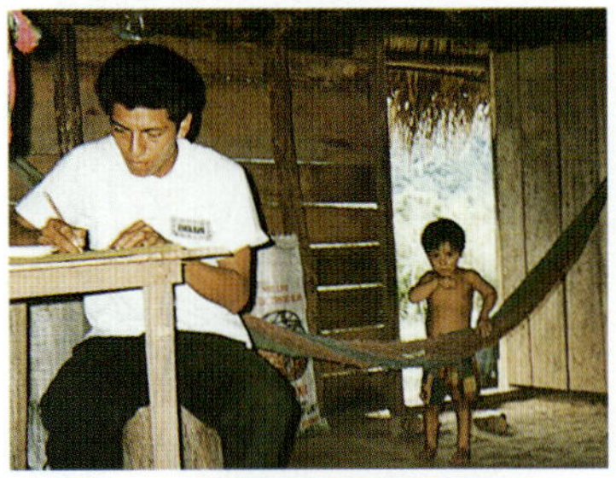
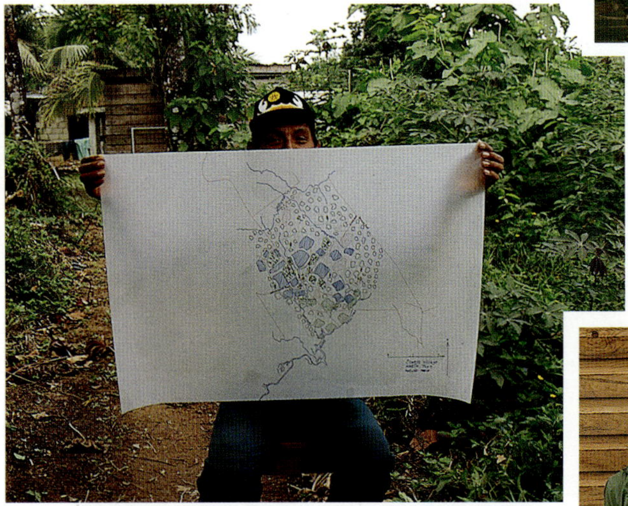
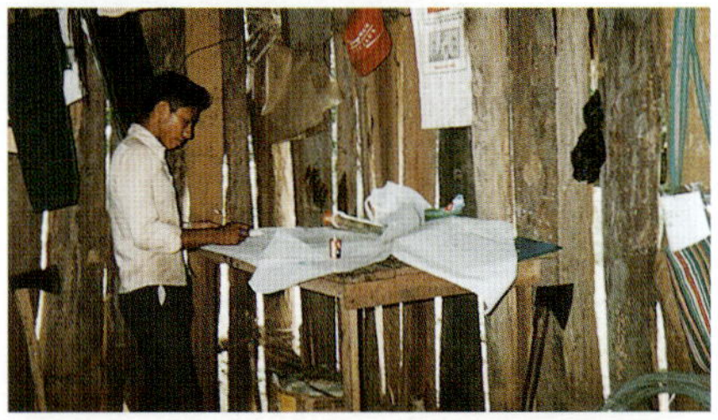
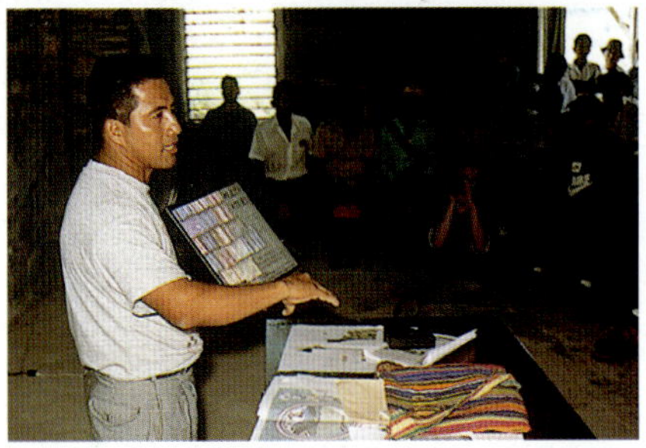
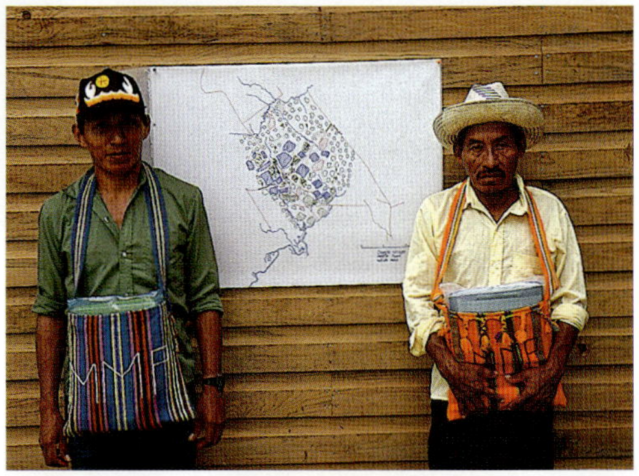
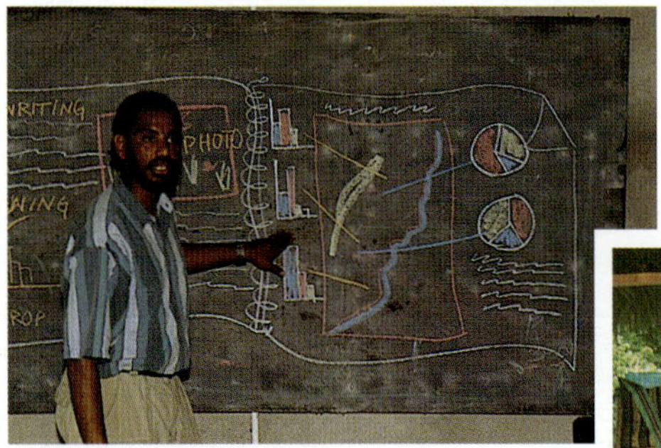
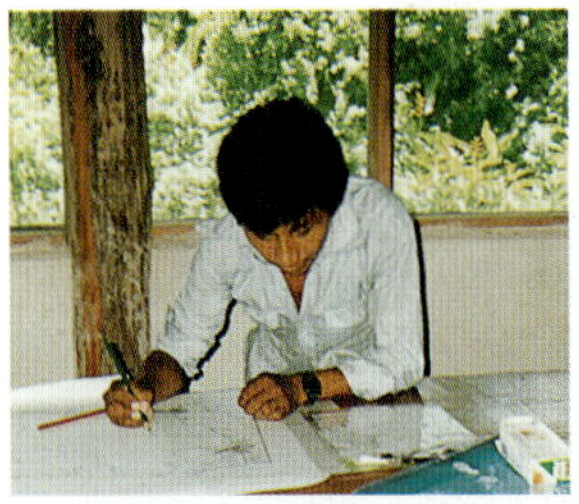
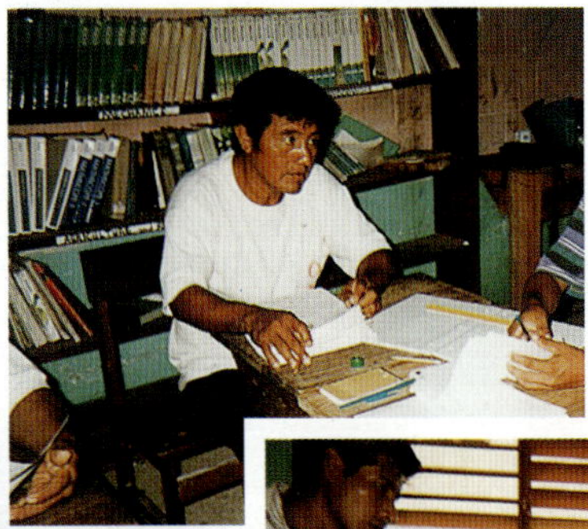
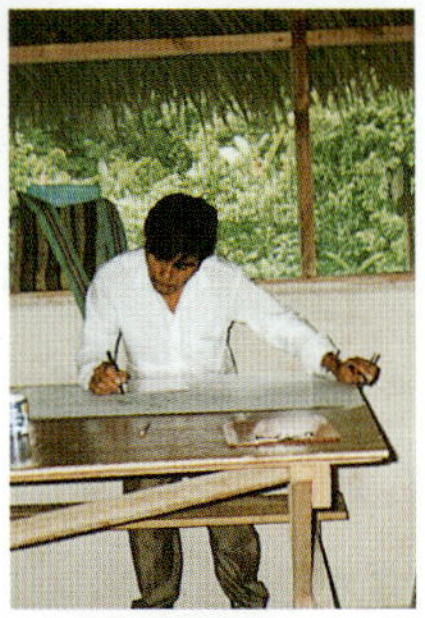
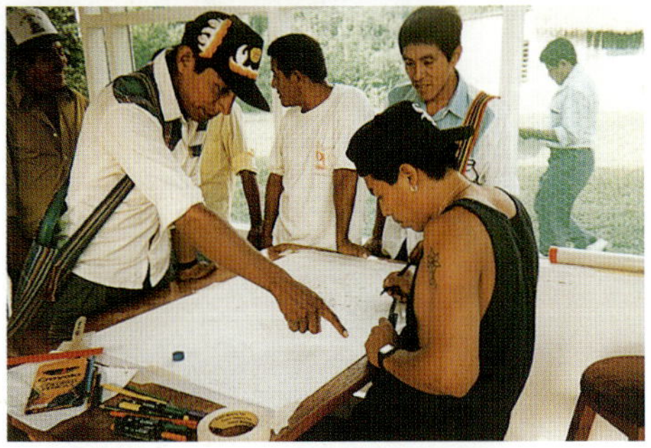
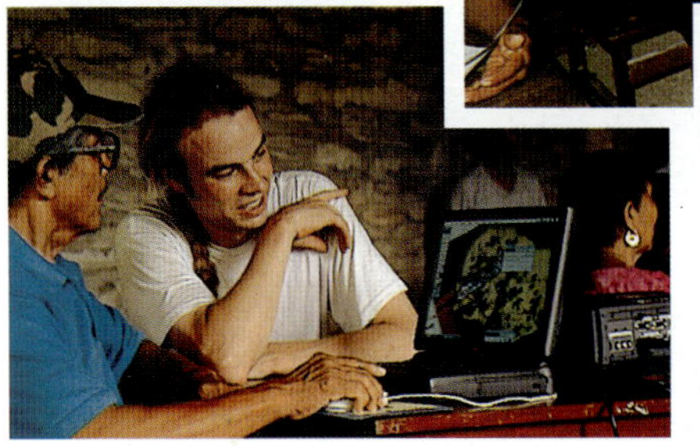
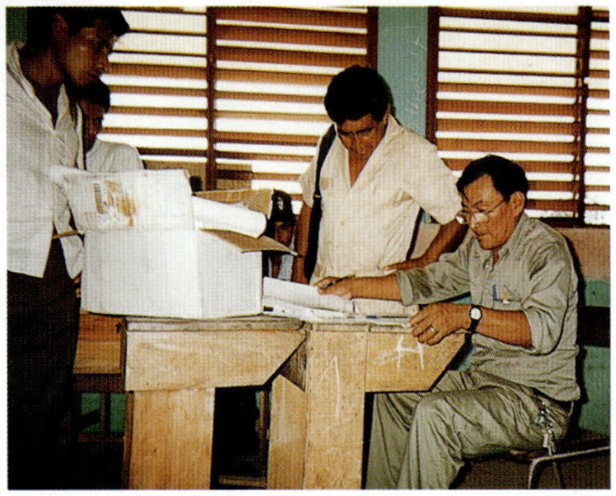
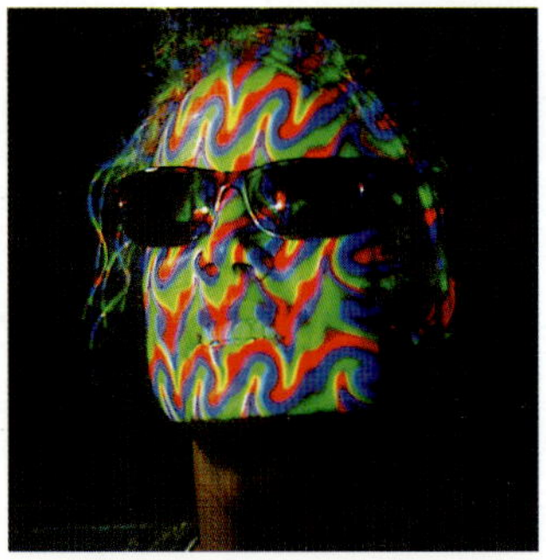
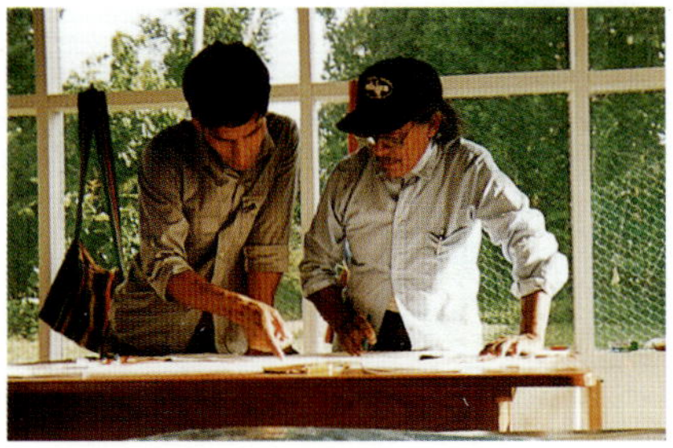

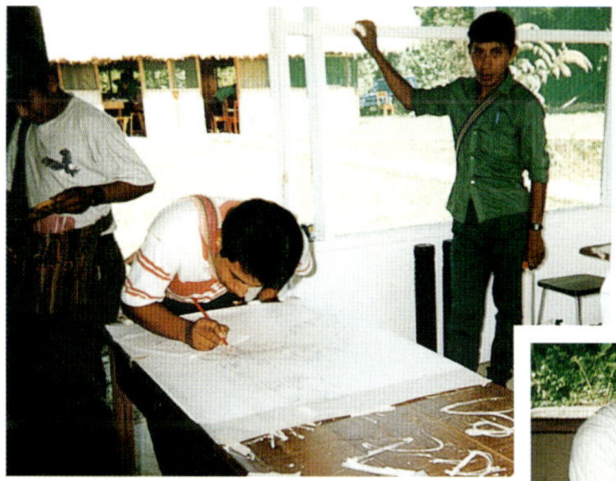
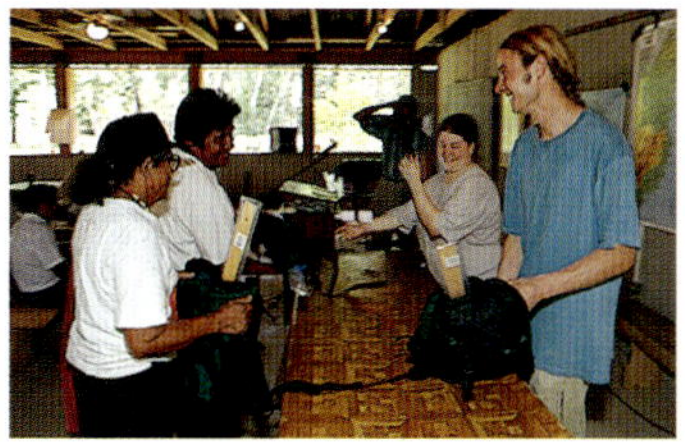
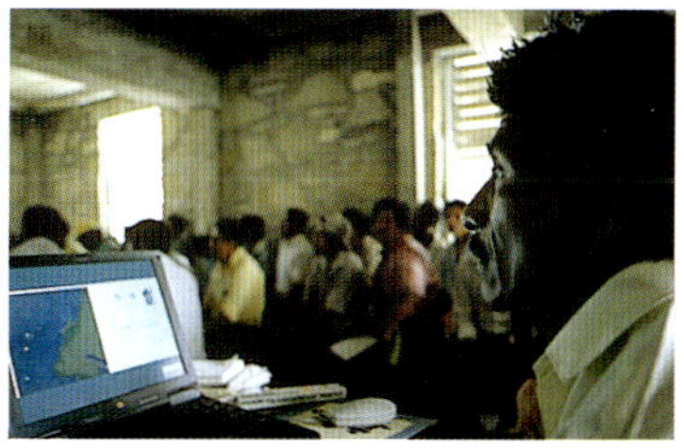
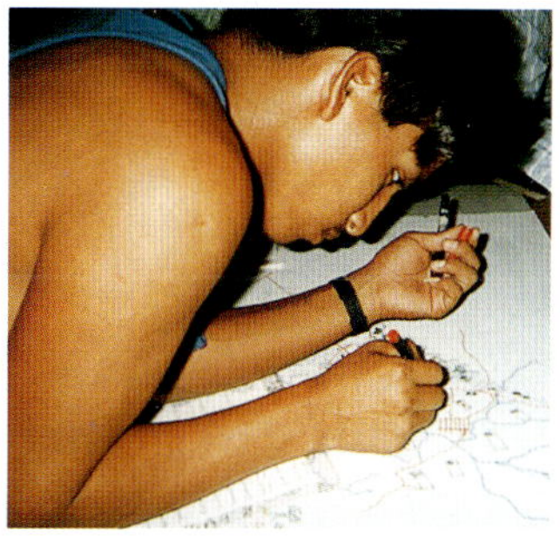
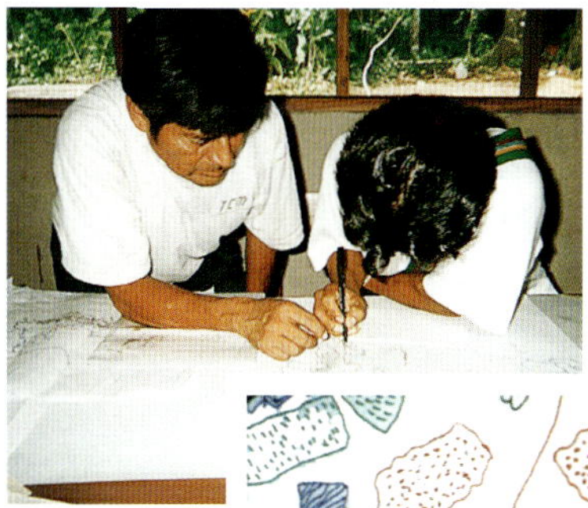
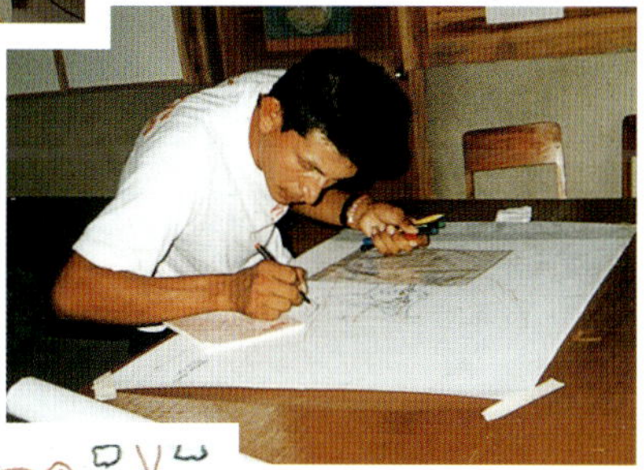
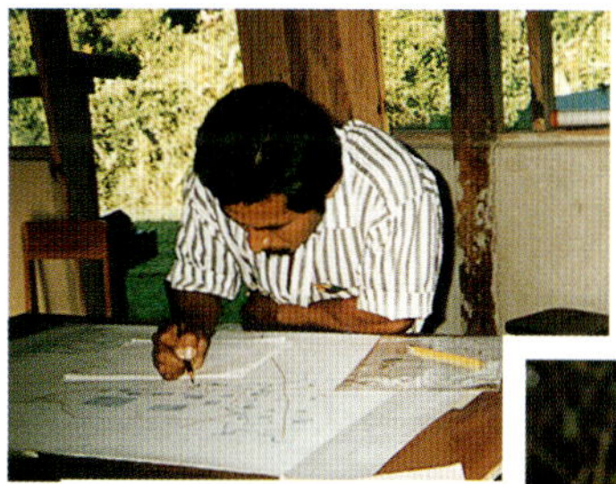
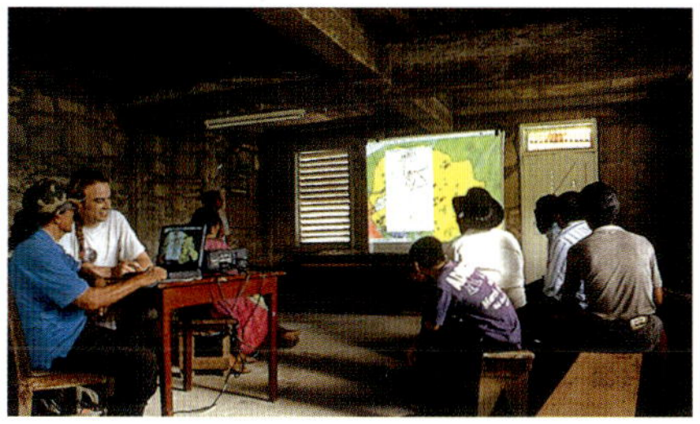
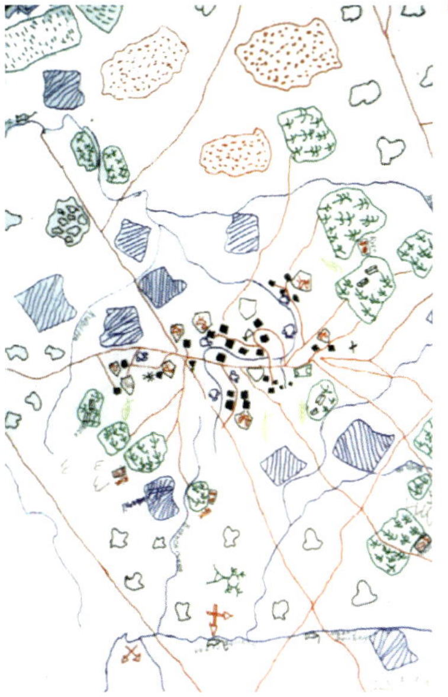
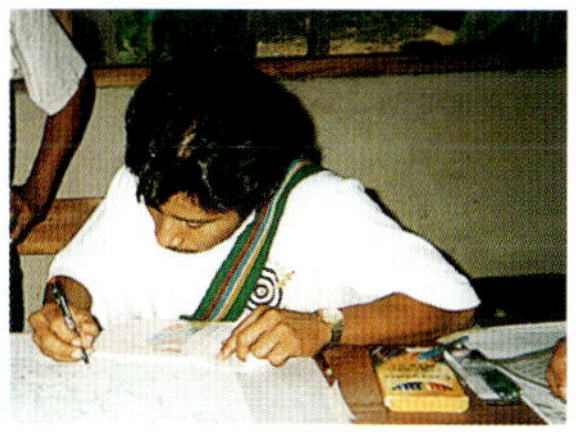
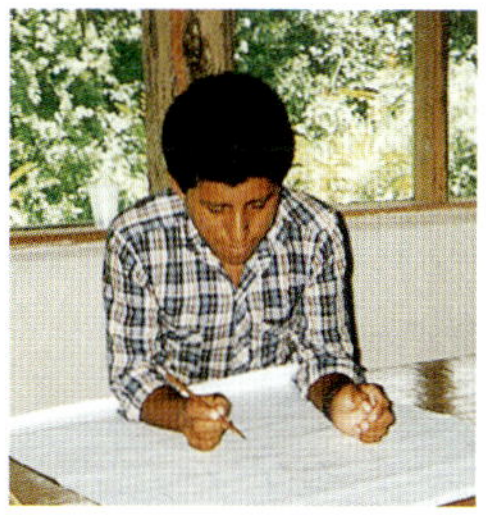
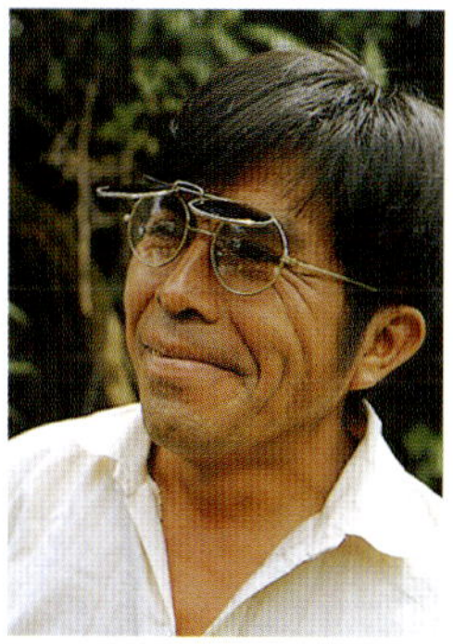
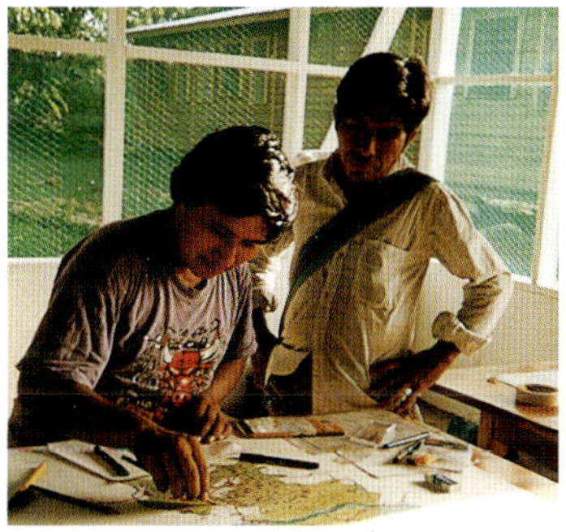
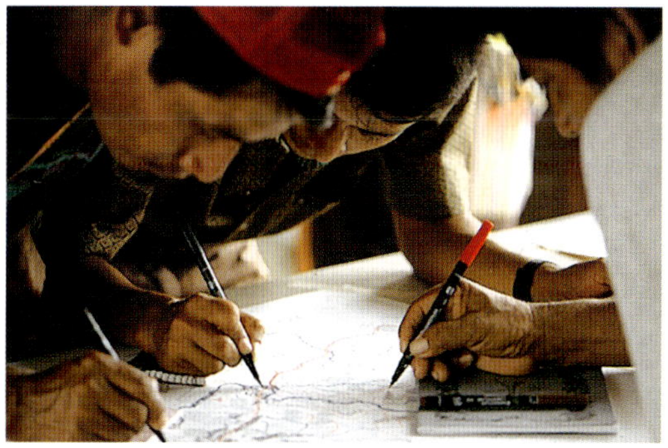
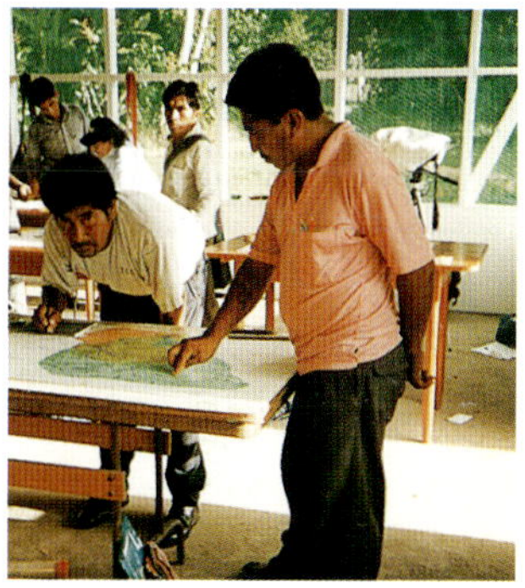
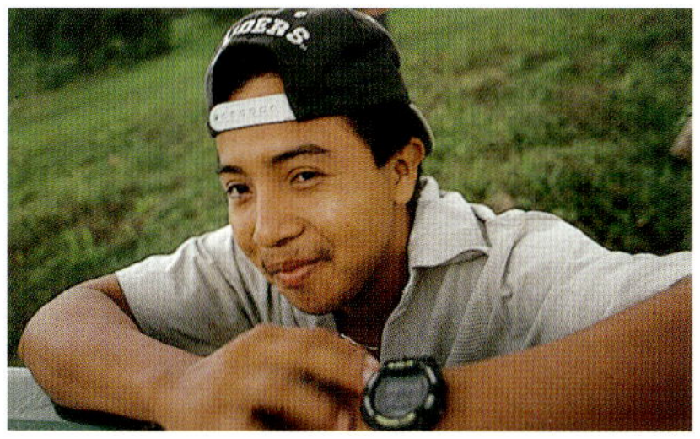
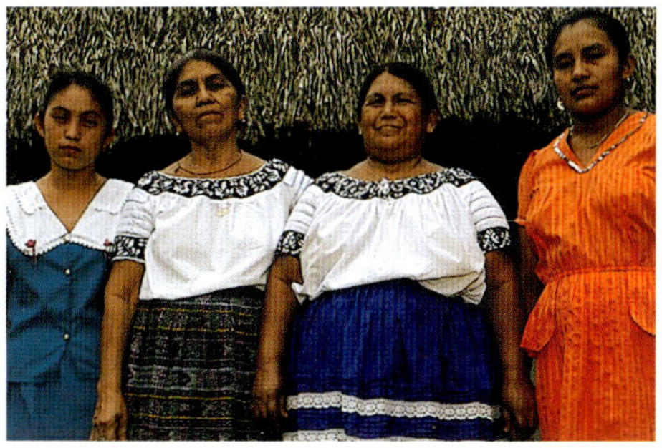
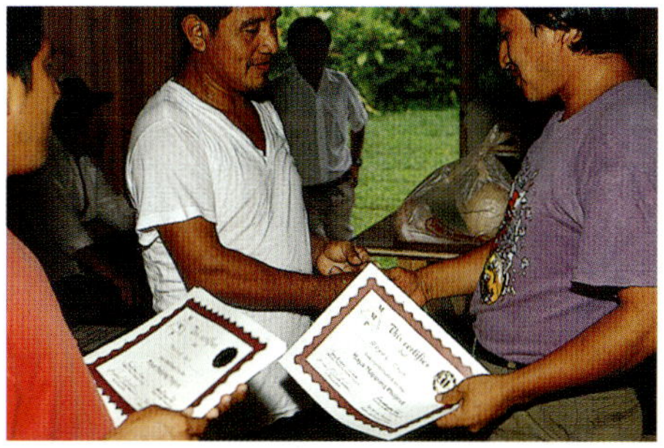
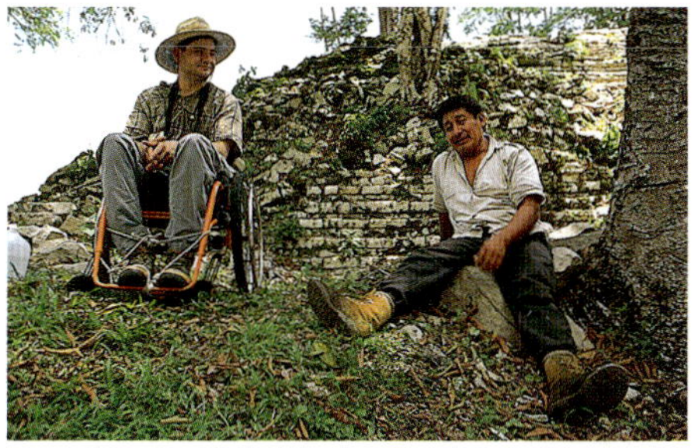
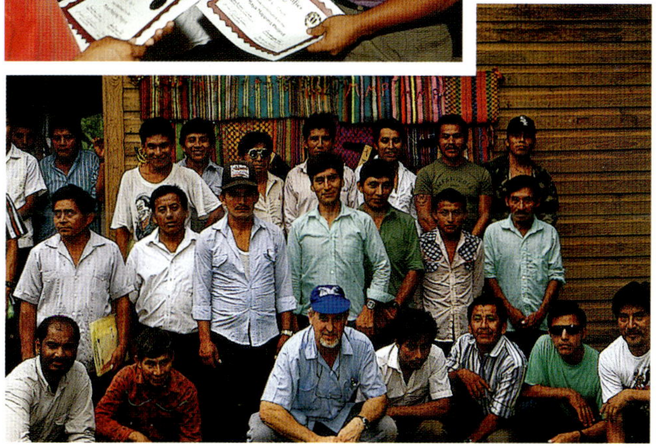
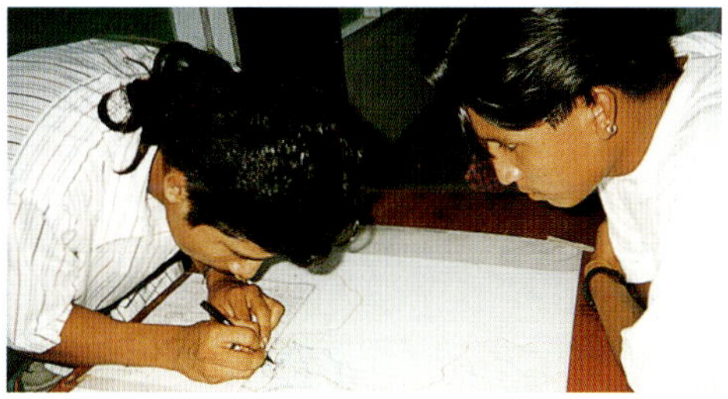
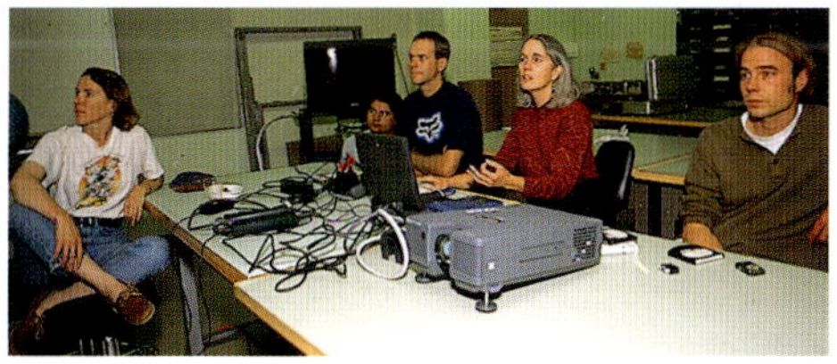

Group Photos

The Cockscomb Workshop

First Row: Sophia Cho, Linadora Bol, Teodora Castellano, Julian Cho, Santiago Chub, Sebastian Shal, Mattido Makin, Dionicio Choc, Everisio Coh, Reyes Chun, Joseph Cal, Marcello Cho
Second Row: Cayetano Ico, Sebastian Choco, Juan Teul, Emeterio Cho, Higinio Chioc, Clara Bol, Julio Saqui, Pio Coc, Marcus Shal, Marcus Bah, Emelino Cho
Third Row: Cruz Cal, Jacinto Max, Mateo Pop, Martin Chen, Jose Coy, Venancio Coc, Domingo Pau, Jose Salam, Domingo Choco
Fourth Row: Martin Tush, Santos Coc, Juan Bo, Andres Coh, Santiago Coh, Regino Cowo, Julio Sanchez, Basilio Ah

The Indian Law Resource Center

First Row: Dalee Sambo Dorough, Deborah Schaaf, Lorna Babby, Marilyn Richardson, Trudy Miller, Armstrong Wiggins
Second Row: Jim Anaya, Tim Coulter, Steve Tullberg, Curt Klotz

GeoMap
Department of Geography
University of California
Berkeley, California

GeoMap was created in 1996 at the University of California by Professor Bernard Nietschmann and a small group of young cartographers to provide mapmaking training and skills to indigenous peoples and local communities. GeoMap takes the best cartographers, the best cartography knowledge, and the best appropriate mapping technology to provide university-based assistance to community-based projects.

Maps are power. Either you will map or you will be mapped. If you are mapped by those who desire to own or control your land and resources, their map will display their justifications for their claims, not yours. Cartographers routinely worked for the governments and corporations of the invaders and occupiers. Recently, however, a new generation of cartographers is inventing a New Cartography, based on a commitment to help indigenous peoples and communities protect the world's two fundamental resources: biological diversity and cultural diversity. The New Cartography is being done using small, powerful computers and handheld GPS (Global Positioning System) receivers to work with and train indigenous peoples who wish to map their traditional knowledge, their territories, and their resources. More powerful and accurate than almost anything that exists in most central governments in most capital cities of the world, this new technology can be carried in a backpack, and, with solar panels, used anywhere.

GeoMap began working with the Miskito people in their autonomous region of northeastern Nicaragua to help them map their traditional sea and coral reef territories. GeoMap's second project was to work with the communities of northeastern Costa Rica to map their aquatic environments and resources. The *Maya Atlas* is GeoMap's third project.

GeoMap
Top: Bernard Nietschmann, Madison Roswell
Bottom: Tim Norris, Steve Rose

At the baseball game; Julio Sanchez, Basilio Ah, Bernard Nietschmann, Tangni Nietschmann, and Andres Coh

Basilio Ah, Andres Coh, Bernard Nietschmann, and Julio Sanchez

Jennie Freeman, Joël Wainwright, Tim Norris, Widdicombe Schmidt, and Charles Tambiah, the first Mapping Workshop, Machaca Camp, June, 1996

North Atlantic Books and GeoMap
First Row: Anastasia McGhee, Steve Rose
Second Row: Susan Bumps, Deborah Schaaf, Diego Bol
Third Row: Madison Roswell, Robin Grossinger, Richard Grossinger, Bernard Q. Nietschmann

Afterword

We are pleased to be able to tell you about our Maya culture and traditions. We hope you understand better the importance of our land and resources to our survival and the continuance of our way of life. If you are interested in learning more about the Maya of Belize, we invite you to get in touch with us. We are proud of our culture, and we welcome you to visit our communities and our people, whether you live in Belize or another country.

We hope you will pass along the information you have learned in our *Maya Atlas* to your friends and colleagues. You would help us by encouraging more cultural exchange about the Maya in schools and institutions both in Belize and abroad.
Perhaps you can help us achieve our goals by offering financial or technical assistance. You can reach us by phone, fax, or letter.
We look forward to hearing from you.

Contact:

Chairman
Toledo Maya Cultural Council
P.O. Box 104
Punta Gorda Town
Toledo District
Belize C.A.
ph/fax (501) 72 2774

Chairman
Toledo Alcaldes Association
Punta Gorda Town
Toledo District
Belize C.A.

Maya Community Phone Numbers
San Antonio (501) 72 2144
San Jose (501) 72 2972
Aguacate (501) 72 2973
San Pedro Columbia (501) 72 2303

In the United States:
Director
Indian Law Resource Center
602 North Ewing Street
Helena, MT 59601
ph (406) 449-2006
fax (406) 449-2031

Index

Topics Index

achiote (Spanish: red annato seeds, *bixa orellana*, used for coloring and flavoring food, *Bixa orellana*) 8
Adventists 58, 109
African bees 133
agouti (*Dasyprocta punctata*) 23
Aguacate 13, 15-18, 42, 43, **52-53**, 57, 117-119, 121, 123-124, 126-127, 139, 150
Aguacate River 52, 53-54
ah'cuab (Ke'kchi: a musician) 36
Alabama (early Maya settlement in Stann Creek District) 110, 113
alcalde (Spanish: a mayor or elected community leader) 1, 3-8, xi, 19, 47, 50, 60, 64, 67, 70, 73-74, 81-82, 85-86, 91, 93, 103-104, 107, 122, 135, 138-139, 145, 150
alcalde system 3-4, 6, 73, 81, 86, 103-104
alkilo (dispersed Maya households, not located close together as in a village) 47, 49, 60, 86
ancestors vii, 7, x, 23, 38-39
ancestral claim 14
ancestral land 1, 9, 76
ancestral territory, 3
ancestral rights 1, 7-8
animals, ancient 27, 40
annual family income 5, 126
antelope (brocket deer, *Mazama americana*) 23
archeological sites 2, 121
arts and crafts 27, 120, 129-133
Asab Shalab (a Maya God for special spiritual concerns) 41
Atlantic Industries sawmill 1-2, 122, 124-125, 151

Atlantic International Ltd. (Malaysian-backed logging) 74, 79, 122, 151-152
atlas, making the **136-147**

ba cajhoc (Ke'kchi: a string made from henequen used to make hammocks) 30
baboon (black howler monkey, *Alouatta pigra*) 23
banana industries 113
bananas (*Musa* sp.) 21, 73, 109
Baptists 47
Barcin (the hunting dog "Spotty" in the Deer Dance Festival) 37, 39
baskets 27-28, 120, 129-130
basket-weaving 49
bass (musical instrument) 26
bayal (Ke'kchi: a natural fiber used to make baskets) 28
beans (*Phaseolus* sp.) 5, vii, 7, x, 21-22, 32, 34-35, 37, 49-50, 64, 69, 104, 109, 113-114, 133
beans, pinto 21, kidney 21-22, white21, black 21, string 21
becan (cohune palm)24
begga bush 22
Belize Constitution 6
Belize Defence Force (BDF) 69, 91
Belize Electric 119
Belize Maya Institute 5
Belize National Selection Exam 70, 134
Belmopan 4-5, 12, 18, 64, 114, 126
Berkeley 1, v, 137-145, 149
bial (Ke'kchi: a natural fiber used to make baskets) 27
Big Falls 1-2, 6, 13, 15-18, 22, 42-43, **102-103**, 117-119, 121-127, 132, 139-140
Big Falls Plantation Limited 103
Big Falls Rice Mill
Big Foot Hairy Man of the forest 23
bitz (fruit from the *bri-bri* tree) 24
Black Creek 19, 58, 83, 90, 102
black hunters (Deer Dance) 36, 38
Bladen Nature Reserve 125, 126
Blanco River 49
Blue Creek 13, 15-18, 22, 42-43, **56-57**, 117-119, 121, 123-124, 126-127, 139
boh (a local rum made from sugarcane) 29
bolouyuuk ikilab ixchquow chalaam (fish poison vine) 24
Boom Creek 13, 15-18, 22, 42, 43, **88-89**, 118-119, 121, 123-124, 139
Boy Scouts 132
bracelets 120, 129
broken ridge 18
bri-bri tree 24
bridges 85
British colonial government 1, 19
British forces 64
British High Commission 60
British Honduras 3, 95
British settlement 3
British woodcutters 7
buluuk (Ke'kchi: a game) 20
buses 4, 114, 118

bus service 4, 9, 118
buul (Mopan: a game) 20
buyul (Mopan: a natural fiber used to make baskets) 27-28, 130
Cabbage Hall Creek 110-111
cabildo (Spanish: town meeting hall and courthouse) 69-70, 103-104
cacao (*Theobroma cacao*) 21, 35, 37, 73, 95, 113, 125
Cacao Creek 95
calabash tree (*Crescentia cujete*) 31, 128
calabash making 31
caldo (Spanish: a meat and vegetable stew) 32, 35-36, 49, 114, 135
ca'intzle (Mopan: a meat and vegetable stew; *caldo* in Spanish) 35
candle 20-21, 24, 34, 37, 40
cane juice 29
Caracol vii, 58
Caracol Hill (an ancient Maya ruin is located near here) 58
carajay (Ke'kchi: boy) 40
cardinal points iv, 36-38, 41
Caribbean Sea 12, 18, 70, 89-90
cartography 137, 139-141, 143-144, 149
cash crops 22, 49, 110, 113
cassava (English: manioc; Spanish: *yuca* ; *Manihot dulcis*) 21, 34
Catholic 70
Catholics 58, 109
cattle 18, 21, 33
cattle hides 33
caves 3, 19, 23, 46, 55-56, 120-121, 140, 142
Cayo District 4, 5, 12-13, 15-18, 42, 118-119, 121, 123-124, 126
cedar 5, 26, 30-31, 35, 60
Cedar Farmers Group 5, 60
ceremonies 3, 26, 36, 39, 41
chachi' (Ke'kchi: a species of fish) 24
cha'kop (Ke'kchi: the 60-foot pole used in the Deer Dance Festival) 37
Cha'n'al (name of one of the dancers in the Cortez Dance) 39
champa (Ke'kchi: a string bag used to carry ears of corn) 30
charcoal 24, 26, 35, 37
charcoal making 24
Che'il 3
che'oreg (Ke'kchi: a plant used to flavor stew dishes) 35
chechah (Mopan: fermented corn beer, chicha in Spanish) 39
chicha (Spanish: a fermented corn beer) 34
chicle (Spanish: the sap of some trees exported to make chewing gum) 3, 49
chicleros (Spanish: gatherers of *chile*) 49
chinams (Mopan: treasurers or people responsible at a Deer Dance Festival) 36
Chiquibul National Park 125-126
Chol 3-6, 104, 138-139
ch'ukcua (Ke'kchi and Mopan: a special occasion sweet tortilla) 34
church 20, 28, 37-38, 44, 47, 49, 52, 55, 57, 69, 79, 85-86, 88, 91, 96, 99, 104, 109-110, 113-114, 119, 145
Church of Christ 47
churches 28, 52, 91, 114
chúyubac' (Mopan: an incense-leaf tree) 28
cilantro (a plant grown to flavor stew dishes) 35
citrus (mostly oranges, *Citrus sinensis*) 8, 19, 21-22, 103, 110, 113-114, 124-125, 133, 144
Classic Period vii
clay 18, 27, 29, 36-37, 41, 120, 129-130
clay pots 27, 129-130
clothing 28, 50, 132
Coban, Guatemala 40
cobañeros (Maya merchants from Petén) 31
Cockscomb 13, 15-17, 42, 110-111, 118-119, 121, 123-124, 126, 142-143, 148
Cockscomb Basin Wildlife Sanctuary 110-111, 126
Cockscomb workshop 143, 148
cohune palm (*Orbignya cohune*) 23, 120
cohune cabbage 35, 120
cohune nuts 3, 35
cocoa (dried, roasted and ground seeds from pods from the cacao tree, *Theobroma cacao*) 5, 8, 20-22, 34, 49, 109, 114
cohune leaf (*becan*) 24
colors 27-28, 31, 37, 137, 140, 142, 145
Columbia River Forest Reserve 5, 60, 122, 124-126
Columbia River Forest Management Plan 122
comal (Spanish: metal pan or sheet used to cook tortillas) 34
communal land system 7, 19, 81
communal work 34
community-based mapping **136-147**
community center 49, 52, 58, 91, 93, 103, 119
community government 135

community phone 119, 150
community researchers 1, 138-139, 141-142
community services ix-x, 5, 63, 118-119
computer cartography 141, 143-144
computer projector 137
computers x, 137, 144-145, 149
Conejo 13, 15-18, 26, 42-43, **84-85**, 86, 117-119, 121, 123-124, 126-127,139
Conservation International 125
cooperatives 133
C'ooxol (a Mayan king and one of the Cortez Dance dancers) 39-40
copal (*Protium copal*) 20-21, 24, 39, 41
Corazon 13, 15-18, 42-43, **80-81**, 117-119, 121, 123-124, 126-127, 139
corn (maize, *Zea mays*) iv-5, 7, 9-x, 10, 18-22, 27-30, 33-37, 39-41, 47, 49-50, 58, 63-64, 67, 69, 73, 85, 88, 91, 104, 109, 114, 125, 129, 131, 133, 135, 137-138
corn cobs 20
corn, mother of all vegetation 39
corn wine 29
corn, divine spirits
corn, harvesting
Corn in the Cave story 9-10
corn planting 19-20, 22, 28, 135, 138
corn seed selection 20-21, 27
cornfield 20-21
cornmill projects 24, 26-27, 128, 131
cornsham (roasted corn grains used to make a coffee-like beverage) 34
coronation 73
Cortez Dance 36, 39-40, 104
cotton 28, 30-31, 134
craboo tree (krabo) 24
crabs 24
crab hunting 22
Cramer Estate 69, 124
Creole 16
Crique Jute 13, 15-18, 42-43, **58-59**, 117-119, 121, 123-124, 126-127, 129-130, 139
Crique Sarco 13, 15-18, 42-43, **70-71**, 103, 117-119, 121, 123-124, 126-127, 143
cultural dances 5, 22, 26
cultural preservation 135
cumla (a offering of chicken meat and tortilla mix) 21
curassow (a large bird, *Crax* sp.) 23, 35
cuxtal (a woven shoulder bag) 27, 31, 120, 140

dance 5, 22-23, 26-28, 36-40, 44, 50, 81, 104
dead, honoring the 6, 10, 22, 39, 79
Deer Dance 22, 36-39
Deer Dance Festival 22, 36-37, 39
deer dancers 36-38
Deep River 4, 12-13, 15-17, 42, 106, 108-109, 118-119, 121, 123-124, 126
development 3-9, 27, 57, 85, 93, 100, 103-104, 110, 113, 119-120, 125-126, 129-131, 133-134, 142, 144
Devil's Dance
dogs 9, 23, 36-39
Dolores 13, 15-18, 42-43, 55, **68-69**, 70, 73, 117-119, 121, 123-124, 126-127
Dolores Estate 73
Dolores Sarstoon 55
dory 31, 55, 88
dory making 31
drugs 132, 134-135
drums 35
dump area 82, 96, 103

East Indians 16, 103
Eastern Morning Star 41
economic development 100, 133
eco-tourism 44, 133
education 3-v, 5, 7, 9, 58, 67, 91, 103, 110, 119, 125-126, 130, 132-135, 139
eels 24
electricity 91, 93, 113, 119
electrification 110, 119
embroidering 31, 129
embroidery 27-28, 104, 107, 120, 129
Environmental, Social, Technical Assistance Program (ESTAP) 126
escabeche (a Maya *caldo* or stew) 32
Evangelists 58
fajina (communal cleaning of a village) 6, 104, 129, 135
fasting 22, 28, 32, 39
Festival of the Village Patron, San Luis (San Antonio village) 22, 36-37
fiddle 36
firewood 6, 8, 23-24, 26, 140, 142
firewood making 24
firewood scarcity 24
fish 1, 18, 22, 24, 28, 31, 44, 47, 49-52, 55, 57, 63-64, 67-70, 73-74, 76, 79, 81-82, 85-86, 88, 91, 93, 95-96, 99-100, 103-104, 107, 109-113, 115, 142
fish poisoning 24
fish poison vine 24
fish soup 24
fishing18, 22, 24, 28, 31, 44, 47, 49-52, 55, 57, 63-64, 67-70, 73-74, 76, 79, 81-82, 85-86, 88, 91, 93, 95-96, 99-100, 103-104, 107, 109-113, 115
floods 22
flute 36, 40
foreign companies 93, 134
foreign investors 7, 93
foreign missionaries 36
forest 2-5, 7-8, 18-20, 23, 30, 33-35, 37-39, 47, 49-50, 58, 60, 103-104, 109, 113, 122, 124-125, 130, 137
Forestry Department 58
Freehold Title 8
fruit trees 7, 109
funding 1, 27, 129, 131, 133-135, 138, 144-145

Garifunas 16
GeoMap 1, v, x-xi, 137-145, 149
gas stoves (propane) 24
General Assembly 5
Georgetown 110
gibnut (paca, *Agouti paca*) 9, 23, 35
Global Positioning System (GPS) 137, 141, 149
Gods 20-21, 26, 37, 40-41
gold 43, 47, 107, 113, 139
Golden Stream 13, 15-18, 42-43, 47, **106-107**, 117-119, 121, 123-124, 126, 139
Government of Belize (GOB) 1, 3, 5-8, 14, 50, 67, 74, 76, 82, 119, 122, 126, 135, 138
Graham Creek 17, 73
grapefruit 109
grassland 18
guest houses 44, 49, 103, 120-121
guitar 26, 36
Guatemala 3-4, vii, 9, 12-18, 22, 31, 40, 42, 44, 50, 52, 62-65, 67, 69-70, 95-96, 113, 118-119, 121, 123-25

hammock 29-30
hammock making 29
handicrafts 27
harp 20, 26, 35-38, 49, 69, 137, 145
harvesting 22, 69
Hawia River 48, 65
healing 28, 32, 39, 41
healing plants 32
health 4-5, 9-10, 30, 32, 41, 52, 69, 103-104, 110, 114, 119, 125-126, 135
health center 52, 114, 118, 119
health post 52, 69, 110
henequen fiber 29
henequen (a fiber plant) 29
Hicatee 13, 15-18, 42-43, **68-69**, 117-119, 121, 123-124, 126
high school 4, 52, 67, 70, 104, 110, 119, 132, 134
Hills and Valleys 21
Hinchosonnes (near Santa Teresa) 55
hix (jaguar, *Panthera onca*) 21, 40
holy deer (Deer Dance Festival) 36-37, 39
Homeland 1-2, 4-5, 7-x, 138, 144
Homeland proposal 4, 7-8
homeland map 4
horse saddle 33
hot peppers 35
house framing 33-34
house woods 34
Hun Utchben Ilma (Mopan kings, queens, priests) 6
Hun Shil (Ke'kchi kings, queens, priests) 6
hunting 10, 18, 22-23, 28, 31, 37, 39, 44, 47, 49-52, 55, 57-58, 60, 63-64, 67-70, 73-74, 76, 79, 81-82, 85-86, 88, 91, 93, 95-96, 99-100, 103-104, 107, 109-113, 115, 122, 140
hunting grounds 18, 23, 122, 140
hurricane 55

illiteracy 5, 85, 122, 126
ilma (Mopan: shaman) 6, 41
ilonel (Ke'kchi: shaman) 41
immigrants 2, 138
incense (important are *copal* and *naba*) 3, 10, **20-24**, 28, 32-33, 36-41, 73
incense burning 3, 28, 32
incense leaves 21
incense uses 28
Indian Creek 13, 15-18, 42-43, **100-101**, 117-119, 121, 123-124, 126-127
Indian Law Resource Center (ILRC) v, 1, 8, 27, 138-139, 143-145, 148, 150
inheritance 19
Inter-American Development Bank (IDB) 126, 144
Inter-American Foundation 1, v, xi, 138
inter-marriages
International Rescue Committees' Quick Impact Project (UNICEF) 60
interviews 2, x, 138

ique'h (a natural fiber used to make rope) 30
isk'ih (Ke'kchi: mint leaves used to flavor stew dishes) 35
Itza (Petén)
Ixbenil Son (Ke'kchi: Maya Anthem) 26
ix'ca'al (Ke'kchi: girls) 40
Ix Chel (goddess of healing) 32

Jacinto Creek 13, 15-17, 42, 92, 118, 121, 123-124
jaguar (also called "tiger" locally, *Panthera onca*) 9, 23, 36, 110, 129, 142
Jalacte 13, 15-18, 42-43, **64-65**, 117-119, 121, 123-124, 126-127, 139
jalacte (Ke'kchi: a species of riverside palm trees) 64
Jamaicans 118
Jimmy Cut 60, 122
jipijapa (a natural fiber used for baskets) 28, 35, 129
Jordan 13, 15-18, 42-43, **56-57**, 118-119, 121, 123-124, 126, 139
jute (Mopan: river snails) 43, 58, 129-130, 139

kaaj (Ke'kchi and Mopan: traditional grinding stone or *metate*) 34
k'ah (Ke'kchi: a beverage made from sweet corn) 34
K'eche Cuink (the name of one of the dancers for the Cortez Dance) 39
keel-billed motmot (*Electron carinatrum*) 125
k'el (Ke'kchi: a metal pan or sheet used to cook tortillas—*comal* in Spanish) 34
Ke'kchi Council of Belize 5-6, 122
kerosene 24
killer bees 133
koton (Mopan: a woman's blouse) 28
ko'yem (Ke'kchi: a corn drink) 20
kua (Ke'kchi: tortillas) 24
KuKue Can' (Gods of Peace) 26
kudzo 22
kumum (a palm with leaves used as brooms) 24

lab (a beverage made from sweet corn) 1, 4-5, 8, 23-24, 27-31, 34, 37, 41, 58, 81, 107, 109-110, 113-114, 120, 129, 131-133, 135, 137-139, 143-144
lagoon 82
Laguna 13, 15-18, 29, 31, 34-35, 42-43, 57, **82-83**, 100, 103, 117-119, 121, 123-124, 126-127, 132, 139
land clearing 22
land owned by outsiders 18, 127
land tenure 5, 122, 125
Land Trust Committee 8
land use vii, ix-x, 18-19, 24, 81, 93, 127, 137-138, 140, 142-144
land use rules 19
legal recognition 14
lightning 10
limosna (Mopan: a ceremonial gift) 39
Lannan Foundation viii, 145
leather making 33
logging 1, 5, vii, 7-8, x, 23, 74, 76, 79, 88, 122, 125-127, 134, 138, 142, 144
logging companies 122
logging concessions 1, 5, 122, 123
logging impacts 122
Lubaantun vii, 94, 121
Luxembourg, government of v, xi, 144

Mabil Ha 13, 15-18, 42-43, **76-77**, 117-119, 121, 123-124, 126-127
MacArthur Foundation 1, v, xi
macapal (one of the sticks used to weave a *cuxtal* bag) 31
machac (a fish) xi, 24, 55, 139-140
Machaca Camp workshop 140, 141
mahogany 3, 26, 30-31, 35, 58, 69
mahogany cutters 58
maize 5, vii, 113
making the *Maya Atlas* 136-147
Malaysian 61, 74, 79, 88, 90, 94, 102, 122, 124-125, 127, 138, 144
Malaysian logging 61, 90, 94, 102, 124, 138
Mamah (Ke'kchi: law man) 6
Man, Wife, Animals story 33
Manci-chol Maya 3
mandolin 36
mango 109
mangrove 18
maps 1, 3, x, 137, 139-144, 149
mapping x, 1, 14, 136-144, 149
mapping workshops 144
Mamah (Ke'kchi: law man)
marcha (Mopan: Mayas' Anthem) 26
market days 22
markets 21, 110, 133-134
marriage 28, 32
marimba 20, 25-26, 32, 36-39, 49-50, 114
masa lab (a corn beverage) 29
matambre (a high-yield field of corn planted alongside rivers or in humid depressions) 18-19, 93
matz (Ke'kchi: sweet corn *lab* with beans) 34
Maya Atlas, making the 1-2, vii, ix-x, **136-147**, 143-145, 149
Maya agriculture 21
Maya Association of Belize, The 5
Maya Centre 5, 13, 15-18, 27-28, 30, 35, 42-43, **110-111**, 117-119, 121, 123-124, 126, 130-131, 134, 139, 142
Maya Centre Indigenous Organization 5
Maya Centre Water Board 110
Maya Centre Women's Group 27, 130
Maya chiefs 6
Maya communal lands x, 4, 123, 127
Maya Flag ii-iii
Maya Gods 40-41
Maya Homeland 1-2, 5, 7-ix
Maya Land v, 5, vii, x, 18, 23, 28, 31, 35, 122-123, 127, 134, 137-138, 142, 144
Maya Mapping Project (MMP) x, 1, 14, 138-141, 144
Maya Mopan 8, 13, 15-18, 42-43, 103, 110, **112-113**, 118-119, 121, 123-124, 126, 139
Maya Mountains 13, 15-18, 42, 94, 115, 117-119, 121, 123-127, 137
Maya Mountains Forest Reserve 125-126
Maya teachers 5, 49
Maya territory 1, 4, 14
Maya Traditional Altar (made with special woods) 36-37
Maya Year (calendar year) 21-22
Maya youth 132, 135
medicinal plants 32
Medina Bank 13, 15-18, 42-43, **108-109**, 117-119, 121, 123-124, 126-127
Mennonites 47, 58
Mestizo 88, 95, 103
metate (Spanish and English: a grinding stone for corn) 34
Mexico 12, 18
Midway 13, 15-18, 28, 42-43, **86-87**, 118-119, 121, 123-124, 126, 139
milpa (Spanish: a small household subsistence farm; the slash-and-burn farming method) 5, 7, x, 18-19, 22, 70, 73-74, 86, 91, 100, 103, 109, 113-114, 125, 135, 140
missionaries 3, 36
moho bark (bark from the hibiscus tree used to make rope and to tie things) 37
Moho River 3, 4, 12-13, 15-17, 19, 42, 52, 54-56, 83, 87-92, 93, 118-119, 121, 123-124, 126
Moho River Aguacate 52
Monkey Dance 36
Moon 33, 41
Morro Dance 36
mortar making 35
mortar and pestle 22, 35
mother of all vegetation 39
Mountain Cave 9
mountain cow (Baird's tapir, *Tapirus bairdii*) 23
mulch 5, 18-19
mulching 18
museum 3, 82
music 3, 26, 32, 36, 39, 49, 114, 132, 145
musical instruments 26, 36
Mutuzum (name of one of the dancers in the Cortez Dance) 39

Na Luûm Caj (Mother Earth Village) 13, 15-18, 42-43, 48, **60-61**, 117-119, 121, 123-124, 126-127, 139
naba (Ke'kchi and Mopan: a very hard wood used to make a sugarcane press; bark used for incense)
National Geographic Society viii, x-xi, 144
Native Lands 138
Nazarenes 58
New Year 22
night walker (kinkajou, *Potos flavus*) 23
nisop (inebriated) 39
Nos Sos Falls (a waterfall near San Antonio)
Notch Winic (Mopan: a law man) 6

ochehelestûk (Mopan: one of the special woods for the Maya Traditional Altar) 37
ohlay acer (Mopan: one of the special woods to make the Maya Traditional Altar) 37
ohleche' (Mopan: one of the special woods used to make the Maya Traditional Altar) 37
orego (Mopan: a plant used to flavor stew dishes) 35
Otoxha 13, 15-18, 42-43, 67, 69, **72-73**, 81, 117-119, 121, 123-124, 126-127 139
outside problems **122-126**
over-hunting 23
owls 23

paca 9, 23
papaya 34, 109
Parent-Teachers Association (Maya Centre) 103, 110
partridge (a bird hunted in the forest) 35
pash (Mopan: a musician) 36-37
pastor 82
pasture 18
Peace Corps Volunteers 82
peccary (collared peccary, *Pecari tajacu*) 9-10, 23, 35
Pepper Camp 114
peppers (various species of chile peppers) 35
Petén 3, 31, 44, 50, 58, 95
Pew Charitable Trusts xi, 144
Phillips Oil Company 58
photography 143
pigs 23, 55, 60, 67, 69, 82, 85
pig-rearing 49
pilón (Spanish and Mopan: mortar) 35
pine ridge 18
pineapple 34
pinol (Spanish and Mopan: a beverage made from sweet corn) 34, 104
plantains 21, 109
plantation (*milpa*) 8, 18-19, 21-22, 24, 34-35, 57-58, 67, 69, 86, 91, 96, 103, 113, 129, 142, 144
Pohlil Kah (Mopan law man; *alcalde*) 6
pohoc (Ke'kchi: henequen fiber used to make a hammock) 29
poison 23-24
poisonous snakes 23
Poite River 8, 14, 24
police 6, 9, 67, 70, 104
political representation 5, 126
pom (resin from the *copal* tree used as incense) 32, 41

Pooc (Ke'kchi: place with plums; first name for Jordan village 20, 34-35, 37, 57
pooch (Ke'kchi and Mopan: a *tamale*-like corn dough boiled or roasted in a *waha* leaf) 20, 34-35, 37
popol (Ke'kchi: a meeting hall-courtroom; *cabildo* in Spanish) 104
Popul Vuh iv
pôôt (Ke'kchi: a woman's blouse) 28
population 1, 9-x, 14, 24, 44, 47, 49-50, 52, 55, 57-58, 60, 63-64, 67, 69-70, 73-74, 76, 79, 81-82, 85-86, 88, 91, 93, 95-96, 99-100, 103-104, 107, 109, 111, 113-114
posol (Spanish: a beverage made from roasted and ground corn kernels) 20, 34
pottery 27-29, 104, 120, 129
pottery making 27-29
prayers 3, 10, 20, 22-23, 28, 32, 39
praying 10, 20-21, 39
precipitation 22
priest 6, 40, 70, 81, 104
primary school 5, 50, 58, 67, 82, 86, 91, 93, 103-104, 109-110, 118-119, 133-134
Progress Ltd.
propane gas 24
Protestants 47
Pueblo Viejo 9, 13, 15-18, 42-43, **50-51**, 58, 107, 117-119, 121, 123-124, 126-127
Punta Gorda (Punta Gorda Town) 3-5, 9, 12-13, 15-18, 22, 27, 49, 52, 55, 67, 70, 74, 88, 93, 103-104, 117-119, 121, 123-124, 126-127, 129, 132, 134, 145, 150
Puscilha 3

qh'echal sha'leb (Ke'kchi: sponsors of the Deer Dance Festival) 37
qku'tej (a rosewood-like tree wood) 26
quam (guan, crested guan, *Penelope purpurascens*) 10, 23, 35, 110
quash (coatimundi, *Nasua narica*) vii, 9, 23
Queen Elizabeth II, coronation 6, 73
quimbal (the figure-eight shape of cotton thread to make a *cuxtal*) 31

rabbit 9
racoon 9
rah rum 38
rain 1-2, iv-vii, 7-8, x, 18, 21-22, 24, 34-35, 39, 49, 69, 88, 103-104, 113, 122, 125, 129, 131-134, 138-144, 149
rainfall vii, x, 125
Raleigh International 67
Red Bank 13, 15-18, 42-43, **112-113**, 118-119, 121, 123-124, 126
refugees 113
regional age distribution 14
Regional Coordinators 142, 145
regional identity 14
regional religious practice 14
religious denominations 47, 50
reinvestment of women's group income 131
reservations 1, 7, x, 99, 123, 125-126
reservation system 7
rice vii, 18-22, 30, 32, 34-35, 37, 50, 57, 64, 67, 85, 88, 91, 103-104, 109, 113-114, 129, 131, 133-135
Rio Blanco 46, 48, 50-51, 57, 93
Rio Blanco Fall 50-51
Rio Blanco Indian Reservation 50, 123, 126
Rio Blanco National Park,50, 126
Rio Grande Cooperative 133
rituals 26, 41
rivers 5, 18-19, 24, 31, 37, 49, 57, 104, 113, 140, 142,
roads iv-5, 9, 58, 140, 144
rock carving 30
rope making
rose-apple 109
ruins 8, 113, 122, 140, 142
Ruj'il (Ke'kchi : a law man) 6

saddle making 33
sa'h (Mopan: sweet corn *lab* with beans) 34
sa'il ûûk (Ke'kchi: a woman's slip) 28
Sajil Cholexil Women's Group (Silver Creek) 104
Salamanca (forestry camp, later outpost for British military forces) 45, 58-59, 61, 94, 117, 127
samaat (a plant with long thin black leaves used to flavor stew dishes) 35
samilakil (one of the sticks used to weave a *cuxtal* bag) 31
San Antonio 13, 15-18, 22, 42-43, **44-45**, 49, 61, 117-119, 121, 123-124, 126-127
San Benito Poite 13, 15-18, 42-43, **66-67**, 86, 117-119, 121, 123-124, 126-127
San Felipe 13, 15-19, 42-43, 91, **92-93**, 117-119, 121, 123-124, 126-127
San Jose 13, 15-18, 42-43, **48-49**, 103, 113, 122, 124, 132, 139, 150
San Isidro Roman Catholic School 103
San Lucas 74, **78-79**, 81, 117-119, 121, 123-124, 126-127, 136, 139
San Luis (Petén) 36-38, 44, 50
San Luis Rey (patron saint of San Antonio) 36
San Marcos 13, 15-18, 31, 42-43, **96-97**, 118-119, 121, 123-124, 126, 139
San Miguel 13, 15-18, 42-43, 94, **98-99**, 117-119, 121, 123-124, 126-127
San Luis, Petén, Guatemala 95
San Pedro Columbia 6-7, 13, 15-18, 42-43, 82, **94-95**, 99, 117-119, 121, 123-124, 126-127, 132-133, 135, 139, 142-143, 150
San Pedro Columbia Rice Growers Cooperative 137
San Roman 13, 15-18, 42-43, 47, **114-115**, 118-119, 121, 123-124, 126
San Vicente 13, 15-18, 42-43, **62-63**, 117-119, 121, 123-124, 126-127, 139
sankil che (a dark red wood) 26
Santa Anna 13, 15-18, 42-43, 86, 88, **90-91**, 93, 117-119, 121, 123-124, 126-127, 139
Santa Cruz 13, 15-19, 42-43, **46-47**, 50, 117-119, 121, 123-124, 126-127
Santa Elena 13, 15-18, 42-43, **50-51**, 117-119, 121, 123-124, 126-127, 133, 139
Santa Rosa 13, 15-19, 42-43, **114-115**, 118-119, 121, 123-124, 126
Santa Teresa (Santa Teresa) 13, 15-18, 28, 42-43, **54-55**, 99, 103, 117-119, 121, 123-124, 126-127, 139, 142
Saving Animals, Vegetation and Environment (SAVE) 39, 104, 132
sa'yuk (Mopan: the 60-foot pole used in the Deer Dance Festival) 37-38
sawmill 1-2, 5, 30, 76, 122, 124-125, 127, 134
sawmill project 5
sawmills 1, 2, 5, 30, 124, 127, 134
scarlet macaw (*Ara macao*) 113
Scarlet Macaws Conservation Project 113
schools 5, 134, 150
primary school 5, 50, 58, 67, 82, 86, 91, 93, 103-104, 109-110, 118-119, 133-134
secondary school 6, 134
tertiary school 134
buses 4, 114
sewing machines 27
school buses 4, 114
Se-Pan (Ke'kchi name for Santa Teresa village) 55
shamans 6, 41
sha'an sho'yuk na (Mopan: a village rest house) 120
sh'mm'ch (a metal pan or plate use to cook tortillas—*comal* in Spanish) 34
si'maatou (Ke'kchi: a ceremonial gift) 39
sign of the cross 20
Silver Creek 6, 13, 15-18, 29, 42-43, 99, **104-105**, 117-119, 121, 123-124, 126-127, 132, 139, 142
Sittee River 12-13, 15-17, 42, 110, 118-119, 121, 123-124, 126
siuk tree (the tree used for the 60-foot pole in the Deer Dance Festival) 37-38
slash-and-burn 5, 18-19, 135
slash-and-mulch 5
snakes 23, 26
snakes, poisonous 23
snook (a fish) 24
social dances 22
Society for the Promotion of Education and

Research (SPEAR) 1, 22, 24, 139, 143, 145
Southern Bee Keeper Cooperative 133
Southern Highway 13, 15-18, 42, 75, 82, 100, 103-104, 109-110, 117-119, 122, 125, 127, 144
Spanish missionaries 3
soursop (*Annono americana*)
species diversity 125
spinach 21
spindle 30
spirit of creation 20
spiritual cardinal signs 20
Stann Creek District x,1, 8, 12-14, 15-18, 39, 47, 110, 118-119, 121, 126, 137, 140, 142
statue 7-38, 50, 55, 69, 79, 95, 99
string beans 21
subbim (a tree) 24
suc pic (Mopan: a woman's slip) 28
Sucootz Maya Organization 5
sugar 29, 37
Sun 21, 28-29, 31, 33-35, 39-41
Sunday Wood 13, 15-18, 25, 42-43, **74-75**, 117-119, 121, 123-124, 126-127, 139, 142
Sunday Wood Creek 74
supa palm 30
sursukil sha'nal cabl (Ke'kchi: a village rest house) 120
swamp 18
sweet potatoes 21
swimming 91, 107, 109, 132

tamal (Spanish: boiled corn meal dough with meat and vegetables wrapped in corn husk) 20, 34
tape recorders 142
Tapir Women's Group, San Antonio 28
Tiger Women's Group, San Antonio 133-134
telephones 117-118
Temash River 4, 12-13, 15-17, 42, 68, 70-72, 74-75, 80, 84-85, 118-119, 121, 123-124, 126
temples 2-3, 7, 23, 39, 103
tenleb (Ke'kchi: mortar) 35
tiââlinbil (Ke'kchi: a meat and vegetable stew; *caldo* in Spanish) 35
tie-tie (a natural fiber used to make baskets) 28
tiger (jaguar) 9, 23, 26, 36-40, 129-130
thanksgiving 20, 22, 39
thread making 30, 129
thunder 9
Toledo Community College 4-6
Toledo Sister Caritas Lawrence CSC (school) 5
TMCC (Toledo Maya Cultural Council) iii-v, xi, 1-8, 60, 122, 136-140, 142-145,150
TMCC mission statement 3-4
Toledo Alcaldes Association (TAA) xi, 1, 4-7, 122, 138, 142-143, 145, 150
Toledo Atlantic International Ltd (Malaysian-backed logging) 122-124
Toledo District x, 1, 3-5, 7-8,, 12-14, 36, 42, 52, 69, 74, 91, 100, 103, 113, 118-119, 121-126, 129, 134, 137-141, 145, 150
Toledo Ecotourism Association (TEA) 120
Toledo Indian Movement 5
Toledo Relief Fund for Refugees 113
Toledo Rural Development Project (TRDP) 57
Tonko (the hunting dog "Charred Tail" in the Deer Dance Festival) 39
tortillas x, 20-21, 24, 27, 32, 34, 114, 135
Torros Dance 36
tourism 7, ix-x, 30, 44, 50, 82, 103, 110, 113, 119, **120-121**, 133
tourists 8, 28, 30, 50, 107, 119-120, 130
toxic waste vii, 138, 144
tradition 2, 6-7, 10, 19-24, 27, 29, 32, 34-39, 44, 47, 49-50, 52, 60, 73, 76, 79, 81, 104, 114, 122, 132-135, 140, 143, 149-150
traditional healers 7, 140
traditional healing 32, 39
traditional healing herbs 140
Traditional Hunting story 10
traditional medicine 140
traditional ways 2, 132
trapiche (a wooden sugar-cane press) 29
tze'h (Mopan: a species of fish) 24
tzuluc (Ke'kchi: a wood frame used to make a hammock) 30

Uch Ben Cah (ancient Maya ruin near Santa Cruz) 47
UC Berkeley v, 137-138, 140-144
University of California 1, 143, 149
ushb' (Ke'kchi: an incense-leaf tree) 28
ûûk' (Ke'kchi: a woman's skirt) 28

video project 5
videography 140, 143
videographer 140, 143
village council 103, 110, 113, 119
village histories 1-2, **44-114**

village maps x, **45-115**, 137, 143-144
village researchers x, 139-143, 145
village survey questionnaires 138, 140-142
village phone 52
violin 26

wah (Mopan: tortillas) 20, 22, 24, 34, 36, 114
waha leaves (for wrapping food) 20
wahmil (secondary, fresh scrub bush) 22, 43
Wal Cua 2
Wal Itza 2
Wal Shucaneb 2
Wal Taca 2
Wapinol (Spanish: a wild fruit tree) 104
wari (white-lipped peccary) 23, 35
water vii, 9, 18, 21, 33, 35, 38, 41, 44, 57, 69, 82, 91, 93, 95, 103-104, 109-110, 119
water, special from secret caves 41
water system 82, 110
water tanks 91
waterfalls 46-47, 55, 61, 103, 113, 120-121, 140, 142
watermelon 34
weavers 28
wedding day 32
wee-wee (wiwi) leaf-cutting ants 9, 21
white beans 21
Whitney's Company 100
wild ducks 23
wild pigs 23
wood carving 30
woodpecker 9-10
women's development 131
women's groups 5, 107, 129-131
women's work 132
World Resources Institute 5
workshops 1, 4-5, 8, x, 131, 135, 137-141, 144

yams 34
youth activities 136
Yum Kax (corn god) 10, 20, 41
yummil oku't (Mopan: the sponsors of a Deer Dance Festival) 37
Yucatecan 3
Yucatán 3, vii, 44

Place Index

Acres Of Love 83, 124
Actun Haleh 61
Aguacate 13, 15-18, 42, **53**, 117-119, 121, 123-124, 126-127
Aguacate Creek 13, 15-17, 42, 118-119, 121, 123-124, 126
Aguacate River 53-54
Aguacate Road 56, 66
alcalde 4, 118
Ambergris Caye 12
American Camp 48
Antonia Creek 89, 92
Aquacate Swamp 17
archeological sites 121
Armado Creek 17, 89, 92
arts and crafts 118, 121
Atlantic Ocean 12

Baca Rea 54
Bahia Chetumal 12
Bareja Creek 90
Barera Creek 87
Barranco 13, 15-17, 42, 90, 117-119, 121, 123-124, 126-127
Barranco Road 90
Belize 12-13, 126,
Belize City 12
Belize District 12-13
Belize River 12
Belmopan 4, 12, 18
Ben-nil San Antonio 61
Ben-nil San Jose 61
Benil Cá 48
Benil Col 48
Benil Punto 48
Benil Santa Cruz 48
Benil Tzôn 48
Bieras Creek 84
Big Falls 13, 15-18, 22, 42, **102**, 117-119, 121, 123-124, 126-127
Big Falls Road 97
Big Falls Waterfall 121
Black Creek 56, 83, 90, 102
Black Creek Lagoon 56, 90
Bladen 12-13, 15-17, 42, 101, 106, 108, 118-119, 121, 123-126

Bladen Branch 12-13, 15-17, 42, 108, 118-119, 121, 123-124, 126
Bladen Nature Reserve 126
Bladen Road 101
Blossom Berry Creek 17
Blue Creek 13, 15-18, 42, **56**, 117-119, 121, 123-124, 126-127
Blue Creek 13, 15-17, 42, 56, 83, 118, 121, 123-124
Blue Creek Cave 46, 56, 121
Blue Creek Road 45, 56
Boom Creek 13, 15-18, 42, **89**, 118-119, 121, 123-124, 126
Bosh Ha 61
Bottle Creek 101
Bouden Creek 101
Bowman 124
Box Ha 51
Broken Ridge 18
Burges 117, 127
bus services 118
Butterfly Road 94

Cabbage Haul Creek 111
Cabbage Haul Fire Lookout 111
Cabbage Haul Gap 111
CaCaowil Ha 68
Calajel Ha 54
Calente Road 71
Calente Stream 71
Caliente Creek 102
Calvary Hill 45
Caraso Creek 17, 89
Carasow Creek 90
Caribbean Sea 12, 18, 89-90
Cattle Landing 16, 117, 127
cave 46, 56, 121
Caweyil Ha 54
Caye Caulker 12
Cayes Branch 13
Cayo District 4, 12-13, 15-18, 42, 118-119, 121, 123-124, 126
Central 17, 48, 117, 127
Central River 17
Chakil Ha 72
Champon Road 105
Chan Quebrada 117, 127
Chano Creek 94
Charles Seller Sawmill 124
Chich Ha 112
Chinese Logging 124
Chiquibul Branch 13, 15-17, 42, 118, 121, 123-124, 126
Chiquibul Forest Reserve 126
Chiquibul National Park 126
Christmas Bridge 45
Chu Ha 80
church 111, 119, 121
Chutamil Cooperative 101
Cirila Creek 92
Cisil Ha 59, 61
Citrus Plantation 124
Cockscomb Basin 13, 15-17, 42, 111, 118-119, 121, 123-124, 126
Cockscomb Basin Wildlife Sanctuary 111, 126
Cocoa Branch 13, 15-17, 42, 118, 121, 123-124, 126
Columbia Branch 13, 15-17, 42, 118-119, 121, 123-124, 126
Columbia River 45, 59, 61, 94
Columbia River Forest Reserve 126
Columbia Spring 94
Commence Bight 126
Communal Lands 18, 123
Conejo 13, 15-18, 42, **84**, 117-119, 121, 123-124, 126-127
Conejo Creek 13, 15-17, 118, 121, 123-124
Conejo Road 84, 87
Corazon 13, 15-18, 42, **80**, 117-119, 121, 123-124, 126-127
cornmill 118
Corozal 12
Corozal District 12
Corozon Road 72
Corozon Trail 75
Costa Rica 12
Cotohel Creek 78
Cramer Estate 124
Creole 16
Crique Arenalosa 112
Crique Jute 45
Crique Jute 13, 15-18, 42, **59**, 117-119, 121, 123-124, 126-127
Crique Jute Road 45
Crique Negro 45
Crique Sarco 13, 15-18, 42, **71**, 117-119, 121, 123-124, 126-127
Crique Sarco Road 68, 72, 80
Crique Troso 94

Cu Blanco 51
Curasow Creek 87

Dan Nil Ha 54
Dancing Pool 111
Dangriga 12-13, 119
Danto Creek 112
Daraskil Ha 83
Deep River 4, 12-13, 15-17, 42, 106, 108, 118-119, 121, 123-124, 126
Deep River Forest Reserve 126
Diosil Ha 54
Doa Creek 108
Dolores 13, 15-18, 42, **68**, 117-119, 121, 123-124, 126-127
Dolores Road 72
Dove Cliff Rock 111
Dump Area 94, 102
Dump Trail 97

Eastern Branch (Belize River) 12-13
East Indian 16
Edward Central 48
Edwards Central 117, 127
Eguen Che Ha 112
El Salvador 12, 18
electricity 118
Esperanza 117, 127
Esperanza Camp 117, 127

Forest 18, 117, 126-127
Forest Home 116, 117, 127
Fresh Water Creek 17,80

Genus Sawmill 124
Georgetown 16, 112
Georgetown Road 112
Glovers Reef 12
Go To Hell Creek 17, 98, 105
Go To Hell River 80
Go To Hell Stream 71, 77
Golden Pippen 111
Golden Stream 4, 12-13, 15-17, 42, 106, 118-119, 121, 123-124, 126
Golden Stream 13, 15-18, 42, **106**, 117-119, 121, 123-124, 126-127
government office 118
Graham Creek 17
Grassland 18
Green Creek 92
Guam Church Bank 111
Guatemala 4, 12-18, 22, 42, 62, 65, 118-119, 121, 123-126
Guatemala City 12
guest houses 121
Gulf of Honduras 12-13, 15-18, 22, 42, 118-119, 121, 123-124, 126
Gulf of Mexico 12, 18

Ha Ah Marto 48
Ha Ill A Che Aj 45
Ha Ill Acrino 45
Ha Ill Aquin 45
Ha Ill Ayin 45
Ha Ill Balum 51
Ha Ill Belente 61
Ha Ill Blanco 48
Ha Ill Bosh 51
Ha Ill Che 48
Ha Ill Chice 45
Ha Ill Chimun 51
Ha Ill Louv 61
Ha Ill Maax 51
Ha Ill Map 45
Ha Ill Prasca 61
Ha Ill Tutu 45, 48, 59, 61
Ha Ill Tutuh Cá 61
Ha Ill Tuzu 45, 59, 48
Ha Ill Tza'c 48
Ha Ill Tzimin Che 61
Hal Back 90
Hellgate Run 111, 124
Henry Kelly Creek 111
Hicatee Creek 13, 15-18, 42, **68**, 117-119, 121, 123-124, 126-127
Hicatee Creek 13, 15-17, 42, 68, 102, 105, 118, 121, 123-124
Hilal Che Road 98
Hishil Ha 97
Honduras 13, 18
Hop Creek 106
Hopkins 16
Hughes 124
Hunting Grounds 18, 127
Hus Hil Ha 98

Ich Ulehiil 59

Independence 16
Indian Creek 13, 15-17, 42, 102, 106, 118, 121, 123-124, 126
Indian Creek 13, 15-18, 42, **101**, 117-119, 121, 123-124, 126-127
Ish Witzil 45

Jacinto Creek 13, 15-17, 42, 92, 118, 121, 123-124
Jacinto River 83
Jalacte 13, 15-18, 42, **65**, 117-119, 121, 123-124, 126-127
Jalacte Creek 53
Jalacte River 65
Jalacte Road 51, 62
Jalawate Ha 80
Janshil Be 83
Jenkins Creek 112
Jimmy Cut 59, 61, 117, 127
Jimmy Cut Hill 61
Jokh'en Wa Patalech 112
Jordan 13, 15-18, 42, **56**, 118-119, 121, 123-124
Jordan Road 90
Joshua Creek 101, 106
Joventud 66, 117, 127
Juan Branch 112

Kallera Pec Road 98
Keky Ha 83
Kikche 54
Kish Pekil Ha Road 72
Kux Ill Ha 111

Lagarto Creek 112
Lagoon 83
Laguna 45, 84
Laguna 13, 15-18, 42, **83**, 117-119, 121, 123-124, 126-127
Laguna Road 83
Laguna Trail 92
Land Owned By Outsiders 18, 127
Lighthouse Reef 12
Logging 61, 90, 94, 102, 108, 124, 127
Logging Concessions 123
Long Cliff 111
Lu Ha 83
Lubaantun (Hubaantunich) 94, 121

Mabil Ha 77
Mabil Ha 13, 15-18, 42, 54, **77**, 117-119, 121, 123-124, 126-127
Mabil Ha Trail 75
Macal River 13
Machaca 66, 77, 97, 108, 117, 126-127
Machaca Creek 97, 108
Machaca River 66, 77
Machakil Ha Road 72
Mafredi 13, 15-17, 42, 45, 118-119, 121, 123-124, 126
Mafredi Creek 13, 15-17, 42, 118, 121, 123-124
Mafredi Lagoon 17
Makil Ha 68
Malaysaian Sawmill 124
Malaysian Logging 61, 90, 94, 102, 124
Managua 12, 18
Mango Creek 16, 126
Mangrove 18
Manzana Stream 51
Mares Nest 13, 16, 42
Marimpil Ha 83
Matambre 18
Maya Centre 13, 15-18, 42, **111**, 118-119, 121, 123-124, 126
Maya communal lands 4, 123, 127
Maya Homeland 4
Maya Land Use 18, 123, 127
Maya Mopan 13, 15-18, 42, **112**, 118-119, 121, 123-124, 126
Maya Mountain Forest Reserve 126
Maya Mountains 13, 15-18, 42, 94, 115, 117-119, 121, 123-127
Maya Reservation 126, 123
medical services 118
Medina Bank 13, 15-18, 42, **108**, 117-119, 121, 123-124, 126-127
Mexico 12, 18
Middle River 13, 15-17, 42, 118, 121, 123-124
Midway 13, 15-18, 42, **87**, 118-119, 121, 123-124, 126
Midway Road 87
Militesh 83, 90
Mill Creek 84, 87
Milpa 18
Mirimar 48, 117, 127
Mirimar Hill 48
Mitchell Creek 111
Mitchell Run 111
Mochochil Ha 92
Moho River 4, 12-13, 15-17, 42, 54, 56, 83, 87, 89-90, 92, 118-119, 121, 123-124, 126

Moho Trail 77
Mokchil Ha 90
Moko Chila 80
Monkey Falls 53
Monkey River 4, 12-13, 15-17, 42, 118-119, 121, 123-124, 126
Monkey River 4, 12-13, 15-17, 42, 118-119, 121, 123-124, 126
Monkey Tail Branch 17
Monto Portio Trail 108
Moody Hill Creek 101
Mopan Ha 112
Mother Point 89, 117, 127
Mountain Pine Ridge 13
Mukbil Ha 68
Mullins River 13

Na Luûm Caj 13, 15-18, 42, 48, **61**, 117-119, 121, 123-124, 126-127
Nasario 117, 127
Nasimento Ha 62
national parks 126
New Mabil Ha 77
New River 12
Nicaragua 12, 18
Nim Li Punit 101, 117, 121, 127
Noh Witz 121
North Stann Creek 12-13

Oceab Ha 45, 51
Old Mabil Ha 77, 80
Old Mabil Ha Road 80
Old Machakil Ha 68
Orange Point 117, 127
Orange Walk District 12
Other Plantation 124
Otoxha 13, 15-18, 42, **72**, 117-119, 121, 123-124, 126-127
Otoxha Creek 53, 56
Otoxha Road 66, 80
Otoxha Trail 77
Owil lHa 77

Pacific Ocean 12, 18
Pakil Ha 80
Palmar Camp 117, 127
parks 126
Pascua Ha 61
Pasture 18
Paynes Creek National Park 126
Pe'cho Paloma 51
Peckil Ha 53, 89, 90, 92
Pine Ridge 13, 18
Placencia 4, 12-13, 16
Plenty 124
Pobaltzi Ha 66
Poite River 66
Poite Road 54, 72, 77
Pol Noh Ha 51
Poxil Ha 112
precipitation 22
Pueblo Viejo 13, 15-18, 42, **51**, 117-119, 121, 123-124, 126-127
Pueblo Viejo Creek 51
Pueblo Viejo Fall 51, 121
Pueblo Viejo Road 51, 62, 65
Puhbal Peck Ha 72
Punta Gorda Road 45, 61, 97
Punta Gorda Town 4, 12-13, 15-18, 22, 42, 117-119, 121, 123-124, 126-127
Punta Negra 16
Pusil Ha 117, 127

Quarry 51, 78, 80, 87
Quebrada 117, 127
Queso Creek 94
Qui Ha 54
Quitam Ha 112

Ramos Creek 17
Raspaculo Branch 13, 17
Red Bank 13, 15-18, 42, **112**, 118-119, 121, 123-124, 126
Red Bank Road 112
Reservation 123, 126
reserves 123, 126
Resumadero 117, 127
Richardson Creek 17
Rio Blanco 46, 48, 51
Rio Blanco 126
Rio Blanco Fall 51
Rio Bravo 12
Rio Grande 4, 12-13, 15-17, 42, 45, 59, 94, 97-98, 102, 105, 118-119, 121, 123-124, 126
Rio Grande Cave 121
Rio Grande Dry Creek 94

Rio Hondo 12
Rio Machiquila 17
Rito Bonillo 61
Rivers Road 105
Riverside 16, 18
Roaring Creek 13, 54, 84, 87, 90
Roaring Stream 75
Roberts Road 92
Rondon Road 98
room for rent 121
Rosh Ha 83
Ruish Pur Ha 72
Runaway Creek 108

Sa Banil Ha 98
Saba Ha 83
Sac-Caril Ha 87
sacred place 121
Saki Kib 72
Salamanca 45, 59, 61, 94, 117, 127
Salawat Creek 78
Salt Water Creek 80
Salt Water Stream 71
San Antonio 13, 15-18, 22, 42, **45**, 59, 61, 117-119, 121, 123-124, 126-127
San Antonio Road 46, 48, 51, 94
San Benito Poite 13, 15-18, 42, **66**, 117-119, 121, 123-124, 126-127
San Benito Poite Trail 53
sanctuaries 126
San Felipe 13, 15-18, 42, **92**, 117-119, 121, 123-124, 126-127
San Felipe Road 90, 92
San Ignacio (Cayo) 12
San Jacint 83
San José 12
San Jose 13, 15-18, 42, **48**, 117-119, 121, 123-124, 126-127
San Jose Road 45, 48, 61
San Lucas 13, 15-18, 42, 77-**78**, 117-119, 121, 123-124, 126-127
San Lucas Road 54, 80
San Marcos 13, 15-18, 42, **97**, 118-119, 121, 123-124, 126
San Miguel 13, 15-18, 42, 94, **98**, 117-119, 121, 123-124, 126-127
San Miguel Road 105
San Pablo 13, 15-18, 42, 118-119, 121, 123-124, 126
San Pedro Columbia 13, 15-18, 42, **94**, 117-119, 121, 123-124, 126-127
San Pedro Columbia Road 98
San Pedro Landing 117, 127
San Roman 13, 15-18, 42, **115**, 118-119, 121, 123-124, 126
San Salvador 12, 18
San Vicente 13, 15-18, 42, **62**, 117-119, 121, 123-124, 126-127
San Vicente River 62
San Vicente Road 65
Sand Creek 108
Sandy Creek 112
Santa Anna 13, 15-18, 42, **90**, 117-119, 121, 123-124, 126-127
Santa Anna Road 92
Santa Cruz 13, 15-18, 42, **46**, 118-119, 121, 123-124, 126
Santa Cruz Creek 46
Santa Cruz Falls 121
Santa Cruz Road 45
Santa Cruz Trail 65
Santa Elena 13, 15-18, 42, **51**, 117-119, 121, 123-124, 126-127
Santa Elena Road 46
Santa Rosa 13, 15-18, 42, **115**, 118-119, 121, 123-124, 126
Santa Rosa Ha 115
Santa Rosa Road 62
Santa Teresa 13, 15-18, 42, **54**, 117-119, 121, 123-124, 126-127
Santa Teresa Road 54, 56, 77
Sarstoon River 4, 12-13, 15-17, 42, 118-119, 121, 123-124, 126
Sarstoon—Temash National Park 126
Savery Branch 17
sawmill 124, 127
Saxi Kib Ha 80
school 118
Se Balom 83
Se Chima 66
Se Holobob 83
Se Kulb 66
Se Pos Ha 54
Se Shal Blanc 83
Se Tamarin 83
Se Ucal Techic 83
Seine Bight 16
Shanil Ha 77, 80, 83, 97

Shbe Keky Ha 83
Shbe Se Calient 83
Shenil Ha 83
Sibun River 12-13
Silk Grass 16
Silver Creek 13, 15-18, 42, **105**, 117-119, 121, 123-124, 126-127
Silver Creek Road 98
Sis-sil Ha Road 45
Sittee Branch 13, 15-17, 42, 118-119, 121, 123-124, 126
Sittee Point 16
Sittee River 12-13, 15-17, 42, 111, 118-119, 121, 123-124, 126
Sittee River Forest Reserve 126
Small Wech Creek 97
Snake Creek 17
Snouk Eddy 111
South Stann Creek 12-13, 15-17, 42, 111, 115, 118-119, 121, 123-124, 126
Southern Highway 13, 15-18, 22, 42, 83, 92, 98, 101, 102, 105, 106, 108, 111, 112, 115, 118-119, 121-127
Stann Creek District 12-13, 15-18, 42, 118-119, 121, 123-124, 126
store 118
Sunday Wood 13, 15-18, 42, **75**, 117-119, 121, 123-124, 126-127
Sunday Wood Road 78, 80, 84
Sunday Wood Trail 77
Swamp 17-18
Swamp Creek 115
Swasey Bladen 126
Swasey Branch 13, 15-17, 42, 118-119, 121, 123-124, 126
Swasey River 112

Tamagas Stream 71, 75
Tambo Ha 112
Tambohil 51
Tambran Creek 75
Tegucigalpa 12, 18
telephone 118
Temash Lagoon 17
Temash River 4, 12-13, 15-17, 42, 68, 71-72, 75, 80, 84, 118-119, 121, 123-124, 126
The Tiger 124
Tikin Columbia 48, 59, 61
Tog Creek 83
Toledo District 4, 12-13, 15-18, 42, 118-119, 121-126
tour guides 121
Trio Branch 17
Tulsey Sawmill 124
Tunich Ha 112
Tunich Wah 48
Turneffe Islands 12
Tz' Ha 83
Tzokotz Ha 51

Union Camp 117, 127
Upper Half Kentucky 124
Uxbenca 46, 121

Vaca Plateau 13, 17

Waha Leaf 4, 17, 115
Waha Leaf Creek 17
Warrie Creek 13, 15-17, 42, 118, 121, 123-124, 126
waterfall 46, 61, 121
Wech Creek 97
Whitney Sawmill 124
wildlife sanctuary 126
Witzil Tout 45, 48, 61

Xha Ajrick 84
Xmas Creek 59
Xpicilha 117, 127

Ya'ax Ha 51
Ya-ax Actun 61
Yancey 124
Yax Ha 48
Yax-cal Stream 71
Yotoch Oxtuul Ti Chup 112
Yukil Ha 72, 80
Yuxil Ha 112

Zanabeh 124